D1272719

McGRAW-HILL PUBLICATIONS IN SOCIOLOGY
EDWARD BYRON REUTER, CONSULTING EDITOR

The City

This book is produced in full compliance with the government's regulations for conserving paper and other essential materials.

McGRAW-HILL PUBLICATIONS IN SOCIOLOGY

EDWARD BYRON REUTER
Consulting Editor

Angell—THE INTEGRATION OF AMERICAN SOCIETY
Baber—MARRIAGE AND THE FAMILY
Bowman—MARRIAGE FOR MODERNS
Brown—SOCIAL PSYCHOLOGY
Cook—COMMUNITY BACKGROUNDS OF EDUCATION
Faris—THE NATURE OF HUMAN NATURE
Hagerty—THE TRAINING OF SOCIAL WORKERS
Haynes—CRIMINOLOGY
Haynes—THE AMERICAN PRISON SYSTEM
Hertzler—SOCIAL INSTITUTIONS
Hertzler—THE SOCIAL THOUGHT OF THE ANCIENT CIVILIZATIONS
Holmes—RURAL SOCIOLOGY
House—THE DEVELOPMENT OF SOCIOLOGY
Karpf—AMERICAN SOCIAL PSYCHOLOGY
LaPiere—COLLECTIVE BEHAVIOR
Landis—RURAL LIFE IN PROCESS
Lumley—PRINCIPLES OF SOCIOLOGY
McCormick—ELEMENTARY SOCIAL STATISTICS
Mead—COOPERATION AND COMPETITION AMONG PRIMITIVE PEOPLES
North—THE COMMUNITY AND SOCIAL WELFARE
North—SOCIAL PROBLEMS AND SOCIAL PLANNING
Parsons—THE STRUCTURE OF SOCIAL ACTION
Queen and Thomas—THE CITY
Radin—SOCIAL ANTHROPOLOGY
Reckless—CRIMINAL BEHAVIOR
Reckless and Smith—JUVENILE DELINQUENCY
Reuter and Hart—INTRODUCTION TO SOCIOLOGY
Reuter and Runner—THE FAMILY
Street—THE PUBLIC WELFARE ADMINISTRATOR
Thomas—PRIMITIVE BEHAVIOR
Thompson—POPULATION PROBLEMS
Young—INTERVIEWING IN SOCIAL WORK
Young—SOCIAL TREATMENT IN PROBATION AND DELINQUENCY

The City

A STUDY OF URBANISM IN THE UNITED STATES

By
STUART ALFRED QUEEN
Professor of Sociology
Washington University

and
LEWIS FRANCIS THOMAS
Associate Professor of Geography
Washington University

FIRST EDITION
SIXTH IMPRESSION

McGRAW-HILL BOOK COMPANY, INC.
NEW YORK AND LONDON
1939

PRINTED IN THE UNITED STATES OF AMERICA

THE MAPLE PRESS COMPANY, YORK, PA.

PREFACE

This is an attempt to present methods of studying cities together with some of the findings now available, especially as they pertain to cities of the United States. This limitation to our own country is due partly to the difficulties of securing adequate data concerning cities of other lands and partly to the apparent fact that the cities of North America differ considerably from those of Europe and the Orient, not to mention other parts of the world. The methods of study discussed and demonstrated are chiefly those which have been developed in this country; to these have been added some adopted from elsewhere.

As we proceed we shall examine the contrasts between urban and rural situations—their environments, populations, groups, institutions, and social processes. We shall build on the foundation of geographic factors which have to do with the location, site, and consequent development of cities, but we shall treat the rise, growth, and other changes in cities as a phase of cultural development. This development will be treated primarily as one of the cultural changes taking place in a specified physical scene through the interaction of persons and groups.

Not only shall we observe differences between urban and rural life; we shall also note the diversity among cities and within each particular city. One of the most significant findings of urban sociology and geography to date is that various parts of a city may differ from each other more than one city differs from another or more than cities in general differ from the country as a whole.

Finally, we shall be concerned with problems of social control in cities. Our interest in the factors affecting cities and the processes through which they change carries over to an interest in predicting and controlling the future of our cities. We shall concern ourselves with whether and how we may become masters of our metropolitan centers rather than their victims.

We are indebted to more persons than we are able to list here for suggestions as to hypotheses, methods of procedure, and sources of material and for supplying actual data. Among those to whom we express special thanks are: Ralph C. Fletcher, Pittsburgh Council of Social Agencies; Harry L. Hornback, Works Progress Administration; Roy Wenzlick, Real Estate Analysts, Inc.; John G. Marr, St. Louis City Plan Commission; Irving Weissman, Social Planning Council for St. Louis and St. Louis County; Donald O. Cowgill, Drury College; Elsie M. Huseman, St. Louis Provident Association; Jessie S. Bernard, United States Department of Labor; Howard W. Green, Real Property Inventory of Metropolitan Cleveland; S. C. Gribble, Washington University; W. H. Reals, Washington University; William I. Thomas, Yale University; Ernest W. Burgess, University of Chicago; Robert E. Park, University of Chicago; William F. Ogburn, University of Chicago; R. D. McKenzie, University of Michigan; Donald C. Marsh, Wayne University.

We also express our appreciation for permission to quote granted by the following publishers and copyright holders: American Geographical Society, American Medical Association, Carnegie Corporation, Thomas Y. Crowell Company, University of Chicago Press, Columbia University Press, Harcourt, Brace & Company, Harper & Brothers, Harvard University Press, Henry Holt & Company, Houghton Mifflin Company, International City Managers' Association, Longmans, Green & Company, The Macmillan Company, University of Minnesota Press, National Municipal League, National Recreation Association, National Resources Committee, National Society for the Study of Education, President's Research Committee on Social Trends, Princeton University Press, Real Property Inventory of Metropolitan Cleveland, Russell Sage Foundation, University of Southern California Press, *The Spectator*, *St. Louis Post-Dispatch*, University of Washington Press, and John Wiley & Sons, Inc.

STUART A. QUEEN,
LEWIS F. THOMAS.

ST. LOUIS, MISSOURI,
January, 1939.

CONTENTS

Part I

THE RISE OF CITIES AND OF URBANISM

CHAPTER I

CHAPTER II

CHAPTER III

CHAPTER IV

Part II

URBAN INSTITUTIONS AND FOLKWAYS

Part III

DISTRIBUTIVE AND SELECTIVE ASPECTS OF THE CITY

CHAPTER XIII

CHAPTER XIV

CHAPTER XV

CHAPTER XVI

Part V

PREDICTION AND CONTROL

LIST OF FIGURES

LIST OF FIGURES

PART I

THE RISE OF CITIES AND OF URBANISM

Chapter I

DEFINITIONS AND HYPOTHESES

Ever since their first appearance several thousand years ago cities have been the objects of pride and of suspicion, of envy and of fear. Books have been written about "The Shame of the Cities" and about "The City the Hope of Democracy." Orators have extolled cities as "the vanguard of civilization" and condemned them as "blots on the landscape." In our own land hostility between city and country is suggested by the pitting of Baltimore against the Eastern Shore, New York against Upstate, Chicago against Downstate, Denver against the Western Slope, Seattle against the Inland Empire. All these popular expressions imply that there is something distinctive about cities, but none of them tells us what that something is.

What Is a City

In the state of Kansas 100 people living near together and meeting certain other requirements set forth by the legislature may incorporate as a city of the third class. A group of Bostonians talking about rural social work once referred to the charities of Northampton (25,000) and Lowell (100,000). Clearly the Kansas lawmakers and the Boston social workers had very different conceptions of city and country. Both were interested in enabling the inhabitants of a locality to organize for the carrying on of joint activities. But one group was thinking of the scattered population of the rolling prairies, while the other spoke from the vantage point of a great metropolitan center.

Evidently the concept of a city is conditioned by the point of view of the person who is observing or studying it. Also, plainly it must be a statement in terms of the setting in which cities appear. Thus Massachusetts is a small, densely populated state. The Fifteenth Census classed 90 per cent of its people as "urban" (living in places of 2,500 and over) and reported 30 places with a population of 25,000 or more. In fact, over half the population lived in metropolitan Boston, 2,300,000 of 4,250,000. The density of the whole state was 529 persons per square mile. Kansas, on the other hand, is ten times as large as Massachusetts but has only two-fifths as many people. Less than 40 per cent of its people were classed as urban in 1930. There were only four places with a population of 25,000 or more, and all of them together accounted for only one-sixth of the population. The density of the whole state was 23 per square mile. To a Bostonian, "city" means a large number of people, perhaps a million, living close together in multiple dwellings, riding to their work in streetcar, subway, elevated, and ordinary railway, working in great office buildings, stores, and factories, enjoying the bright lights of movie and dance palace, or possibly the subdued lights of orchestra hall and art museum. To a Kansan, "city" means any incorporated place with its water tower rising above the prairie, its cottages, stores, schools, and churches clustered amid trees that break the horizon, its main street, and its courthouse square. Apparently the marks of identification are varied and numerous.

Simply as a preliminary statement, we may say that a city is a collection of people and buildings, large for its time and place, and characterized by distinctive activities. This will not do for a permanent definition. But before revamping it, we shall examine some of the criteria proposed by various students of cities.

Criteria

Every student should acquaint himself with the criteria proposed by such authors as Gist and Halbert, Sorokin and Zimmerman, Park and Burgess, Weber, Bedford, and others.[1] The various characteristics which they use to identify cities may be summarized and criticized through the following questions and comments.

Is a city primarily a collection of buildings? If so, of what kinds and how many? When we tour across the country we are conscious of approaching a city, or at least a town, when we see water towers, smokestacks, and tall buildings. We have no difficulty in classifying Denver, Indianapolis, or Buffalo as a city.

[1] Noel P. Gist and L. A. Halbert, *Urban Society*, 1933; Pitirim Sorokin and C. C. Zimmerman, *Principles of Rural-urban Sociology*, 1929; Scott E. W. Bedford, *Readings in Urban Sociology*, 1927; Adna F. Weber, *Growth of Cities in the Nineteenth Century*, 1899; R. E. Park and E. W. Burgess, *The City*, 1925.

But how about North Platte, Carlsbad, or Winchester? After all, stores are found in country villages, factories in mill towns, hotels and theaters (of sorts) throughout the land. Perhaps apartment houses and office buildings are distinctively urban structures.

Is the city a large number of people living in a given district? How many people make a city? The Bureau of the Census now calls any place of 2,500 inhabitants a city, but it formerly drew the line at 8,000. Other countries set the mark anywhere from 500 to 24,000. State laws vary greatly in regard to the minimum number of people who may establish a city government. In view of the fact that the persons counted are those who happen to live within certain more or less arbitrary lines, we may do well to abandon the numerical criterion and use population figures merely as statistical conveniences. However, the Bureau of the Census has recently defined a kind of urban unit that we can use to advantage. A "metropolitan district" is a local area containing at least 100,000 people, of whom at least 50,000 live in a central city or cities (incorporated municipalities) and the remainder are found in "adjacent and contiguous civil divisions having a density of not less than 150 inhabitants per square mile, and also as a rule, those civil divisions of less density that are directly or nearly surrounded by minor civil divisions that have the required density."[1] There were, in 1930, 96 such metropolitan districts in the United States. This definition has the advantages of referring only to population aggregates that are indisputably urban and of including the whole of areas within which some common conditions of living obtain. Most of our study will be of such large metropolitan aggregates, but we shall not insist that they alone are urban.

Some thoughtful students have urged that density be the criterion, or perhaps density and total numbers considered together. Mark Jefferson suggests 10,000 per square mile as evidence of city life, while Willcox regards 1,000 as an appropriate figure.[2] The actual variation in density of American cities is

[1] Fifteenth Census, *Metropolitan Districts*, pp. 5–6.

[2] Mark Jefferson, "The Anthropogeography of Some Great Cities," *Bull. Amer. Geog. Soc.*, 41 (1930), 542–544; Walter F. Willcox, "A Redefinition of City in Terms of Density of Population," *The Urban Community*, edited by E. W. Burgess, pp. 115–121, 1926.

Both proposals are discussed by Gist and Halbert, *op. cit.*, pp. 4 *ff*.

enormous. Thus in 1930 the density of the Duluth metropolitan district was 350, while for metropolitan New York it was 4,336. For New York City it was 23,178, and in five New York census tracts it was 276,253.[1] As in the matter of total population, it is probably not profitable to debate the exact demarcation of urban and rural, but it is plain that a relatively high degree of congestion, as well as a relatively large number of inhabitants, tends to identify the city. A great body of folk living in a given area must take some account of each other which would not be necessary if their numbers were smaller. If they are crowded very closely together, they must give still more thought to the requirements of housing, transportation, sanitation, and the like.

To many persons the distinguishing mark of a city is the fact of legal incorporation. Until recently the United States Census has reported only political units; however, as we observed earlier, it is now agreed that a city is not always confined to the political boundaries or corporate limits. For this reason we really need to have separate terms for the legally created unit of government on the one hand and for the total urban population and the area it occupies on the other. For the latter, the term "metropolitan district" is coming into common use. For the former, we may perhaps use the term "municipality." If we are going to reach beyond the official boundaries, then the question will arise: How far out shall we call the area and population urban? This is a problem to which we shall devote considerable attention later; for the moment we may simply agree that it shall be the built-up area in which people come and go daily for work, shopping, and recreation.

Some students make much of the point that occupations distinguish cities from rural districts. Thus tilling the soil, animal husbandry, and the extraction of various products from nature, as in fishing and forestry, are accounted the occupations of rural folk, whereas urban trades have to do, it is said, with the transformation of raw materials into various products of industry, the exchange and transportation of such articles, and the accompanying financial functions. But we may observe that an agricultural village will usually have a bank, some stores, and possibly a small factory or two. Does it thereby become a city?

[1] Fifteenth Census, *Metropolitan Districts;* Walter Laidlaw, *Population of the City of New York,* 1890–1930, p. 204.

On the other hand, is it sound to call a logging camp, fishing village, or mining town rural, merely because it lives by extracting raw materials from nature? Perhaps a more important distinction is one having to do with the number and variety of occupations, that is, minuteness of the division of labor and degree of interdependence. Thus in a country district there might be found not over a dozen different vocations, while in a large city there are sure to be several hundred. The countryman is often a jack-of-all-trades; the city man more commonly performs a single operation on an assembly line. The rural community produces much of its own food, fuel, and (formerly) clothing. The city gathers its necessities from many sources and sends its products far and wide.

Again there are those who would make personality types the criteria of city and of country. Some claim that there are distinctly urban types, or at least certain varieties of personality, found only or chiefly in cities. The evidence on this point is not very satisfactory but does warrant further inquiry into this question: Are there characteristic urban habits and attitudes, and is the behavior of city dwellers fundamentally different from that observed elsewhere? Specifically, are the social contacts distinctive as to number, variety, intimacy, or permanence? Some observers report that urban contacts tend to be temporary, casual and superficial, rather varied, and very numerous. Yet we know that some of the loneliest people live in cities. Many urbanites have little to do with persons outside their own class. There is intimacy between some city folk and social distance between some country people. Hence the last three observations may legitimately be questioned. But as to the relative permanency of rural and urban contacts there appears to be less doubt.

In similar fashion we may ask whether there are social groups and types of social relations that mark the city. Are professional associations, criminal gangs, and luncheon clubs distinctively urban? Or are cities characterized less by particular sorts of groups than by their size, number, and variety?

Then there is the question of social institutions. Are there any which are peculiar to the city? For example, real estate board, taxi-dance hall, church federation, chain store, community chest? Can it be shown that any institutions now quite general originated in the city? Is this true of parent-teacher association, family welfare society, the movies, community church, park, and playground? Are basic institutions such as church, school, and family different in the city and in other settings? If any or all of these questions should be answered affirmatively, then we would be on the road to a definition of much greater consequence to sociology than any that might be based upon mere numbers or legal status.

Another question of importance to students of the city pertains to the relative complexity of city and nonurban populations. That is, are there particularly involved relations between persons, groups, and institutions within a city, between cities, or between cities and the rest of the country or the world? It is very generally held that complexity is a mark of urbanity. On the whole, common observation will support this theory; however, there should be further inquiry before it is accepted without reservation.

Mobility is frequently proposed as a distinguishing characteristic of the city. This term refers to several varieties of behavior. Sometimes it is applied to the daily coming and going to and from work, trade, recreation, and the like. Another use of the term is its application to changes of residence, employment, and social status. On the surface it appears that city people shift about more than those who live in villages and the open country, but with the development of hard roads and the wide use of automobiles, the time may not be very distant when rural people will travel farther and faster than city people. It also has been observed that agricultural laborers in the West and tenants in the South are moving about a great deal, perhaps as much as any important group of city dwellers. Possibly mobility is negatively correlated with ownership of property to the point that future differences between urban and rural mobility will vary only with differences in opportunity to own real estate. This in turn may be expected to change with the life cycle of communities and regions. First settlers are likely to be owners; later arrivals are more often renters. Owners stay put; renters move.

Another popular criterion is heterogeneity. The common implication is that cities contain a great variety of ethnic groups, languages, occupations, abilities, codes of behavior, groups, institutions, economic levels, etc. There is considerable evidence to support this observation, and it may well be that heterogeneity will remain one of the important criteria of urban life.

Finally the cultural anthropologists have afforded another clue. It is that cities are the principal centers of cultural innovation and diffusion. Certainly they are today the centers of fashion, art, music, literature, and business practice. Whether there are other important traits and complexes that originate outside of cities ought to be studied, but certainly casual observation indicates that cities are cultural centers.

These then are the possible marks of urbanization: numbers and density of population, compactness and size of buildings, legal status, functions, division of labor, personality types, social groups and contacts, institutions, complexity, mobility, heterogeneity, and cultural innovation.

Some Rural-urban Contrasts

A rural-urban dichotomy seems to be firmly fixed in our traditions and has existed in the Western world at least for many centuries. From the laments of the Hebrew prophets to the last meeting of the Louisiana legislature, there is evidence that country people and city people commonly regard each other as different and often as hostile. Such prejudices and antipathies may rest on contemporary differences; they may be traditions handed down from the past. Even in antiquity it may have been divergence of interest rather than of other characteristics that pitted city and country against each other. Common-sense observations of seemingly fundamental differences, therefore, must not be accepted at their face value but must be examined critically.

Ogburn has made a statistical analysis of available data to determine whether cities are more alike than rural units, and whether their supposed similarity minimizes the differences between regions of the United States.[1] His findings did not support the original hypothesis that cities are more alike than are rural units but did show that there are significant differences between groups of cities and the regions of which they are parts. He made 108 comparisons of cities of different regions with the nonurban areas of the same regions. In 52 instances the inter-

[1] W. F. Ogburn, "Regions," *Social Forces*, 15 (1936), 6–11.

city resemblance was greater than the rural resemblance, while in 56 it was not. These comparisons had to do with such items as size of family, school attendance, percentage married, home ownership, automobiles, telephones, and birth and death rates. This result was confirmed when he brought together all the cities of a given population class and computed the standard deviation to determine how great was the scatter or cluster. He made 36 comparisons of these standard deviations with the same measure of deviation in rural counties. In exactly half, the scatter was greater for cities than for rural counties. A third test was to compare the traits of whole regions, urban and rural, with the traits displayed by their cities. This indicated that the average of the cities in one region resembled the average of the cities in another region more than the whole regions resembled each other in 58 comparisons and less in 50. He then sought to discover whether the differences within a region were greater or more numerous than differences between regions. This was determined, first, by comparing rural-urban differences within a region with differences between the cities of two regions. In 142 out of 216 comparisons the former were greater than the latter. In like manner he compared rural-urban differences within a region with the differences between rural areas of two regions, and secured almost identical results. Thus he showed beyond a doubt that the differences between cities and their surrounding territory (regions) are greater than the admittedly marked differences between regions of the United States. For further information about the nature of these distinctions we turn to other sources.

Perhaps the most systematic summary of the differences believed to obtain between urban and rural situations has been made by Sorokin and Zimmerman.[1] They present quantitative data from a number of countries showing important differences in occupation, size of community, density, homogeneity, mobility, differentiation, and stratification. Their evidence with reference to the types and varieties of occupation lead them to conclusions which require qualifications like those suggested in the preceding section; likewise, their data concerning the number and density of population. They point out furthermore that numbers and density are definitely and naturally related to the occupations

[1] Sorokin and Zimmerman, *op. cit.*, Chap. 2.

of city and country folk respectively. Farming, forestry, and similar occupations require a relatively sparse population, while manufacturing, banking, and the like favor the concentration of people in considerable numbers. As to heterogeneity and homogeneity, Sorokin and Zimmerman indicate that city populations are recruited from many different regions, not only from within a given country but from various parts of the world; while farming districts usually have low percentages of people who have come from other regions. In general these seem to be the facts. However, at different stages in the life cycle of a community different situations may obtain. During a period of rapid growth immigration may bring a very mixed population, but as numbers become stabilized, through declining migration and otherwise, there is likely to be greater biological homogeneity through amalgamation and greater cultural homogeneity through assimilation. These cyclic changes may be found in both rural and urban districts.

With reference to mobility, the same authorities present evidence bearing on change of residence in relation to change of employment and ownership of property. Their data indicate that as yet urban populations are more mobile than rural, both in a physical sense and in respect to the changes of employment and social status. Sorokin and Zimmerman also discuss at length certain differences in the system of social interaction, holding, first, that the physical range of contacts is greater for city dwellers; second, that face-to-face contacts are a smaller proportion of the whole than for country people; third, that most of the relationships of city folks are impersonal; hence, fourth, "casual, superficial, and short-lived." All these various characteristics are held by these two students of rural-urban contrast to be closely related.

Some of the points made by Sorokin and Zimmerman seem to be adequately established, but in support of others their evidence is by no means convincing. Thus, more data are needed concerning the relative proportion of face-to-face contacts in city and in country. Also it should be remembered that the number, variety, permanence, and intimacy of social contacts vary greatly for different classes and different districts in a city. Nevertheless, we are indebted to these two men for the careful assembling of an important body of material which helps to bring us out of the realm of casual observations and guesswork into the realm of objectively established generalizations.

Another student of the same problem, Georg Simmel,[1] has offered some hypotheses concerning rural-urban differences which are similar to those already discussed but which make a somewhat different approach. These have been presented most simply by another European, Nicholas Spykman. Simmel, as interpreted by Spykman, holds that the social structure of urban communities is dominated by interest groups rather than kinship and locality groups as in rural areas. He holds that social circles are larger and that each individual is the meeting point of numerous distinct groupings, whereas in the country many individuals belong to a number of almost identical circles. This is reflected in the greater freedom of the city dweller to select his associations, the countryman's groups being pretty well predetermined. Concerning the behavior of individuals, we are told that the city man is less restrained, more individualistic, more emotional, more formal, more objective, and more self-assertive. It is only fair to observe that there is a lack of convincing data to support these generalizations. However, if we regard them as hypotheses to be tested, as problems to be solved, they may be very useful to the student of city life.

The reader should be warned to approach all these propositions with at least moderate skepticism. Some of them are undoubtedly true, others may someday be shown to be true, still others are so general as to be useless, particularly when they pertain to conditions which are widely different in the various parts of a city. Especially is there need for further and more objective study of urban and rural personality traits. Perhaps the most widespread and yet the most questionable of generalizations concerning urban and rural personalities is the one to the effect that city dwellers are more individualistic than rural folk. On equally good authority we are informed that "extreme individualism is one of the outstanding attitudes of the farmer."[2] There are similarly conflicting statements about the restraint, emotionalism, and assertiveness of urban and rural people. Whenever such a hypothesis is presented, the student should examine care-

[1] Nicholas J. Spykman, *The Social Theory of Georg Simmel*, especially Chap. 2, 1925.

[2] N. L. Sims, *Elements of Rural Sociology*, p. 226, 1928.

fully the evidence that is offered in its support and should also look for evidence pointing in the opposite direction. Particularly is he advised to read, along with the works on urban sociology, corresponding treatises on rural life.[1]

TYPES OF CITIES

Gist and Halbert[2] have classified cities as (*a*) production centers, (*b*) centers of trade and commerce, (*c*) political capitals, (*d*) resorts for health or recreation, (*e*) cultural centers, (*f*) defense cities, (*g*) diversified cities. This might be considered a functional classification. Wirth[3] suggests in addition that cities be classified according to age (by which he probably means maturity), means of communication, site and location, planning or its absence. Obviously there are real differences between old cities and those that have sprung up recently, *e.g.*, between Boston and Seattle. Also it is evident that the importance of a city is related to dominant modes of transportation and communication. When river traffic was supreme, New Orleans was our fifth largest city and St. Louis dominated the Middle West. With the shift from river to rail, this supremacy passed to Chicago. As to planning and its absence, the classic American illustration is the contrast between Washington's radial pattern and Boston's cow paths. This comparison, however, is not quite fair, for differences of topography may have had quite as much influence as those of planning. A better contrast would perhaps be that of Salt Lake City and Los Angeles.

Returning to the categories of Gist and Halbert, it should be noted that most cities today are hard to place in any one category; in this sense they are "diversified." Ancient cities may have been places of defense, but modern cities are quite vulnerable in war. All cities are doubtless "cultural centers"; but many universities are in small towns, and in the cities themselves institutions for the promotion of art, music, letters, and science are almost lost sight of in the midst of business, politics, sports, and "society." Recreation centers are commonly on the fringe

[1] Sims, *op. cit.;* J. H. Kolb and E. de S. Brunner, *A Study of Rural Society*, 1935; Dwight Sanderson, *The Rural Community*, 1932; C. R. Hoffer, *Introduction to Rural Sociology*, 1934; C. J. Galpin, *Rural Life*, 1918.

[2] Gist and Halbert, *op. cit.*, p. 18.

[3] Louis Wirth, "A Bibliography of the Urban Community," *The City*, edited by R. E. Park and E. W. Burgess, pp. 175–182, 1925.

of great cities or far from any cities; health resorts are usually smaller places. In the ancient world political capitals and great cities were almost synonymous, but not in the middle ages. Today it is only small cities or towns that are primarily political capitals. The economic functions probably offer the most satisfactory basis for classifying modern cities.[1] Thus there are marked differences in the appearance, population, and organization of life in manufacturing cities like Akron, Birmingham, and Lowell and in commercial cities like Seattle, Denver, and Houston. Also there are important differences between one-industry cities like Flint, Tulsa, and Lowell, and places with diversified industries like Chicago, St. Louis, and Minneapolis–St. Paul. Among the cities dominated by a single industry there are variations according to the nature of that industry. Thus a steel town, like Youngstown, looks and is different from a textile town, like Fall River.

So far we have considered the more tangible features of urban life. But there is another sort of difference between cities which merits more careful study than it has yet received; it is that elusive something called "individuality" or "atmosphere." Certainly there are differences between San Francisco, Los Angeles, St. Louis, Chicago, New Orleans, Philadelphia, Boston, and New York which are barely hinted at in the categories previously named. It is important to consider these intangibles, although their analysis must await the development of new techniques. An interesting suggestion as to how the individuality of cities may be studied comparatively has been made by Thorndike and Woodyard.[2] They studied 117 cities in terms of 120 items of measurable fact. Some of the items were: infant death rate, median size of family, average rent paid, rate of growth from 1900 to 1930, per capita expenditure for teachers' salaries, per capita expenditure for recreation, per capita number of homes owned, per capita number of telephones, income per capita, per capita number of arrests for certain offenses, and per capita circulation of certain magazines. They computed for each item pertaining to each city its deviation from the median

[1] William B. Munro, "City," *Encyclopaedia of the Social Sciences*, vol. 3, p. 478.

[2] E. L. Thorndike and Ella Woodyard, "Individual Differences in American Cities: Their Nature and Causation," *Amer. Jour. Sociol.*, 43 (1937), 191–224.

of the whole group of cities, and thus were able to show graphically how each city differs from the others. It also showed certain recurrent groupings of positive and negative deviations. This is only a pathfinding study, but it opens up some very attractive possibilities of objectively studying the individuality of American, and doubtless other, cities. Although the items studied belong to the category of tangibles, they definitely suggest intangibles, which, after all, can be dealt with only by way of inferences from objective data.

Sociology and Geography of Cities

Cities have long been the object of study by historians and political scientists. What have geographers and sociologists to add? Why should four groups of specialists study cities? Admittedly their interests overlap. But each has a special objective and responsibility. For the political scientist it is municipal government. For the historian it is the narrative of cities' roles in national and world affairs. The geographer's concern is with location, site, natural resources, means of transportation. He studies the distribution of cities, and of various traits within a given city, in their relation to the physical setting. The sociologist is interested primarily in social organization in urban environments—the groups, institutions, customs, traditions, attitudes, and relations that characterize the city as a type of human aggregation. His special task is to see what uniformities he can find in the social organization of urban life; how organization arises, gives way to disorganization, and then to destruction or to reorganization. In the pages that follow our attention will be centered chiefly on the geographic and sociological aspects of the city, but they will be related to the historical, economic, and political views of the same complex aggregate of persons, groups, institutions, and their physical equipment. In other words, we shall endeavor to present the city as a distinctive cultural development in a characteristic physical setting, the product of a certain kind of evolution.

General Works on the City

Carpenter, Niles: *The Sociology of City Life*, Longmans, Green & Company, 1931.

Davie, Maurice R.: *Problems of City Life*, John Wiley & Sons, Inc., 1932.

GIST, NOEL P., and L. A. HALBERT: *Urban Society*, The Thomas Y. Crowell Company, 1933.

MCKENZIE, R. D.: *The Metropolitan Community*, McGraw-Hill Book Company, Inc., 1933.

MUMFORD, LEWIS: *The Culture of Cities*, Harcourt, Brace & Company, Inc., 1938.

MUNTZ, EARL E.: *Urban Sociology*, The Macmillan Company, 1938.

SOROKIN, PITIRIM, and C. C. ZIMMERMAN: *Principles of Rural-urban Sociology*, Henry Holt & Company, Inc., 1929.

WOOLSTON, HOWARD B.: *Metropolis: A Study of Urban Communities*, D. Appleton-Century Company, Inc., 1938.

Our Cities: Their Role in the National Economy, National Resources Committee, 1937.

OGBURN, W. F.: *Social Characteristics of Cities*, International City Managers' Association, 1937.

Chapter II

THE RISE OF CITIES

It is very difficult for a modern person, particularly one who has lived most of his life under urban conditions, to realize that mankind is overwhelmingly rural. In fact, until fairly recently in the evolution of man our ancestors were exclusively rural. This cannot be stated in terms of dates and percentages, because the chronology of man's evolution is very far from precise. Nevertheless, a few generalizations may be ventured. It is pretty well agreed that there have been human beings of one kind or another for a half million to a million years. For twenty-five to fifty thousand years there have been men very much like ourselves. But until five or six thousand years ago there was nothing which we could recognize as a city. Against the background of man's history, the period of city dwelling is short indeed. But even that five thousand years has found only a small fraction of the human race urbanized. As recently as 1800, only 4 per cent of the population of the United States lived in places of 8,000 or more. In various European countries corresponding percentages ranged from 3 to 21.[1] Today over half the people of the United States and of Europe may be classed as urban. In 1927 there were 182 great cities (100,000 or over) in Europe, as against only 21 in 1801. At the beginning of the nineteenth century, so far as we know, there was no city over 100,000 outside of Europe. By 1927 there were 355 on other continents.[2] But we know that, the great cities of China, Japan, and India notwithstanding, the majority of Asiatics are villagers. The same thing is true of Africa and South America. This means that even today many more people live in villages, towns, and the open country than are found in cities.[3] Perhaps

[1] Adna F. Weber, *The Growth of Cities in the Nineteenth Century*, pp. 144–145, 1899.

[2] Mark Jefferson, "Distribution of the World's City Folks," *Geog. Rev.*, 21 (1931), 446–465.

[3] Weber, *op. cit.*, Chap. 2.

we might sum up the whole matter thus: A short time ago there were no cities at all. Just yesterday they became large and important. Even yet their dominance is not complete.

PRECURSORS OF CITIES

Just what points have marked the transition from rural to urban living may never be established. However, we do have some information about various sorts of primitive communities and how they grew up. We need not go back to those distant ancestors who lived in trees and caves, gathering berries, nuts, and roots, killing small animals, and moving about from place to place. Their way of life was about as completely unlike that which we call urban as it is possible for us to conceive. Let us start with men who planted and cultivated grasses, roots, and trees.

Childe has called the cultivation of plants the first great economic revolution. It began to give man more control over his food supply and began to attach human groups to fixed places of residence. Wheat and barley seem to have been especially significant because of their combined food value, ease of storage, relatively high return, and fairly limited labor requirement. With such tillage, and also with the domestication of some animals, came an increase in population. Children could be useful in weeding the crops, chasing away birds, and tending sheep. Now the development of tillage and domestication did not necessarily mean the adoption of a sedentary life. Even today there are in Africa, Asia, and South America peoples who clear a patch in the jungle, reap a few crops, and leave to repeat the process somewhere else when the productiveness of the first tract of land has been used. Nevertheless, cultivation of the soil was a first step toward permanent residence, which in turn had to come long before there could be any such thing as a city.

Once people settled even temporarily, their groups became somewhat larger. Other things appeared which tended to make possible development in the direction of urbanism. One was cooperative effort. It was necessary for the whole group to work together in clearing a place in the forest, draining a marsh, making dikes to protect against floods, building irrigation canals, and erecting walls for defense. Through such cooperative activities men must have learned a great deal about the kind of teamwork which must be done if they are to live together in large groups and in permanent settlements.

Thus we have to observe that through most of human history (in the actual, not merely in the written sense) the way of life followed by human beings might be described as nomadic and collectional. This gave way to a seminomadic and cultural economy which was in turn succeeded by primitive agricultural villages. Some of these villages must have grown to towns of a few thousand; some of them developed trade with peoples at a distance, but in general their activities and interests were localized, their numbers were small, and they were very unlike anything we would recognize as a city.[1] Nevertheless they were settled abodes where material goods might accumulate. The relative scarcity of desirable sites, the labor required for their improvement, the time needed for growth of orchards and vineyards, all contributed to stability. So did the storehouses, irrigation ditches, and walls for defense. Living close together within a limited area, forced to act together in military and engineering projects, and dependent on common sources of water and food, these neolithic villagers doubtless developed numerous social institutions. Their standard of living rose; they must have been envied and attacked by nomads from adjacent districts.

The Earliest Cities

It is probable that the earliest settlements that we would accept as urban appeared in the great stretch of semi-arid lands reaching from Egypt to India. They developed along the valleys of the Nile, Tigris, Euphrates, and Indus rivers. No doubt they started as neolithic villages which developed in one way and another into walled cities, some of which became the capitals of great empires. Their growth was probably associated with the necessity of assembling inside strong walls for defense, the attraction to a common shrine for religious purposes, or the development of a market for the exchange of various goods.

[1] The story of cultural development before the appearance of cities and the kinds of communities that preceded the existence of cities have been presented in the following works: V. Gordon Childe, *Man Makes Himself*, 1936; Niles Carpenter, *The Sociology of City Life*, Chap. 1, 1931; Dwight Sanderson, *The Rural Community*, Chaps. 2–3, 1932.

These river valleys which were good places for the raising of certain crops were poor in other raw materials, particularly stone and timber; hence trade must have developed very early. Now, in order that trade might be carried on there had to be a surplus of some local produce for exchange, and it was necessary for a local group to support a body of traders and transport workers. They had to have craftsmen who could work up the imported articles; they needed soldiers to protect goods in transit, clerks to keep records of transactions, and public officials to adjudicate disputes. All these represented developments in the direction of numbers, heterogeneity, and complexity, which we associate with city life. Apparently it was about the middle of the third millennium B.C. that some of these cities became imperial capitals. Doubtless this resulted from clashes between rival cities, union of some sort for protection against hostile forces, the prestige of outstanding warriors, judges, or priests.

In general, the conditions attending the appearance of these first cities have been summarized by Carpenter as: (*a*) mild climate, (*b*) growth of cereals, (*c*) relative freedom from attack, (*d*) soil and climate which favored people's living close together.[1] To Carpenter's list Gras[2] adds transportation facilities by land and by water, a respectful distance from possible rivals, and a fairly wide free-trade area. In the areas described, these conditions obtained; but whether they were all essential to the rise of cities or whether cities might have arisen under other conditions it is impossible to say. It is at least worth noting that the Incas in Peru, the Aztecs in Mexico, and the Mayans in Yucatán developed many features of an urban civilization in quite different environments. The freedom from attack mentioned by Carpenter was very real in Egypt but far from complete in Mesopotamia. His fourth point seems to us more important. The fertile valleys were narrow and were surrounded by wide deserts. These conditions promoted the cooperation for flood control, irrigation, and other purposes discussed in the preceding section. In any event, further research is necessary before we can assess the importance of the various factors associated with the appearance of cities in the Near East.

[1] Niles Carpenter, *op. cit.*, p. 21. By permission of Longmans, Green & Company, Inc.

[2] N. S. B. Gras, "The Rise of the Metropolitan Community," *The Urban Community*, edited by E. W. Burgess, pp. 183–191, 1926.

Another problem concerning the earliest cities pertains to their dominant functions. It is frequently held that they were primarily places of defense or seats of government. It is observed that they were also centers of worship and to a certain extent headquarters of trade. Which of these functions was primary in time and which was supreme in importance are questions much less easily answered than may appear to the casual student. Again it may be that further historical research will enable us to make more definite statements on these matters. For the present we can merely observe that the earliest cities seem to have performed for their inhabitants these four functions.

Cities of the Mediterranean World

While some really great cities were appearing in Egypt, Babylonia, and India, Europe was inhabited by rude pastoral peoples whose lives were crude and whose communities were small. However, beginning with the seaports of Phoenicia, cities grew up one after another around the eastern Mediterranean and Aegean seas. They spread into the western Mediterranean and then northward into Gaul.

In their development it appears that the usual sequence was something like this: (*a*) Several clans or tribes settled together for common defense, worship, and trade. (*b*) A tribal village grew into a big town, retaining, however, the kinship type of social organization with the elders of the clans often forming a council or senate. (*c*) As trade developed, individuals not important in the clans sometimes came to the fore, sought emancipation from the kinship system and elevated one or several of their number to positions of authority. Thus appeared the tyrants in Greek city-states. (*d*) The numbers of ordinary traders, soldiers, and artisans increased; the tyrants were perhaps overthrown, and a semidemocratic government was set up, representing usually, however, only the slaveowners.

Now this cannot be accepted as a universal sequence. In fact, it may not have been followed precisely in a single instance. Nevertheless, something like this order of events does seem to have occurred often enough to warrant our using it as a pattern of the general trend. In the next chapter we shall see how the development of these ancient cities was bound up with location and site. Whether changes in the physical pattern bore any relation to changes in the social pattern has not been established. But there are some indications that a common sequence was: (*a*) a defensive hilltop settlement, expanding to include (*b*) a market place in a valley, and (*c*) a harbor on a river, estuary, or bay. (*d*) The original hilltops became aristocratic residential sections or the sites of temples and other public buildings. (*e*) The lowlands were occupied by residences of poorer people and by expanding business.

There is evidence that some of these cities of antiquity grew to very great size. The Greeks had several cities which undoubtedly reached 100,000 in population. Weber thinks that Carthage may have attained the figure of 700,000. Rome grew to more than half a million and quite likely contained at one time nearly a million people. It is interesting, in view of this significant development in the Roman Empire, that cities subsequently declined and that by the beginning of the sixteenth century there were only a half dozen in the 100,000 class.

The cities of 2,000 years ago were both like and unlike those of today. In Rome some of the streets were paved; water was brought down from the mountains; sewers emptied into the Tiber; there were public baths; and, in the reign of Augustus, systems of fire and police protection were highly developed. First in Rome and later in provincial cities the concept of a municipal corporation evolved, *i.e.*, Roman cities became legal entities, artificial persons. However, most cities of antiquity lacked some or all of the urban characteristics just mentioned.

The appearance of Periclean Athens (fifth century B.C.) has been described in words which show it to have been a real city, yet something very different from a modern metropolis.[1] On a high hill called the Acropolis were stately temples to the gods, but below it was a "sea of low flat roofs," without a single chimney. There were no attractive houses, but mostly one-story dwellings with blank walls of sun-dried brick. They had few windows, dirt floors, no plumbing or drainage, but many beautiful utensils, some lovely furniture, and some books. The streets were narrow, crooked lanes without pavement or sidewalks. All household rubbish and garbage were thrown directly into the streets. There were no sewers and no system of street cleaning. At the foot of the Acropolis was an outdoor theater

[1] J. H. Breasted, *The Conquest of Civilization*, Chap. 15, 1926.

ooden seats. Farther down the slope was a market place. entire city covered the equivalent of about 150 modern ›cks, though it was not laid out in any such orderly fashion. Surrounding the whole was a wall, with a double wall reaching down to Piraeus, the seaport. The urban population was perhaps 100,000 including a large number of slaves and some foreigners. Another 100,000 lived in outlying parts of Attica, dependent on Athens as a market, administrative, religious, and military center. But other sections of ancient Greece were much more rural, as were most parts of the Mediterranean world.

Perhaps the change from classical antiquity to the so-called dark ages was not really as great as we sometimes imagine. After all, in spite of the truly great cities that existed, most people were residents of little villages. Hence, when the northern tribesmen and villagers swept down into southern Europe we may say that they were merely making apparent what had been really true all the time, namely, that the bulk of mankind was rural and the city dwellers were rather exceptional. In other words, the mere presence of cities does not mean that a region has been truly urbanized. As Carpenter puts it, "In an urban society the city dominates the scene. It is the center of gravity, politically, socially, and culturally."[1] Moreover, the country is economically dependent upon it. Each city not only dominates its own hinterland but is in close touch with other urban centers. By way of contrast, in nonurban societies cities are small, communication is slow and uncertain, trade is mostly local, the city is economically dependent on the country, but the latter is almost self-sufficing. This hypothesis is worthy of further study. Certainly there is a great difference between an agricultural civilization, with occasional cities as centers of government, religion, and trade, and an urban society like that of present-day England. However, one should not be too hasty in assuming that the cultures of the ancient world were all nonurban.

Medieval Towns

We have suggested that the cities of classical antiquity declined and in some instances disappeared. This was not because the Germans came to destroy the cities but rather because they did not know how to live in them. This urban decline was likewise

[1] Carpenter, *op. cit.*, p. 19. By permission of Longmans, Green & Company, Inc.

bound up with the encroachments of the Mohammedans, so that by the end of the eighth century Charlemagne's empire was inland, isolated, and practically without foreign commerce. Rome itself had declined from a possible 1 million inhabitants to less than 20,000. Now the towns that remained were for the most part fortresses, feudal administrative centers, or ecclesiastical headquarters. Economically they were bound up with the neighboring countryside. They were not part of a far-reaching nexus of commercial activities and relations. Pirenne has said:[1]

> It is, therefore, a safe conclusion that the period which opened with the Carolingian Era knew cities neither in the social sense, nor in the economic sense, nor in the legal sense of that word. The towns and burgs were merely fortified places and headquarters of administration. Their inhabitants enjoyed neither special laws nor institutions of their own, and their manner of living did not distinguish them in any way from the rest of society.

Some of these medieval towns apparently grew through their markets, fairs, and otherwise into cities possessing those features with which we are familiar; but the actual urban development of the late middle ages and early modern period seems most often to have involved an external stimulus and an accretion of strangers. The external stimulus seems to have been bound up with the Crusades and the expanding influence of Venice. Now this city had a unique history. It was founded by people who were fleeing before the advancing Huns. They found a refuge on some barren islands which lacked even drinking water. Hence they were forced to become traders in order to survive. In the beginning they exchanged salt and fish for wheat and other necessities. Thus they escaped conquest by the Germans and remained under the sovereignty and influence of Constantinople; thus they maintained an urban tradition in an era of ruralization. But Venice did not attain importance until the Crusades created a great demand for supplies and ships to carry men and equipment to the Holy Land. She was relatively well prepared to supply these wants, because of her location, because she had many ships, and because she had a business system. While

[1] Henri Pirenne, *Medieval Cities: Their Origins and the Revival of Trade*, p. 76, 1925. By permission of Princeton University Press.

Europe as a whole was engaging in local barter, Venice was carrying cargoes between distant points, operating a credit system, keeping books, making commercial treaties. In due time other Italian cities began to imitate and rival Venice; ere long, merchants from these places were finding their way to the markets of various lands in western Europe.

Thus there come to be a conspicuous number of traveling merchants, peddlers, and foot-loose adventurers who went about in groups for mutual protection, sometimes organized themselves into brotherhoods, and usually invited the suspicion of those who lived settled lives under the feudal order. Now these wandering merchants needed a point to which they could return between trips, during the winter, or otherwise as convenience might dictate, so some of them settled down usually just outside the walls of some burg or episcopal town. Presumably they had not merely a place of temporary residence but one where goods might be stored and transferred. For defense they often erected a wall about their little settlement. Sometimes a "newburg" grew entirely around the old town, and ultimately the public interests and governments of the two tended to merge. To the merchants were added persons who engaged in transportation, the manufacture of boats and vehicles and other accessories of the developing commerce. Industries were drawn in from the country, *e.g.*, the making of wool. Now these new towns, of course, found it necessary to come to some sort of terms with the feudal proprietors of the soil. The merchants did not fit into the old order. They were a new sort of folks. Pirenne calls them *de facto* free men because their original status was unknown. But many of their servants and artisans came from near-by demesnes whose lords sometimes tried to identify and reclaim them. This made trouble, as did intermarriage of the two groups. Other ways in which feudalism hampered the development of trade included the fees charged for the holding of markets, use of bridges, and crossing the boundaries of petty states. Finding it difficult, if not impossible, to carry on business under feudal limitations, townsmen entered upon a struggle which was basically for four or five concessions. First of all, the city dwellers wanted freedom to transfer and mortgage their property without securing the permissions and paying the fees required of feudal tenants. Second, they wanted a new legal system eliminating the old-fashioned compurgations and ordeals and offering a more dependable, more rational system of justice, to be operated by their own magistrates. In the third place, they wanted to administer some of their own affairs independently and to raise taxes for these municipal purposes, which included water supply and fortification. In general, they wanted the abolition of feudal dues, the regulation of new laws, the appointment of their own officials—in short, a new social status. The acquisition of these prerogatives resulted in the recognition of "free cities" or city-states with more and more of the traits we associate with urbanism. In Germany several score of cities united in the great Hanseatic League to win and defend such concessions as we have just mentioned. In France, England, and other countries they made individual agreements with the nobility or secured royal aid in escaping from ancient requirements. Thus in one way or another there emerged not only a new agglomeration of people and buildings but also a new commerce, a new form of government—in short, a new way of life, urbanism.

The history of Paris[1] involves many of the features we have mentioned but is unique on account of the important role which government played in its development. Near the convergence of several navigable rivers and actually occupying an island in the Seine, Julius Caesar found Lutetia, the principal town of the Parisii. Two wooden bridges connected the island with the north and south banks respectively. The Romans built a town on the south bank with a theater, an arena, baths, villas, an aqueduct, and a highway. About A.D. 300 this luxurious town was destroyed; with the debris the island was walled. Only a fortified bridgehead remained on each bank. Early in the sixth century the Frankish chief Clovis made himself master of most of Gaul and established himself in the island town, now known as Paris. He and his successors founded numerous religious institutions on both banks of the river; around these gathered feudal estates and villages. In the ninth century Normans captured Paris, which was presently rebuilt, and devastated the surrounding country, whose inhabitants were forced to seek refuge within the town. In the tenth century Paris was still a fairly small town ruled by a bishop. Not until the twelfth

[1] A. Demangeon, *Paris: la ville et sa banlieue*, pp. 10–14, 1933; Lucien Gallois, "The Origin and Growth of Paris," *Geog. Rev.*, 13 (1923), 345–367.

century did the Capetian kings make it really the capital of France; not till then did it attain commercial importance.

But by 1200 Paris had become a city of some consequence. Structurally and functionally it consisted of three parts. The island, now called "La Cité," was the center of government and the site of the cathedral. It had narrow streets and was connected with the banks of the river by two bridges. On the north bank, where boats anchored, were a market and the houses and shops of merchants, but there were also many empty spaces, orchards, and vineyards interspersed with churches. On the south bank were schools and convents occupied by students, teachers, and writers, together with tradesmen who catered to their needs. In the thirteenth century the group included such illustrious foreigners as Thomas Aquinas and Albertus Magnus. Surrounding the whole city was a wall with towers and fortified gates, started by Philip Augustus in 1180. But the city could not be confined within these limits. The commercial section spread out toward the north so that in 150 years another wall was needed. Shortly before its erection a census was taken, in 1329, which enumerated 61,000 "hearths," *i.e.*, households, including possibly 290,000 persons.

The Industrial Revolution and the Development of Cities

It is impossible in such a work as this to follow the fortunes of other medieval towns as they grew into modern cities. The basic principles of their emergence and growth were established in such ways as have just been indicated. By the end of the eighteenth century there were in Europe possibly 300 towns and cities of 10,000 inhabitants or more; there were 21 cities of over 100,000 inhabitants.[1] The next great culture change associated with the development of cities is that complex series of events which we call the industrial revolution. As a matter of fact, this was not only industrial; it was also a revolution in agriculture, in transportation and communication, in social control, and in urbanization.

It is generally agreed that this great social change manifested itself first in England, probably first of all in the textile industry. England had a good climate for textile manufactures, farm lands

[1] Weber, *op. cit.*, Chap. 2.

were being enclosed to provide more wool for the spinners, British imperialism had opened the way for widespread markets for the finished products. Presently under some impetus, improvements were effected here and there in the making of woolen and cotton cloth. One invention followed another until the output was enormously increased and the number of employed workers multiplied manyfold.

Something of the same sort happened in the metal trades. Whether it was the reduced availability of charcoal that necessitated the use of coal and hence forced a change in the process of manufacturing iron and steel, or whether other influences would have brought this about, we need not pause here to inquire. We need only observe that in this industry another series of inventions took place which considerably changed the character of metalworking. The new development of mechanical power may have been stimulated by considerations of economy and desire for greater output in the industry just mentioned. Perhaps the need for new and greater power to pump water out of the mines, or perhaps still another stimulation, should be held accountable. In any case, the latter part of the eighteenth century and early part of the nineteenth saw the rapid displacement of man power by water and steam. Now this new mechanical power could be utilized most effectively in the operation of large machines or large groups of machines, hence it was natural that factories should appear and mass production should begin. But the development of factories meant the getting to them of great numbers of workers. So factory towns and cities grew up.

The changes that took place during the same period in agriculture facilitated the growth of cities in at least two ways. As new methods of tilling the soil and new farm implements were introduced, as lands were enclosed for the raising of sheep, there was a surplus labor supply crowded off the rural estates and available for employment in the factories. As agricultural production increased there was a surplus of foods and other raw materials by means of which urban populations could be supported.

Still a third revolution had to accompany the industrial and agricultural revolutions. There was a tremendous change in means of transportation and communication. The earlier roads and vehicles and ships could not possibly have carried from the farms to the cities sufficient food at a price and within a length of time that would have permitted large industrial communities to develop. But with the application of steam to both water and rail, this new urban growth was greatly facilitated. No less important has been the later development of canning, refrigeration, and cold storage. Since the conduct of business was no longer limited to local or even national markets, it required much better communications. The steamboat and the railroad carried people to and fro faster than ever before. The regular mails sped up the transmission of messages, the newspaper printed on a steam press disseminated general information to those concerned with the market. Long after, there came, of course, the telegraph and telephone, the radio, electric railway, automobile, and airway—all of which have made possible the transacting of business over large areas, economically uniting groups of great cities.

One of the first great cities to be developed in the industrial revolution was Manchester, England. But its origin was much earlier. Apparently the site was first occupied by a Roman camp. Subsequently a Saxon community grew up. In Norman times it was part of a feudal estate with a market, a fair, and a borough court. There is evidence that the textile industry had taken root before 1300. This received an impetus from the coming of Dutch and Flemish workers invited by Edward III. Through the sixteenth century the raw materials were wool and flax; by the middle of the seventeenth some cotton was being imported. The stuff was given out to be taken home, carded, spun, woven, bleached, or dyed, and returned to the merchant-clothier—the so-called domestic system. Hence, there was no large population in the town. In 1650 Manchester had less than 5,000 inhabitants.

But the domestic system was not very efficient. A weaver sometimes had to walk three or four miles in the morning to collect enough yarn to keep him busy through the day. By 1750 there were master weavers who, instead of giving out homework, brought together journeymen and apprentices in shops with 5 to 20 looms apiece. As a result of this centralization the population of Manchester had grown to 17,000. But industry and urban development were alike hampered by primitive transportation facilities. We read of wagons and caravans of packhorses going weekly to London and Bristol. During the next half century good roads were built and waterways were opened connecting Manchester with Liverpool and with inland towns.

In 1769 water power was applied to spinning machines, and soon mills were set up wherever there was a good water-power site. Industry was again decentralized, leaving to Manchester certain finishing processes and marketing. But by 1800 available water-power sites had nearly all been utilized. Meanwhile development of the steam engine and of near-by coal fields helped to reverse the trend and to bring about a new concentration of mills in Manchester. By 1800 the city had 70,000 inhabitants, of whom 10,000 were Irish immigrants. Naturally the city spread out, but it also became more congested in the center. New residential districts grew up in outlying sections, but near the heart of the city old houses were turned into converted tenements, where whole families were crowded into single rooms. Newer dwellings were put up in "gloomy little courts and blind alleys," while hundreds of families lived in dark, damp cellars. New streets in outlying districts were wide and straight, but those in the central and older section were narrow, winding, and for the most part unlighted and unpaved. In 1776 there was some widening, but not until 1821 was there a more general clearance. Moreover, its purpose was to facilitate traffic rather than to improve the public health. In 1830 the opening of the Manchester and Liverpool Railway brought another aid to urban development. By 1850 the population had risen to nearly 400,000. Thus grew up one of the first great industrial cities.[1]

Summary

Without attempting a recapitulation of culture history, we have attempted to show that the appearance and development of cities have been associated with various accretions to the cultures of the Near East and the Western world. Until there were settled abodes, arts and crafts, accumulation of material goods, and written records, cities were out of the question. Once established, they tended to become centers of administration, religion, defense, wealth, leisure, and the amenities. Such were the

[1] G. H. Tupling, "Old Manchester: a Sketch of Its Growth to the End of the Eighteenth Century," *Jour. Manchester Geog. Soc.*, 45 (1935), 5–23; R. S. Atwood, "Localization of the Cotton Industry in Lancashire. England," *Econ. Geog.*, 4 (1928), 187–195.

cities of the Mediterranean world in classical antiquity. But urbanism, as we know it, is not the result of a steady development from ancient cities. There was a partial, almost a total, eclipse lasting several centuries before urbanism was much in evidence. The Crusades stimulated a revival of commerce which spread gradually over western Europe and then to all parts of the world. The development of strong central governments favored the growth of cities, not only by weakening the feudal nobility but by creating wide areas within which trade might move freely. Protestantism contributed its bit indirectly through the encouragement of thrift, investment, and profit taking. Then came the factory system with the assembling of large numbers of workers. Mass production, like trade on a large scale, involved huge investments. Capital was supplied by persons who did not otherwise participate in the industrial process. Two social classes acquired new prominence—the owners and managers (bourgeoisie) and the wage-earning workers (proletariat). Finally, the development of great cities has depended on the use of faster and faster means of transportation and communication. In short, the evolution of urbanism since the middle ages has involved corresponding developments of commerce, government, religion, industry, agriculture, and transportation. Capitalism, nationalism, Protestantism, industrialism, and urbanism have all grown together in the modern world.

Selected Readings

Childe, V. Gordon: *Man Makes Himself.* Watts & Co. (London), 1936. Deals with the backgrounds of urbanism from the neolithic revolution to the formation of real cities.

Carpenter, Niles: *The Sociology of City Life.* Longmans, Green & Company, 1931. Chapter 1, The Beginnings of City Life, traces the development from neolithic "workshops" to the cities of classical antiquity, with special attention to Europe.

Adams, Thomas: *Outline of Town and City Planning.* Russell Sage Foundation, 1935. Chapters 1, 2, and 3 deal with the development of cities in the so-called ancient, medieval, and Renaissance periods—chiefly, but not exclusively, from the standpoint of planning.

Pirenne, Henri: *Medieval Cities: Their Origins and the Revival of Trade.* Princeton University Press, 1925. Describes the breakdown of urbanism during the Germanic invasions and its revival during the commercial revolution.

Mumford, Lewis: *The Culture of Cities.* Harcourt, Brace & Company, Inc., 1938. Chapters 1 and 2 offer a brilliant account of the development of medieval and early modern cities.

Chapter III

THE GROWTH OF CITIES SINCE 1800

Urbanization throughout the World

In Chap. II we pointed out how very recent is the development of cities and urban ways of life. We emphasized this by showing that in 1800, which roughly marks the beginning of the period of the industrial revolution, the percentage of our (United States) population that was urban (living in places of 8,000 or more) was less than 4. For all Europe it may have been equally small, though in Great Britain and the Netherlands it was somewhat greater. In the whole world there were only 21 cities of 100,000 or over, and these were all in Europe.[1] By 1927 Mark Jefferson was able to account for 537 such cities, half of them in Asia and 90 in North America. It is interesting to note that the continent on which the first cities may have appeared (Africa) is now the least urbanized, while the last to be settled (Australia) is the most completely urbanized. This suggests that urbanism has been slow to take hold of old populations, but that when people with city experience settled in new regions they quickly built up a thoroughly urban culture. At all events it stresses again the relation of urbanism to the new civilization. However, too much importance should not be attached to this fact. It was only in the Nile Valley, a very small corner of Africa, that cities appeared "spontaneously." In Australia cities were not indigenous at all; until the nineteenth century neither physical nor cultural conditions were favorable to urban development. It was the migration to Australia of people already habituated to city life that imposed an "exotic" urban civilization on this continent.

Turning from continents to countries, we note in Table 2 several interesting facts. First, there has been a tremendous increase in urbanism as measured by the number of great cities, by their population, and by the percentage of the total population

[1] Mark Jefferson, "Distribution of the World's City Folks," *Geog. Rev.*, 21 (1931), 446–465. It should be said that data concerning Asiatic cities are too meager to warrant this statement without qualification.

living in them. But the development has been far from uniform. Thus the number of great cities in both China and the United States rose in a century and a third from practically none to about 100. But the combined population of such cities in the United States was more than double that in China. Also the percentage metropolitan (*i.e.*, living in cities of 100,000 and over) was seven times as great in the United States. Italy, the scene of urban development for many centuries, and Japan, a newcomer in this field, had almost the same number of great cities and the same percentage of population metropolitan. Russia and France each had three great cities in 1800. By 1930 they had increased to 31 and 17 respectively, but the percentages metropolitan were 7 and 20.

TABLE 1.—URBANIZATION BY CONTINENTS, 1927[a]

Continent	Great cities (over 100,000)	Percentage urbanized (percentage of total population living in great cities)
Australasia	9	44
North America	90	24
Europe	182	19
South America	20	11
Asia	224	5
Africa	12	2.5
Total	537	

[a] Mark Jefferson, "Distribution of the World's City Folks," *Geog. Rev.*, 21 (1931), 446–465, By permission of the American Geographical Society.

Both Table 1 and Table 2 involve some estimates and some conflicting reports. They indicate, therefore, the approximate rather than the absolute truth. In some countries no census was taken until long after 1800. The most recent counts have not all been made in 1930; but for our present purpose this is unimportant. The actual dates range only from 1927 to 1932. For the United States we report metropolitan districts rather than municipalities. The boundaries of some countries have been greatly changed, some of them several times. For these and other reasons the figures in Table 2 must be used with discretion. Nevertheless, they display a genuine trend toward urbanization. When 1940 data are available, the table can be revised. Meanwhile the interested student can use the sources we consulted and see what trend is indicated for countries other

TABLE 2.—URBANIZATION, 1800–1930
In 15 Selected Countries[a]

Country	Percentage of population living in great cities		Number of great cities		Population of great cities	
	1930	1800	1930	1800	1930	1800
Great Britain	49	10	58	1	22,900,000	865,000
United States[b]	45	0	96	0	55,000,000	
Australia	43	0	5	0	3,050,000	
Germany	30	1	53	1	19,950,000	200,000
Argentina	30	0	8	0	3,750,000	
Canada	22	0	7	0	2,320,000	
France	20	3	17	3	8,625,000	765,000
Italy	15	4	22	4	6,175,000	800,000
Japan	14	0	21	0	9,200,000	
Brazil	10	0	10	0	4,000,000	
Mexico	8	0	4	0	1,400,000	
Russia	7	1	31	3	11,000,000	500,000
Turkey	7	?	3	3	1,000,000	1,000,000
China	6	0	112	3	22,000,000	?
India	3	0	38	0	11,900,000	

[a] Data for this table were derived from Adna F. Weber, *The Growth of Cities in the Nineteenth Century*, 1899; Mark Jefferson, "Distribution of the World's City Folks," *Geog. Rev.*, 21 (1931), 446–465; Fifteeth Census; *The World Almanac*, 1937.

[b] Fifteenth Census, *Metropolitan Districts*.

TABLE 3.—PERCENTAGE OF TOTAL POPULATION LIVING IN PLACES OF 10,000 AND OVER[a]

Country	1930	1890	1850	1800
England and Wales	80	62	39	21
France	50	26	14	10
United States	47	27	12	4
Australia	45	41		

[a] Data for first three periods are from Adna F. Weber, *The Growth of Cities in the Nineteenth Century*, pp. 144–145, 1899. For 1930 they are based on sources used in constructing Table 2 and are intentionally in round numbers.

than those listed. With the aid of Weber's classic study, he can supply figures for intermediate dates, thus showing the parts of the period 1800–1930 during which cities grew most rapidly in number, size, and share of the total population. To illustrate the sort of project which may well be undertaken we present Table 3.

From Table 3 it is easy to see that England started the nineteenth century with a larger percentage urban than did the three other countries. Moreover, England held this lead throughout the 130 years. France started out one-half as urban as England and two and a half times as urban as the United States. Yet by the middle of the century the United States had almost overtaken France. Since that time they have run "neck and neck," and have cut down England's lead. Australia made a late start, but was markedly urban from the outset. Similar data may profitably be assembled for other countries and for other dates, perhaps every 10 years beginning with 1890. Data for 1940 should be included as soon as they are available.

So far we have been considering urban development without reference to particular cities. In Table 4 we present data which indicate how very large certain cities have become and how they have grown since 1800. The general impression likely to be derived from this table is essentially correct. However, in detail many qualifications and corrections need to be made. Thus London did not double, nor did New York treble, in size from 1900 to 1930. The later figures cover the "greater" city, or the metropolitan district, while the earlier data represent only the "inner" city, or the political unit. Corrections of this sort can be made from the footnotes. Some data are missing altogether, because no census was taken or no reliable estimate is at our disposal. Nevertheless, the table strikingly portrays a period of rapid urban expansion. In 1800 there were no cities of one million, and less than 25 of 100,000 inhabitants. Now there are about 40 in the "million class." During this century and a third individual cities have grown at an amazing rate. Even old London multiplied ninefold, if we may assume that city and metropolitan district were approximately identical in 1800. Greater New York multiplied a hundred fold and Sydney nearly five hundred fold. Because a new census will soon be taken in many lands, students of the city should plan to supplement this table between 1940 and 1942.

One more comment should be made before we turn from worldwide urbanization to the growth of cities in our own country.

TABLE 4.—LARGEST CITIES IN THE WORLD[a]

	1930[b]	1900	1850	1800
London	8,200,000[c]	4,535,000	2,360,000	865,000
New York	10,900,000[d]	3,435,000	695,000	80,000
Tokyo	5,300,000	1,820,000		
Berlin	4,250,000	2,710,000	430,000	170,000
Shanghai	3,550,000	455,000		
Chicago	4,365,000[e]	1,700,000	30,000	
Paris	4,935,000[f]	2,660,000	1,050,000	550,000
Moscow	2,800,000	1,175,000	330,000	190,000
Leningrad	2,785,000	1,440,000	485,000	220,000
Osaka	2,600,000	1,000,000		
Buenos Aires	2,215,000	725,000	150,000	
Philadelphia	2,850,000[g]	1,295,000	120,000	40,000
Vienna	1,875,000	1,725,000	445,000	230,000
Detroit	2,105,000[h]	285,000	20,000	
Rio de Janeiro	1,500,000	690,000	165,000	
Calcutta	1,485,000	1,270,000	800,000	
Canton	1,370,000			
Peiping	1,300,000	1,000,000		
Nanking	1,300,000			
Los Angeles	2,320,000[i]	100,000	1,600	
Sydney	1,235,000	490,000	55,000	2,500
Rome	1,200,000			
Warsaw	1,200,000	640,000		
Bombay	1,160,000	775,000		
Hamburg	1,130,000	720,000	195,000	
Milan	1,120,000			
Montreal	1,100,000			
Barcelona	1,100,000			
Glasgow	1,090,000	760,000	345,000	80,000
Budapest	1,060,000		155,000	60,000
Cairo	1,060,000	570,000		
Birmingham	1,000,000			
Madrid	1,000,000			155,000
Boston[j]	2,310,000	560,000	135,000	25,000
Pittsburgh	1,955,000	450,000	70,000	1,500
St. Louis	1,295,000	575,000	80,000	
San Francisco	1,290,000	345,000	35,000	
Cleveland	1,195,000	380,000	17,000	
Istanbul[k] (Constantinople)	675,000	1,125,000		

[a] Principal sources for this table are *Whitaker's Almanack*, 1937, p. 206; W. S. Thompson, *Population Problems*, 1930, p. 273; Adna F. Weber, *The Growth of Cities in the Nineteenth Century*, Chap. 2; *Statesman's Year-book*, 1937; Fifteenth Census of the United States.

[b] These cities are ranked as in *Whitaker's Almanack*, 1937. Some reports include suburbs; others do not. The seemingly irrational ranking of American cities is due to the fact that the *Almanack* reported only the city proper, whereas we have reported the metropolitan district. For other cities, and probably for all cities in 1900 and earlier, only the city proper is considered.

[c] Administrative County of London in 1931 had a population of 4,385,000.

[d] New York City in 1930 had 6,930,000.

[e] The city of Chicago in 1930 had 3,375,000. But Chicago's urbanism really includes Milwaukee and South Bend. With their addition the "conurbation" about the lower end of Lake Michigan contains nearly 5,500,000 people.

[f] According to A. Demangeon, *Paris: la ville et sa banlieue*, p. 3, 1933, the population of the Département de la Seine was a fairly accurate statement for the metropolitan district. In 1931 the city proper had 2,870,000.

[g] The city of Philadelphia in 1930 had 1,950,000.

[h] The city of Detroit in 1930 had 1,570,000.

[i] The city of Los Angeles in 1930 had 1,240,000.

[j] We add five American cities whose metropolitan districts place them in the million class. The population in 1930 of each inner city alone was: Boston, 780,000; Pittsburgh, 670,000; St. Louis, 820,000; San Francisco, 635,000; Cleveland, 900,000. Note that their rank as indicated in the table would be considerably altered if we considered only the main city instead of the entire metropolitan district.

[k] Istanbul (Constantinople), though no longer in the class of cities of a million inhabitants, is included because of its previous size.

It is that urban development has been in part an aspect of general increase in population. It has been estimated that the world's population in 1750 was 660 million, that in 1850 it was 1,098 million, and that in 1930 it was 1,800 million.[1] In other words, we may assume that for the period 1800–1930 the human race doubled in number. This alone directly implies a great increase in city dwellers. Indirectly it has still further implications, for the improvements in agriculture which added to the world's food supply released surplus workers for urban commerce and industry. Hence it is quite natural that cities should grow much faster than their rural hinterlands.

The Growth of Cities in the United States

As might be expected, the growth of cities has been especially marked in our own country. With "a continent to conquer," unbelievable natural resources, a growing flood of immigrants (until 1914), new inventions appearing at an accelerated rate, and a philosophy of "bigger and better," what could be more natural than a great urban development? As shown in Table 2, we had in 1800 no city of 100,000 inhabitants. By 1930 we had 96 metropolitan districts with populations ranging from 100,000 to 11 million. Another way of regarding the trend toward urbanization is presented in Table 5. We see a great and a steady increase in the number of cities and in the percentage of the total population that is urban, whether the line be drawn at 8,000 or 100,000 or 1 million. Places of 8,000 and over have multiplied two hundred fold in 140 years, their population four hundred and sixty fold. In 1810 New York was the only city to exceed 100,000. It did not pass the 1 million mark until 1860, and no other city reached this size until 1890. Truly our great cities are very new. The repeated emphasis on the recency of this metropolitan development is necessary because we of this generation take our great cities so for granted. Grime and deterioration give them a superficial appearance of great age which belies the fact of their newness.

Another significant aspect of our urban trend is that the proportion of the total population that lives in urban centers has increased more in great cities than in small ones. It is true that small cities are continuing to grow. In fact, from 1920 to 1930

[1] Walter F. Willcox (ed.), *International Migrations*, vol. 2, Chap. 1, 1931.

cities of the 25,000–50,000 class showed a higher rate of actual increase than did those of any other size. This, however, is because many cities (municipalities) of that size were really parts of metropolitan districts. But considering the percentage

TABLE 5.—URBANIZATION OF THE UNITED STATES[a]
Number of Places of 8,000 or More, 100,000 or More, 1,000,000 or More; Percentage of Total Population in Each Group: 1790–1930

Year	Places of 8,000 and over		Places of 100,000 and over		Places of 1,000,000 and over	
	Number of places	Percentage of total population	Number of places	Percentage of total population	Number of places	Percentage of total population
1930 (Metropolitan districts)	....	....	96	44.6	10	25.0
1930 (Separate cities)	1208	49.1	93	23.6	5	12.3
1920	924	43.8	68	26.0	3	9.6
1910	768	38.7	50	22.1	3	9.2
1900	547	32.9	36	18.8	3	8.4
1890	445	29.0	26	15.4	3	5.8
1880	285	22.7	19	12.8	1	3.8
1870	226	20.9	14	11.6	1	3.8
1860	141	16.1	8	8.6	1	3.7
1850	85	12.6	6	5.8		
1840	44	8.5	3	3.5		
1830	26	6.7	1	1.8		
1820	13	4.9	1	1.5		
1810	11	4.9	1	1.6		
1800	6	4.0				
1790	6	3.0				

[a] Fifteenth Census, *Population*, vol. 1, pp. 9–21, and *Metropolitan Districts*, pp. 7–13.

of the total population in urban places of specified size in 1890 and 1930, and computing the ratio of the latter to the former, we get the results shown in Table 6.

Associated Factors

This great upsurge of urban development did not occur in a vacuum. It was accompanied by a host of other social changes, some of which we have identified in connection with the industrial revolution. In speaking of these we shall not assume any particular causal relation; we shall proceed rather on the assumption that all of them are somehow interrelated as integral parts of our cultural development. First let us note the increasing numbers of mechanical inventions. In the decade ending with 1850 the United States Patent Office issued approximately 9,000 patents. In the decade ending with 1930 it issued 423,000.[1] It is not necessary to suppose that all or even a majority of these patents represented important innovations; we are not even sure that the relative number of significant inventions has been the same throughout this period. A forty-seven fold increase, however, must mean not merely an accumulation of new devices but also an accelerated rate of innovation. Thus mechanical invention has played an ever more important role from the industrial revolution until now.

Table 6.—Proportionate Rates of Growth by Size of City[a]

	Percentage of total population in places of given size		Ratio of 1930 percentage to 1890 percentage
	1890	1930	
2,500 or more	35.4	56.2	1.59
10,000 or more	27.6	47.6	1.72
25,000 or more	22.2	40.2	1.81
50,000 or more	18.6	35.0	1.88
100,000 or more	15.4	29.6	1.92
500,000 or more	7.1	17.1	2.44
1,000,000 or more	5.8	12.3	2.12

[a] Based on Fifteenth Census, *Population*, vol. 1, p. 14.

From the very beginning of city life, as we have pointed out, it has been necessary that there should be a surplus both of foodstuffs and of laborers over and above what would be required in a strictly agricultural civilization. With this observation in mind we note that the production of cereals in the United States increased from 600 million bushels in 1840 to 4,600 million bushels

[1] *Recent Social Trends*, vol. 1, p. 126.

in 1930.[1] During approximately the same period the number of wage earners employed in manufacturing in the United States increased from less than 1 million to about 9 million.[2] Not only was there this tremendous increase in both agricultural and industrial production; there was a corresponding increase in trade as measured by our exports and imports. In 1840 the sum total of our foreign trade was valued at about $240 million. In 1920 it had risen to $13,500 million. This was very definitely the period of rapid urban growth in the United States, and the association of these facts can hardly be accidental.

The growth of cities during this time, with their expanding commerce and industry, would have been very unlikely, if not impossible, without a parallel expansion of our facilities for transportation and communication. In 1830 we had only 40 miles of railroad; by 1930 we had 250,000 miles.[3] Beginning even earlier there was a tremendous development of roads and highways. Exact figures for most of this period are not available, but by the beginning of the twentieth century there were 2 million miles of roads (not counting city streets), of which 150,000 miles were surfaced and less than 150 miles were paved. By 1935 the total mileage had passed 3 million. Surfaced roads had increased to 700,000, and there were well over 100,000 miles of paving. A major factor in the expansion and improvement of our highways was the automobile. Cars appeared first toward the end of the nineteenth century; their number passed 1 million just before the World War and reached 23 million before the last depression.[4]

Much older than the automobile is the post office. Indeed, there was a postal system of sorts before the Declaration of Independence, but it was not until 1863 that a uniform rate was fixed. Free delivery, registration of letters, and a money-order system came about the same time. Special delivery came 20 years later, parcel post after the turn of the century. Data are not at hand to show the volume of mail handled in the nineteenth century, but in a little over 20 years preceding the last depression first-class mail increased from 7 billion pieces per year to 17

[1] Adna F. Weber, *The Growth of Cities in the Nineteenth Century*, p. 26, 1899; *The World Almanac*, 1935, p. 354.

[2] *The World Almanac*, 1935, p. 311.

[3] Weber, *op. cit.*, p. 25; *The World Almanac*, 1933, p. 391.

[4] *Recent Social Trends*, vol. 1, pp. 172–176.

billion pieces, *i.e.*, from 80 per capita to nearly 140 per capita.[1] It was during the period of our urban expansion that the telegraph, the ocean cable, and the telephone made their first appearance. From tiny beginnings our telegraph lines have increased to over 250,000 miles and are reported to have carried 160 million messages in 1934. In similar fashion the telephone has spread over the land until there are now over 80 million miles of wire and more than 150 million telephones, carrying more than 30 billion calls a year.

We have made no mention of commercial aviation, the air mail, wireless telegraph, and radio. Doubtless these will greatly affect the further development of our cities, but their appearance has followed rather than preceded our major urban growth to date.

Another mark of the great change in American life from rural, agricultural folkways and institutions to urban, commercial,

TABLE 7.—OCCUPATIONAL SHIFTS[a]
Percentage of Gainfully Occupied Persons in Certain Occupational Groups: 1870 and 1930

Occupation	1870 Percentage	1930 Percentage
Clerical	1.7	8.2
Professional	2.7	6.5
Trade and transportation	9.1	20.7
Manufacturing and mechanical	22.0	28.6
Domestic and personal service	9.6	11.3
Agriculture	52.8	21.3

[a] *Recent Social Trends*, vol. 1, p. 284. By permission of the President's Research Committee on Social Trends.

and industrial patterns is the measure of occupational shifts. The 60-year decline in the percentage engaged in agriculture is nothing less than startling. All the other major groups show increases which are relatively greatest in clerical occupations, professions, trade, and transportation, in the order named. We might have expected manufacturing to absorb a larger part of the former agricultural population. But in recent years factories have occupied a decreasing share of the gainfully employed.

[1] *Ibid.*, pp. 191–194.

Since 1910 the greatest gains have been made in clerical occupations and in trade, *i.e.*, in selling.

Periods of Urban Development

McKenzie offers an interpretation of urban development in the United States in relation to three periods, each with a corresponding type of transportation—water, railroad, motor.[1] The first period, according to his analysis, was that of development along the seacoast, lakes, and navigable rivers. This era lasted to 1850 and was marked by a predominantly rural population living east of the Mississippi River, in fact, mainly east of the Alleghenies. The second period was marked by rapid westward expansion of the railroad, occupation of new lands, and the development of cities at junctions and convenient shipping centers. The third period, which McKenzie dates from about 1900, is one of what he calls "city regionalism." Both wholesale and retail trade, the marketing of farm produce and the distribution of manufactured goods are centered in great cities and handled largely by motor transportation.

A slightly different interpretation, although one not incompatible with McKenzie's, has been offered by Mark Jefferson.[2] It is graphically presented in Fig. 1. In this chart the name of a given city appears in the period during which it reached a population of 100,000; it appears in the vertical column which represents the major transportation facility at its disposal. Progression from period to period through the development of ocean, river, lake, and railroad transportation is quite obvious from this chart. From checking the chart with the histories of these cities it is interesting to find that they had been founded in periods following approximately the same order as those in which they reached 100,000. When we view the location of these cities on a map, we wonder why they did not develop first along the Hudson-Mohawk-Great Lakes route. Physically this was an easier way to the West than that which crossed the mountains between the Potomac and the Ohio valleys. Perhaps the conflict between France and England held the English-speaking people back from the Great Lakes region until a strong move-

[1] R. D. McKenzie, *The Metropolitan Community*, Chap. 1, 1933.

[2] Mark Jefferson, *op. cit.*, p. 462. Figure adapted by permission of the American Geographical Society.

ment toward the southwest had already been established. Moreover, the Mohawk Valley has been much more useful as a rail route than as a waterway. The lake cities are all important railroad centers.

Rise of Great Cities in Relation to Transportation

Period	Ocean	River	Lake	Railroad
1800–1840	New York Baltimore Boston New Orleans			
1840–1870	Philadelphia San Francisco	Cincinnati St. Louis Pittsburgh Louisville	Chicago Buffalo	
1870–1900	Providence Fall River	Memphis	Cleveland Detroit Milwaukee Toledo	Minneapolis Rochester Kansas City Omaha Indianapolis Denver Columbus Worcester Syracuse New Haven Paterson Los Angeles Scranton

Fig. 1.

Without dividing the last century and a third into periods, McKenzie has suggested another possible basis of classification. On the whole, population has moved from east to west, but more and more it appears to be turning back, so that instead of the ratio of westward to eastward movement being 9:1 as in 1900, it was only 3:1 in 1930. A similar change has been taking place in the movement of population between the North and the South. After the Civil War there was a marked movement into the South. By 1900 more people were moving north than in the opposite direction and by 1930 the ratio of northward to southward movement was approximately

2:1.[1] The manner of computing the data which support these statements is briefly this: Take the census reports for each state, the people born in it and in other states; people born in a state to the east are counted as representing a westward movement. The same principle is, of course, applied to all four directions of the compass. Still another basis of dividing our urban development into periods is suggested by the census data concerning the percentage of the population urbanized in different regions at various dates. Thus in 1880 New England was the only section that showed more than half the population urban. In 1890 this predominant urbanization was also evident in the North Atlantic states. By 1910 it had extended to the East North Central and Pacific groups. Undoubtedly this southwestward trend is associated with the development of transportation and other factors previously discussed.

In the early years of our republic, there was a steady stream of settlers pouring into the West, pushing steadily on to new frontiers; but about 1890 there ceased to be any new frontiers to occupy, and in place of dispersion we began to see a very marked concentration of population. To be sure, there had been long before this a definite increase in the percentage of population that was urban, but the end of the nineteenth century seemed to mark a special sort of turning point. So great was this change that by 1930 only 27 counties contained one-fourth of our entire population. Two-thirds of our people lived within 50 miles of the seaboard or the Great Lakes. Nearly one-half lived in our 96 metropolitan districts. Not only that, but of the increase in population for 1920–1930, three-fourths occurred in 63 metropolitan zones.[2]

Finally, the development of American cities may be divided into periods according to the dominant ethnic groups which contributed to their growth. In the first half of the nineteenth century our own rural white folk furnished most of the accretions to our urban population. From the Civil War to the World War it was immigrants from abroad. Since 1900, rural Negroes from the South have been an increasingly important element in urban growth. These changes will be discussed further in Chap. XVI.

[1] McKenzie, *op. cit.*, p. 12.

[2] *Ibid.*, pp. 19–21.

TABLE 8.—RANK OF THE 10 LARGEST AMERICAN CITIES AT VARIOUS TIMES AND THEIR POPULATIONS IN THOUSANDS

City	1790		1810		1830		1850		1870		1890		1910		1930	
	Rank	Population	Rank	Population	Rank	Population	Rank	Population	Rank	Population	Rank	Population	Rank	Population	Rank	Population
New York	1	49	1	120	1	242	1	696	1	1,478	1	1,912	1	4,767	1	6,930
Philadelphia	2	28	2	54	3	80	4	121	2	674	2	847	3	1,549	3	1,950
Boston	3	18	4	33	4	61	3	137	6	250	4	363	5	671	9	781
Baltimore	4	13	3	46	2	81	2	169	5	267	6	332	7	558	8	805
New Orleans	..	..	5	17	5	46	5	116	8	191	10	216				
Cincinnati	..	..	..	...	6	25	6	115	7	216	7	255				
St. Louis	..	..	..	...	..	...	7	78	3	311	5	351	4	687	7	822
Chicago	..	..	..	...	..	...	..	...	4	299	3	503	2	2,185	2	3,376
San Francisco	..	..	..	...	..	...	..	...	9	149	9	234				
Pittsburgh	..	..	..	...	10	15	..	...	10	139	8	235	8	534	10	670
Buffalo	..	..	..	...	..	...	9	42	..	.....	..	.....	10	424	..	573
Cleveland	..	..	..	...	..	...	..	...	..	.....	..	.....	6	560	6	900
Detroit	..	..	..	...	..	...	..	...	..	.....	..	.....	9	465	4	1,569
Los Angeles	..	..	..	...	..	...	..	...	..	.....	..	.....	..	.....	5	1,238
Providence	5	6	6	10	8	17	10	42								
Richmond	6	4	7	10	9	16										
New Haven	..	..	9	6												
Washington	..	..	8	8	7	19										
Springfield, Mass.	7	2	10	3												
Louisville, Ky.	..	..	..	...	..	...	8	43								

Each of these suggestions concerning periods of urban development may be helpful in understanding the changing ranks of cities from decade to decade. Table 8 shows the position and population (in thousands) of the 10 urban leaders at the time of every other census. Note that New York has held first place from the beginning. But observe that New Orleans, after holding fifth place from 1810 to 1850, a period of river transportation, dropped out of the first 10 after 1890 when railways had spread over the whole country. The late appearance of Detroit in the list is associated with the fact that the automobile industry arose about 1900 and happened to be centered in that city. The story of Los Angeles will be told in the next chapter. In the case of Boston an important correction must be made. Although in 1930 it ranked ninth as a city, it ranked fifth as a metropolitan district, for most of the people of Greater Boston lived outside the city limits in various satellite, or suburban, places. To facilitate similar corrections for the other cities we present Table 9.

TABLE 9.—COMPARATIVE RANK OF CITIES AND OF CORRESPONDING METROPOLITAN DISTRICTS, 1930[a]

City	Rank as city	Rank as metropolitan district
New York	1	1
Chicago	2	2
Philadelphia	3	3
Detroit	4	6
Los Angeles	5	4
Cleveland	6	10
St. Louis	7	8
Baltimore	8	12
Boston	9	5
Pittsburgh	10	7
San Francisco	11	9
Milwaukee	12	16
Buffalo	13	14
Washington	14	18

[a] Compiled from Fifteenth Census, *Metropolitan Districts*, pp. 10–13.

SELECTED READINGS

WEBER, ADNA F.: *The Growth of Cities in the Nineteenth Century*, Columbia University Press, 1899. This remains the most important statistical study of the period in question.

McKenzie, R. D.: *The Metropolitan Community*, McGraw-Hill Book Company, Inc., 1933. This is one of the monographs prepared under direction of the President's Research Committee on Social Trends. It covers the period from 1900 to 1930, for the most part statistically.

Mumford, Lewis: *The Culture of Cities*, Harcourt, Brace & Company, Inc., 1938. Chapters 3 and 4 depict the development of cities from the industrial revolution to the present. Both narrative and interpretation.

Schlesinger, Arthur M.: *The Rise of the City*, The Macmillan Company, 1933. Chapters 3–5 and 9–11 constitute a narrative of the rise of cities and of urbanism in the United States since the Civil War.

Chapter IV

HABITATS OF CITIES

In Chap. II we observed that the rise of cities was clearly related to a minimum development of culture and to a certain kind of physical setting. The former included the growing of some cereals, some use of metals, building with bricks, wheeled carts and sailing vessels, and some system of records. The latter involved a mild climate, fertile river valleys surrounded by deserts, mountains, and oceans. The rivers furnished water for domestic use and irrigation of crops; they provided a basis for transportation. The deserts and mountains afforded some freedom from attack; they favored living close together on land that was arable. Both the general setting (location) and the immediate setting (site) were involved in the rise and growth of cities. Each of these phases of the urban habitat will now be discussed in some detail; but for the moment we may say simply that location is a matter of regional characteristics, including resources and their development, general climatic conditions, raw materials, fuel, power, transportation facilities, markets, labor, capital, and nearness of competitors. Site, on the other hand, is the ground space on which a city is built, with its surface, geological structure, water supply and waterways, vegetation, and climate.

Urban Sites: Features of the Simple Site

The site of a city, to state it in other words, is the area occupied by it, the features of this area, and the pattern of construction and land use which is imposed upon it. We shall consider the various features of sites in terms of the following: (*a*) size and shape of land and water areas, (*b*) surface, (*c*) terrain, (*d*) climate, (*e*) water supply, (*f*) bodies of water, (*g*) native vegetation.

a. Size and Shape of Land and Water Areas.—The site which offers the simplest relations for the development of an urban center is that of an extensive tract of smooth land. The physical features of such a site offer a minimum of conditions to which the urban pattern must be adapted. The usual design is that of a square or checkerboard pattern. In most instances the streets are oriented along north-south and east-west axes. As Chicago spread across the low, flat lake plains, this type of pattern was projected monotonously. In many cities where the site affords only small areas of smooth land surface, regular squares are laid out even though they may be surrounded by crooked, winding, or diagonal streets. Occasionally a site with an extensive smooth surface has lent itself to intricate designs of circles, squares, and diagonals, as in the case of Washington, D. C., and the newer part of Berlin.

As the site comprises both land and water areas, the size, shape, and placement of these areas determine the major structure of the urban pattern. In Venice a group of small sand-bar islands in the delta of the Po River has been developed by means of enlarging the islands for building sites and using the distributary channels of the river as canal-streets. The site of Boston consists of partially submerged glacial deposits as represented by numerous islands, estuaries, marshes, promontories, and peninsulas. As a consequence Boston, which was established on a small peninsula, has spread over the metropolitan site by developing numerous nucleuses on the separated land areas. Some of the hills have been leveled and some of the marshlands have been filled in, but characteristics of the site are an outstanding feature of the Boston metropolitan pattern. Greater New York has similar conditions in its site. The original nucleus on Manhattan spread northward across the Harlem River into the Bronx, across the East River into Brooklyn on Long Island, across New York Bay to Staten Island, across the Hudson to Jersey City, and across the Hackensack Meadows to Newark. As the site is on the shore of a large body of water, one-half of a symmetrical pattern is displayed, as in the case of Chicago and of Cleveland.

If the site of an urban center is crossed by an important river or water channel a bi-core pattern will probably be developed. There are many so-called twin cities illustrating this type, such as St. Louis–East St. Louis, Omaha–Council Bluffs, and Cincinnati–Covington. If the river is relatively small and one municipality is on both sides, there usually develops a bi-core nucleus in the pattern at the important bridgehead connecting them. If the site is at the confluence of two rivers, a tri-core is probable. An outstanding example is Zanesville, with its famous "Y" bridge. Various combinations of the above site arrangements of land and water areas may be found.

b. The surface forms found in urban sites are those of plain, hill, plateau, and mountain. The basic contrast in these forms is the relief, *i.e.*, the difference between the highest and the lowest elevation. As was pointed out in the preceding section, a plain surface with slight relief permits the uniform expansion of an urban center in all directions with equal ease.

A hilly site is characterized by steep short slopes and necessitates a deliberate modification of pattern to surface. In a truly hilly site a contour street pattern is typical, *i.e.*, the long blocks are on streets at right angles to the steep slopes. In such patterns, cross streets are commonly absent, or at least exceedingly rare. In many cases inclines or steps lead from one contour level to another. Cincinnati has several examples of such adaptations. In most hill regions which become the sites of urban centers there are valley floors along which the major streets are laid out, and at the convergence of one or more valley floors is the major core. Such small cities as Butte, Mont., and Bingham, Utah, are excellent examples.

Some cities are located at the edge of a plateau escarpment. This is the case in Duluth. A long major street parallels the lake front at the base of the escarpment. Short cross streets end at the shore and at the steep slopes of the escarpment. An inclined railway leads from the lower city to the suburb on the edge of the plateau. With the development of modern highway building, expensive roads with hairpin loops climb the face of the escarpment, culminating in a scenic sky-line drive.

The adaptation of urban-center plans to mountain sites differs from their adaptation to hilly sites, chiefly in degree. The cost of developing an urban pattern on a long, steep mountain slope is generally sufficient to discourage much expansion.

c. The adaptation of an urban center to its geological terrain involves the composition of the mantle-rock and bedrock. The principal significance is the texture and depth of the mantle-rock. If it is deep and can be easily moved, the development of an urban pattern may greatly modify the original surface of the site. For example, a considerable part of the site of St. Louis is underlain by deep, fine-textured loessial clays. With modern grading machinery, the high, rugged slopes can be peeled off and dumped into narrow, shallow ravines, resulting in a gently undulating surface.

At Seattle a major hill composed of glacial sands and gravels obstructed the expansion of the city, but by means of hydraulic flushing the hill was washed away, filling up adjacent marshlands over which Seattle could expand.

If there is no mantle-rock and the hard bedrock is exposed at the surface, great expense is involved in removing hills and knolls which interfere with the expansion of the urban pattern. On Manhattan many of the original hard-rock irregularities have been blasted away and the monotonously uniform checkerboard pattern has been extended over the island. The features of the original terrain are somewhat preserved in Central Park. At Rio de Janeiro a high mountain rose abruptly at the edge of the city, obstructing its expansion and interfering with the health-giving breezes. This mountain was cut away at great expense, giving room for the expansion of the city and improving the healthfulness of the site. The mantle-rock was used to fill in low places along the shore and thus added to the beauty of the site. If the bedrock hills and ridges are too large and numerous to be removed, tunnels can pierce them and thus provide access to other valley lands for urban expansion. Such tunnels have been constructed at Pittsburgh and Los Angeles.

Where the bedrock is exposed at the surface or the mantle-rock is exceedingly shallow, the laying of water mains, sewer mains, gas mains, and telephone and electrical conduits is exceedingly expensive, owing to the fact that the ditches must be blasted cubic foot by cubic foot. Also, under such conditions the cost of excavating cellars or basements for buildings is prohibitive and they are set on top of the ground. Large cities which require many subways must spend many millions of dollars in construction in such bedrock. New York City is an outstanding example.

The presence of bedrock near the surface is an advantage in the construction of tall skyscraper buildings, because the steel skeleton must be firmly keyed. Such keying is essential in regions subject to earthquakes, as has been demonstrated in San Francisco. The buildings which were keyed into the bedrock suffered slight damage from the earthquake, whereas those constructed on "made land" and not keyed into the bedrock suffered great damage.

Where the mantle-rock is deep and moist, the construction of large, tall buildings is greatly handicapped by the lack of a firm foundation. An outstanding example is found in the Loop district of Chicago, where expensive piling and concrete mats must be constructed as a foundation. Similar conditions prevail in New Orleans. Where the depth of mantle-rock varies markedly in an urban site, this results in localizing the development of skyscraper districts. Such localization may be noted in the upper and lower Manhattan skyscraper districts, which are built on shallow bedrock, and the intervening space, which is underlain by deep, unconsolidated sands and gravel. Another instance is Minneapolis, where the surface is a smooth glacial plain which buries irregular preglacial rocky surface. Thus it is that a small group of city blocks have shallow mantle-rock and are suitable for skyscrapers. Adjacent to them are many blocks under which the bedrock is so deep that suitable foundations are not found. In cities which are underlain with limestone-country rock, curious subsurface drainage may develop. For example, in Bellevue, Ohio, such subsurface drainage lines take care of the city's sewerage system. In St. Louis subterranean caves and channels have been filled with quicksand adding greatly to the cost of construction of the buildings on such sites.

d. The features of climate which are important in the development of an urban site involve temperature, precipitation, and wind. The usual interpretation is in terms of healthfulness or unhealthfulness. A hot, humid climate generally imposes conditions favorable for sunstroke, malaria and other fevers, and dysentery diseases. In cool, moist, raw climates, handicaps to health are in the categories of the lung diseases and rheumatism.

It is obvious that the design and appearance of cities in these contrasted types of climates present marked contrasts. In hot climates exposure to the free sweep of winds is very desirable. As a consequence, in well-planned cities in such locations the streets are wide and the houses are low and widely spaced. Most of the buildings are constructed of light materials and have wide, screened verandas and large windows and doors. In urban centers developed in cold regions, where the exposure of building walls to cold winds means increased heating cost, buildings are close together along narrow, canyonlike streets. Most of them are several stories high and have small doors and windows.

The appearance of cities in arid regions is generally different from that of cities in humid regions. Where there is little or no precipitation, flat roofs are common. The adobe pueblos of southwestern United States and the flat sky line of Cairo are typical examples. Where the precipitation is abundant, steeply pitched roofs are necessary for the rapid runoff of water or the slipping off of snow. The steep roofs of Switzerland and the peaked huts of Burma are excellent examples.

The amount and distribution of precipitation are also critical in the design of storm-sewer systems. If the rains are torrential, drainage lines of large capacity must be constructed adequately to carry off the heavy precipitation.

e. The problem of water supply increases rapidly as urban centers develop in size. Some cities derive adequate supplies from springs or wells. The larger cities tend to depend upon large rivers, lakes, or artificial storage basins. It has been necessary for London to reach farther and farther into its hinterland for an adequate supply of water, utilizing sources as remote as the Welsh hills. In a similar fashion New York City has tapped the Catskill Mountains for its water. There is keen rivalry between Boston and the cities of the Connecticut Valley for urban water supplies. San Francisco has reached across the San Joaquin Valley into the Sierra Nevadas. The critical struggle of Los Angeles for an adequate water supply involves long pipe lines to Owens Lake in the Sierra Nevadas and across the deserts to the Colorado River. In contrast, cities on the Great Lakes and the large rivers of the central states have plenty of water near at hand. The problem of water supply for growing cities in regions with scanty precipitation and inadequate ground water amounts almost to a crisis.

f. Bodies of water include oceans, lakes, rivers, swamps, and marshes. Urban sites on ocean coasts are subject to tidal ranges and commonly to severe storms. If the coast is low the problems of handling tidal flats arises. A notable example of such a site is that of Galveston, where a large part of the site has been reclaimed from the shallow waters of the bay and lagoons. The low elevation of this reclaimed land affords little protection from the hurricanes which at irregular intervals sweep across the

Gulf of Mexico. Tremendous damage to the city has occurred in the past, and in self-defense the city has built a sea wall to minimize the hazards. In the New York district many of the urban nucleuses were separated by extensive tidal flats or meadows. Many of these have been reclaimed, as at Newark and on the west end of Long Island. Similar made land forms a part of the water front of San Francisco, where it constitutes a serious hazard because of the earthquakes which occur in that vicinity. Along the western coast of Europe many city sites were established at the head of navigation at times when the draught of ocean-going vessels was relatively shallow. With the designing of ships of increased draught, particularly large transatlantic vessels, two alternatives have presented themselves. At Hamburg, *e.g.*, the estuary of the river has been deepened at tremendous cost in order to accommodate vessels of deep draught. Where the cost has been prohibitive, as at Bremen, an outer port, like Bremerhaven, has been developed. Some American cities have declined as ocean ports because of the change in ship design. An unusual situation occurs at New Orleans because, as the delta is built into the Gulf, the distance from the Gulf to New Orleans gradually increases. In Iraq, Basra was once a coastal city, but because of the growth of the Shat el Arab area it is now several miles inland. The cities of England have experienced great difficulty in adapting themselves to the high tidal range of the estuaries. At London large docks or basins have been built into which the vessels come at high tide and remain until a succeeding high tide.

Sites on large lakes are similar to those on ocean coasts, the main differences being the less violent character of storms and the absence of tidal range. Sites on rivers are affected by the characteristics of the stream. If the site is on a flood plain, the problem of handling floodwaters requires much adjustment in the form of levees. Cairo, Ill., is completely encircled by high embankments to keep out the floodwaters of the Mississippi and Ohio rivers. New Orleans is similarly protected from the floods of the lower Mississippi. Many cities have a tendency to encroach and build a line on the channel of the stream and thus increase the hazards of flood damage. Paris has repeatedly suffered great damage because of the backing up of floodwaters through the sewer mains of the city, thus reversing their normal flow. On account of the wide flood range of the Ohio River most of the cities along its banks are periodically flooded.

Marsh sites have generally been avoided in the development of cities. Some marshes, however, have been located in such strategic positions that cities have been built in spite of them. Venice is the classic example of the use of such a marsh area. Even Rome has had its marshland problems. Shanghai has been created by foreign interests in the marshlands of the Yangtze delta. New Orleans also has been built in the midst of vast swamplands. The suburbs of Miami have been encroaching upon the Everglades.

g. The native vegetation of a site is only a temporary factor. The site may be forest, savanna, prairie, grassland, steppe, or desert. Of these, the forest offers the problem of clearing and, in particularly rainy areas, the problem of keeping the forest from encroaching upon the site. The grassland affords the best of conditions for the laying out of a city, since no problem of clearing presents itself. In deserts the cities develop at oases. Such cities are commonly inconvenienced by drifting sands accompanying the migration of sand dunes.

Generally the type of native vegetation is reflected in the planting of trees along streets in parks and playgrounds. Tropical cities are noted for their magnolia drives and palm-lined boulevards. New England is famous for its elms and western Europe for its oaks and lindens. Northern cities are featured by pines and spruces.

Urban Location

The location of cities commonly determines their potential development. Urban sites are strategic with regard to the direction of movement of people or commerce and the occurrence of resources.

The movement of people or commerce is commonly focused at straits, islands, capes, isthmuses, passes, elevations, confluences of rivers, river crossings, and river bends. Singapore, Batavia, and Gibraltar are examples of cities which have developed at straits. Honolulu and Havana are cities located on strategic islands. Capetown is a lone example of an important cape site; Panama and Suez are outstanding isthmus cities which have had their importance enhanced because of ship canals. Many of the cities of Europe have developed around medieval castles, which for purposes of defense were located on strategic elevations rising abruptly above surrounding lowlands. Belfort, Vienna, Albany, Lanchowfu, Yarkand, and Kashgar have developed relative to passes or water gaps. The list of cities located at the confluence of rivers is long; Pittsburgh, Paris, Manaos, Hankow, and St. Louis are excellent examples. Many cities have been located at convenient river crossings, *e.g.*, Paris, London, and Budapest. Cities developed at river bends generally mean a break in transportation between river and overland routes; Kansas City and Cincinnati are examples.

Changes in the means of navigation due to the change in the vessel draught are important in determining strategic sites. Chief of these is the change from oceanic to inland waterways. The most important ports are examples of such sites, *e.g.*, Hamburg, Le Havre, and Rotterdam. Changes in the depth of river channels are usually determined by the confluence of important rivers and are sometimes significant, as at St. Louis and St. Paul. Interruptions of river routes by falls and rapids necessitate portages which account for such urban sites as those at Louisville and Leopoldville.

Changes in the means of transportation from oceanic to continental are also reflected in the development of port cities. Overland transportation may be by means of caravan, highway, or railroad. The larger the network of continental lines which focus at a port city, the larger is the potential development of that city. New York, Hamburg, and Buenos Aires are examples of port cities with extensive railway nets.

Functions of Urban Location

The type of urban center which is developed at a given site is determined by the features which are characteristic of its regional locations, such as animal husbandry, agriculture, forestry, mining, and manufacturing. Some of the functions which characterize locations favor the concentration of population in cities, others do not. Some functions are symbiotic, *i.e.*, mutually complementary, and some are parasitic, *i.e.*, dependent on other functions. Some of the locations are characterized by simple, homogeneous economic environments, and others are complex, with interrelated, diversified functions. Whether the economic environment is simple or complex, the functions of the environment are reflected in the economic functions of the urban centers. In regions characterized by fur trading, the business activities of the city reflect that occupation in the warehouses and offices of the fur companies. Where fisheries are important, the water front is marked by fish wharves and houses. If the region produces wheat, elevators and flourmills form part of the city landscape. Sawmills and wood-milling factories reflect forestry conditions. Mines and smelters indicate mining activities.

The various business activities which handle and process the commodities produced in the economic environment are housed in buildings and plants designed to meet the characteristics of the various types of commodities, which are consumed in the surrounding economic environment. The executives and wage earners engaged in the various businesses contribute the personalities to the urban social structure.

Some urban centers possess strategic locations with respect to transportation, commerce, government, finance, culture, recreation, and health. Executives, clerks, administrators, teachers, doctors, clergy, entertainers, domestics, and miscellaneous service employees compose the social structure of such centers.

The great cities of the world are complex in their economic and social structure. Cities are likely to be characterized by special attributes which give an urban individualism to each of them in physical appearance, economic structure, and social atmosphere. Thus, some urban centers may be readily characterized by a single word or phrase, as: Detroit—automobiles; Tulsa—oil; Washington—capital; Pittsburgh—steel; Fall River—textiles; Minneapolis—flour; Los Angeles—movies; Duluth—iron ore; Atlantic City—amusements; Miami—resorts; Hot Springs—sanitariums; Rome—Vatican; Oxford—colleges; London—Lloyd's; Benares—temples; New York—Wall Street; Chicago—Loop; Paris—Louvre; Seattle—lumber; Johannesburg—gold; Bagdad—dates; Butte—smelters; Geneva—dynamos; Dresden—china; Bombay—cotton; Tokyo—silk; Calcutta—tea; Glasgow—ships. The list could be lengthened easily: Philadelphia is sometimes called "the world's workshop" because of the great size and variety of its manufacturing plants. Cairo is "where East meets West," Panama is "a human melting pot." One of the world's trade centers, Victoria, Hong Kong, is "a bit of

England in the Orient." Chinatowns in many occidental cities are fragments of the Orient.

The resultant combination of natural sites, economic functions, and social structures produces a geographic profile. Its basic characteristics are determined by the natural surface on which the cultural functions take place. The sky line is composed of cultural features such as housetops, church steeples, temples, cathedral domes, skyscrapers, massive lofts, and factory chimneys. If the topography is smooth, the cultural sky line is dominant and is usually transitional, as will be described in Chap. XIII. If the topography is rugged or broken by bodies of water, certain districts become specialized and land uses are concentrated.

The conventionalized concentric pattern, which will be described more fully in Chap. XIII, represents the areal distribution of the features indicated in the urban profile. Thus in Kansas City, railroads enter by following the Missouri and Kaw rivers or by climbing easy ridges from the east and southwest. Along the rivers factories are built, thus dividing some sections of the cities which are otherwise residential and almost surrounding others.

Urban Cycles and Sites

Cities which are founded on strategic sites usually conform to a conventional growth profile in population as a resultant of the combination of functions. The curve usually starts with a slow increment of growth, accelerating rapidly through a period of youthful expansion until maturity brings a slowing down which culminates in a flattened slope of old age. The varying rates of growth are commensurate with the rates of expansion of activities and the concomitant population increases to carry on these activities. For example, a city which is a center of agricultural functions increases by commerce and manufacture as the land is occupied and cultivated by the rural population. When all the acreage suitable for agriculture has been utilized, the increase in rural population becomes exceedingly slow, if it does not stop. During the period of expansion, raw materials from the farms increase rapidly and the distribution of goods to the agricultural communities increases correspondingly. Again, a city which is the center of mining activities may grow rapidly to the point of efficient mineral production and then be stabilized for a number of years until the raw materials are exhausted. If there are no other sustaining functions in the region, the city will rapidly decline, and it may be eventually abandoned. Cripple Creek and Central City, Colo., are excellent examples. If the city is a center of manufacturing activities, growth will expand rapidly to a point of stabilization, which is determined by the size and purchasing power of the sphere of influence. The building of branch factories and competing factories in other cities for efficient distribution beyond that sphere will result in a decentralization of manufacturing and a consequent flattening of the city's growth curve. As a result of the combination of site features and functions the center or core of development within the urban center may shift. Many river towns which developed large and impressive warehouse and business districts on the water front have undergone a shift to points removed from the river, resulting in considerable deterioration if not abandonment of the original core.

Cities which have established their urban patterns under the dominant influence of one function may undergo rejuvenation when new functions are added. This is illustrated in many European cities which were well developed before the industrial revolution. The new functions are commonly distributed to industrial satellites around the old city. Thus it seems that the present-day urban center is a resultant not only of present conditions but of combinations throughout its historical evolution.

Examples of Urban Habitats

The principles stated above may be used in an interpretation of Old World city-states. In ancient Egypt three urban centers on an agricultural background developed, as commercial, political, educational, and religious centers. They were Thebes in Upper Egypt, Memphis in Middle Egypt, and Cairo in Lower Egypt. As the Valley of the Nile progressively increased in density of population and agricultural wealth, these urban centers grew and flourished. When the point of saturation was reached they became thoroughly stabilized. For many centuries no other functions penetrated them, because of the isolation of the Nile Valley, which was effected by the vast deserts on three sides, the Mediterranean and the swampy delta of the Nile, on the other. When Lower Egypt came under the influence of the Greek Empire, a new city, Alexandria, arose on the westernmost distributary of the Nile delta. This city became a portal, or gateway, city between Greece and Egypt. It flourished on commerce. Subsequently Roman and West European influences entered Egypt through the same gateway.

Babylon, the site of modern Bagdad, rose to great prominence under nearly the same conditions as the agricultural cities of the Nile Valley. Because the bordering areas were not uninhabited, barren desert lands but were peopled with nomadic tribes, Babylon came under the influence of successive invasions of powerful steppe-land peoples. The result was the building of a great empire capital, which spread its influence over the entire extent of southwestern Asia. Babylon, like the cities of Egypt, was a river city. It was built between the Tigris and the Euphrates and was frequently surrounded by the floodwaters of those rivers.

In upper Mesopotamia a similar city, Nineveh, the site of modern Mosul, was erected. In the vicinity of Mosul the Tigris occupies a rather deep trench in the plains, and Mosul is saved from the hazards of floods. The discovery of vast petroleum fields in the vicinities of Bagdad and Mosul has markedly changed the economic significance of these cities.

The distribution of Greek cities has been studied by many people, who have noticed that characteristically their sites are small intermountain valleys, separated by greater or less expanses of sea and mountains. It is obvious that the limited area of these plains resulted in an early saturation and necessitated the development of far-flung commercial activities. The development and maintenance of such commerce was reflected in the fleets of vessels which sailed the waters of the Mediterranean, Aegean, and Black seas. These activities converted the Greek cities into military and commercial centers. Greek cities commonly had two centers, the peacetime core on the water front and the military core on near-by fortified heights. The city of Athens in its present pattern still displays these two centers.

The rise and development of Rome is believed by some historians to have been largely influenced by its strategic site at the constriction and focus of routes between the mountains and the coast of west central Italy. The dominant functions of Rome have been military, political, religious, and cultural. Its actual site had many disadvantages, particularly the low, flat, marshy lands along the Tiber. Persistent in the descriptions of Rome is reference to the Seven Hills, which served as fortification sites during the many centuries of military development. Coincidently with the development of political and military power, religious prestige gained influence, and this is reflected in the Vatican as a distinct core in the pattern of Rome.

In western Europe there developed in the middle ages a group of cities known as the Hanse towns. The coastal cities of this Hanseatic League were located generally at the head of navigation, for the vessels of that period were built to penetrate inland as far as possible in order to avoid the more expensive land transportation. These sites were also favorable for defense, since they were not subject to sudden raids of enemy vessels sailing the open seas. As has been pointed out, with the development of larger vessels of greater draught, there has been increasing difficulty in maintaining these sites as modern ports. As a consequence, outer ports have commonly been developed nearer the mouth of the river. A typical example is Bremerhaven. Although these pairs of sites may be miles apart, they represent two cores with regard to the functions of original cities involving the loss of their dominant port functions.

The site of London is called a "bridgehead" site. At this point the Thames River narrows to a width which was practicable for bridgebuilding in early days. As a consequence the street pattern of old London radiates from each end of the bridge, flaring out over the gently undulating plains on either side. The bridge thus artificially determined the head of navigation for seagoing vessels and focused governmental and commercial activities in its vicinity. The growth of London has been the focus of the British Empire both politically and commercially. In recent years, London has added to its many functions a number of modern manufacturing satellites, which dot its periphery.

The site of Paris was determined by a small island practically at the head of navigation of the Seine. The island offered desirable defense features. It also afforded a good bridge site for a river crossing. Thus the heart of Paris developed at the intersection of an overland route and a river route. Like London, Paris attained its major development as a commercial, political.

and cultural center. Like London, in recent years it has been affected by modern factory development. Owing to the hilly and rocky terrain, the manufacturing satellites have been projected along the banks of the Seine, both upstream and downstream. The rocky heights between the complicated meanders of the Seine have been largely utilized for high-class residential districts.

One of the first cities of importance to be developed in the new world was Panama, on the Pacific shore of the Isthmus of Panama, at the end of a transisthmian trail. The Pacific slope was preferred to the Atlantic on account of its more healthful climate. The east coast is characterized by a more or less uniformly high temperature, abundant precipitation, and high relative humidity, which make it an extremely unhealthful climate for Europeans and North Americans. The west coast has these characteristics for only a part of the year and experiences relatively fair dry weather in the remainder. The western site was also efficient as a focus of shipping along the North American and South American coasts as well as to and from the Philippine Islands. It therefore served as a funnel through which commerce poured across the isthmus.

Rio de Janeiro developed on one of the world's finest harbor sites. The large bay is practically landlocked by low mountain ranges which afford safety from storms and ample anchorage for many ships. The disadvantage of the site is the lack of adequate smooth low ground for a large city. As a consequence the business functions are congested on a limited acreage of lowland, while the residential sections spread out on high escarpments and uplands adjoining the inner city. The slopes are so steep that these uplands must be reached by elevators, aerial tramways, and inclined railways. Recently a motor road has been constructed with numerous intricate hairpin turns.

The site of Buenos Aires, on the right bank of the Río de la Plata, affords easy access to the Atlantic Ocean but has the severe handicap of silting along the water front. As a consequence, new port facilities have had to be constructed in order to assure adequate depth for ocean commerce. The city spreads like a fan over the smooth plain of the pampas; expansion has been so easy that it occupies an unusually large area for its population. A fan-shaped railway net spreads over the pampas from a focal point on the water front. Because of the absence of congestion and of high land values, there is a notable absence of skyscraper districts.

The core of greater New York City was established by the Dutch on the lower end of the island of Manhattan. This site was the waterway focus from Long Island Sound via the East River, the Hudson River, Newark Bay, and Raritan Bay via Kill Van Kull and the lower harbor of New York. Manhattan is a rock-ribbed island suitable for the building of a great city on firm foundations. As the metropolis grew in size the water barriers around the island assumed significance. Harlem River, on the north, offered the least formidable challenge. The Brooklyn Bridge was the first to span the East River barrier. Other bridges have supplemented it. In recent years tunnels under the Hudson and the George Washington Bridge over the Hudson have facilitated that crossing, supplementing to a large degree the hundreds of ferries which operate on the river. Brooklyn, on the west end of Long Island, has almost unlimited room for expansion eastward across the morainic hills and plains of that island. Newark, on the shores of Newark Bay, has gradually expanded its urban area by reclaiming the tidal flats of the Hackensack Meadows and Newark Bay. Staten Island for many years has been predominantly a residential area. The contrast in homogeneity of development between New York and Buenos Aires is very obvious.

The site of New Orleans was selected at the river end of a portage, between the Mississippi River and Lake Pontchartrain. This site is strategic with regard to coastwise and river transportation, but it is hazardous with respect to floods. From the very beginning New Orleans has waged a relentless conflict against the Mississippi River floods. Dikes and canals have been enlarged and strengthened as the city has grown. Located on the inside curve of a large meander, New Orleans is known as the Crescent City. The laying out of major streets parallel to the water front has given an unusual pattern to the city. Its contacts with the opposite shore have, on account of the width and depth of the Mississippi River, been largely by ferry, with the result that the opposite bank is lined with small villages. With the completion of the Huey Long Bridge, greater growth may be expected on the opposite bank. The city has expanded northward to Lake

Pontchartrain, reclaiming the low swamplands. The portage has been converted into a modern ship canal.

The site of San Francisco on the tip of a peninsula is somewhat analogous to that of New York on the island of Manhattan. As long as San Francisco served as a gateway to gold fields along the Sacramento River, its position was ideal and the city grew steadily over the rugged rocky hills of the peninsula. The width and depth of the Golden Gate and the size of the bay necessitated the use of ferries in reaching San Francisco from eastern and northern points. Railroads obtained extensive tracts of land for their yards and depots, and Oakland grew rapidly as a heavy industrial city. Similar towns and cities grew up adjoining Oakland. In recent years gigantic bridges have spanned these waters, affording easier access to the heart of San Francisco. The northern side of the Golden Gate will now undoubtedly experience rapid urban development.

The core of Detroit was a fort at a convenient crossing on the Detroit River. This site constituted the hub of numerous trails which evolved into roads, streets, and boulevards as the basis of the fan-shaped pattern of modern Detroit. When the automobile manufacturing stage developed at Detroit a number of industrial satellites grew up in the periphery of the city, notably Highland Park, Dearborn, and River Rouge.

The site of Chicago was determined by the mouth of the Chicago River, which afforded an easy route to a short portage to the Illinois River, thence to the Mississippi. The original site was too swampy, but so strategic was the core thus started that the Loop district has been maintained at terrific cost. In that vicinity it was found that the bedrock was deep beneath the surface, which necessitated expensive pilings and concrete mats for the skyscrapers which now cover the area. The north and south forks of the Chicago River converge a short way upstream from the lake. These waterways have become industrialized and lined with railroads. As a consequence, residential Chicago is divided into a North, a West, and a South Side. As Chicago grew, encircling terminal railroads were built successively. These terminal belt lines became industrialized, forming a series of concentric manufacturing zones around the central core. The outermost belt now connects a series of satellite cities, remote from the Loop district.

The pattern of Birmingham has been conditioned by the long, narrow parallel ridges and valleys of the south part of the great Appalachian Valley. The mountain ridges contain iron ore, the valley floors contain limestone, the near-by Cumberland escarpment contains coal; the proximity of these resources constituted the basis of the growth of Birmingham as a great iron and steel manufacturing center. The district is dotted with furnace towns on the valley floors, separated from each other by wooded hills devoted to residences. The result has been a metropolitan area exceedingly disjointed but with units exceedingly similar in type because of a common function.

A casual glance at a map or air view of metropolitan St. Louis shows the levee to be the hub of natural and artificial structural features such as waterways, railways, and highways. The dividing line between the river traffic of the upper and lower Mississippi River is at the levee. The railroads of the west side diverge from the levee to the north, the west, and the south. The railroads of the east side converge at great terminal warehouses opposite the levee. For many years the only bridge crossing, the Eads Bridge, was at the levee. The ferries which served the levee for many years connected the roads of Illinois and Missouri. These roads radiate from the ferry landings like the strands of a spider web and are connected by many concentric roads which complete the pattern of the web. In the mosaic of metropolitan St. Louis these roads have become boulevards and major highways whose concrete slabs constitute the artificial skeleton of the urban area.

The broad, placid waters of the Mississippi River divide the urban area into two distinct parts. The Missouri River forms part of the northwestern boundary of the area. Low gray limestone cliffs and brown loessial bluffs stand out in mild relief. Hills are clothed with woods or crowned with mansions, schools, or churches. The intervening billowy surface mirrors the light from a multitude of roofs, streets, and highways, or presents open spaces in parks, country clubs, cemeteries, airports, and idle property. Standing out prominently are the congested business districts of St. Louis, East St. Louis, Alton, Belleville, and St. Charles, with their blocks of stores, office buildings, and loft factories.

Stretching along the main, connecting, and belt lines of railroads on the west side are compact industrial districts which appear as veins in the pattern and divide the mosaic into irregular patches. North, south, and west from the levee extend the North Broadway, South Broadway, and Mill Creek districts, respectively. The Northwest, River des Peres, Oak Hill, and Carondelet sections are outlying industrial districts. All the west-side districts are dominated by small, light manufacturing plants, although there are some rather large factories. The buildings are usually multiple-story.

On the east side are Monsanto, East St. Louis, Belleville, Collinsville, Edwardsville, Madison, Granite City, East Alton, Wood River, Hartford, and Alton—each noted for one or more large-scale factories of the heavy industry type. The large acreage, massive structures, and towering chimneys are high lights in the landscape; around them are oriented systematically laid-out residential plots. The haphazard distribution of the heavy industries and clusters of houses has resulted in a patchwork pattern in the mosaic.

The former courses of the Mississippi and Missouri rivers are marked by sloughs and oxbow lakes, such as Creve Coeur, Horseshoe, and Pittsburgh. The floods of the streams necessitate dikes, levees, and drainage districts. The navigation of the rivers has been improved by wing dams and dikes and will be further improved by the new Alton Dam. The difficulty and cost of spanning the Mississippi River have kept the number of bridges low and have contributed to the imposing appearance of the few which have been built. The Chain of Rocks, Madison, and Howards Bend waterworks, with their settling basins, add an artificial touch to the aqueous elements of the mosaic.

The diversity of features in the metropolitan St. Louis mosaic is due to the multiplicity of adaptations of urban development to site, and to the hinterland which has furnished the materials for its growth.

Selected Readings

Van Cleef, Eugene: *Trade Centers and Trade Routes*, D. Appleton-Century Company, Inc., 1937. A geographer's interpretation of the location, growth, structure, and functions of commercial cities.

Huntington, C. C., and F. A. Carlson: *The Geographic Basis of Society*, Prentice-Hall, Inc., 1933. A general treatise incidentally dealing with the habitats of cities.

White, C. L., and G. T. Renner: *Geography, An Introduction to Human Ecology*, D. Appleton-Century Company, Inc., 1936. Another general treatise.

Carpenter, Niles: *The Sociology of City Life*, Longmans, Green & Company, 1931. Chapters 2 and 3 deal with site and location.

Gist, Noel P., and L. A. Halbert: *Urban Society*, The Thomas Y. Crowell Company, 1933. Chapter 3 deals with site and location.

Dickinson, Robert E.: "The Metropolitan Regions of the United States," *Geog. Rev.*, 24 (1934), 278–291. Discusses the relation of great cities to their hinterlands.

Chambers, William T.: "Geographic Areas of Cities," *Econ. Geog.*, 7 (1931), 177–188. Internal diversification of cities in relation to physical and other factors.

Ridgley, D. C.: "Geographic Principles in the Study of Cities," *Jour. Geog.*, 24 (1925), 66–78.

Chapter V

THE GROWTH OF INDIVIDUAL CITIES

We have already discovered that cities have varying degrees of importance at different times. Some have an early period of rapid growth and then settle down to a more moderate rate. Thus Cincinnati increased more than forty fold in the 40 years 1810–1850. But in the forty years 1890–1930 it did not even double its population. From 1830 to 1860 Lowell multiplied sixfold; from 1860 to 1890 it more than doubled; from 1890 to 1920 it grew about 50 per cent; from 1920 to 1930 it actually lost 10 per cent. The history of Cincinnati is bound up with that of the Ohio River and of the railways built after the Civil War. The history of Lowell involves the changing fortunes of New England's textile industry. It is impossible at this point, because of limited space, to offer other examples. Instead we present Table 10 to facilitate and stimulate the contrasting of slow-growing and fast-growing cities within a given period. The reader is invited to apply the same method to the study of other cities in which he may be interested. He is also urged to select one or more cities for more detailed study on the basis of the Census Bureau's summary of cities having 100,000 inhabitants in 1930, and their population decade by decade from 1790 to 1930.[1] As he makes his analysis he should note the changing rates of growth from decade to decade, especially sudden accessions, occasional losses, and changes in rank. Then let him search for accompanying events that may help to account for these variations, *e.g.*, annexation, development of new industries or means of transportation, discovery or exploitation of new natural resources, economic development of the hinterland, rise of rival cities, fires, tornadoes, floods, earthquakes, epidemics, strikes, removal of factories to other regions. After the Sixteenth Census has been taken and reported there should be careful scrutiny of the figures to see whether new trends are indicated. To illustrate further

[1] Fifteenth Census, *Population*, vol. 1, pp. 18–21.

the sorts of factors a student may find associated with urban growth we shall present the story of several individual cities.

TABLE 10.—SOME SLOW-GROWING AND SOME FAST-GROWING CITIES[a]

	Central city		Metropolitan district	
	1890	1930	1920	1930
Slow-growing cities:				
Albany	94,923	127,412	377,185	425,259
Baltimore	434,439	894,874	817,646	949,247
Boston	448,477	781,188	2,007,425	2,307,897
Cincinnati	296,908	451,160	630,896	759,464
Fall River	74,398	115,274		
Louisville	161,129	307,745	330,048	404,391
New Orleans	242,039	458,762		494,877
Omaha	140,452	214,006	238,440	273,851
St. Louis	451,770	821,960	1,071,529	1,293,516
Fast-growing cities:				
Akron	27,601	255,040	288,371	346,681
Cleveland	261,353	900,429	935,854	1,194,989
Detroit	205,876	1,568,662	1,252,909	2,104,764
Houston	27,557	292,352		339,216
Jacksonville	17,201	129,549		148,713
Los Angeles	50,395	1,238,048		2,318,526
Memphis	64,495	253,143		276,126
Oklahoma City	4,151	185,389	100,773	202,163
Seattle	42,837	365,583	350,678	420,663

[a] Adapted from Fifteenth Census, *Population*, vol. 1, pp. 18–21, and *Metropolitan Districts*, pp. 10–13.

ST. LOUIS

The development of St. Louis has geographic significance in the analysis of the metropolitan mosaic. The growth of the city may be divided into stages of evolution characterized by the adjustments of the city to certain phases of its regional environment. The effect is similar to multicolor printing, where each imprint intensifies, mixes, or neutralizes the previous impressions in making a finished colortype.

The first imprint was made about the middle of the eighteenth century when French pioneers from the lower St. Lawrence Valley and Gulf settled in the vicinity in little farm villages such as Cahokia, Prairie du Pont, French Village, and Carondelet.

The farm lands which these early immigrants tilled have changed their appearance and function. Then they were subsistence farms supporting a thrifty, complacent, independent people. Today some of the lands are parts of large general farms, some are intensively cultivated in truck and market gardens, and some have been blotted out by urban uses such as railroads, factories, commercial buildings, and residences.

The second imprint began with the founding of St. Louis in 1764. Unlike the farm villages, which grew by gradual accretion as settlers moved into the vicinity, St. Louis began as a full-fledged fur-trading post, some 30 citizens arriving all at once as representatives of a famous New Orleans fur-trading company. The center of interest in the village was the substantial stone building which housed the trading post, and which was located on the water front in what is now the levee district.

The third imprint began with the great tide of farmer and miner emigration into the prairies and mountains of the West. St. Louis was not only the most important outfitting center but the gateway through which moved the increasingly large volume of supplies needed by the emigrants. The coming of the first steamboat in the early 1800's was followed by hundreds of steamboats which facilitated trade on the many miles of waterways. The development of numerous overland trails, notably the Santa Fe, California, and Oregon, enlarged the sphere of commercial influence of St. Louis. Again the levee district responded to the stimulus, and great wholesale and jobbing houses crowded the congested water front, where steamboats tied up.

The fourth imprint began with the advent of many manufacturing activities which sought to provide a local supply of the great volume of goods moving through the city. The reasoning went thus: Why should the St. Louisans buy their merchandise in Boston, New York, Philadelphia, and Baltimore, when they could manufacture much of it themselves? Consequently, when a company's business reached a sufficient volume, it branched out into manufacturing. Other companies boldly entered the manufacturing field directly. Foundries, machine shops, brickyards, flour mills, tanneries, chemical shops, tobacco factories, shoe factories, drug factories, sawmills, and printing establishments crowded close to the wholesale houses and spread northward and southward along the banks of the Mississippi River and westward up the shallow valley of Mill Creek.

The fifth imprint began with the building of the railroads from St. Louis westward, and to East St. Louis from the east. The railroads, with their associated terminal depots, connections, yards, and shops, added new and large-scale features to the growing urban area and provided a structure for commercial movements. The railroad stage of development favored an east-west alignment, raw materials going east and manufactured goods going west. Warehouses and factories shifted to railroad and trackage sites, and rails were laid to form an intricate terminal web.

The sixth imprint was facilitated by the development of the railroad net focusing on St. Louis, and involved the businesses utilizing the mineral resources of the St. Louis territory. The low-priced, excellent coal easily obtainable from the fields of southern Illinois was a stimulant to the local manufacture of products from near-by and distant mineral deposits. During the latter decades of the nineteenth century the iron and steel business of St. Louis was stimulated by the mining of a high grade of iron ore at Iron Mountain, Mo. Numerous iron furnaces were built in Carondelet.

The seventh imprint, which began about 1860, might be considered an embossment, since it involved the raising of dikes and digging of ditches. Major dikes protect the low flood plains on the Illinois side from the high waters of the Mississippi River. Before such dikes were constructed, water at high flood stages covered the entire American Bottoms. To protect the low ground from floods originating on the Illinois prairie uplands, diked channels were constructed to carry the water across the flood plain from the bluffs to the river. In order to converge the drainage into a few large channels a master ditch, some 200 feet wide, was dug along the base of the eastern bluffs.

The eighth imprint appears as a lacy grid covering the whole area with towers and power lines which radiate from large steam electric plants and which also tie into regional hookups with hydroelectric plants at Keokuk and Bagnell dams. The high degree of electrification of the urban area is made visible by the distribution net connecting the various parts and satellite cities.

The ninth imprint brought out the neighborhood residential and shopping cores. Many of the neighborhoods originated as independent suburban cities, towns, and villages but have been enmeshed in the expanding pattern of residential growth. Some neighborhood business cores have evolved or crystallized at the intersections of major highway arteries, such as the Grand-Olive.

The tenth imprint, which is in progress, involves the beautification of the metropolitan area by major boulevards, plazas, civic centers, parks, and outer park systems. Notable on account of its size and the monumental buildings of public and private types is the Memorial Plaza. The various lakes and bluff strips afford natural themes for treatment with drives and playgrounds. The new lake above the Alton Dam is expected to be especially worthy of landscape treatment for recreational purposes. It is probable that this tenth imprint will include slum clearance or rehabilitation which will further enhance the desirability of the St. Louis metropolitan area for work and play.

The story of St. Louis as told in the preceding paragraphs displays only part of the characteristic factors which may affect the placement and the growth of the city. Two French officers were rewarded for their services in Indian wars by a grant of trading rights with the Indians in the Missouri Valley. They came up the river to Fort Chartres. Then, learning that the east bank of the Mississippi had been ceded to England, they moved on to a site on the west bank. Near the present location of the Eads Bridge in St. Louis they found a happy combination of limestone cliffs, which afforded protection against floods, with wood and water. As to location, they were not far from the junctions of the Missouri, Illinois, and Ohio rivers with the Mississippi. They were in a position to tap a great trade area reaching to the Rocky Mountains and into Canada. After the Louisiana Purchase the little town which these Frenchmen had started became the capital of the territory, but for 40 years its chief claim to importance lay in its fur trade. In the 1840's there occurred some events which might have provided a setback. There were a great fire, a flood, and a cholera epidemic. These threats to the growing city were, however, offset by immigration from Germany and Ireland. It was changes in the dominant modes of transportation, and particularly the route of the Santa Fe Railroad, that actually impeded the rapid growth of St.

Louis. The blockades of the Civil War helped to change the main trade routes from north and south on the Mississippi River to east and west by the railroads. The first railroads had their terminals on the east side of the river, hence it was necessary to ferry across, an expensive and time-consuming procedure. When the first bridge was completed, in 1874, traffic became tremendous through St. Louis. Meanwhile, the Sante Fe Railroad had been constructed from Chicago to Kansas City, passing by to the north and cutting off a large part of what had been previously included in St. Louis's trade area. Presently there grew up rival cities at the fringe of the St. Louis hinterland. First and greatest was Chicago, which did not overtake St. Louis in population until after 1870. Then came a number of lesser cities (Little Rock, Springfield, Des Moines, and others), each of which, however, has taken away a portion of the region that formerly contributed to the prosperity of St. Louis–Kansas City. Offsetting these losses there were from time to time newly discovered resources. In the sixties iron, in the eighties lead and zinc. Out of this complex of forces has come a slow-growing city with a narrowed but apparently stabilized hinterland, diversification of industry, and in general what might be called a maturity of development. St. Louis's period of rapid growth is long past. It has settled down to a fairly steady but slow development, relatively free from rapid or striking change.

Los Angeles

We turn now to a very different city and a very different setting. Los Angeles has been widely advertised as possessing great natural advantages. Many people believe it to be actually natural superiority rather than superior promotion that has produced this metropolitan district of 2 million inhabitants. There is much for us to observe that is contrary to popular impression. Los Angeles started with very serious natural disadvantages. It was in an extreme corner of the country, isolated by mountains, deserts, and great distances. It had a small arable hinterland and a limited water supply. It possessed no natural harbor, and its site was on an earth fault entailing the danger of earthquakes. On the other hand, it had a mild climate and was "at a respectful distance from possible competitors." Throughout the period of the missions, when the Southwest was dominated by Spanish-speaking people, Los Angeles remained a village. By the time of the war between the states it had only 4,500 inhabitants. But in the next 20 years increasing numbers of "Americans" drifted in to engage in small farming. They started the growing of oranges, and after the first railroads came through they began to advertise for tourists. By 1885 they were ready for the first great boom. The Southern Pacific and the Santa Fe railroads were bidding for passengers with amazingly low rates. The next two years were marked by feverish speculation in land and the two following by a building boom. A Chamber of Commerce was organized and active promotion became a major activity in this nascent metropolis. From 11,000 inhabitants in 1880 it leaped to 50,000 in 1890, doubling again by 1900. During the nineties there was a slowing down, however. The nationwide depression left its mark on Los Angeles, and many individuals suffered severe losses. But by 1902 a new boom was on, which continued with only a temporary interruption until the opening of the World War. Henry E. Huntington acquired and integrated a system of interurban lines promoting suburbs to furnish passengers for his cars and reaping a large reward from the rapid rise in the prices of real estate. Presently came a new railroad from Salt Lake City and another down the coast from San Francisco.

The population had already reached a point that made the water problem acute. The earthquake of 1906 and the depression of 1907 also contributed to the temporary interruption, but the completion of the aqueduct bringing water from the Owens Valley, the Panama Canal facilitating trade with the Atlantic seaboard and with Europe, the annexation of San Pedro and other water fronts, the building of a breakwater, and the coming of the movies carried Los Angeles forward in an enthusiastic growth which seemed to have no end. This combination of engineering feats—the bringing of water 250 miles and the building of a harbor 25 miles away—with the constant promotional efforts—had by 1910 made a city of 320,000 people. Then came the World War. Construction and the real estate business were hard hit, as elsewhere. Midwestern farmers found it profitable to remain at home and raise wheat or corn at high prices; industrialists and laborers found eastern attractions. But once the war was over and the depression of 1921 past, a third boom set in which lasted until the great depression of 1929. The postwar "prosperity" of the country was revealed in the thousands who flocked into the Southwest to retire or to invest and have an easy living. The automobile made possible the filling in of areas not tapped by the interurban lines. New oil developments, accompanied by excessive drilling and high-pressure salesmanship, drew thousands of new residents and millions of new dollars. All these trends, which might have gone forward of themselves, were accelerated, if not forced, by the advertising of the Chamber of Commerce and the "All Year Club," heralding to the world the "health, beauty, and romance" to be found in Sunny Southern California and especially in Los Angeles. Here, then, is the tale of a city built by man's ingenuity in engineering feats and his persistence in propaganda—the two quite overcoming the natural disadvantages which might have prevented the spot from producing any important urban development.

Seattle

The story of Seattle is still different from that of Los Angeles, as the latter in turn differs from the history of St. Louis. Certain aspects of the development of the metropolis of the Northwest have been interestingly and effectively presented by McKenzie.[1] The first white settlers from the eastern part of the United States appeared in the Puget Sound region at about the same time they were moving into southern California, but the character of their life was very different. They found a region rich in fish and lumber. Later there was coal, and still later gold. The first settlements about Puget Sound were pioneer villages. Each of them sent its products directly by boat to distant markets and received its supplies directly by boat from outside centers. These small mill towns were relatively isolated from one another and were located chiefly on the western rim of the Sound.

A second period of growth began about 1880. It was marked by the increasing size of lumber mills, the development of wholesale business, the coming of steam railroads, and the development of local electric lines. This was a period of intense rivalry, especially between Tacoma and Seattle, each of which wanted to be the center of this rapidly developing commercial and industrial

[1] R. D. McKenzie, "Ecological Succession in the Puget Sound Region," *Pub. Amer. Sociol. Soc.*, 23 (1929), 60–80.

life. For a time Tacoma seemed to have an advantage—which so frightened the residents of Seattle that they threatened to build a railroad connecting them with the Canadian Pacific unless their city instead of Tacoma was made the terminal of lines this side of the border. By 1890 Seattle had begun to pull ahead, but the margin of difference was slight indeed. By 1900 Seattle had again doubled its population, while Tacoma had almost stood still. From the time of the World War on, business was increasingly centralized and Seattle became increasingly dominant. Lumber was no longer handled from separate camps and mills directly to distant markets. Instead, logging was scattered and mills were concentrated in fewer centers under larger corporations, with their offices increasingly in Seattle. The cooperative marketing of agricultural products was largely carried on through Seattle headquarters. The management of chain stores partook of the same pattern. This centralization could not possibly have developed so long as the city was dependent upon water transportation. Even the railroads could scarcely have brought it to the point it has now reached. The paved highway, the automobile, and the motor truck seem to have been essential to the development of a great metropolitan center—of a single city in which the economic life of a whole region is bound up.

Other Cities

More briefly we may comment on several other cities. Duluth is located at the head of lake navigation, where there is a natural break between land and water transportation. It began as a center for traders in furs. As this activity declined, lumbering became the dominant industry. Presently the discovery and exploitation of iron ore displaced even lumber in importance, and now wheat seems likely to take precedence over the natural resources which earlier contributed to the development of Duluth.

The story of Fall River is the tale of a city which early developed into a place of some consequence because of its convenient location for receiving raw materials and shipping manufactured products, together with the nearness of water power. First iron works and then textile mills were the chief industrial establishments and the economic base of the community. In spite of a disastrous fire in the forties and serious labor difficulties in the seventies, Fall River moved ahead steadily, passing the 100,000 mark in 1900. But with the turn of the century came a rapid development of cotton manufacturing in the South, aided by lower taxes, cheaper labor, lack of labor organization, laxer legislation, and nearness to the supply of raw materials. Despite all this, 1920 was a banner year for manufacturing in Fall River, but the depression which followed immediately gave this industrial city a serious setback. From 1926 to 1931 there was a loss of 1½ million spindles and 33,000 looms, destroying the jobs of 11,000 operatives in 34 mills. It seems that the cotton manufacturers had all along discouraged the coming of other industries. Hence, when their single major source of livelihood met with the competition of the South, there was little for the people to fall back upon. Very likely the absentee ownership of mills also meant a lack of interest in the town. At all events, it appears that Fall River has seen its best days. It has been definitely declining in population, and in 1930 it had had fewer people than in either 1920 or 1910.

The growth of Birmingham illustrates another type of urban evolution. Prior to 1880 Birmingham was not listed in the census statistics. In that year the population was 3,086; by 1900 it was 38,415. This period represents a slow pioneer exploration of the iron, coal, and limestone resources of the vicinity. The occurrence of these resources constituted an ideal setting for the growth of the iron and steel industry, since it is not necessary to transport any of them a considerable distance. By 1910 the population had increased to 133,000, and by 1930 to 260,000. The large numbers of common laborers needed in the iron and steel industry have progressively increased as the number and size of plants have increased. The great majority of them are Negroes.

The different parts of Birmingham represent residential districts and neighborhood businesses, each group clustered around the plant of a large company. Thus Birmingham is a spread-out agglomeration of distinct units, in some places separated by low hilly ridges and in others by high mountain ridges. The whole is bound together by a network of railroad switches and belt lines. At the southern end of the metropolitan area, at the head of navigation from the Gulf on the Warrior River, is Birmingham Port. During periods of business prosperity, when the plants are operating on full schedule, the days are clouded by the smoke from the furnaces and the nights are illuminated by the brilliant flares from the converters. In the Fairfield district is a planned city, with its segregation of employees according to color and economic status, around the large mills and furnaces. The district possesses one of the largest and finest equipped hospitals in the South. The tremendous development of Birmingham has stimulated the growth of many small cities up and down the valley, cities which are industrial in type and which specialize in some particular commodity. Rayon mills, weaving and knitting mills, and cottonseed-oil mills are typical. Because of its rapid growth, centered in one basic industry, there has been little opportunity to develop the typical commercial activities generally associated with a city of this size.

The growth of Detroit affords an example of another type of city development. Founded as a fort and fur-trading post in the early 1700's, Detroit experienced very slow growth, since most of its functions were scattered over a wide territory and demanded little in the way of population concentration. By 1820 the population had increased to 1,400. When westward migration from New York and the New England states began, Detroit grew as a distributing point for southern Michigan and by 1860 possessed 45,000 inhabitants. As the agricultural development became more and move intensive, Detroit grew more and more rapidly, until by 1900 its population was 285,000. At this stage of its evolution, Detroit had become fairly stabilized and was growing quite slowly. In the early 1900's the automotive industry started in Detroit, and the successive decades exhibited almost miraculous growth. In 1910 the population was 465,000; in 1920 it was 995,000; and by 1930 it was 1,570,000. The rapid expansion of the automotive industry in Detroit and in the Detroit urban region represented the building of large-scale plants and the intricate subdivision of manufacture in allied fields. The well-known assembly line requires many thousands of employees. The management and administration of such plants and employees require thousands of other workers. The development of the automotive industry in Detroit has approximately reached its maximum of efficiency as is witnessed by the fact that the parent companies have established scores of branch factories and assembly plants, scattering them through many cities of the United States and the world.

Tulsa, popularly referred to as the oil capital of the world, is another "miracle city" in rapidity of population growth. The vicinity of Tulsa constituted a part of the Indian Territory, which in 1890 barely mustered a population of 400. In that year petroleum was discovered and people of all sorts flocked by the thousands to the oil fields of southeast Oklahoma. The town grew rapidly and by 1910 possessed 18,182 inhabitants.

On account of its central location in the developing fields, Tulsa soon became the refining, supply, and administrative center for many oil fields. As a consequence, its population is now about 140,000. If its growth had been confined to the activities of one field, undoubtedly Tulsa would be losing its population, as some of its neighbors are. It may be thought of as a "super" oil town, whose wealth and prosperity are based upon a broad function in relation to scores of oil fields. As the production from one field begins to decline, others are discovered and begin to take their place. Eventually all of the near-by oil fields will be found and exhausted, and the black gold which has given untold prosperity to Tulsa will cease to flow. Such a condition is probable in the near future. Meanwhile the great wealth of this city is reflected in its boulevards lined with costly mansions, its elegant shops, and its palatial hotels. Tulsa has, thus, as its economic base an exhaustible one-commodity resource in a region of extremely poor background.

Oklahoma City, not far from Tulsa, illustrates the development of an urban center in a rich, diversified material background, which has been topped off with the wealth of oil production in recent years. Like Tulsa, the vicinity of Oklahoma City was retarded because of its situation in the Indian Territory. By 1890 it had 4,150 inhabitants, thus exhibiting at an early date the beginnings of a rich agricultural background. To the north of Oklahoma City are the vast winter-wheat fields which yield year after year millions of bushels of this grain. To the west are the high grazing plains, which have supported thousands of head of cattle. To the southwest are the cotton fields, with their yield of millions of bales.

Surrounding Oklahoma City is a diversified crop and stock farming system. These various activities, as they have gradually expanded and intensified, have resulted in the growth of a great commercial center. The city is dotted with slaughterhouses, elevators, flour mills, gins, and cottonseed-oil mills. The agricultural population has required much and varied merchandise to carry on its activities. Thus by 1930 Oklahoma City had grown steadily and rapidly to 185,000 inhabitants. Within the last few years oil has been struck on the very site of the city, and oil derricks are thickly distributed wherever space will permit; the drillers may obtain the privilege of putting down wells on the state capitol grounds, on the lots of private residents. This new burst of wealth has given added prosperity to a city already richly endowed.

Fort Worth is an excellent example of a city which has grown steadily because of the many activities associated with the processing of the raw materials of its urban region. In 1880, there were 6,700 inhabitants in Fort Worth. Each decade has witnessed a steady growth toward a population of 165,000 in 1930.

One of the first economic stages of the Fort Worth urban region was characterized by ranching. In time the stockyards and meat-packing industries of Fort Worth became of national consequence. The number and quality of the herds has steadily progressed, from the early longhorns to the present-day shorthorns. Much of the urban region is still dominated by ranches. In the Edwards plateau, in the southwest part of the Fort Worth region, goat raising for mohair is an outstanding industry, with a very sparse population density. The semi-arid high plains specialize in beef cattle. In the northern part of the high plains around Lubbock there was an extensive cultivation of wheat and cotton for a number of years, during the period of high prices for those commodities. As a consequence, Fort Worth is noted for its elevators and flour mills, its compresses and oil mills. During the last three decades a large part of the Fort Worth region has witnessed progressively expanded production of petroleum. Pipe lines conduct vast quantities from the various fields to the large oil refineries of Fort Worth. The handling of these commodities has resulted in the focusing of all the important railroads of Texas in this city, with numerous shops and yards. As these various industries increase in volume and intensity, Fort Worth will doubtless experience a slow and steady growth.

Dallas has developed a marked contrast to Fort Worth because of its concentration of commercial activities. Dallas in 1880 had 10,000 inhabitants and has grown rapidly to 360,000 in 1930.

For many years the distribution activities of the Southwest were promoted by railroad lines from St. Louis and Kansas City to the Southwest through Dallas. Thus this city has become the center for wholesaling and jobbing houses for a large number of companies. The salesmen, clerks, and executives employed by such companies dominate the economic activities of Dallas. In the last two decades, remarkably large petroleum fields have been developed in eastern Texas, and Dallas has profited by the increased wealth of that area. As these activities reach their maturity the rate of growth will flatten slowly and the commercial prestige of the city will possibly decline. Already Dallas is gradually being overshadowed by Houston, which has the advantage of coastwise shipping and transportation.

Miami exhibits the growth of a city which has capitalized its resort features, namely, mild winters, sun bathing, and fishing. In 1900 Miami had a population of 1,700; in 1910 it had 5,500; in 1920 it had 30,000. Then came the Florida boom, and Miami miraculously grew to 125,000 in 1930. The chief features of the city are determined by the serving of winter tourists sometimes estimated at 500,000. As a consequence, Miami is a city of palatial hotels, furnished apartments, and cottages. The vacationist brings to Miami many millions of dollars to spend on pleasure and luxuries.

Miami has made consistent attempts to "sell" itself as a center for summer vacationists but so far has met with only mediocre success. The urban region of Miami may logically be considered as the immediate environment of the city plus outlying resort centers. Factories and general business hold an exceedingly small proportion of the city's interest; thus retailing through a great variety of shops and stores dominates the business activities of Miami. Its growth and prosperity are contingent upon the number and spending power of its transient customers.

Salt Lake City represents a very peculiar growth among American cities. It began with the westward trek of the Mormons as they were driven out of the Middle West. In 1860 Salt Lake City had 8,000 inhabitants, and it has grown with a steady increase to 140,000 in 1930. This growth is entirely commensurate with the progress and intensive development of the Utah oasis. Nature built an admirable stage for this agricultural evolution. The fertile beaches and terraces of the vast sea which once occupied the region were naturally smooth and graded for the development of irrigation districts. The outwash of the mountains to the east provided streams, which in turn gave ample water for the fields. The position so remote from the agricultural markets of the world necessitated a specialization in a crop which would yield high value for small bulk; the sugar beet provided such a commodity. The thousands of agriculturalists drawn to Salt Lake City provided numerous and willing workers in the wheat fields. Thus there developed a diversified agricultural population producing great wealth. In recent years mining has become an important industry, as in Bingham Canyon with its copper. Therefore Salt Lake City has expanded smelters and mining machinery businesses.

The Mormon Church has dominated the social, educational, economic, and political life of the district, thereby giving unusual unity to the program. It integrated farm production, farm consumption, and urban manufacturing for the common good.

Summary

The narratives in this chapter display in a variety of ways the interrelation of geographic and cultural factors in the development of American cities. St. Louis shows the significance of changes in dominant modes of transportation and of the limitation and maturation of its surrounding region. Los Angeles offers a remarkable history of the overcoming of natural disadvantages by engineering and promotion. Seattle is an interesting case of changing natural resources and transportation with a concomitant centralization. Duluth has grown in part through the replacement of one resource by another. Fall River, depending too narrowly on a single industry, is one of four large cities that lost in population before 1930. Birmingham illustrates effectively the advantage of complementary raw materials —iron, coal, limestone—and of relief of the land. Detroit is an example of economic factors outweighing geographic; without automobiles it was a small city and there was nothing about its site and location that gave it a marked advantage over Toledo and Cleveland. Tulsa and Oklahoma City present the contrast of a one-industry town and a center based on varied resources and activities. Forth Worth and Dallas also present a contrast—Fort Worth being a market for the products of ranch, farm, and oil field, while Dallas is a center of wholesale distribution. Miami represents the tourist town. Salt Lake City has a unique history, not only because of its intermountain setting but, especially, because of its founding and development by a religious sect.

Selected Readings

Hoyt, Homer: *One Hundred Years of Land Values in Chicago,* University of Chicago Press, 1933. The story of Chicago's growth and of the factors involved, largely from the economic point of view.

Wagner, Anton: *Los Angeles: Werden, Leben und Gestalt der Zweimillionen Stadt in Südkalifornien,* Bibliographisches Institut (Leipzig), 1935. An excellent account of the rise of Los Angeles by a German geographer. Unfortunately not translated into English.

Schmid, Calvin F.: *Social Saga of Two Cities,* Minneapolis Council of Social Agencies, 1937. An ecological and statistical study of social trends in Minneapolis and St. Paul.

McKenzie, R. D.: "Ecological Succession in the Puget Sound Region," *Pub. Amer. Sociol. Soc.,* 23 (1929), 60–80. The emergence of Seattle as a center of dominance in relation to changing modes of transportation and other factors.

James, Preston E.: "Vicksburg: A Study in Urban Geography," *Geog. Rev.,* 21 (1931), 234–243. The development of a small southern city.

Catlin, George B.: *The Story of Detroit,* Detroit News, 1923. A popular account that is useful if supplemented by more recent data.

PART II
URBAN INSTITUTIONS AND FOLKWAYS

Chapter VI

DOMESTIC INSTITUTIONS AND FOLKWAYS OF THE CITY

The central problems of Part I, which we have just completed, are: How have cities come to be, and what is the series of cultural changes through which urbanism has developed? We come now to a more intensive examination of the characteristic institutions and folkways of urban society. Our central problems now are: What culture traits and complexes are peculiar to cities, and how do they differ from those that we find in rural districts? Unfortunately there are many aspects of family life concerning which our data are limited. But the data are sufficient to warrant such generalizations as these: Marriage is less frequent in cities than in the country. Urban families and households are smaller than rural. Cities have more broken homes. Family functions are declining more rapidly in cities. There appear to be trends toward more equalitarian family organization, more individualization of members, and decline of the *Grossfamilie*, or kinship group. The urban family is less an integral part of its immediate social milieu. There are differences in various domestic folkways, such as those of courtship and contraception. The housing of urban families is more commonly multiple, rented, and expensive. The evidence bearing on these propositions will constitute the bulk of this chapter. In addition to rural-urban differences we shall consider differences that occur within any given city.

The Family

The Frequency of Marriage in Urban and in Rural America. "City life may . . . be said to discourage marriage about 10 per cent."[1] This was Ogburn's conclusion after careful analysis of 1920 data for American cities. The situation in 1930 was

[1] E. R. Groves and W. F. Ogburn, *American Marriage and Family Relationships*, p. 448, 1928. By permission of Henry Holt & Company, Inc.

different in detail but not in general outline. In Chap. XIX we shall present the percentage married in 1930 and some relationships between this and sex ratio, age distribution, ethnic groups, and regional differences. It has not yet been feasible for us to study these relationships with the statistical methods employed by Ogburn. Hence we shall summarize briefly some of his findings.

Contrary to expectation, the highest percentage married was not found where the sexes were equal in number but where there was a slight excess of men. The highest percentage married appeared in the age class thirty-five to forty-four, but the greatest difference between urban and rural percentages occurred in the age class twenty to twenty-four. In no age class was the urban percentage as high as the rural. The same statements are apparently valid for 1930. However, the sum of married males in all age classes and married males whose age was unknown constituted a larger percentage of all males over fifteen in cities than on farms. The significance of color and nativity seemed to be about the same in 1920 as in 1930, the greatest difference between urban and rural percentage married being that of the children of immigrants. As to general divisions of the United States, the greatest difference between rural and urban percentage married was in the eastern South Central states. This was still true in 1930, although the rank of some other divisions was changed.

Since 1890 there has been an increase in the percentage of each sex married in the general population. This increase has appeared chiefly if not wholly in the age classes under thirty-five. It has been greater for males than for females. It has been greater in cities than in the country. Since 1900 the percentages widowed have not changed much, but the percentages divorced have increased. Hence, there has been for both sexes a decline in the percentage of those who have never married. This is important to note because it is popularly believed that the period of rapid urbanization has been accompanied by postponement of marriage, *i.e.*, increasing age of persons at the time of their wedding. Yet, while stressing the trend toward early marriage, we must recognize that it has apparently been checked. Table 11 summarizes the evidence that for urban young people of both sexes the percentage married before twenty-five was standing still or declining. Only country girls continued the trend of the previous 30 years. During the depression we know that the general marriage rate fell sharply. Hence the reversal of the 1890–1920 trend still holds. Since 1935 the marriage rate has increased, but we do not anticipate a revival of the trend toward earlier marriage.

The distribution of urban and rural folk with reference to marital status in 1930 is shown in Table 12. Ogburn has made a more refined analysis by separating large cities (over 500,000) from small cities and computing the percentage married in each age group. For both sexes under age thirty he found the highest percentage married in villages (rural nonfarm), next highest on farms, next in small cities, and lowest in large cities. Over age thirty he found the highest percentage married on farms but the lowest still in large cities and next lowest in small cities.[1] Sorokin and Zimmerman present data from a dozen countries which may be summarized thus: City people are less likely than country people to marry. City people marry later than country people, this being especially true of women. City people live less commonly in families, *i.e.*, they have more single, widowed, and divorced persons. Thus the contemporary American situation differs somewhat from conditions found in western Europe a decade or so ago.[2]

TABLE 11.—EARLY MARRIAGES AS INDICATED BY THE PERCENTAGE MARRIED AT AGES FIFTEEN TO TWENTY-FOUR, 1920 AND 1930[a]

	1920		1930	
	Urban	Rural	Urban	Rural
Males 15–19 years	1.7	2.4	1.3	2.2
Females 15–19 years	10.7	14.5	10.2	15.5
Males 20–24 years	25.8	31.1	25.8	31.1
Females 20–24 years	47.6	58.4	47.1	58.8

[a] Fifteenth Census, *Population*, vol. 2, p. 848; E. R. Groves and W. F. Ogburn, *American Marriage and Family Relationships*, p. 230, 1928.

[1] W. F. Ogburn, "Recent Changes in Marriage," *Amer. Jour. Sociol.*, 41 (1935), 285–298.

[2] Pitirim Sorokin and C. C. Zimmerman, *Principles of Rural-urban Sociology*, Chap. 10, 1929.

TABLE 12.—MARITAL STATUS OF URBAN AND RURAL POPULATION, 1930[a]
Percentage of Males and Females Single, Married, Widowed, Divorced

Marital status	Male			Female		
	Urban	Rural nonfarm	Rural farm	Urban	Rural nonfarm	Rural farm
Single	33.7	32.1	36.5	27.8	23.0	25.2
Married	60.5	61.1	57.9	58.5	63.9	66.0
Widowed	4.3	5.3	4.8	11.8	11.8	8.1
Divorced	1.2	1.2	0.7	1.7	1.1	0.6
Unknown	0.3	0.3	0.1	0.3	0.2	0.1

[a] Fifteenth Census, *Population*, vol. 2, p. 848.

The Size of Urban Families and Households. The divergence in size of family between urban and rural America is made evident in Tables 13 and 14. Very obviously in 1930 city families were smaller than rural families. Comparison with earlier dates cannot be made with precision because of varying definitions. For 1930 the Bureau of the Census defined the family "in general as a group of persons related either by blood or by marriage or adoption, who live together as one household, usually sharing the same table. Single persons living alone are counted as families, however, as are a few small groups of unrelated persons sharing the same living accommodations as 'partners.'"[1] In earlier censuses institutional, hotel, and boardinghouse groups had been treated as families.

In general the greatest contrast is between urban and farm families, with the rural nonfarm, chiefly villagers, falling in between. Considering various factors that may be associated with the difference in size between city and farm families, we note first that the divergence is greatest in the South and least in New England. It is greatest among the foreign born and least among Negroes.[2]

Ogburn has analyzed census data in such a manner as to show how much or little the composition of families varies with the size of cities. From Table 15 we see that there is surprisingly little difference in the median households of large and of small cities. Cities over 300,000 have fewer small children than do

[1] Fifteenth Census, *Population*, vol. 6, pp. 5–6.

[2] *Ibid.*, p. 37. Also found in *Amer. Sociol. Rev.*, 2 (1937), 641.

cities below this size. Lodgers are kept more frequently in large cities.

Elsewhere Ogburn has reported the diversification of structure in a sample of metropolitan and farm families. Table 16 summarizes his findings. Studies of five smaller cities show less striking results.[1]

TABLE 13.—SIZE OF AMERICAN FAMILIES, 1930[a]
Percentage Distribution of Urban and Rural Families

Family size	Urban	Rural nonfarm	Rural farm
1 person	8.0	10.4	5.2
2 persons	25.1	23.8	18.3
3 persons	22.1	20.2	18.0
4 persons	18.1	16.6	16.6
5 persons	11.6	11.4	13.3
6 persons	6.8	7.3	10.0
7 persons	3.8	4.5	7.1
8 persons	2.1	2.7	4.8
9 persons or over	2.2	3.0	6.7
All families	100.0	100.0	100.0

[a] Fifteenth Census, *Population*, vol. 6, pp. 14–15.

TABLE 14.—FAMILIES HAVING CHILDREN UNDER TEN YEARS OF AGE, 1930[a]
Percentage Distribution of Urban and Rural Families

Number of children under ten	Urban	Rural nonfarm	Rural farm
No child	62.4	57.4	50.7
1 child	19.4	18.8	19.1
2 children	10.9	12.3	13.7
3 children	4.6	6.7	8.8
4, or more, children	2.7	4.8	7.7
All families	100.0	100.0	100.0

[a] Fifteenth Census, *Population*, vol. 6, pp. 19–20.

In general the trend of American families has been toward smaller and smaller families.[2] From an average of 5.7 persons in 1790 and 5.0 in 1880 it has dropped steadily to 4.1 in 1930.

[1] Mildred Parten and Ruby Reeves, "Size and Composition of American Families," *Amer. Sociol. Rev.*, 2 (1937), 649.

[2] *Ibid.*, p. 638.

This decline has been somewhat more marked in cities than in the country and more marked in large cities than in smaller ones. Thus Ogburn found the percentage decreases in size of households from 1900 to 1930 to be: on farms 0.6 per cent, in small towns 3.5, in cities 4.5, and in a metropolis 21.2 per cent.[1] In the farming area which he studied, unbroken families actually increased from an average of 4.21 to 4.32 persons per family. In small towns there was a slight decline. In cities the drop was greater. In Chicago the average fell from 3.22 to 2.85.

Thus the evidence at our disposal indicates not only that urban families are smaller than rural families but that they have been declining somewhat more rapidly. This, however, is unlikely to continue. As rural standards of living rise and the art of contraception spreads we may expect rural families to decrease more rapidly than urban families. Perhaps the 1940 census will show that this reversal of previous differences in trends has already begun.

The Frequency of Broken Homes. Census data already cited show in general higher percentages of divorced and widowed

TABLE 15.—VARIATIONS IN FAMILY COMPOSITION BY SIZE OF CITY, 1930[a]

	Median household		Per cent of families with no children under 10 at home	Children under 5 per 1,000 women 15–44	Per cent of families of 5 persons or more	Per cent of households with lodgers
	Including all families	Excluding one-person families				
1,000,000 and over	3.21	3.39	64	484	26	14
600,000–1,000,000	3.22	3.45	65	514	27	13
300,000–600,000	3.15	3.35	66	479	24	12
100,000–300,000	3.25	3.45	62	535	26	12
50,000–100,000	3.27	3.45	62	532	27	11
25,000–50,000	3.23	3.42	62	562	27	
10,000–25,000	3.22	3.43	61		27	
2,500–10,000	3.18		62			
Farm		4.18		872	42	

[a] Adapted from W. F. Ogburn, *Social Characteristics of Cities*, pp. 11–12, 1937. By permission of the International City Managers' Association.

[1] *Recent Social Trends*, vol. 1, pp. 682–683. By permission of the President's Research Committee on Social Trends.

TABLE 16.—DISTRIBUTION PER 1,000 OF DIFFERENT TYPES OF FAMILIES IN CHICAGO AND ON FARMS, 1930[a]

Type of family	Metropolis	Farms
Husband and wife only	398	163
Husband, wife, and one child	229	205
Husband, wife, and two children	122	202
Husband, wife, and three or more children	61	249
Husband or wife alone	135	39
One parent and one or more children	55	42

[a] Adapted from *Recent Social Trends*, vol. 1, p. 684. By permission of the President's Research Committee on Social Trends.

persons in cities than on farms and in villages. (An exception is the lower percentage of urban than of rural widowers.) In the study of recent social trends, Ogburn examined a special sample of urban and rural families to determine the relative frequency of homes that were broken before the wife was forty-five years old or before the husband was fifty.[1] The percentages of broken homes were: metropolitan district 19.0, cities of the 100,000 class 16.7, villages 14.7, and farms 8.1. The percentages of such broken homes containing young children showed a similar distribution, *i.e.*, most in the metropolitan district and fewest on farms. Moreover, he found an increase, from 1900 to 1930, in the relative number of broken homes with children; this increase was greatest in the metropolitan district and least on farms. Other studies, though less representative in character, indicate the same sort of rural-urban differences.

A special study of marriage and divorce by the United States Census Bureau some years ago showed that from 1870 to 1900 urban counties had a larger number of divorces per 100,000 population than did rural counties.[2] Mowrer has analyzed the data in terms of divorces per 100 marriages for rural and urban areas through the years 1887–1924. Until 1910 the ratios were nearly the same, first one and then the other running ahead, but after 1910 the urban ratio increased very much more rapidly than the rural.[3] Unfortunately, more recent studies do not separate urban from rural data, hence we can only infer that

[1] *Ibid.*, vol. 1, pp. 689–691.

[2] Bureau of the Census, *Marriage and Divorce*, 1867–1900, p. 17.

[3] Ernest R. Mowrer, *The Family*, p. 150, 1932.

divorce is still more prevalent in American cities than in the country. Sorokin and Zimmerman found convincing evidence "that in practically all countries the divorce rate has been higher in the urban than in the rural population and that the agricultural class has rates for divorce possibly lower than any of the large urban occupational classes."[1]

Concerning desertion we have less satisfactory data, but it is quite generally conceded that this mode of family disruption is distinctively urban. No doubt a major factor in this rural-urban difference is economic. A majority of farms are occupied by their owners. A man does not often run away and leave such an investment or inheritance. However, as the numbers of tenants and laborers increase this restraining influence will decline. After all, it is not often that a homeowner or business proprietor in the city deserts his family. "Desertion characterizes the poverty group."[2] Aside from economic factors, it is probable that urban mobility and the decline of neighborhood life increase the incidence of desertion. The city man is less frequently controlled by the opinions and gossip of a stable group of neighbors than is the farmer or villager. Another hypothesis pertains to the influence of religion: Catholics are more numerous in American cities than in our rural districts; the Catholic Church rejects divorce; hence the only practical recourse for an unhappy spouse of this faith and of small means is desertion. Such an interpretation seems plausible, but it needs to be examined in the light of more data than we now have at hand.

The Cost of Maintaining the Family. On the basis of relative size country families should be more expensive to maintain than city families. Yet the popular impression is that living is cheaper under rural than under urban conditions. Perhaps the matter may be summed up thus: (*a*) Cash outlays are undoubtedly greater in cities, because rural families often produce many articles for home consumption; (*b*) standards of living may be higher in cities; hence (*c*) the differences in goods and services required by an urban and a rural family may not be very great. Some evidence bearing on these points will be presented in the succeeding chapter.

[1] Sorokin and Zimmerman, *op. cit.*, p. 334. By permission of Henry Holt & Company, Inc.

[2] Mowrer, *op. cit.*, p. 89.

The Decline of Family Functions. For some time observers have been calling attention to what they regard as a decline of the institutional functions of the family, particularly in our cities. However, there has been some uncertainty as to how much importance should be attached to such conclusions because they have been based on casual observations and general impressions rather than on systematic enumeration and measurement. Also there is some question as to what was implied in the word "function." For ourselves, we shall mean by function what the members of a group (in this case the family) customarily get from their participation in it, what they habitually do in and through it rather than through other channels. Activities carried on and results accomplished will interest us more than what anyone happens to think ought to be the functions of the family. Moreover, we shall not have to depend on guesswork, as we fortunately have access to some objective data bearing on this point.

As part of the study of recent social trends Ogburn examined the various functions of American families from such viewpoints as were amenable to statistical treatment.[1] We shall not here reproduce his data, since they are so easily accessible to all students, but we shall summarize them briefly.

As to the economic function, the rural family is very commonly a productive unit. The members work together on the farm to produce both goods for sale and articles for home use. Members of the urban family more commonly are employed away from home as individuals although they may put their earnings into a common treasury. What they do together is more frequently to spend the earnings of one or more members for rent, food, and other goods. Families in general and urban families in particular do less baking, less canning, less cleaning and dyeing, less making of clothes than they did a generation ago. Laundering, too, has been removed from the urban home to a certain extent, but the high cost of commercial laundering and the wide sale of electric washers and irons has slowed down this particular change. Because urban families in large numbers live in multiple dwellings they have less responsibility for heating their quarters. Indeed, they have smaller quarters to care for in every way. For work that is done in the home electric power has partly displaced

[1] *Recent Social Trends*, vol. 1, pp. 661–679.

human muscles. Women have less space, smaller families, and more power equipment, and spend less time in doing housework. Hence we seem to be completely justified in saying that the economic function of the family has diminished and that many activities formerly domestic in character have been removed from the urban home.

In less detail but in similar fashion it may be shown that the family performs less of an educational function in cities than in rural areas; this was especially true a few years ago. Country girls more often than city girls learn the practical arts of home-making in their own homes from their own mothers. City girls either devote very little time to these accomplishments or take courses in home economics. Country boys more often than city boys learn their trade working at home. City boys often learn no trade at all or take vocational courses at school or learn through employment outside the home. In general the percentage of children attending school has been increasing; school terms are longer and children spend more years in school than at the beginning of the century. All these changes are more marked in the city than in the country; thus educational functions are less commonly vested in the urban than in the rural family.

Recreation affords a similar picture. There has been a trend away from recreation in the home and from recreation outside the home in which the family engages as a unit. This change, too, has been more in evidence in cities than in the country. Ogburn found that there was more reading aloud in country than in city homes, more singing and playing of music, more going together to movies, picnics, and homes of friends. In the city the members of the family attend baseball games, play golf, go to meetings of bridge clubs, the theater, etc., as individuals. There is, however, considerable going out together in the family car and some joint listening to the radio. Further study is needed before we are justified in generalizing about these last activities.

The decline in religious functions of the family seems to parallel that in the field of recreation. City families less often than rural engage in Bible reading, religious discussion, family prayers, and family attendance at church.

In the country it is commoner than in the city to provide home care for the sick, afflicted, defective, orphaned, and others who seem to need special protection. In the city the protective function has been, not wholly but to a considerable extent, transferred to juvenile courts, hospitals, and institutions for children, old people, defectives, and delinquents.

In these five phases of group life the urban family seems clearly to have experienced a loss of function. In other phases the evidence is by no means clear. It is held by some students that the rural family is more an agency of social control than the urban, that it plays a more important part in restraining its members from forbidden behavior and in disciplining them when guilty. The development and activity of juvenile courts in cities suggests that this may be true. However, there is still need of further study on this point. The procreational function, which a popular audience might mention first, continues in both the urban and the rural family, but we have noted that the birth rates are declining, and apparently faster in the city than in the country. Illegitimacy, which might be said to represent the procreational function detached from the family, is apparently much more common in the city than in the country. However, the presence in cities of maternity homes patronized by rural girls compels us to be skeptical about such statistics as we possess.

Some people feel that the affectional function is expanding and intensifying enough to offset the decline in other functions of the family. What they mean is that formerly members of the family were bound together by economic and other necessity. Today in cities it is possible to live very comfortably and respectably outside of matrimony. Hence mutual affection must be a more important influence both in leading city people to marry and in stabilizing their relations in marriage. It is possible that there is actually a more highly developed love life in contemporary urban than in rural families, especially those of an earlier day. However, at the present time we have no means of knowing whether this be true. It is an interesting hypothesis, but one which will not be easy to test.

Personal Relationships within the Family. From the data used in studying family functions we are warranted in drawing some inferences about family relationships. It seems evident that members of urban families spend less time together, work together less, play together less, and go out together less frequently than do rural families. Moreover, there appears to be a continuing trend toward fewer and fewer cooperative activities. Nevertheless, there should be periodic restudy of this hypothesis.

A frequent generalization concerning the American family, especially in the city, is that it displays a marked trend away from the authoritarian type toward the equalitarian. As yet this proposition has not been reduced to concrete elements suitable for quantitative study. However, it should not be impossible to secure information concerning the management of money, title to property, selection of residence, planning for children, and choice of recreation. Do husband and wife consult together or are decisions made by either alone? Are children consulted, and under what circumstances? With specific answers to such questions from a representative sample of city and country families we should know more definitely whether urban families are really more nearly equalitarian than are rural families. Sorokin and Zimmerman would test this hypothesis by examining the relative frequency, urban and rural, of genuine monogamy, equal rights in dissolution of marriage, equal freedom in choice of mate, equal rights to the ownership and disposal of property, and (they might have mentioned) equal privileges and obligations in respect to guardianship of children. So far as the United States alone is concerned, these criteria seem unlikely to serve our present purpose, for the laws governing such matters presumably operate alike in rural and in urban areas.

Individualization is often held to characterize members of the urban more commonly than members of the rural family. To test this proposition we need to learn the relative numbers, urban and rural, who are gainfully employed outside the home. Especially do we need to know the numbers of wives and children with independent incomes. Census figures on occupations are suggestive but not conclusive on this point. Another test of individualization would involve the assembling of data concerning the frequency with which members of urban and of rural families carry on specific activities (attending or staying away from school or church, staying out at night, playing bridge or poker, scattering ashes, papers, or clothing about the house, etc.) despite the protests of other members.

Another hypothesis which has received less attention and study than it deserves is the one holding that in the city the *Grossfamilie*, or kinship group, is disintegrating more rapidly than in the country. This could be tested by such means as measuring physical separation, frequency of visits, letters, gifts, mutual aid in emergencies, reunions, etc., as they involve parents and grown children, grandparents and grandchildren, brothers, sisters, cousins, and other near relatives. There should also be a study of the ways of caring for superannuated kinsmen in urban and in rural families. Our impression is that they are less frequently provided for in the homes of their children in cities than in the country.

Finally, our attention is called to possible occasions of tension in urban and in rural families. In the city there appears to be a great deal of confusion and conflict as to the appropriate roles of husband and wife. If this really is greater in the city than in the country, it may be related to cultural heterogeneity and to the frequency with which husband and wife have divergent backgrounds. It may be involved in the wife's frequent economic independence before marriage, coupled with a tradition of economic dependence after marriage. It may be associated with a lack of useful work for middle- and upper-class women; their husbands may want them to be domestic ornaments, whereas they crave careers; they may have regarded marriage as a retirement from work and then fret for lack of something else to do. These are only a few of the possibilities.

The relative frequency of tension between parents and children is also in the realm of speculation. Presumably it is greater in cities than in villages and on farms. Children are more commonly and for longer periods economic liabilities in cities. "Only" children, more common in cities, are likely to be emotionally involved with their parents. In the city it appears that projection of parental ambition more frequently clashes with goals supported by school, gang, or other group. In the city there is more frequently an "educational differential" between parents and children. Sometimes this even involves use of the English language. All these statements are made very tentatively for the purpose of stimulating further study.

The Changing Relation of Family to Community. Not only does it appear that relationships within the urban family are different from those within the rural family; it also appears that urban families differ from rural families in their relation to the community. We are here using the term "community" as a shorthand expression for groups and agencies with which a family may come into direct contact.

Common observation indicates that city families have less to do with their "nigh-dwellers" than do countryfolk. So far as we know, no quantitative study has verified this hypothesis, but a procedure has been worked out for dealing with such a problem. Jessie S. Bernard devised an instrument for measuring the relative amount of neighboring in various parts of a city. It dealt with such matters as visiting, exchanging articles and services, going out together, asking or giving advice, and membership in neighborhood groups such as parent-teacher associations. She also devised a simple system of scoring the schedule.[1] Thus it was possible for her to compare different areas and also to correlate neighboring with other aspects of the local life.

A similar problem has to do with the relative use made of such local agencies as church, school, playground, and store. It appears that rural families make more consistent use of strictly local facilities than do cityfolk. But until comparative studies have been made we cannot be sure. We know that many city families attend churches at a distance from their homes and do their trading at various centers. But most of them send their children to near-by schools and playgrounds. It may be that with good roads and automobiles rural families are enabled to scatter their institutional contacts and affiliations in similar fashion.

The city family pretty certainly has more competition with other groups and institutions for the attention, time, and loyalty of its members. There are scout troops, schools, businesses, adult clubs, gangs, and informal groups which not only draw members of the family away from home, but present patterns of behavior and codes of conduct that are often in conflict with those of the family. In addition there are often near-by families belonging to other culture groups. As the members of such different families become acquainted at school, work, or play, their varied folkways and mores may prove rather confusing, especially to the youth. Now we do not have the data to support

[1] Jessie S. Bernard, "An Instrument for the Measurement of Neighborhood, with Experimental Application," unpublished doctoral dissertation, Washington University, 1935. Dr. Bernard's schedule is duplicated in part in Chap. XV of this text.

an unqualified statement that these intergroup rivalries and culture conflicts are more common in city than in country, but it is our impression that this is definitely the case. Neither do we know whether they involve a weakening or a strengthening of the family.

On all three points—neighboring, patronizing local agencies, and struggling against rival groups and institutions—we have the further impression that the urban family is less and less an integral part of its immediate social milieu. But we also suspect that a similar change is occurring in rural America. Again there is real need for objective study of these hypotheses.

Miscellaneous Folkways and Mores. There are numerous other patterns of behavior in which rural and urban families seem to differ. One has to do with courtship. In the country, a young person commonly "goes with" someone from the immediate vicinity, hence with a similar cultural background and well known to the family. Often the two have attended the same school and church. Hence they have a great deal in common, the question of their compatibility is not serious, and their conduct is more or less under the eye of the neighborhood. At least this is the picture we carry from personal experience and observation. On the other hand, city youth very often find lovers and friends of the opposite sex whose cultural and personal backgrounds are very different; they do not belong to a common group whose standards guide their conduct; they carry on their courtship in an atmosphere of anonymity—in the park, on the excursion steamer, at the dance hall. They may proceed less directly, from "dating" to serious courtship and from that to matrimony, or they may profess love at first sight, marry in haste, and repent at leisure. We are unable to assert that this is typical of urban courtship in contrast with rural love-making, but we are anxious to have this matter studied in order that we may know what differences and similarities are truly characteristic of city and country.

Another such issue has to do with birth control. We know from the presence of birth control clinics and drugstore displays in cities that urban dwellers are aware of contraception and make use of various devices for the regulation of parenthood. But we also know that powerful ecclesiastical groups in the same cities offer bitter opposition. In the country we suspect that much less is known and hence that there is less practice of contraception, but again we are not sure. There have been for centuries empirical devices and procedures to prevent conception, and while they may be inefficient they are not wholly unknown to farmfolk. This is a problem which does not readily lend itself to quantitative study, but there is no reason for neglecting it entirely.

The Ecology of the Urban Family. If one examines the variation in types and numbers of families in different parts of a city, he may get the impression either of a crazy quilt or of an interesting pattern. Figure 2 shows for St. Louis in 1930 variations in the average size of families found in the 128 census tracts of that city. In general, large families are found most often in the outlying parts of the city, small families near the center. In fact, there is a belt of very small families straight through the middle, from east to west. This is a part of the city that is undergoing fairly rapid change—from private residential, to rooming house, to commercial. The eastern, or near-downtown, half of this belt is marked by poverty, disease, vice, crime, mobility, and deterioration; but the other half is an area of fairly high economic status, low death rates, and less than average disorder. The whole belt is one of multiple dwellings, some of them erected as such, others old residences converted into tenements. It is losing population to the north and south sides and to the suburbs.

The distribution of married persons of both sexes corresponds pretty well to the size of families. The newer parts of the city, southwest and northwest, have the largest percentages of both sexes married. These are areas in which single residences predominate. The population is more stable. The social "pathologies" are at a minimum. It would be valuable to discover the areas in which families remain intact longest and those in which they are most frequently broken. This work has not yet been done in St. Louis.

Mowrer has made studies in Chicago, however, which display the spatial distribution of various types of families and of family disorganization.[1] Near the downtown district known as the Loop he found nonfamily areas, occupied largely by men, some

[1] Mowrer, *op. cit.*, pp. 187–193, 1932. By permission of the University of Chicago Press.

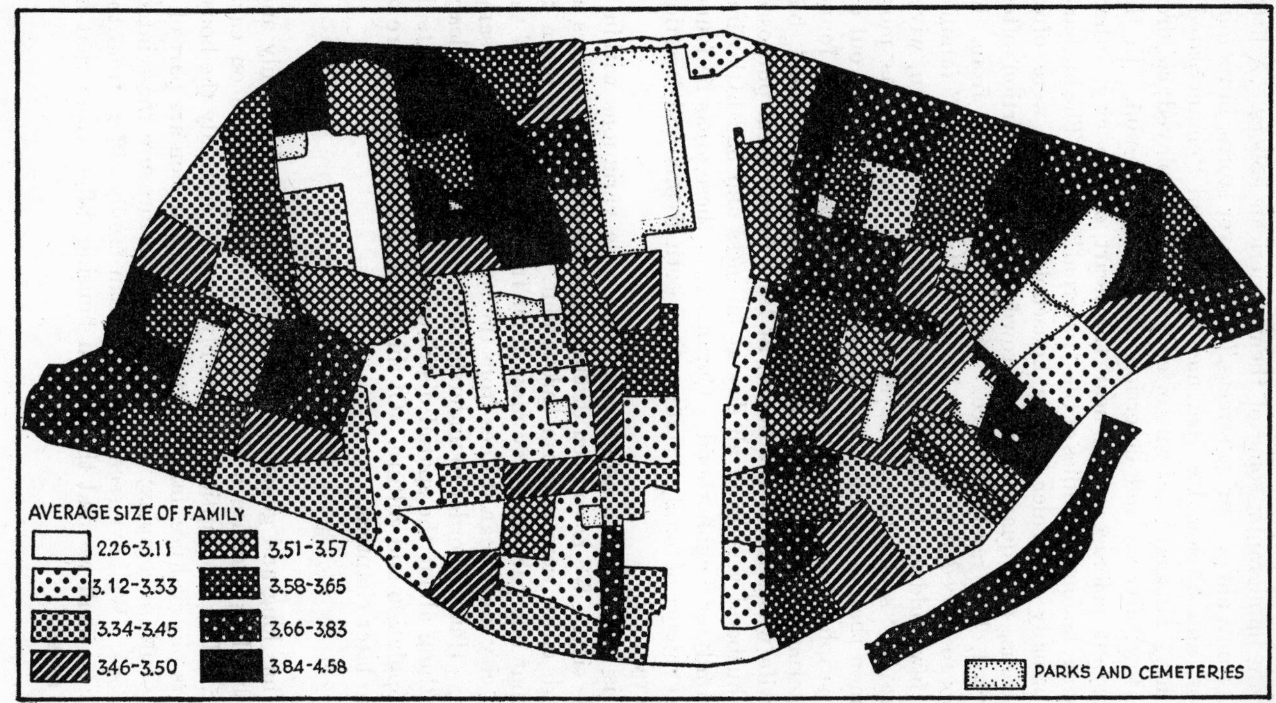

FIG. 2.—Average size of family, St. Louis, 1930.

of them immigrants, some of them American hoboes. A little farther out, along "string streets," living over stores, in rooming houses, and kitchenette apartments, he found "emancipated" families. Husband and wife often were both employed; children were few; divorce and desertion alike were common. In the immigrant colonies, some near the heart of the city, others outlying, he found families of the "paternal" type. The husband was usually the ruler of the household, children were often numerous, and quarters were crowded. Here desertion often occurred, but rarely divorce. More than halfway from the center to the edge of the city he found "equalitarian" families with few children, husbands professional or businessmen, wives active in "social" or civic affairs. Here divorce was more common than desertion, though both occurred. Finally, out on the periphery of the city and in the suburbs, Mowrer found "maternal" family areas. Here, too, families were small, but the wife was head of the house, at least for all local purposes. The husband was away all day at business and had little time for family or neighborhood. Curiously, in these areas he found little evidence of family disintegration; both divorce and desertion were rare.

It is important to appreciate these wide variations within a single city. We have been discussing rural-urban differences as though cities were uniform throughout. But now we begin to see that one part of a city may differ from another part of the same city more than it does from the rural districts of the same state. Hence in order to understand a city it is essential to learn something about the spatial distribution of various elements of its population and culture. Of this we shall have much more to say in later chapters.

Housing

It has long and generally been assumed that the family and the dwelling exercise a direct and intimate influence on each other. This assumption is probably correct; certainly the house and its physical use, family structure, and function are part of a single culture complex; but we have yet to measure these interrelations. We have seen that the urban family differs from the rural; so shall we find that urban housing differs from that in rural areas.

The dwellings of city people differ from those of countryfolk first by being more frequently multiple, less frequently owned by the occupants, and more expensive. These points we can demonstrate statistically. Concerning other aspects of housing we have impressions and hypotheses, but their verification and measurement await further research. It seems evident that the city man's home is usually some distance from his place of employment, while the countryman commonly lives and works on the same piece of land. It appears that city homes are smaller than country homes, even in relation to the size of the family; but this is one of our undemonstrated hypotheses. Farmers and villagers often live for several generations in the same house; those who move about go from one dwelling to another of the same sort—tenant cabin, bunkhouse, etc. But city people, at least those of the middle class, are observed to pass through a cycle. In childhood they often live in a single dwelling in a village or town. After dormitory life while away at school, they spend their early business or professional years in rooming houses or clubs near the center of a city. Early married life finds them in apartments farther out. The period of child rearing often brings a return to the single dwelling, this time on the periphery of the city or in the suburbs. Then, in middle and later life, there is a return to apartment, or possibly a residential hotel, toward the inner city. Perry has offered this hypothesis, which obviously is less applicable to low-income families than to those commonly described as middle-class and upper-class.[1]

To indicate the extent to which urban housing is multiple rather than single we pass from the casual impressions which everyone has of flats, apartments, converted tenements, and hotels to some statistical data. Gist and Halbert have assembled from scattered reports of the United States Bureau of Labor Statistics evidence that over an 11-year period, 1921–1931 inclusive, the proportion of new housing that took the form of single homes declined, as did the proportion of duplexes, whereas there was a marked increase in the proportion of families provided for in new apartments and other buildings for three or more families.[2] McKenzie has shown that in the period just preceding

[1] C. A. Perry, "Neighborhood and Community Planning," *Regional Plan of New York and Its Environs*, vol. 7, p. 25, 1929.

[2] Noel P. Gist and L. A. Halbert, *Urban Society*, p. 370, 1933.

the depression of 1929 the percentage of multiple dwellings increased sharply, and increased more in large cities than in small ones.[1] These data will be referred to presently in a discussion of urban housing.

TABLE 17.—PERCENTAGE DISTRIBUTION OF HOMES OCCUPIED BY OWNERS, 1930[a]

Value classification	Urban	Village, rural nonfarm
Under $1,000	3.1	18.1
$1,000–1,499	3.1	10.8
1,500–1,999	3.5	8.8
2,000–2,999	9.1	16.0
3,000–4,999	22.9	21.0
5,000–7,499	25.7	12.8
7,500–9,999	11.9	3.5
10,000–14,999	11.0	3.1
15,000–19,999	4.2	1.0
20,000 over	4.2	1.4
Not reported	1.4	3.5
Total	100.0	100.0

[a] Fifteenth Census, *Population*, vol. 6, p. 17.

TABLE 18.—PERCENTAGE DISTRIBUTION OF RENTED HOMES, 1930[a]

Rental	Urban	Rural nonfarm
Under $10	5.3	39.2
$10–14	8.1	20.4
15–19	10.0	12.6
20–29	22.5	13.7
30–49	31.1	6.8
50–74	15.1	1.5
75–99	3.5	0.3
100–149	1.6	0.2
150–199	0.5	0.1
200 and over	0.5	0.1
Not reported	1.8	5.1
Total	100.0	100.0

[a] Fifteenth Census, *Population*, vol. 6, p. 17.

[1] R. D. McKenzie, *The Metropolitan Community*, p. 218, 1933.

In 1930 the Bureau of the Census found 42.8 per cent of urban homes occupied by owners, while 52.3 per cent of farm homes and 52.6 per cent of rural nonfarm homes were occupied by owners. Tables 17 and 18 show conclusively that city homes are much more expensive than those in villages. Note that the tables take no account of farm homes, which would be hardly comparable to those of city dwellers. Speaking generally, villages have many more homes worth $3,000 or less, while cities have many more worth $3,000 and over. As to rentals, villages have more homes at less than $20 per month, while cities have more homes at $20 and over. There can be little doubt that the expensiveness of city homes, the fact that they are frequently multiple, and the predominance of tenants over owners are interrelated aspects of the same situation. It would be difficult to prove that any one is the cause of any other, but the three obviously go together.

There are other observations which might be made about the difference between city and country homes. Thus in the city there is greater land crowding, less storage space, and more frequent occupying of dwellings erected for an entirely different set of folks. On the other hand, city homes have more adequate sanitary facilities and more generally have such utilities as gas, electricity, running water, and telephone. We do not at all agree with Davie when he says that "the housing problem is primarily a city problem."[1] After seeing the dwellings of Southern tenant farmers, Western ranch hands, and workers in the oil fields, lumber camps, and on construction jobs, our observation would be that housing problems appear throughout America but are different in the city and in the country.

Trends in Urban Housing. Contrary to popular impression, the percentage of urban homes occupied by owners has not been dropping; from 1890 to 1930 it was actually increasing. Table 19 displays the surprising facts bearing on this point. However, it should be observed that the category of owner includes persons and families who have made a down payment and assumed from one to three mortgages. We know that after 1929 many thousands of these people lost the homes for which they were paying, either by foreclosure of mortgage or by sale for nonpayment of taxes. Whether this occurred more frequently in cities than in

[1] Maurice R. Davie, *Problems of City Life*, p. 93, 1932.

the country we do not know as yet; hence until 1940 data are available we shall not know whether the trend toward more home ownership in the city has really been checked. Returning to the predepression trend, in 1930 there were 20 large cities in which over one-half of all homes were occupied by their owners. Moreover, in each of these cities the percentage of homeowners had increased during the preceding 20 years. At the other end of the scale there were 11 large cities in which less than 30 per cent of homes were occupied by the owners. In each of these, however, the trend had been upward from 1910 to 1930. Of this latter group 5 cities were in New England, 3 in metropolitan New York, and 3 in the South. Among the cities with over 50 per cent of

TABLE 19.—TENURE OF HOMES, FARM AND NONFARM, UNITED STATES, 1890–1930[a]

Type	1930	1920	1910	1900	1890
Farm homes:					
Owned	52.5	56.7	62.7	63.9	65.9
Rented	44.5	40.8	37.1	35.3	34.1
Tenure unknown	3.0	2.5	0.2	0.7	
Nonfarm homes:					
Owned	45.2	40.0	37.1	34.7	36.9
Rented	53.2	57.9	59.6	60.5	63.1
Tenure unknown	1.6	2.1	3.3	4.8	

MEDIAN SIZE OF FAMILY, 1930[b]

Urban owners	3.48	Rural farm owners	3.89
Urban tenants	3.12	Rural farm tenants	4.21

PERCENTAGE OF HOMES OWNED, 1930[c]

District	Urban	Rural farm	Rural nonfarm
United States	42.8	52.3	52.6
Middle Atlantic	38.7	77.0	59.4
West North Central	48.5 (high)	55.0	59.4
South Atlantic	38.9 (low)	46.5	40.1
East South Central	39.3	42.3 (low)	39.1 (low)
New England	40.2	85.2 (high)	59.4
East North Central	47.6	66.0	64.0 (high)

[a] Fifteenth Census, *Population*, vol. 6, p. 11.
[b] *Ibid.*, p. 16.
[c] *Ibid.*, p. 35.

homes owned, 12 were in the Middle West, 5 in the Middle Atlantic states, and 3 on the Pacific coast. We do not, however, know what significance, if any, should be attached to these regional variations.

McKenzie has shown that in the decade ending with 1930 there was relatively more new housing in large urban areas than in small ones. He showed that the proportion of multiple dwellings was increasing most in great cities. The structural unit was becoming larger but the dwelling unit, *i.e.*, the individual apartment, house, or other space occupied by a single household was decreasing.[1] Later we shall show that the areas of greatest density in our cities are steadily losing population to outlying districts. The centrifugal flight, therefore, is reducing land crowding but it is not necessarily reducing room crowding or in other ways improving the housing situation.

Objections to Much Urban Housing. In reading the reports of housing surveys, which usually deal with the central portions of our cities, we are struck with evidence concerning houses that are dirty, dark, noisy, out of repair, internally poorly arranged, poorly located with reference to work, shopping, play and school, unpleasantly surrounded, and universally expensive. In some cities there is very little yard space. Rear tenements are not uncommon even in New York City. Ford found over 1,300 Class A multiple dwellings with water closets in the yard and over 24,000 such dwellings with toilets in public halls.[2] It has been widely charged that such objectionable housing is directly responsible for much of the disease and delinquency found in our cities. There is no doubt that those areas where housing is most antiquated, least sanitary, and most crowded are also the areas in which we find high indexes of poverty, delinquency, and disease. Thus in St. Louis, where a careful check was made of such dwellings, a high correlation was found between this factor on the one hand and on the other hand density, death rates, venereal disease, illiteracy, relief, juvenile court cases, and several other indicators of deprivation and disorganization. A study made by the Federal Emergency Administration of Public Works in 1936 seemed to demonstrate a close relation between housing conditions and delinquency. However, the authors of the report were careful

[1] McKenzie, *op. cit.*, pp. 217–219.

[2] James Ford, *Slums and Housing*, vol. 1, p. 265, 1936.

"to avoid referring dogmatically to 'cause' of crime, and to think in terms of relationships between sets of phenomena."[1] Unfortunately, this precaution has not been observed by all students of housing, and it is frequently alleged that the dwellings per se are directly "the cause" of various and sundry circumstances and behavior. Thus a report of the Michigan Housing Association holds that "it is generally conceived that apartment life has a deleterious or even destructive effect upon American ideals and institutions, the basis for which has been the traditional integrity of the American home."[2] Elsewhere in the same report it is alleged that apartment life tends to inhibit motherhood, retard the mental and physical development of children, and destroy the unity of family life. This may be an extreme statement, but it illustrates the general tendency to attribute to housing other conditions and forms of behavior without adequate analysis of objective data. In this particular instance the Michigan inquirer asked numbers of people their opinions and based his conclusions upon a summation of the casual judgment of some 1,300 apartment dwellers.

A much more careful examination of the possible relations between housing on the one hand and disease, death rates, and crime on the other has been made by Ford in his study of slums and housing in New York City. He concludes that "most diseases are unrelated to housing, and even among those in which a relation is demonstrable other conditions such as malnutrition . . . inevitably play a larger role."[3]

As to crime in relation to housing, Ford thinks there is some evidence that dark hallways and cellars provide opportunity for sex misbehavior and that noisy, crowded, unattractive quarters drive young people, especially, to the streets and to commercial recreation to spend their leisure time. In so far as these observations are correct they represent an indirect relation and a sharing in a total situation of which housing is only one factor among many. Our remarks are intended in no sense as a defense of

[1] *The Relation between Housing and Delinquency*, Public Works Administration, Housing Division, Research Bulletin No. 1, p. 8, 1936.

[2] S. James Herman, *Why Do You Live in an Apartment: A Study of a Sinister Trend in American Life*, p. 5, 1931.

[3] Ford, *op. cit.*, vol. 1, p. 374. By permission of Harvard University Press.

deteriorated and insanitary dwellings. They are only a warning that generalizations should be based upon factual data rather than upon casual impressions.

The Sources of Unsatisfactory Urban Housing. The drab, often dirty, and usually obsolescent housing of our inner cities has been variously attributed to the avarice of landlords, the carelessness of tenants, and, less frequently, to a complex of factors not easily identified with any particular set of persons. We are inclined to regard the issue as primarily an economic one. The expense of providing anything like an acceptable dwelling is so great that a large part of our urban population must perforce accept secondhand or shoddy dwellings in poor repair and in undesirable locations.

Behind the expensiveness lie a number of interrelated factors. First is the cost of construction. This involves the employment of a host of separate trades carrying on semi-independent handicraft processes on a retail basis. They get their supplies through a horde of jobbers, material and equipment dealers. They quarrel with each other about the right to do particular parts of the work, they promote the use of fads and gadgets, they operate often under codes which give monopolies to certain materials and involve expensive inspection. Second, there is the high cost of land. Our method of subdividing urban real estate involves inefficient use of land, premature expansion of public utilities, and wasteful methods of sale. Next is the cost of financing. Houses are rarely bought for cash. Moneylending with mortgages as security is not a charitable enterprise. In a boom period values are set high and loans are made on a basis which is insupportable when depression comes. Nevertheless, owners strive to maintain prices, hoping to avoid the loss of their investments. Even cities help to bolster artificial prices of land and buildings because their income depends largely on taxes levied on real estate. If we were to plan the use of land in our metropolitan districts along lines that have been intelligently worked out, if construction were more generally on a large scale, if building codes were revised in the interest of efficiency and economy, if people who cannot afford to buy homes were not induced to sign contracts, and if assessors were realistic about real estate values, housing could be provided for much less money than at present. But these things will not readily come to pass because too many people are dependent upon the existing scheme of things for their own living—realtors, contractors, subcontractors, craft unions, dealers in materials, and many others.

To restate the problem in somewhat different fashion, urban housing is unnecessarily expensive, because of (*a*) our bent for individual action in place of large-scale planning and building, (*b*) our habit of speculation in real estate, instead of subdivision and construction with an eye to needs and capacity to pay, (*c*) our practice of regarding real estate as a field for investment rather than as a means to the satisfaction of a need and, not least of all, (*d*) the uneven distribution of buying power. Some students believe that our system of taxation rests too heavily on improvements and too little on the unearned increment in land values.

Still another way of viewing the matter is this: When a city is small, all homes are near the business district. As the city grows, business invades the residence section. Those who can, move farther out, but they do not immediately sell their old homes. They hold them with the expectation that demand for the lots as sites of commercial or industrial establishments will raise the price and enable them to recover their investments, even though the houses must be demolished. Pending such increase in land values, they rent the houses. But since persons able to pay an adequate rent for a good single dwelling are unwilling to live near the business district, the owner divides the old home into a number of units. It becomes a converted tenement. Now, if the city grows rapidly, such a converted tenement does not have to be held many years before it ceases to be used for human habitation. But if the city ceases to develop rapidly, if the business district ceases to expand, then the converted tenement persists for many years. It deteriorates, and large numbers of such buildings make the inner city one of those areas of blight sometimes called slums.

In thus attempting to interpret the sources of unsatisfactory urban housing we are bringing charges against no one—neither landlord nor tenant, neither private citizen nor public official. We are simply calling attention to conventional ways of behaving which seem automatically to involve things which no one likes and of which no one knows how to get rid. This complex involves the organization of building trades, our system of financing, our practices of subdividing, the general mobility of the urban population, especially centrifugal flight, and the uneven distribution of incomes. Occasionally there is sheer congestion due to geographic limitations and problems of transportation, as on the island of Manhattan and the San Francisco peninsula, but in general we do not consider this a fundamental cause of defective housing in American cities.

Programs for Dealing with Urban Housing. For many years a minority of interested and earnest citizens has sought to find some way of correcting the housing situation. As to auspices, control, and finances, the programs have varied from limited dividend companies to out-and-out government owned and operated housing projects. The difficulty of a limited dividend company's raising capital from interested citizens with an appeal sometimes described as "philanthropy at 5 per cent" is apparent, and there have not been many such ventures. While they have provided some rather satisfactory housing, it has not been cheap enough to meet the needs of those who now occupy the most dilapidated, crowded, and insanitary dwellings. Cooperative housing, which has made some headway in Europe, has not appealed to many Americans. The part of government is chiefly that of enacting and sometimes enforcing restrictive legislation. Sometimes there have been subsidies in the form of remitted taxes or of out-and-out gifts or of loans at low rates of interest.

One of the amazing things of the depression period has been the extensive discussion of housing problems, the impressive promises that the government would through the construction of new dwellings both relieve unemployment and provide more acceptable quarters for low-income groups. But an equally amazing thing is the small amount of new housing that has emerged from all this discussion and all these promises. The Reconstruction Finance Corporation lent eight million dollars for a single housing project in New York City. The housing division of the Public Works Administration set out to encourage limited dividend corporations, but they encountered difficulty in raising the necessary money, the suspicion of property owners, and efforts to unload poor investments on these ventures. Ford lists some 50 projects set up under this governmental unit.[1] The Public Works Emergency Housing Corporation was created

[1] Ford, *op. cit.*, vol. 2, pp. 634–635. By permission of Harvard University Press.

to purchase or lease land and construct buildings directly, but this body encountered various legal difficulties and soon became inactive. The National Housing Act of 1934 set up an organization to guarantee loans and insure mortgages. Beyond this it has not participated directly in housing or even in furnishing funds. The Home Owners Loan Corporation granted 15-year 5 per cent amortized loans to homeowners in danger of losing their homes by foreclosure or forced sale.

An older and more highly developed program of home building and ownership is that of building and loan associations. Their maximum expansion was reached between 1925 and 1930, when their number was over 12,000 associations with 10 to 12 million members and assets ranging from 5½ billion to nearly 9 billion dollars.[1] They attract principally middle-class folk, skilled artisans, white-collar workers, small merchants, and professional people. Their system of financing is too expensive for those who are most in need of new houses. However, they do represent a useful form of semicooperative enterprise in this field.

In general we can say that private enterprise has failed to provide adequate housing for city populations. It has approximately sufficed for families of relatively large incomes, but it has failed utterly to provide decent housing at prices within the reach of wage earners and persons with modest salaries.

With reference to planning and location, housing programs have varied from slum clearance to the creation of garden suburbs. The slum clearance projects have been intended to remove the blight which so often surrounds the central business district and to put in its place housing that is healthy, decent, and inexpensive. Incidentally, such housing programs have been highly esteemed because of what they might contribute toward reemployment. Nevertheless, slum clearance is inevitably expensive and unless subsidized by the government cannot rehouse the original populations of blighted areas. Some studies have been made of what happens to the original occupants when a slum area is cleared. In general they move into adjoining districts that are little, if any, better than their original homes, while the new houses are occupied by people who are on a somewhat higher economic level. This may be no fundamental difficulty, as in the long run a larger part of the population has

[1] *The World Almanac*, 1937, p. 287.

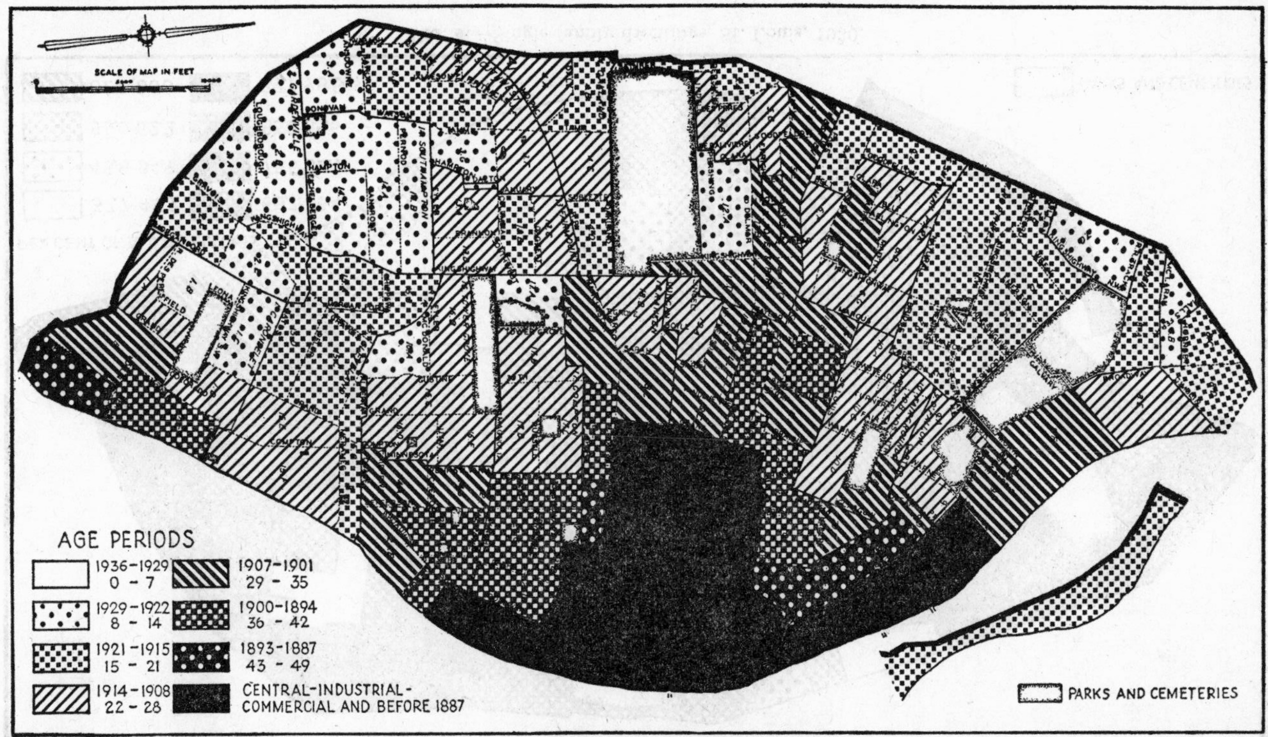

FIG. 3.—Age of dwellings, St. Louis, 1930.

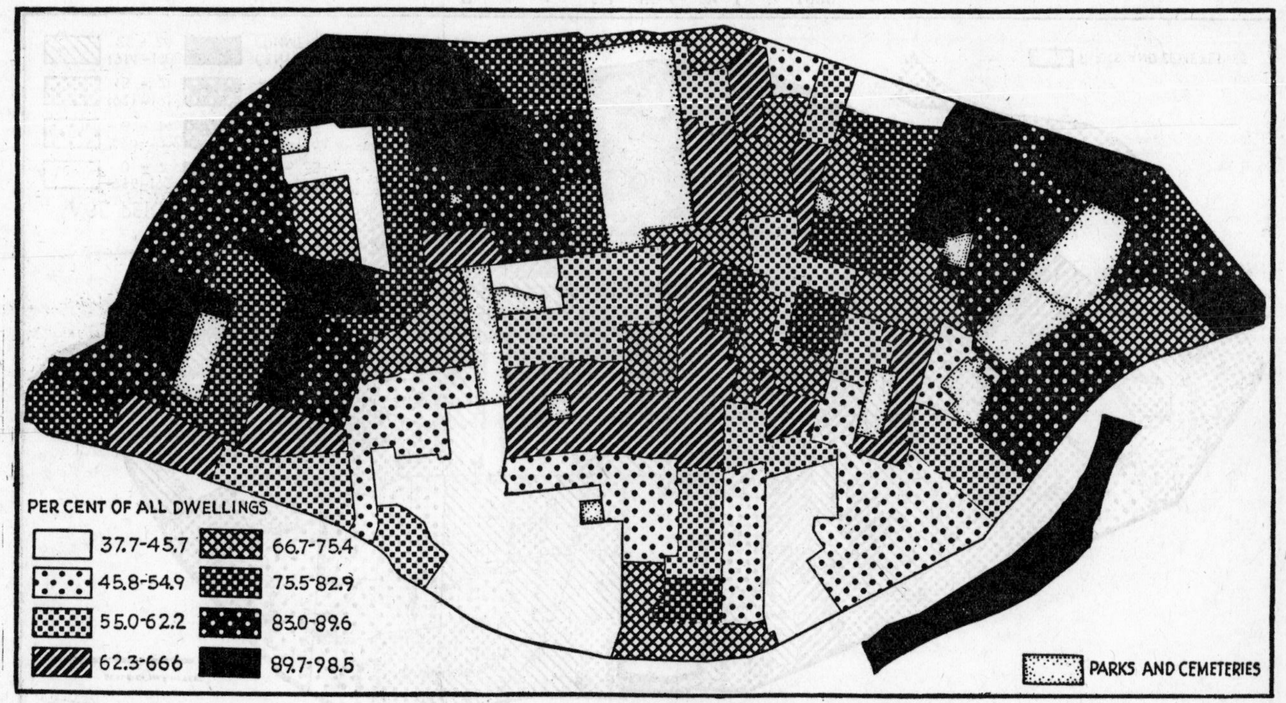

FIG. 4.—Single family dwellings, St. Louis, 1930.

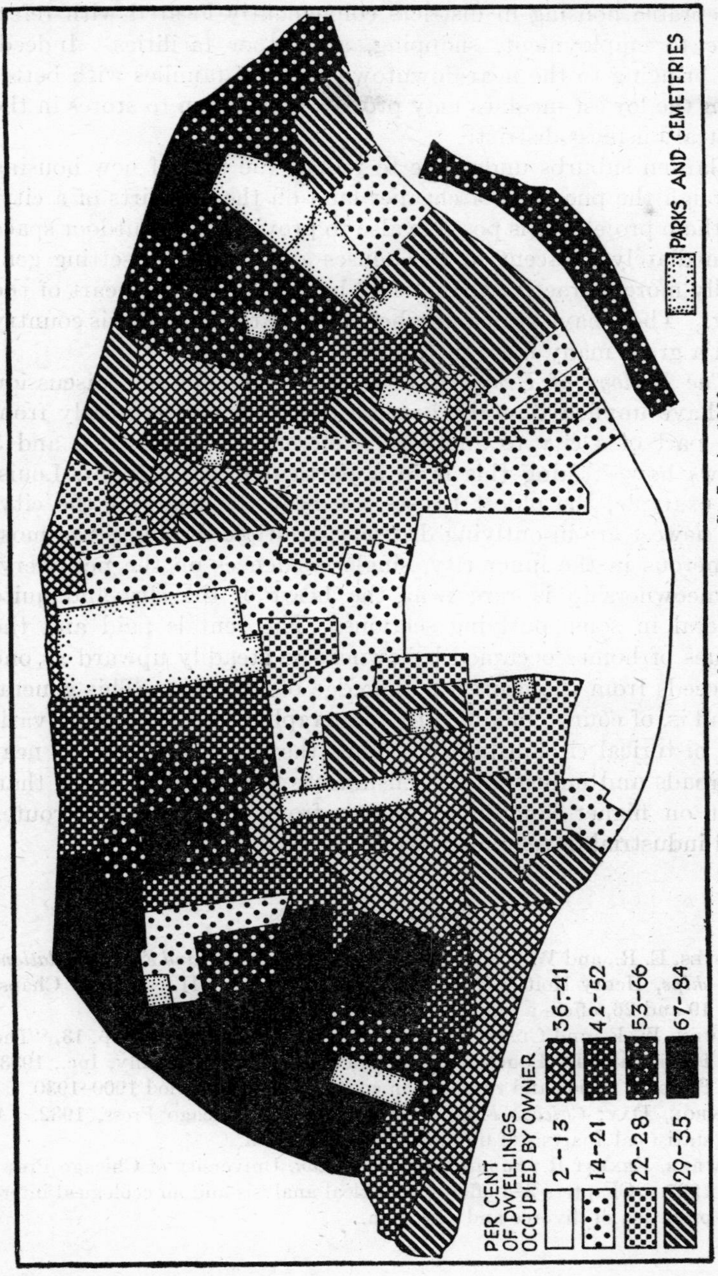

FIG. 5.—Homes owned by occupants, St. Louis, 1930.

acceptable housing in districts conveniently located with reference to employment, shopping, and other facilities. Indeed, the bringing to the near-downtown areas of families with better than the lowest incomes may prove a great boon to stores in the central business district.

Garden suburbs undertake to reduce the cost of new housing through the purchase of cheaper land on the outskirts of a city. In these projects it is possible also to provide more outdoor space immediately adjacent to the houses and make the setting generally more attractive than would be possible in the heart of the city. There have been a number of such attempts in this country and a great many more in Europe.

The Ecology of Urban Housing. Throughout our discussion we have implied that the housing situation varies greatly from one part of a city to another. Reference to Figs. 3, 4, and 5 shows how striking this is in a particular city. In St. Louis, for example, the oldest houses are near the heart of the city, the newest are in outlying districts; multiple dwellings are most numerous in the inner city, single residences on the periphery. Homeownership is rare near the heart of the city and quite general in some outlying sections. The rentals paid and the values of homes occupied by owners go steadily upward as one proceeds from the center to the edge of the city. This general trend is, of course, modified by topographic features and by various historical circumstances. Thus the housing in valleys near railroads and industrial establishments is generally poorer than that on higher land more remote from transportation routes and industrial developments.

Selected Readings

Groves, E. R., and W. F. Ogburn: *American Marriage and Family Relationships,* Henry Holt & Company, Inc., 1928. Part II, especially Chaps. 19 and 26, offers a valuable statistical analysis.

Ogburn, W. F., and Clark Tibbitts: *Recent Social Trends,* Chap. 13, "The Family and Its Functions," McGraw-Hill Book Company, Inc., 1933. Presents trends and rural-urban contrasts for the period 1900–1930.

Monroe, Day: *Chicago Families,* University of Chicago Press, 1932. A statistical analysis of unpublished census data.

Mowrer, Ernest R.: *Family Disorganization,* University of Chicago Press, 1927. Chapters 3–5 offer a statistical analysis and an ecological interpretation of divorce and desertion.

MOWRER, ERNEST R.: *The Family*, University of Chicago Press, 1932. Chapter 9, "Family Disorganization and Urbanism," is especially significant.

BAUER, CATHERINE: *Modern Housing*, Houghton Mifflin Company, 1934. Deals with urban housing in Europe and America in the nineteenth and twentieth centuries, including programs of reform.

ABBOTT, EDITH: *The Tenements of Chicago*, University of Chicago Press, 1937. The development of tenements, types, ownership, occupants, problems presented, and legislation enacted, especially 1908–1935.

FORD, JAMES: *Slums and Housing*, Harvard University Press, 1936. A thorough study of the history, present conditions, and policies affecting housing in New York City.

MUNTZ, EARL E.: *Urban Sociology*, The Macmillan Company, 1938. Chapters 7–11 deal with various aspects of housing in Europe and America.

CHAPTER VII

ECONOMIC INSTITUTIONS AND FOLKWAYS

It is a matter of common observation that the economic organization of urban and of rural areas is quite different. Rural economy centers about agriculture; urban economy is more concerned with manufacturing, trade, transportation, and finance. Country people talk about crops, livestock, the weather, and prices of farm products. City people talk about wages, stocks, bonds, income tax, and bargains. Great numbers of country people are self-employed and work in small units. In the city large organizations (corporations or municipal departments) provide for masses of people goods and services which in the country individual families provide for themselves—water, fuel for heating and cooking, light, fire protection, certain foods (vegetables, fruits, dairy and poultry products), and disposal of waste (ashes, garbage, and rubbish).

This means that country people do a great many different kinds of things, while city people tend to specialize. We have known rural villages in which the only occupations were those of farmer, blacksmith, merchant, physician, clergyman, teacher, and housewife. In large cities the number of occupations often runs to several hundred. The 1930 census listed for cities of 100,000 and over in New York State, nine broad divisions of occupation, with the number of subdivisions of each, as follows:[1]

Forestry and fishing	10
Extraction of minerals	17
Manufacturing and mechanical	280
Transportation and communication	89
Trade	82
Public service (not otherwise counted)	19
Professional	63
Domestic and personal	46
Clerical	15
	621

[1] Fifteenth Census, *Population*, vol. 4, pp. 1088–1103.

In the city there are much greater inequalities of income. To be sure, the millionaire may have a country home, but his principal residence is usually in one of a very small number of large cities. Poor people are numerous in both urban and rural districts. In Chap. XXI evidence will be presented which indicates that the burden of poverty is somewhat greater in cities than in the country. If this be true, then there are in urban centers more individuals and families at the extremes of the economic ladder, as well as a greater disparity of incomes. This suggests the possibility of sharper economic conflicts in cities than in the country. At least it guarantees that persons in low-income groups will be kept aware of those who receive a great deal more.

This last is one of several items in which rural and urban folk are known to differ qualitatively; whether or not they differ quantitatively we have not yet discovered. In the city there are clashes between employers and employees, stockholders and directors, industrial and craft unionists, "independent" merchants and chain stores, rival corporations, and trade associations. In the country farmers are often pitted against merchants, bankers, and commission men, landlords against tenants, and farm operators against farm laborers. Farmers work together through the Grange, Farmers' Union, and various cooperatives. Urban businessmen work together through manufacturers' associations and chambers of commerce. As yet we have no measure of the relative amount of cooperation and competition in city and country areas.

Waste has been an outstanding characteristic of our American folkways, but whether it is more common among urban or among rural folk we do not know definitely. In some rural districts we find erosion, deforestation, soil depletion, and the permanent destruction of many natural resources. In cities we find waste in manufacturing and marketing, frequent changes of styles, alternation of rush and idle periods, poor personnel work, sabotage by workers to prolong jobs, sabotage by employers to keep prices high, overproduction of some articles and underproduction of others, interference with management by manipulators of stocks and bonds, excessive numbers of retail outlets, multiplication of salesmen, "talking points" in place of improvements—in general, too few people regularly engaged in production and too many people "muscling in" on the distributive process. Consider the amount of time during which factories are idle. Count the number of milk wagons that pass any city door. Take a census of door-to-door salesmen, real estate salesmen, automobile salesmen.[1] Compute the sums that are spent for competitive (rather than educational) advertising, which stresses the unimportant, misrepresents quality, and sometimes promotes the sale of articles that are useless or dangerous. Farmers are often condemned for their inefficiency, but it is yet to be demonstrated that they are as wasteful of time, energy, and money as city people.

This brings us to the plight of the consumer in city and in country. In both instances the buyer is often uncertain as to the quantity of goods he is getting; he purchases by the package, bottle, or basket, rather than by weight. Unless sophisticated, he is unaware that price is a poor index of quality. Sometimes the merchant is as ignorant as his customer, but in general there is a disparity in the information at the disposal of the two. In so far as country people produce for their own consumption they have an opportunity to escape some of these difficulties. In so far as they depend on catalogues of mail-order houses, statements printed on containers, and the words of village merchants, their troubles are quite as great as those of city folk. Moreover, they do not have such protection as better business bureaus can provide against gross fraud.[2]

There was a time, not long past, when farmers were considered economically secure. Even if hail, drought, grasshoppers, or boll weevils destroyed a crop, farmers had their homes and something stored up for the winter. As a matter of fact, they were not very secure even in those days, but now that they have the additional risks of an international market they are even less so. With two-fifths of all farms mortgaged and another two-fifths operated by tenants, with share croppers being evicted and farm laborers being discharged to make way for new machinery, life in rural America seems to be about as insecure as it is in our cities.

[1] City people may be confronted with either of two extremes. One is the excess number of stores, salesmen, etc. The other is monopoly. The latter may be quite as expensive as the former to the consumer.

[2] Of late there has been some headway made toward standardizing both containers and quality of goods. But in general, advertisements and labels are not very informative as to weight or quality.

Nevertheless, a larger proportion of urban than of rural folk are directly dependent on others for means of making a living. For both groups seasonal and cyclical fluctuations of employment and prices are very great. Hence the relative insecurity of country and city presents another unsolved problem for future research.

Control of economic processes is much more centralized in urban than in rural areas. Not only do a few corporations dominate certain cities; sometimes a few individuals rule those corporations. Moreover, through the development of holding companies, financial jugglers in one city may control the destinies of investors, workers, and consumers in many others. The cases of Insull and the Van Sweringens are recent enough to make this point vivid. In *Middletown in Transition* the Lynds show how completely one family controls the economic life of a small Midwestern city. Such complete dominance is more difficult to achieve in larger centers, but a very few automobile manufacturers may be said to hold the fate of Detroit in their hands. As for the other side of the case, wheat farmers have long found their income determined as much by elevator companies, millers, railroads, and speculators in the produce exchange as by weather conditions and their own efforts. Cotton growers have struggled against similar odds. The livestock men have been pretty much at the mercy of large packing companies. All of them have been greatly affected by changes in the international market. Recently the Agricultural Adjustment Administration has sought to regulate production and, indirectly, farm incomes. In sober truth the farmer is very far from being his own boss. Yet control is by no means so highly centralized in the case of agriculture as in that of industry. It is more scattered in rural economy than in urban economy.

Economic Structure: Manufacturing

A major hypothesis of this chapter is that the economic structure of a city is reflected in the habits and attitudes of its population. But since very little research has borne directly on this basic problem, we shall approach it through some of the outstanding facts about the distribution of manufacturing and commerce, together with some general observations about social concomitants. Table 20 shows clearly the centralization of industry in cities, especially in those of 100,000 or over. At each of the last three census dates cities had factories and industrial wage earners in much larger proportions than their share of the total population of the United States. Their raw materials and power used, wages paid, and finished products were all much greater than would be expected on the basis of their population. However, this is merely a statistical statement of what is already generally known. What may not be so well known is that the centralization of manufacturing is greater in large than in small cities. A still more important difference, which is not displayed in this table, is that an industrial establishment of a given size in a small city assumes a place in the lives of the people quite distinct from that of a similar establishment in a large city. That is, a textile mill employing 500 workers in a city of 10,000 may be quite dominating, but if it were in a city of 100,000 it would probably inspire much less both of fear and of respect. The owners and managers would take their place along with other industrialists. Wage earners would have more alternative possibilities of employment. Another point not brought out by this table is that there is a great difference between a city which depends on a single industry and one whose manufacturing is diversified. Neither prosperity nor depression is likely to strike the latter so suddenly or so devastatingly as the former. When, in addition to dependence on a single industry, a city finds its economic life dominated by a single corporation, its entire social organization is likely to bear many resemblances to feudalism. As was stated above, these propositions are based on general observations that appear to be correct. But before they are accepted with complete assurance they should be tested by the systematic study of representative cities.

Another kind of research which we commend to students of the city is an examination of relations between types of industries (steel, textile, clothing, tobacco, rubber) and composition of the population. Certain industries make extensive use of women and adolescents; others employ chiefly adult men. Some industries require many skilled workmen; others are constantly drawing the unskilled from the most recently tapped reservoir (southern Europe, Mexico, the Ozarks, the cotton belt). We anticipate finding correlations between types of industry and "race," sex ratio, marital status, age distribution, etc.

McKenzie has emphasized a little-known fact, that the percentage of our urban population engaged in manufacturing has been declining for some time.[1] In 1890, 19 per cent of city dwellers were factory workers, while in 1930 the percentage was only 12.8. In particular urban centers the number of industrial wage earners actually decreased from 1920 to 1930, while the total population was increasing. Thus in San Francisco and Oakland population increased 34.9 per cent while the average number of workers in manufacturing establishments decreased 11.4 per cent. In Boston population grew 12.8 per cent while industrial workers dropped 22.7 per cent. In Kansas City population rose 25 per cent while the number of wage earners in manufacturing remained constant. These data indicate in part diversification of employment and in part chronic unemployment. The extent to which each has occurred in given cities can be determined by analysis of general census data and of special reports of employment and unemployment.

TABLE 20.—SUMMARY OF MANUFACTURING IN UNITED STATES CITIES OF 10,000 AND OVER, 1909, 1919, 1929[a]

Percentage of United States Total in Cities

	All cities over 10,000			10,000 to 25,000			25,000 to 100,000			Over 100,000		
	1909 or 1910	1919 or 1920	1920 or 1930	1910	1920	1930	1910	1920	1930	1910	1920	1930
Population	37.0	42.3	47.1	6.0	6.6	7.1	8.9	9.8	10.3	22.1	25.9	29.6
Number of establishments	50.6	57.2	67.3	7.1	7.8	7.7	10.1	10.8	11.1	33.4	38.7	48.6
Wage earners	65.1	70.4	71.2	10.2	10.7	10.1	16.9	18.0	17.3	38.0	41.7	43.8
Horsepower			61.3			12.1			17.3			31.9
Wages			75.1			9.8			17.5			47.8
Cost of materials	68.2	71.6	73.1	9.5	9.5	9.4	17.9	16.8	16.8	40.8	45.3	46.9
Value of products	69.1	72.6	74.8	9.5	9.7	9.2	17.4	17.2	17.0	42.2	45.7	48.7
Value added by manufacture	70.3	74.1	77.0	9.4	9.9	8.9	16.7	17.9	17.2	44.2	46.3	50.9

[a] Fifteenth Census, *Manufactures*, 1929, vol. 1, p. 307.

Another suggestion for research is in order at this point. It is that studies be made of cities from which factories are removing

[1] R. D. McKenzie, *The Metropolitan Community*, pp. 53–58, 1933. By permission of the President's Research Committee on Social Trends.

and of the cities to which they are going. That the transfer of certain textile mills from New England to the South Atlantic states has very serious consequences no one can doubt. But just what adjustments are made in the North and what new problems are presented in the South are questions worthy of extended study.

Economic Structure: Commerce

Wholesale trade is obviously a function of cities, and for the most part of large cities. It is one of the principal ties that binds a city and its hinterland together. The "sphere of influence" of an urban center is substantially the territory through which its wholesale houses distribute their goods. The importance of wholesaling in any city depends in part on the size and wealth of the trade area and in part on the development of other business enterprises in the urban center. In general the wholesale function is more highly centralized than is manufacturing. In 1929 as few as 51 counties contained one-half of all factory workers in the United States. But in the same year as few as 10 counties contained establishments that did one-half of the wholesale business of the entire country. The centralization of retail trade was much less, but even it was surprisingly great. In 1929 as few as 72 counties contained stores that did one-half of the retail business of the country.[1] This means that opportunities for employment in these various fields are quite different in different places. We shall presently illustrate this fact with data from four selected cities.

Like manufacturing and wholesaling, retail trade may be regarded as offering employment—incidentally, a very different sort of employment. But it is more significant as the immediate source of consumers' goods. A study of the sales made by different groups of stores reveals something of the buying habits of people in cities of different sizes. Thus Table 21 shows that food stores sold relatively less in cities over 30,000 than in cities between 10,000 and 30,000, whereas for restaurants the ratios were reversed, so that total sales of foodstuffs were probably about the same. People in large cities "eat out" more than do those in small cities. The inhabitants of cities of every size

[1] *Ibid.*, pp. 55, 60.

spend relatively more for food than do those who trade in villages. The latter undoubtedly produce a considerable part of their victuals at home. Both city and country people patronize stores that handle a wide range of goods; in the large city they go to department and variety stores, while in the village they buy from general stores. The sale of automobiles, together with gasoline and other supplies, bulks larger in villages than in cities, while the reverse is true of clothing and furniture. Apparently many people, especially in large cities, find streetcars and busses more practical than private cars, while the automobile has become a necessity for large numbers of villagers and farmers. It is probably true that countryfolk buy fewer clothes and pieces of furniture than do city people, but they do a part of this buying in cities. Why lumber and other building materials should bulk larger in the sales of village stores than in those of cities

TABLE 21.—RETAIL DISTRIBUTION, UNITED STATES, 1929[a]

	Cities over 30,000	Cities 10,000 to 30,000	Places less than 10,000
Retail stores	683,751	164,871	694,536
Full-time employees	2,466,407	460,311	906,863
Net sales per store	$41,700	$35,400	$21,300
Total pay roll per store	$5,150	$3,630	$1,550
Full-time employees per store	3.6	2.8	1.3
Percentage of all stores:			
Single-store independent	61.5	70.6	66.6
Second and third store independent	10.7	9.1	4.8
Local chains	8.2	5.2	4.4
Sectional and national chains	15.1	13.7	7.2
Percentage of total sales by:			
Food group	22.7	24.1	20.0
Restaurants	5.3	3.3	2.8
General stores	0.1	0.5	16.9
General merchandise (Department and variety stores)	16.9	12.1	6.3
Automotive group	16.6	24.4	23.5
Apparel group	11.6	8.1	3.2
Furniture and household-furnishings group	6.7	5.8	3.6
Lumber and building group	4.2	6.4	7.1

[a] Adapted from Fifteenth Census, *Retail Distribution*, part 1, pp. 8, 969–976.

we do not know, unless urban contractors secure many of their supplies from wholesale dealers.

The size of the stores in a place indicates something of the assortment of goods from which purchasers may make their choice. Hence it is significant that annual sales of individual retail stores in cities over 30,000 are double those in places under 10,000. The number of full-time employees per store is nearly three times as great in cities over 30,000 as in places under 10,000. But more important than sizes of stores are types of merchandise handled and the sales of each. These will be illustrated presently in a comparative study of four cities.

Standards and Levels of Living

It is popularly assumed that city people demand more and live better than country people, in other words, that they have higher standards and actually achieve higher levels of living. It is also generally believed that the cost of living on any given level is greater in large than in small cities. Unfortunately, there have been few studies of standards in the sense of what goods and services various groups consider necessary and are fairly content with. But there have been numerous studies indicating what goods and services are essential to physical health and comfort. We may assume that standards in the physiological sense are not radically different for city and for country or for cities of different sizes. Hence it is practical to study comparative costs of maintaining a minimum, or any other, level of living. Periodically the United States Bureau of Labor Statistics prices identical or equivalent articles in various cities and publishes the results in its bulletins or in the *Monthly Labor Review*. Also, for several years it has been collecting data concerning actual expenditures made by families of wage earners and clerical workers with small salaries. Tables 22 and 23 summarize a few of the findings in five Pennsylvania and five California cities. The reader will note several interesting variations. The total of current expenditures was greater for families in the California cities than for those in Pennsylvania. The California families spent a higher percentage of their total for automobiles and medical care, while the Pennsylvania families spent a higher percentage for food and housing. Expenditure for clothing was not very different in the two areas. On the whole,

TABLE 22.—COSTS OF LIVING IN FIVE PENNSYLVANIA CITIES, 1933–1935[a]

Items	Philadelphia	Pittsburgh	Scranton	Johnstown	Lancaster
Total current expenditures	$1,603	$1,484	$1,413	$1,182	$1,312
Per cent of expenditure for:					
Food	36.2	33.1	35.6	31.9	33.7
Clothing	10.7	10.4	11.0	10.5	11.2
Housing	15.4	19.1	18.6	17.6	16.2
Automobile	3.5	4.5	2.8	5.2	4.0
Medical care	3.2	4.0	3.8	4.8	4.1

[a] *Monthly Labor Review*, 44 (1937), 1493–1508. Data for white families only.

TABLE 23.—COSTS OF LIVING IN FIVE CALIFORNIA CITIES, 1934–1935[a]

Items	San Francisco and Oakland	Los Angeles	San Diego	Sacramento	Modesto
Total current expenditures	$1,657	$1,525	$1,470	$1,520	$1,464
Percentage of expenditure for:					
Food	33.1	30.9	32.3	31.2	30.2
Clothing	11.0	10.9	9.4	10.3	11.4
Housing	16.6	15.3	15.2	15.5	13.1
Automobile	6.7	11.2	11.0	8.0	11.3
Medical care	4.6	4.1	4.4	5.6	4.9

[a] *Monthly Labor Review*, 44 (1937), 663–675.

these facts bespeak different habits as well as different climates. The severe winters of Pennsylvania mean shorter seasons for outings in the country and more expensive food and housing. It is curious that they are not accompanied by greater expenditures for clothing and medical care. Within each state there are also interesting variations. The Philadelphia families spent less money and smaller percentages of their total for automobiles and medical care than did Pittsburgh families. Perhaps the two are regularly associated! Housing costs much more and food less in Pittsburgh than in Philadelphia. San Franciscans spent much less on automobiles than did families in Los Angeles, putting most of the difference into food. The former also spent more for housing and medical care. To those who know the two cities these figures represent real differences in folkways. Many Los Angeles families live in small, inexpensive cottages, bungalows, or house courts; drive their own cars to work, to the beach, and to the mountains; belong to healing cults or, curiously, to cooperative health associations. San Francisco families more commonly live in apartments, ride electric trains and ferryboats, and utilize conventional facilities for medical care. Other differences among the several cities deserve attention, but the items we have discussed should suffice to indicate the possibilities of this type of research.

The only study that we have found to report costs of comparable items for urban and rural folk in the same region dealt with a small sample of Virginia white families in 1928–1929.[1] This bit of research indicated that costs of housing, automobile, and medical care were greater for urban than for rural families. The same was true of clothing except on the lowest income level, where costs were about the same for city and for country groups. The value of food consumed, including that produced at home, was greater for urban than for rural families, except in the case of those of intermediate incomes ($1,200 to $2,800). More comparisons of this sort would be very valuable to students of both urban and rural sociology.

The Comparative Study of Cities

Throughout our discussions we have stressed the importance of comparing cities. Studies of individual cities, like the Lynds' intensive examinations of Middletown,[2] give valuable insight into particular situations and suggest generalizations. But for the latter we need comparative studies to discover what traits of our economic complex regularly occur together, and under what circumstances. Already it is possible to make a beginning of such analysis, using data published by the United States Departments of Commerce and Labor. Merely to suggest what any student may do, we present, in Table 24, some data concerning four selected cities. Akron is a manufacturing city devoted

[1] Wilson Gee and W. H. Stauffer, *Rural and Urban Living Standards in Virginia*, 1929.

[2] Robert Lynd and Helen M. Lynd, *Middletown*, 1929, and *Middletown in Transition*, 1937.

largely to the rubber industry. Denver is an inland commercial and tourist center. New Orleans and Seattle are seaports, but with very different hinterlands. Seattle serves an area in which lumbering, fishing, mining, and small farming are dominant. New Orleans is in a region of large plantations devoted to the raising of cotton, rice, and sugar cane. We claim no special merit for our choice of cities except their diversity.

The extent of Akron's dependence on industry is shown by the fact that over one-half of its gainfully employed persons were in 1930 engaged in manufacturing and mechanical trades. Less than one-seventh were found in any other occupational group. Wholesaling employed an almost negligible percentage. Professional persons were relatively few, and so were domestic servants, clerical and transport workers, and even those employed in retail trade. Retail stores per 10,000 population were less numerous, but their per capita sales compared favorably with the three other cities. Akron people evidently invested heavily in automobiles and accessories; they spent relatively large amounts in variety (*e.g.*, five-and-ten) stores. But for books, or at least in book stores, they paid out almost nothing. Here, then, was a city of factory workers, nearly one-third immigrants or their children, men earning the living, women keeping house, and children going to school. Their recreation came in part through the radio and the family car, but not at all through books. They spent almost as much in food stores as the people of Denver and a little more in restaurants than the people of New Orleans. Their relatively large purchases in variety stores may have offset the little they spent in jewelry stores.

Of the four cities, Denver had the lowest percentage of gainfully employed persons in manufacturing and mechanical occupations and the highest percentage in retail trade. It ranked close to Seattle in wholesaling; it was also second to Seattle in per capita sales of clothing, jewelry, and food stores and restaurants. It was highest in the per capita sales of radio and music stores and of department stores (Seattle department stores not being reported). It seems strange that Denver should rank only third in sales of automobiles and that its restaurants should not exceed those of Akron by a larger margin. Perhaps more of the tourists than might be expected came in trailers or took light-housekeeping rooms. Also it would be helpful to learn how much

TABLE 24.—COMPARISON OF FOUR CITIES, 1930[a]

	Akron	Denver	New Orleans	Seattle
Population	255,000	288,000	459,000	366,000
Percentage of population gainfully employed	41.7	45.3	44.6	43.0
Percentage of wage earners employed in establishments				
Manufacturing	56.5	12.5	11.0	13.1
Wholesale	2.5	8.1	5.1	8.5
Retail	10.9	14.8	9.8	13.4
Percentage gainfully employed in occupational groups				
Manufacturing and mechanical	52.5	25.8	26.4	29.5
Transportation and communication	6.1	9.3	13.8	9.4
Trade	13.4	20.4	16.9	19.1
Professions	6.4	10.0	6.3	9.2
Domestic and personal	9.8	15.0	19.6	13.0
Clerical	9.8	14.8	12.6	13.4
Wholesale establishments per 10,000 population	8	32	16	33
Net sales per capita	$415	$1375	$1315	$1575
Retail stores per 10,000 population	120	154	173	154
Food stores per 10,000	45	47	87	52
Clothing stores per 10,000	18	11	9	13
Sales per capita:				
Food stores	$129	$130	$79	$141
Restaurants	29	32	28	45
Auto sales	110	85	34	95
Clothing stores	52	61	44	65
Furniture stores	24	21	12	18
Radio and music	8	9	4.50	8
Book stores	0.25	2.35	1.10	3.00
Jewelry stores	6	9	6	10
Variety stores	15	10	9	10
Department stores	82	131	47	

[a] Adapted from Fifteenth Census: *Population*, vol. 4; *Occupations*, pp. 232 *ff.*; *Manufactures*, 1929, vol. 1, pp. 293–305; *Wholesale Distribution*, pp 13–14; *Retail Distribution*, part 1, pp. 102, 476, 728, 914.

the economic structure is affected by health seekers, migratory laborers, and Mexican immigrants.

New Orleans presented a very different picture from those we have just sketched. Occupationally, its people were more evenly distributed among the various major groups. It ranked highest in the employment of married women and of children, hence lowest in the percentage of families depending on a single worker. It had fewer wholesale houses than Denver, but their per capita sales were nearly as high. Per capita sales of retail stores were lower than those in the other three cities, with the sole exception of book stores. This indicates a low level of living, which is doubtless related to the fact that 27 per cent of the population was Negro.

As to occupational distribution, Seattle did not rank first or last in any group. However, it had the most wholesale houses per capita and their sales were largest. It had the largest percentage of families with a single wage earner. Its retail sales were highest in stores handling foods, clothing, books, and jewelry, also in restaurants, thus indicating a relatively high level of living. Along with this, it had the largest percentage (48) of population of foreign birth or parentage.

The reader should beware of drawing hasty conclusions from limited data about four cities, but we hope that he will be interested in analyzing similar facts about these and other urban centers until he can establish correlations between significant factors in their economic life.

The Localization of Economic Features of a City

So far we have been discussing cities as wholes. Now we want to emphasize the fact that they are not alike throughout. Every large city has a central business district with its department stores, office buildings, banks, and specialty shops. Near by are railway terminals and sometimes docks and piers. Adjacent to both are warehouses and wholesale establishments. Along the water front or on lowlands abutting railroad lines are heavy industries. At various sites, but commonly not far from the central business district, will be found light industries. Scattered throughout the metropolitan area, especially at the intersections of major thoroughfares, are minor business districts or subcenters.

This distribution of business activities may be illustrated with the case of St. Louis.[1] On the upland which rises directly from the west bank of the Mississippi, spreading out from the point of first settlement, is the downtown area, where are found the

[1] Lewis F. Thomas, *The Localization of Business Activities in Metropolitan St. Louis*, 1927.

principal retail, wholesale, financial, jobbing, and light manufacturing activities. Along the river to the north are lumberyards and woodworking factories, established there because in early days logs were floated down the Mississippi and had to be stopped before they could interfere with shipping near the business center. South along the river are smelters, foundries, and chemical plants to which railroads bring raw materials from southeast Missouri. Through the center of the city in the Mill Creek and Des Peres valleys are warehouses, clay-using plants, and miscellaneous industries. In the northwest and southwest sections are various light industries reached by branch lines of the railroads. Across the Mississippi in Illinois is a broad flood plain occupied in part by railroad lines and heavy manufacturing plants. Near the downtown section are residential districts on a low economic level. Other poor districts are found on the east side and near some of the outlying industrial areas. But in general the economic level rises as one progresses from the center toward the periphery. As we go out from the heart of the city we find rising rents and fewer people on relief.

Turning from the general economic pattern to the distribution of retail activities, we find a central shopping district, mid-city and outlying subcenters, "string streets," scattered stores, and sometimes public markets. A study of Baltimore in 1929[1] showed that three-fifths of all retail stores were scattered, but they did only two-fifths of the total volume of business. One-sixth were in subcenters, and they did one-sixth of the business. Downtown were only 6 per cent of the stores, but they made 28 per cent of the net sales. Along "string streets" were 6 per cent of the stores, doing 6 per cent of the business. Several factors were found to be related to the retail marketing pattern. The first was population density. In the mid-city district, where density was highest, were the largest numbers of scattered stores and of subcenters. Moreover, here were most of the Class A subcenters (those in which nine principal commodity groups were represented). Where density was moderate, chain stores were most numerous. The "independents" predominated where density was very low or very high. Similar to the significance of density is that of income level. Independent stores did best where incomes were very high or very low; chain stores throve

[1] McKenzie, *op. cit.*, Chap. 19, prepared by Inez K. Rolph.

in areas of moderate purchasing power. Subcenters also developed most frequently in sections of intermediate incomes. The third factor, topography, and the fourth, the transportation structure, were closely related. Topographic features were found to determine where people travel and hence where they shop. At important intersections, especially transfer points, subcenters grew up. Finally, the segregation of ethnic groups affected the distribution and character of retail stores. In cheap residential sections occupied by immigrants and Negroes were found both subcenters and scattered stores handling goods which appeal especially to these groups.

No doubt similar patterns would be found in other cities. But further discussion of the localization of business activities will be deferred to Chap. XIII.

Summary

We have verified what common observation suggests, that the economic organization of urban and of rural areas is quite different. Moreover, the economic life of different cities presents a variety of situations. Finally, within each separate city there is a localization of economic levels and activities. Manufacturing and wholesaling belong primarily, though not exclusively, to large cities. The picture varies from dominance of a single industry, even of a few corporations, to diversified industries taking their place along with wholesale and retail trade. The populations attracted by different kinds of employment seem to display different buying habits and different levels of living. This much can be stated in general terms, but further details must await future analysis. The correlation of various features of the economic structure is a fascinating field for research.

Selected Readings

McKenzie, R. D.: *The Metropolitan Community*, McGraw-Hill Book Company, Inc., 1933. Chapters 10–12 deal with the economic interrelations of cities; Chaps. 15 and 17 with the real estate business; Chap. 19 presents the pattern of retail marketing.

Woolston, Howard B.: *Metropolis*, D. Appleton-Century Company, Inc., 1938. Chapter 6 is a general discussion of business in the city.

Stecker, Margaret L.: *Intercity Differences in Costs of Living in March, 1935, 59 Cities*, Works Progress Administration, Research Monograph 12, 1937.

LYND, ROBT. S., and HELEN M. LYND.: *Middletown in Transition*, Harcourt, Brace & Company, Inc., 1937. A brilliant discussion of getting a living and business class control in a small city.

THOMAS, LEWIS F.: *The Localization of Business Activities in Metropolitan St. Louis*, Washington University Studies, 1927.

WARE, CAROLINE F.: *Greenwich Village*, Houghton Mifflin Company, 1935. Chapter 3 describes business and work in a part of New York better known for other activities.

KLEIN, PHILIP: *A Social Study of Pittsburgh*, Columbia University Press, 1938. Chapters 3 and 4 present the chances for a living, labor organization, and social legislation.

Chapter VIII

EDUCATIONAL INSTITUTIONS AND FOLKWAYS

It has been said that among the outstanding characteristics of North American culture are mass schooling and belief in education as a solution for all social problems. The second part of this statement may be somewhat exaggerated, but both the faith and the practice seem to us characteristic of contemporary civilization in the United States. An investment of $12 billion in school property and endowment, an annual expenditure of $3 billion, the employment of a million teachers, and the instruction of 30 million children and youths in 275,000 schools are evidence that education is a major complex in our culture.[1] Moreover, it is most elaborately developed in our urban areas. Although the urban and rural school population (ages five to seventeen) are almost the same, and although the number of rural schools is much greater than the number of those in cities, the urban enrollment is larger than the rural, the school term is longer, attendance is more regular, the number of teachers is only a little less, annual expenditures and the value of property are much greater, and the curriculum is much more elaborate.[2] But these are only a few of the differences between urban and rural schools. In addition to public schools, cities have many private schools—parochial, "progressive," commercial, and exclusive. In the cities are found a host of supplementary services that appear rarely or not at all in the country. These include medical and dental examinations, public health nursing, psychological clinics, attendance departments, visiting teachers, vocational counseling, supervision of classrooms and playgrounds, and research. City systems have developed special classes and schools for handi-

[1] U.S. Office of Education, *Biennial Survey of Education*, 1930–1932, Preface, pp. 1–12.

[2] *Ibid.*, p. 36.

capped children, continuation schools for employed youths, night classes for adults, junior colleges, teachers' colleges, and municipal universities. Such a proliferation of educational structure and functions may fairly be regarded as the product of urbanization added to the democratic and scientific movements.

The relation of universities to urbanism is not altogether clear. The early European universities were established in cities and most of them are still urban in character. This gives them a cosmopolitan setting and makes readily available varied contributions in art, music, literature, science, business, and politics. Probably the traditional freedom of European universities—now diminished in totalitarian states—is a direct result of their location in cities, for it was cities that first escaped from the feudal "cake of custom." In the United States, colleges and universities have been placed in both urban and rural settings. Many of the church schools and state institutions have been located in small towns far from "the wicked city." But because of the handicaps to professional education, notably medicine, engineering, and business, and because of limited employment for impecunious students, there is unlikely to be an expansion of this sort of thing. Some of our older universities were founded in cities: Columbia, Harvard, Pennsylvania, Brown. Not a few of the denominational—and formerly denominational—colleges and universities are urban: Catholic University of America, Loyola, Duquesne, Chicago, Northwestern, Southern California, Drake. The same is true of several state universities: Minnesota, Washington, Ohio. Numerous privately endowed but nonsectarian universities are found in cities: Johns Hopkins, Pittsburgh, Western Reserve, Tulane. The expansion of metropolitan areas is making others truly urban universities: Princeton, Yale, Stanford, California, Georgetown. Two other groups are the newer municipal universities: Cincinnati, Omaha, Wayne (Detroit); and the technical schools: Massachusetts Institute of Technology, Carnegie, Armour, Stevens. Thus it is evident that university education is coming to be very closely bound up with urbanism. But it must not be forgotten that many institutions of higher learning, especially state universities and colleges of agriculture, are essentially rural both in site and in orientation.

The Development of City Schools[1]

Obviously so complex an establishment as a city school system could not have sprung suddenly into existence. Its development covers a long period of time. In ancient Greece and Rome there were few schools. In the middle ages such schools as existed were generally found in towns and cities, although education was associated with the Church rather than with urbanism. In colonial America public schools took their rise in the towns of New England, parochial schools in the middle colonies, charity schools and "select" pay schools in the South. As early as 1642 Massachusetts passed a law requiring the towns to establish schools and parents to see that their children were in attendance. A little later every town with 50 households was ordered to employ a schoolmaster to teach reading and writing; every town of 100 families was to establish a grammar school to prepare boys for the university. This last was a private institution intended primarily to train clergymen for the dominant church. In the middle colonies no single sect or denomination constituted a majority, as in New England. Here education was left mainly to the various religious bodies—Lutherans, Moravians, Quakers, Catholics, and others—which early established parochial schools. In some of the larger towns, private pay schools were also opened. In the southern colonies, with their caste system, education took still another form. Children of the well-to-do were taught by tutors in the home, were sent to select private schools, or were educated in England. Children of the poor were either neglected, trained as apprentices, or taught in "pauper" schools. Negro slaves received practically no formal education. It was natural that schools should develop most rapidly in the middle and northern colonies, where more people lived in towns, and slowly in the Southern ones, where a sparse population was scattered over an immense territory.

By 1850, public elementary schools had been generally established in the North; their development in the South came some-

[1] For a more detailed account, which is, however, less complete than may be found in histories of education, see Maurice R. Davie, *Problems of City Life*, Chaps. 15, 16, 1932. Part of the data in this section is derived from Davie's book with his permission and that of the publishers, John Wiley & Sons, Inc.

what later. In 1821 Boston founded the first high school in the country. In 1827 the state of Massachusetts required every town of 500 families to set up a high school. From here the idea spread slowly to other northern and eastern states. After the Civil War high schools developed more rapidly, but their principal growth in enrollment did not come till after 1900. Previously there had been numbers of Latin (college preparatory) schools in northern cities and private academies in various parts of the country. In all the secondary schools, public and private alike, college entrance requirements dominated curriculum making, and little attention was paid to the needs of boys and girls who would never attend a college or university. But since 1900 this situation has been changing.

With the growth of urban populations and with the passage of compulsory-attendance laws, enrollments in both elementary and secondary schools increased greatly. Many of the pupils were financially unable to go to college, uninterested in higher education, or intellectually unqualified for further schooling. Their presence in the classroom compelled educators to reconsider the assumption that all should follow the same curriculum and advance at a uniform rate. The rapid influx of immigrants further complicated the situation, especially in large cities. Here many children spoke a language other than English at home and possessed a cultural background quite different from that of their American-born schoolmates. In response to these changing conditions, city school systems were gradually reorganized.

One important change has been the introduction of vocational schools. So long as trades and business activities were relatively few and simple, so long as boys followed in their fathers' footsteps and girls kept house after the manner of their mothers, so long as there was little application of science to most vocations, it could be assumed that most of the necessary training would be given at home. But the numbers of vocations were increasing; boys were following pursuits little understood by their fathers; girls were entering more and more into commerce and industry; new knowledge and new skills were being required. Obviously the necessary training could no longer be given at home. Hence, in the eighties, manual arts were introduced into city high schools, at first for the direct benefit of prospective industrial workers, later as part of the general education of all. Especially in the junior high schools, a twentieth-century development, are courses in woodworking, drawing, sewing, and the like, regarded as prevocational. In addition to, and sometimes preceding the setting up of, foundation courses, there have been established in many cities trade schools to prepare boys and girls definitely for specific vocations. The first was founded in 1881 in New York under private auspices; since 1906 there has been increasing public provision for trade instruction. A similar innovation was the part-time, or continuation, school, first established in Cincinnati in 1909 for machine-shop apprentices. Borrowed from Germany, this idea spread rather rapidly to the cities of 30 states. During the same period there was an even more rapid expansion of commercial schools and courses. Many of these were privately operated, but by 1930 two-thirds of the boys and girls preparing for business were enrolled in public high schools.

Logically, vocational counseling should have preceded vocational education. But the actual sequence was the reverse of what might have been expected. After trade schools had been functioning for some time it was discovered that many children were attempting to prepare themselves for occupations in which they were unlikely to succeed, either because of limited ability of the kind required or because of limited opportunities in the field. The pioneer venture in vocational guidance was initiated under private auspices in Boston about 1900, taking form in a vocational bureau in 1908. By 1916 nearly 150 cities claimed to be carrying on vocational guidance in their high schools. At its best this service rests on two basic activities: (*a*) the development of tests to discover those traits which may have a bearing on one's occupational life and (*b*) the analysis of various occupations in order to determine their requirements as to numbers and abilities, probable remuneration, future development, and effects on persons therein engaged. On the basis of such individual tests and general job analyses, conferences are held and readings suggested for the purpose of helping each youth to select a vocation in which he is likely to find an opportunity to make a satisfactory living. The counseling may include guidance into and through appropriate general and vocational courses, placement on a job, and even aid in making subsequent adjustments.

Another part of the effort to adapt the educational system to the needs of various kinds of persons has been the development of special classes and schools for handicapped and superior children, far more attention being devoted to the former than to the latter. Classes for mentally deficient children were established first in 1896 in Providence and a little later in Chicago, Philadelphia, Los Angeles, and other cities. Work for the blind, long carried on only in private and state schools, was undertaken by the city system of Chicago in 1900; Cincinnati, Milwaukee, New York, and others followed. Soon it was realized that the number of totally blind children was very small as compared with those whose vision was defective and in danger of deterioration. To meet their needs there were established in Boston and Cleveland in 1913, and presently in many large cities, sight-saving classes. A day school for the deaf was opened in Boston as early as 1869; by 1900 there were about 25 cities and by 1927 over 80 cities with special classes or schools for children who were deaf or had seriously defective hearing. The first public school system to provide for crippled children was that of Chicago in 1899. By 1930 about 85 cities had special classes or special schools for this group. In contrast to the increasingly generous provision for handicapped children, little has been done for those of superior talents. However, through individual attention they are sometimes given enriched programs of work, afforded opportunities to advance more rapidly than their fellows, encouraged to engage in extracurricular activities. Very rarely they are placed in special classes. Table 25 shows the number of exceptional children enrolled in special classes and schools in 1934.

One of the most interesting innovations of the twentieth century has been the adaptation of social case work to the needs of children in the public schools of several cities.[1] The practitioners in this field are called visiting teachers. They are required to have had training and experience in both classroom teaching and social case work. However, their duties are performed almost entirely outside the classroom and have to do with personal adjustments rather than with formal instruction; hence the term "visiting teacher" is a bit misleading. Children are referred because of retardation, irregular attendance, dirty and unkempt appearance, disturbing behavior in classroom or on playground, "nervous" habits, stealing, lying, and other evi-

[1] A very few visiting teachers have been employed in rural schools, but so far this movement is almost wholly urban.

dences of maladjustment. After careful inquiry, efforts are made to correct physical conditions, home situations, relations with other children, and emotional "sets" which seem to be hindering the child's adjustment in school. This movement started under private auspices in Boston, Hartford, and New York about 1906. Social settlements, an educational association, and a psychological clinic carried on the work through a period of experimentation and demonstration, after which it was taken over by the boards of education. In other cities, such as Rochester and Cleveland, visiting teachers were introduced directly by the school authorities. Despite the impetus given the movement by the Commonwealth Fund, which in the twenties financed and directed demonstrations in 30 localities, the American Association of Visiting Teachers reported only 200 members in 1937. However, their influence is apparent in the changing character of attendance departments, whose staffs are ceasing to function as truant officers and becoming more and more like social case workers.

Another modification of the conventional school organization is the platoon system. Under this system, the children are divided into two large groups; each group has the same program, but while one platoon is in classrooms the other is in gymnasium, shop, auditorium, or playground. In this way much more efficient use is made of the school plant and capital expenditures are materially reduced. When evening classes and social and recreational centers are conducted in the same buildings the taxpayers' return from their investment is even greater. We are unable to report the exact number of cities that make some

TABLE 25.—EXCEPTIONAL CHILDREN ENROLLED IN SPECIAL SCHOOLS AND CLASSES, 1934[a]

507 Cities Reporting

Mentally deficient	84,458
Speech defective	52,153
"Delicate"	22,962
Crippled	17,725
Socially maladjusted	14,520
Deaf and hard of hearing	6,365
Blind and partially seeing	6,133
Mentally gifted	3,834
Total	208,150

[a] U.S. Office of Education, *Biennial Survey of Education*, 1932–1934, Chap. 3, p. 25.

extended use of their school equipment in one or more of these ways, but before the depression of 1929 over 100 cities had at least part of their schools organized on the platoon system and about 700 were using some of the buildings and grounds as recreation centers.

Conventionally the public schools are closed from June to September, but during the twenties several hundred city school systems conducted summer sessions. In 1928, when this development was about at its peak, 447 systems employed over 14,000 teachers, principals, and supervisors, enrolled over 450,000 pupils, and spent nearly $3,250,000 for their summer schools.[1] These were for children of school age. But much earlier some cities had developed evening classes for adults. In fact, it was in 1856 that Cincinnati opened a public evening high school. In 1930, 664 systems employed over 24,000 teachers, principals, and supervisors, enrolled over 1 million students, and spent nearly $10,700,000 for their night and Americanization schools.[2] Besides the public schools, such agencies as the social settlements, the Y.M.C.A., the Y.W.C.A., university extension divisions, correspondence schools, and trade-unions are engaged in formal instruction of adults. Informal education is a feature, sometimes major and sometimes minor, of men's and women's clubs, churches, libraries, museums, radio programs, and the newspapers.

However, the impression must not be allowed to prevail that adult education is exclusively an urban phenomenon. The Chautauqua and lyceum movements were primarily rural. Extension divisions of agricultural colleges have been very active in rural areas. As a matter of fact, we do not know whether a higher percentage of rural or of urban adults are participating in educational programs. Similar uncertainty prevails with reference to vocational training. The teaching of agriculture and home economics has become widespread in rural consolidated and high schools. In general, consolidation, transportation, state and federal aid, higher legal requirements for the certification of teachers, and county units of administration are among the changes through which country children are coming to

[1] U.S. Office of Education, *Biennial Survey of Education*, 1932–1934, Chap. 3, p. 23.

[2] *Ibid.*, p. 24.

enjoy many of the advantages previously confined to those who could attend city schools. Nevertheless, important differences remain, as we shall see in the following section.

Availability of Education in City and Country[1]

In 1934 there were in the United States about 28,000 urban and 213,000 rural schools, each group serving about the same population of school age (five to seventeen years). Obviously a larger number of schools is needed to serve country children scattered over an enormous territory than to provide for the same number of city children. But despite the multiplying of educational units and the operation of school busses, a 1930 study covering parts of eight states showed that nearly one-fourth of the rural pupils had to walk or provide their own transportation for a distance of at least one and a half miles. Attendance of these children, especially the younger ones, was less regular than of those who lived nearer to a schoolhouse. Elementary pupils in cities rarely have to travel so far to school. When they do, there are usually streetcars or busses to carry them. City high school pupils often have to cover greater distances but usually have the benefit of public transportation facilities.

Naturally city schools are larger than those in the country. In 1933–1934 the actual differences were these: average number of pupils per building, urban 480, rural 61; average number of teaching positions (teachers, principals, supervisors) per building, urban 14.5, rural 2.2. Sixty-five per cent of all rural schools were of the one-room variety; only 8 per cent were consolidated. Now when classes are small there is likely to be a lack of stimulating competition among pupils. When one teacher has to instruct half a dozen grades in as many different subjects there is danger that the instruction may be poor.

[1] Data in this section are drawn chiefly from the following sources: U.S. Office of Education, *Biennial Survey of Education*, 1932–1934; Availability of Public School Education in Rural Communities, *Bull.* 34, 1934; National Survey of the Education of Teachers, *Bull.* 10, 1933, vol. 2; National Society for the Study of Education, "The Status of Rural Education," *Thirtieth Yearbook*, 1931, Part 1. Other sources will be indicated when used. Data from the *Yearbook* are used by permission of the National Society for the Study of Education.

The ratio of enrollment to population of school age (five to seventeen) in 1933–1934 was 0.855 in cities and 0.820 in rural districts. Curiously, boys constituted 51 per cent of the pupils in both types of schools. The ratio of average daily attendance to enrollment was 0.862 in cities and 0.836 in the country. The average length of school term was 182 days in cities and 161 days in rural districts. Pupils enrolled attended, on the average, 156 days in city schools and 134 days in country schools. Put somewhat differently, the average number of days attended was 150 or over in the cities of 30 states but in the country schools of only 19 states. The average number of days attended was less than 130 in the rural schools of 10 states but in the city schools of no state. Taken together, these figures demonstrate that considerably less schooling is available to rural than to urban children.

But the case is even stronger than we have made it. The percentage of youths (fourteen to seventeen) attending high school has been consistently lower in the country than in the city. After correcting for rural pupils in city high schools and city pupils in secondary schools located in rural areas, it appeared that 39 per cent of rural youths and 58 per cent of city youths were attending high school in 1932.[1] Several studies have been made of the grades attained or completed before dropping out of school. One such study in New York State revealed that out of every 1,000 children who entered the public schools those completing the eighth grade numbered 556 in cities, 479 in villages, and 415 in the open country. Corresponding numbers completing the twelfth grade were 13, 20, and 7. Clearly city children in general get more schooling than do those who live in the country.

The quality of education is much less amenable to measurement. We approach this problem indirectly through data bearing on personnel, curriculum, and finances. City teachers are older. In 1930–1931 the median ages of teachers in elementary schools were: open country, twenty-four; villages, twenty-six; small cities (under 10,000), twenty-eight; middle-sized cities (10,000–100,000), thirty; and large cities (over 100,000), thirty-

[1] U.S. Office of Education, *Bull.* 17, 1932, Monograph No. 4, pp. 6–7.

four. This indicates longer experience and possibly greater stability in the teaching profession in urban centers. In both country and city schools, men teachers were in the minority, but they were more numerous in rural than in city schools—22 per cent contrasted with 16 per cent. Another index of quality is the training of teachers. In some rural schools this is unbelievably low. A study of 22 counties in 5 states in 1930 indicated that one-fourth of the teachers in one-room rural schools had received no more than six weeks of professional training. Another study covering one-half of all country schools in the United States showed that counties in the first decile (lowest 10 per cent) employed teachers whose total schooling averaged less than one year beyond high school.[1] City schools no longer accept many teachers with less than two years of training on a collegiate level. In 1930–1931 elementary teachers in large cities reported nearly one-fifth with bachelors' degrees, while in one- and two-room country schools the ratio was only 1:40. Of course, one may graduate from a teachers' college or university and still be a poor teacher, and there are doubtless good teachers with limited training; but it is hard to believe that quantitative differences as great as those discovered are not accompanied by qualitative differences.

We have two other crude measures of the kind of teachers to be found in city and country schools—transiency and remuneration. Not only are city teachers older than those in rural districts; they are more stable. In 1930–1931 in large cities 62 per cent of the elementary teachers had been employed in only one school system; whereas in one- and two-room country schools the percentage was 46, and in villages, 35. In large cities 22 per cent had served in three or more systems; whereas in small country schools, 31 per cent had this varied experience, and in villages, 38 per cent. The median in years of actual teaching was 6 for villages and 12 for large cities. In 1933–1934 the average salary of the professional personnel (teachers, supervisors, principals) was $1,735 in cities and $787 in country schools. A sampling in 1930 yielded an average of $2,030 for city schools and $814 for those in the country. Some allowance should be made for differences in the cost of living, but hardly in the ratio

[1] J. H. Kolb and E de S. Brunner, *A Study of Rural Society*, p. 412, 1935.

of 5:2. Moreover, good salaries are no guarantee of good teaching, but poor salaries certainly discourage competent persons from entering and remaining in schoolwork. Hence we are disposed to infer that on the whole city teachers are more competent than those in country schools.

If the quality of instruction is difficult to measure, that of the curriculum is still more so. But we know in general that elementary schools in cities commonly have the benefit of special teachers of art, music, and manual training, in addition to the advantages that accrue from separation of the various grades. In urban high schools the curriculum has been greatly enriched in recent years. Particularly have efforts been made to devise different programs for youths of varying capacities, interests, and vocational opportunities. On the other hand, we must not overlook the development of courses in agriculture and home economics, music and art, in many rural high schools. Both rural and urban schools seem to be moving away from the older, more rigid curriculum with its emphasis on preparation for college. Whether one group has succeeded better than the other we hesitate to say, although it is clear that variety and flexibility are greater in cities than in rural districts.

We come finally to the matter of finances. Although school populations in city and country are about the same, investment in school buildings and equipment is much greater in cities, in 1933–1934 averaging $347 for each city pupil enrolled and $151 for each rural pupil. Current expenditures (less interest) per capita of daily attendance were $83.67 in city and $50.30 in country schools. In 15 states the average for city schools was $90 or over, but in only 9 states was the average for rural schools so high. On the other hand, in 10 states the average for rural schools was less than $40, but in only 4 states was the average for city schools so low. Indebtedness per capita of daily attendance was $187 in cities and $79 in country districts. Obviously city schools are much more expensive than country schools, but admittedly the herding of large numbers of children in attractive buildings on expensive sites is no assurance that their education will be satisfactory. On the other hand, relatively adequate financing should be no handicap, while lack of funds does impose serious restrictions. So once again it appears that the advantage lies with city schools.

Pupil Status and Achievement

Having considered the development and structure of city school systems, we turn now to the children and young people they serve. Particularly shall we concern ourselves with the relative status and achievement of urban and rural pupils. One of the best sources of data on this subject is a special report made to the National Society for the Study of Education in 1931.[1] The first item dealt with was the comparative chronological age of children in the various grades of city and country schools. The results of studies made indicate less difference than might be expected. The median age of pupils in each of the lower grades was nearly the same in urban and in rural schools. In the middle grades city children were definitely younger than those in country schools; in the seventh and eighth grades they were just a little younger. This similarity in median age is accompanied by balancing deviations. Thus rural schools were found to have both more under-age and more over-age children than city schools. No doubt varying distances between home and school and varying demands of home and farm work have much to do with the uneven age-grade status of country pupils. Data from one state, North Carolina, indicate that in each grade the percentage of pupils promoted was higher in city than in country schools. Hence the percentage of the total enrollment in each grade differed in urban and in rural schools. The latter had a larger share in the first grade and a smaller share in the upper grades than were found in city schools; in the middle grades there was little difference. In another state, Illinois, a comparison of rural and urban schools having annual promotions displayed a larger percentage of country school children than of village and city children making rapid progress, a larger percentage making regular progress, and a smaller percentage making slow progress. Causes of nonpromotion were in general much the same in city and in country schools. A California study showed more failures due to absence on account of illness in city schools than in country schools. But mental subnormality was more frequently a cause of failure in country than in

[1] National Society for the Study of Education, "The Status of Rural Education," *Thirtieth Yearbook*, 1931, Part 1, pp. 25–53. Data used by permission of the society.

city schools. This same study indicated that city children were more often weak in reading, language, spelling, and writing, while country children failed more frequently in arithmetic, geography, history, and grammar. All in all, the data now available concerning pupil status leave us somewhat in doubt as to the relative merits of urban and rural schools.

We turn now to evidence of pupil achievement in city and country schools. One of the best studies we have found was made in Minnesota by Van Wagenen,[1] who tested the seventh- and eighth-grade children in 150 city and town systems and 1,000 rural schools. In reading for comprehension he found pupils of city and village schools superior to those of rural schools. Among the latter, incidentally, children in nine-month schools surpassed those in eight-month schools. But pupils in large-city schools outranked those in small cities by a very narrow margin. Similar results were derived from tests of reading for interpretation. The range of information in American history was definitely narrower among seventh-grade pupils in urban than in rural schools. However, in the eighth grade the relation was partly reversed. Tests of the "thought phase" of American history yielded similar results. In both the history tests, pupils in very small-city schools did better than those in large cities. Seventh-grade pupils in city schools showed a wider range of information in geography than that displayed by children in country schools. But eighth-grade pupils in cities were inferior to those in nine-month rural schools. In the "thought phase" of geography urban pupils were definitely superior to the rural groups. The same was true of the fundamental operations of arithmetic. In ability to solve arithmetic problems eighth-grade city pupils surpassed country children, but seventh-grade city pupils did not. Incidentally, children in very small cities did better than those in large cities. In spelling and English composition city pupils of both seventh and eighth grades were found superior to those in rural schools. To summarize, Van Wagenen found city pupils superior in reading, the "thought phase" of geography, fundamental operations in arithmetic, spelling, and English composition. He found rural pupils of

[1] M. J. Van Wagenen, *Comparative Pupil Achievement in Rural, Town, and City Schools*, 1929. Data used by permission of the University of Minnesota Press.

the seventh grade superior in history, and those of the eighth grade superior in information in geography. On the whole, the advantage lay with city children.

Another source of data concerning the relative achievement of urban and rural school children is the state scholarship contest for eighth-grade pupils conducted by the Kansas State Teachers College of Emporia.[1] The scores of 3,500 pupils were submitted for consideration for the awards. Those from nine-month grade schools in cities and villages were consistently, but only slightly, better than those from eight-month rural schools. A more detailed study of 1,100 pupils showed the urban and village groups to be superior in arithmetic, reading, and spelling. The rural pupils did not excel in any subject, but their scores were nearly the same as those of city children in history, civics, and English.

A North Dakota study utilized the New Stanford Achievement Tests in comparing 6,500 rural, town, and city pupils.[2] In each grade and in each age group the city pupils ranked highest, the rural pupils lowest, the town group being intermediate. With only a few exceptions the same was true of each test. In no case did the rural children outrank the others, but in 10 out of 100 instances town pupils surpassed those in city schools. Thus children of the eighth grade in town schools excelled in paragraph meaning, spelling, physiology and hygiene, and arithmetic reasoning. Seventh-grade pupils in town schools surpassed those of the same grade in city schools in word meaning and physiology and hygiene. Town children in the third, fourth, fifth, and sixth grades respectively surpassed city children of the same grades in a single test. Thus in North Dakota the size of community seems to bear a direct relation to pupil achievement.

One other study may well be considered here, because its results do not correspond to those of the studies already described.[3]

[1] H. W. McIntosh and H. E. Schrammel, "A Comparison of the Achievement of Eighth Grade Pupils in Rural Schools and in Graded Schools," *Elem. School Jour.*, 31 (1930), 301–306.

[2] Robert D. Cole, *Educational Achievement in North Dakota City, Town, and Rural Schools*, 1931.

[3] Nora A. Congdon, "Differences in the Achievement in Geography, Civics and History, and General Science of Teachers College Entrants from

Tests in geography, general science, civics, and history were given to students entering 26 teachers' colleges. Their analysis revealed an advantage in favor of small high schools (those with graduating classes of less than 50) over large high schools (graduating classes over 250) in geography and general science. In history and civics the difference was too small to be statistically reliable.

What is to be inferred from these several pieces of research? On the whole they show less difference than might be expected between urban and rural schools. But so many independent studies indicate that city pupils surpass those in country schools that their results cannot be ignored. Only specialists in educational tests and measurements can determine whether the criteria employed are valid measures of relative merit. Perhaps the kind of schooling needed for success in rural life differs sufficiently from that required in the city to discredit the results of tests devised under urban conditions. Perhaps as consolidation proceeds, as rural school terms are lengthened, and as rural teachers are better trained, the achievements of country and city pupils may cease to show significant differences. Perhaps if intelligence levels were held constant we might find that rural children progress as rapidly as their city cousins. Further research in this field is awaited with interest.

Schools of Large and Small Cities

In its biennial surveys the United States Office of Education reports certain facts pertaining to the school systems in cities of various sizes. For the year 1933–1934 it presented data for four classes of cities: (*a*) 100,000 and over, (*b*) 30,000 to 100,000, (*c*) 10,000 to 30,000, (*d*) 2,500 to 10,000. In these several classes there were respectively 90, 211, 643, and 1,943 cities. Thus for the kinds of data included the coverage is fairly complete.[1]

Cities of the first class (*a*) led in the percentage of pupils enrolled in kindergarten, vocational, and trade schools. Cities of the second class (*b*) had relatively fewer pupils in their elementary schools and relatively more in their high schools than did cities of

---

Different Sections of the Country and from Rural and Urban Populations," *Jour. Exper. Educ.*, 5 (1937), 274–277.

[1] U.S. Office of Education, *Biennial Survey of Education*, 1932–1934, Chap. 3.

classes *a* and *c*. Cities of class *c* had relatively fewer pupils in kindergarten, vocational, and trade schools, and relatively more in elementary schools than did cities of the first and second classes. The ratio of attendance to enrollment was higher in classes *c* and *d* than in classes *a* and *b* from 1922 to 1934. During that time there was a general upward trend, from 0.825 to 0.861, in the average of all cities. Just why the percentage of time lost should be higher in large than in small cities we do not know. However, the average number of days attended by each pupil was larger in great cities than in small ones, because school was in session more days per year.

As to the teaching staff, we have already noted the facts that large-city teachers are older, more experienced, and better trained. But the highest percentage of men teachers is found in cities of class *d*. This was true both in 1924 and in 1934. The average annual salaries varied directly with the size of city for all types of schools—kindergarten, elementary, junior high, senior high, and vocational. Similarly the annual current expense per pupil in average daily attendance varied directly with the size of city. This was true in 1924, 1930, and 1934. Likewise the value of school property per pupil in average daily attendance in 1933–1934 varied with the size of the city. In 1934 there was the same kind of relation between bonded indebtedness and size of city, but in 1924 cities of class *b* had greater bonded indebtedness per pupil in average daily attendance than did cities of classes *a* and *c*.

In the study by Van Wagenen previously referred to[1] there is a comparison of large and small cities in addition to that of urban and rural ones. In reading comprehension he found seventh- and eighth-grade boys in large cities superior to those of very small cities, but girls in large and small places showed no difference. In reading interpretation the pupils of small cities generally surpassed those of large cities. Small-city pupils were also superior in American history, both range of information and the "thought phase," except that eighth-grade boys in large cities were slightly superior in information. In range of information in geography seventh-grade pupils in large cities outranked those in small cities, but the reverse was true of eighth-grade boys, there being no difference in the case of eighth-grade girls. In the "thought phase" of geography small-city pupils surpassed those of large

[1] Van Wagenen, *op. cit.*

cities. In the fundamental operations of arithmetic large-city pupils were slightly better than those in small cities, while the opposite was true in the solution of arithmetic problems. In spelling the large-city pupils were superior. Thus, in brief, small-city pupils were superior in reading for interpretation, in American history, in the "thought phase" of geography, and in the solving of arithmetic problems. Large-city pupils were clearly superior only in spelling and the fundamental operations of arithmetic. On the whole, pupils in the schools of small cities did better than those in large cities. This leads us to the observation that while the experience of participating in a large school system is undoubtedly different from being one of a small group, it is not necessarily more beneficial and may even prove to be a disadvantage.

Urban Ecology and Education

So far we have been treating urban education as though it were alike throughout a city. Yet even a moment's consideration will suffice to remind us that there must be great variations in different parts of a city and in different periods of time. In sections occupied by immigrants there are often parochial (Catholic, Lutheran, Hebrew) schools. Both in these and in public schools instruction must be modified because the folkways and mores, often the very language, of the home are different from those of the school. Some ethnic groups attach great importance to education, offering both encouragement and sacrifice to keep their children in school. Others are more impressed with immediate financial needs and send their children to work as early as the law permits. In sections where native Americans of rural origin predominate, teachers often have to deal with children whose parents are largely unschooled and whose homes provide little in the way of music, art, and literature. Negroes present the same problems as rural whites, complicated by varying degrees of segregation and race prejudice.

As the various population elements displace one another the character of particular schools changes. During a period of transition, teachers must not only instruct a heterogeneous lot of pupils; they must also deal with "racial" antagonisms.

While a city, or some part of it, is growing, the school authorities must face problems of overcrowding and redistricting. According to the funds available, they may build additions to existing schoolhouses, set up temporary structures, or erect new buildings. On the other hand, a declining population reverses the situation and presents problems of unused equipment. Thus a board of education needs to be constantly alert to the changing pattern of the city, so as to adapt its building program, districting, curriculum, and personnel to varied social situations.

SUMMARY

Educational machinery is most elaborate in cities. They have more provision for very young children and for older adolescents, more special schools for pupils with special abilities and disabilities, more varied curricula, and more extracurricular services. But these have not always existed. They have been accumulating since colonial times. Innovations have most frequently been made in cities and have then, after some delay, been imitated in the country.

The structure of public school systems differs in city and in country. Urban school systems are not only more specialized; units are larger and more accessible to pupils. In enrollment, attendance, length of term, and grade attained before dropping out—in all these, city schools appear to better advantage. Urban teachers are older, more experienced, hold their positions longer, have more professional and general education but include fewer men than are found among rural teachers. Finances differ sharply. In cities salaries are higher, expenditures are larger, and the value of property is greater—all in proportion to the number of pupils actually in school.

In measures of pupil status and achievement city children usually appear to better advantage than do those in country schools. However, there are many exceptions, and it is by no means established that country children do worse in school than their city cousins. But even if urban pupils have on the average an advantage over rural pupils, this may be expected to diminish with the continued improvement of country schools.

Differences between large- and small-city schools are, like rural and urban differences, difficult to determine except in relatively superficial matters. Such data as we possess suggest that pupils in small cities may have an advantage over those in large cities. But this is still an open question.

Within any given city are quite diverse situations. In some sections teaching of the three R's is quite overshadowed by Americanization, in others by the urbanization of rural Americans. The expansion and contraction of population, as well as the shifting of ethnic groups, require many adjustments in the educational system.

Selected Readings

DAVIE, MAURICE R.: *Problems of City Life*, John Wiley & Sons, Inc., 1932. Part IV deals with the development of education in American cities.

MUNTZ, EARL E.: *Urban Sociology*, The Macmillan Company, 1938. Part IV deals with the development of education in American cities.

KLEIN, PHILIP: *A Social Study of Pittsburgh*, Columbia University Press, 1938. Chapter 8 describes the Pittsburgh public schools.

LYND, ROBERT S., and HELEN M. LYND: *Middletown in Transition*, Harcourt, Brace & Company, Inc., 1937. Chapter 6 reports changes in education in a small American city.

National Society for the Study of Education: "The Status of Rural Education," *Thirtieth Yearbook*, Part I, Public School Publishing Company, 1931. Includes a statistical study of rural-urban differences.

GAUMNITZ, N. H.: *Comparative Status of Secondary Education in Rural and Urban Communities*, U.S. Office of Education, Rural School Leaflet, No. 44, 1928.

VAN WAGENEN, M. J.: *Comparative Pupil Achievement in Rural, Town, and City Schools*, University of Minnesota Press, 1929.

Chapter IX

LEISURE TIME FOLKWAYS AND INSTITUTIONS

Having considered the folkways and institutions that have to do with homemaking, earning a living, rearing and training children, we turn now to those involved in relaxing, playing, and having a good time.

When people are "off duty" and not under compulsion to produce useful goods or services—whether in the shop or in the home—when they are not pursuing such ends as prestige and business connections, when they are relatively "free" to do as they please, or at least to choose among several alternatives, they may be said to be enjoying leisure. Leisure time may be spent in resting or in activity which is enjoyed for its own sake, not because it is "good for one" or because "one should be nice to certain people" or because "it will be worth while to be seen there." The unemployed are experiencing idleness rather than leisure, for they often feel strain rather than relaxation.

Urban and Rural Differences

It has frequently been stated that the leisure time of city people, in contrast to that of countryfolk, is more passive, more vicarious, more frequently planned, directed, or sold. Another hypothesis is that the differences are less in kinds of recreation than in frequency of indulgence. Thus we find that villagers play golf, tennis, and bridge, attend movies, and listen to the radio. But it appears that they do so less than cityfolk. To determine whether these impressions are correct, and whether the difference between rural and urban leisure time habits is great or small, requires more careful inquiry than is usually given this matter.

In 1925 the Lynds found that the leisure of Middletown was becoming "more passive, more formal, more organized, more mechanized, and more commercialized," but in 1935 they found a change toward more spontaneous, informal, and simple play, entertaining, visiting, gardening, etc. This was doubtless in consequence of the depression, but whether it represents a reversal of the earlier trend or a temporary interruption only the future can reveal. Even if the trend identified in 1925 should again be apparent, let us say in 1945, we need to compare it with trends in rural life, which may prove to be very much the same.

In order to pursue this matter more thoroughly we shall have to break the general field of leisure time interests and habits into rather definite and manageable units. First of all we must consider the various sorts of personal behavior which are identified with leisure time. We might undertake to classify them as (*a*) rest and relaxation, *e.g.*, taking sun baths or smoking, (*b*) active participation involving physical exertion, *e.g.*, playing tennis, (*c*) active participation that is primarily mental, *e.g.*, playing bridge, (*d*) group enjoyment that is shared rather passively, *e.g.*, listening to the radio, and (*e*) solitary, passive enjoyment, *e.g.*, reading. By using diaries and schedules such as have been employed in a number of studies we might discover the proportion of each sort of leisure time behavior in rural and in urban areas respectively. As yet we have only very crude indications of these differences; thus we find country people relaxing a good deal in the winter, city people rather more in the summer. City people work shorter hours, but by no means all their time away from their job is spent in recreation or relaxation. Perhaps the information we possess about the rural and urban differences in these several kinds of leisure time behavior can best be indicated as we proceed with other aspects of our problem.

Another aspect of leisure time, and one which might be studied more easily, is that of facilities available for leisure time use in city and in country. In regard to this, it is not difficult to discover impressionistically that places in which to gather for enjoyment, such as theaters, parks, billiard parlors, and dance halls, are very numerous in cities and rather scarce in country districts. Equipment for games, such as tennis courts, golf courses, and gymnasiums, are pretty definitely identified with cities and have only recently made their appearance in rural areas. Equipment for noncompetitive enjoyment, *e.g.*, the radio, the family car, and the public library, is definitely more common in the city than in the country. Some data pertaining to these various facilities will be presented later in this chapter.

Finally, we have found it most convenient to classify leisure time activities and facilities in terms of the auspices under which they are carried on. They are either (*a*) public, tax-supported, usually municipally owned and operated, (*b*) semipublic, semiphilanthropic, (*c*) commercial, (*d*) organized, private, self-maintaining or cooperative, or (*e*) unorganized and under no particular auspices.

We approach the problem of rural-urban differences again in terms of the generally observed characteristics of American country life a generation or so ago. Until fairly recently most rural recreation might be described as informal and homemade—picnics, socials, parties, celebrations of special days, and various kinds of bees. Statistics are not available, but there is no question about the relative absence of recreation under governmental, philanthropic, and commercial auspices. To be sure, there were county fairs with horse racing, games of chance, merry-go-rounds, and side shows, and there were some village "opera houses" that presented small stock companies in one-night stands, a few billiard parlors, dance halls, saloons, and village prostitutes in some parts of the country. Folk from the open country partook of these varied forms of entertainment along with folk from the towns, though probably less frequently. In the past, country people enjoyed, as they still do, hunting, fishing, gathering nuts, swimming, visiting with the neighbors, and other informal, spontaneous, and undirected leisure time activities.

In recent years the increased use of agricultural machinery has lessened the occasions for cooperative work-play such as barn-raisings, husking bees, and quilting parties. The automobile and the hard road have enabled farm people to attend "shows," dances, ball games, and other recreational events in town. Both farmers and villagers go frequently to cities to spend some of their leisure time. They take vacation trips, play golf, listen to nation-wide radio hook-ups, and read magazines of national circulation. All this suggests that in their leisure time behavior they are becoming more like city people.

Another aspect of this seeming convergence of rural and urban recreation is that city people go to the country to hunt, fish, picnic, camp, hike. They have adopted and adapted such rural sports as skating, swimming, skiing, horseback riding, horseshoes, etc.

Thus it is evident that countryfolk and cityfolk are not utterly different in their uses of leisure time. Each has borrowed from the other. But on the whole there appears to have been more diffusion of recreational traits from city to country than in the opposite direction.

Consider, for example, the spread of golf. Introduced in cities of the North Atlantic seaboard, it was largely confined for a long time to northern and eastern cities. But by 1930 over half the golf courses in the United States were found in the western and southern states. Although the greatest number were in states with the largest urban population, some of the rural states outranked these urban states in golf courses per 100,000 people.[1] Steiner has similarly indicated the diffusion of tennis and boxing.[2]

The theater in all its forms apparently originated in cities. For the most part it has never reached rural people. Neither grand opera nor vaudeville, neither the high-class play nor the burlesque show, has appeared as frequently in villages and towns as in great cities. But with the coming of motion pictures, countryfolk have been enabled increasingly to enjoy the same entertainment as city dwellers. Steiner has shown that by 1930 the diffusion of the movies was so general that there was no longer any apparent relation between the population per theater and the percentage of the population living on farms.[3]

An equally striking instance of urban-rural diffusion of a leisure time trait is afforded by the history of radio. Starting with a single station in 1920, the broadcasting of entertainment had spread to 625 stations in 1936.[4] By 1930 two-fifths of our 30 million families had radios: one-half of all urban families and one-fifth of all farm families. In the three depression years 1933–1935, over 12 million radio sets were sold, so that by the beginning of 1936 there were nearly 23 million in use. How many of these were in urban and how many in rural homes we have no

[1] Jesse F. Steiner, *Americans at Play*, pp. 71–72, 1933. By permission of the President's Research Committee on Social Trends.

[2] *Ibid.*, pp. 68, 96. By permission of the President's Research Committee on Social Trends.

[3] *Ibid.*, p. 161. By permission of the President's Research Committee on Social Trends.

[4] *The World Almanac*, 1937, p. 534; Jesse F. Steiner, *Americans at Play*, p. 118, 1933. By permission of the President's Research Committee on Social Trends.

means of knowing, but it is almost impossible for the increase to have been less in the country than in cities.[1]

Similar, though much less rapid, diffusion has occurred in the development of the Y.M.C.A. and the Y.W.C.A. Both had urban origins, about the middle of the nineteenth century. Neither expanded into rural districts until the twentieth. In 1930 the Y.M.C.A. had only 106 town and country associations, compared with 722 city associations.[2] A similar history marks the spread of school social centers. The use of school buildings as social centers seems to have started in New York, Boston, and notably in Rochester between 1900 and 1910. By 1930 there were reported 164 such cases in towns of 2,500–5,000 and 372 in towns of less than 2,500.[3] Luncheon clubs, known to their members as "service clubs," began with the Rotary movement in Chicago in 1905. At first all the Rotary, Kiwanis, Lions, and other such groups were found in large cities, but between 1925 and 1929 over half of the new clubs were organized in towns under 2,500.[4]

Active and Passive Uses of Leisure Time

We observed at the outset of this discussion that many people regard urban leisure time as spent more passively than the leisure time of country people. As a matter of fact, there are many lines of evidence which support this belief. In the first place, our cities are the sites of great stadia wherein assemble spectators by the tens of thousands to witness sports of various kinds and to enjoy them as observers rather than participants. In 1937 there were over 50 such stadia, each seating from 20,000 to 125,000 persons.[5] With the exception of the very few located in college towns, these are all urban institutions. An even more striking evidence of the vicarious enjoyment of sports is the use of the radio to follow baseball, football, and hockey games,

[1] Fifteenth Census, *Population*, vol. 6, p. 10; *The World Almanac*, 1937, p. 534.

[2] Maurice R. Davie, *Problems of City Life*, pp. 640–642, 1932. By permission of the author and of John Wiley & Sons, Inc.

[3] Jesse F. Steiner, *Community Organization*, rev. ed. p. 182, 1930; *Americans at Play*, p. 157, 1933.

[4] C. F. Marden, *Rotary and Its Brothers*, pp. 5–9, 1935; Jesse F. Steiner, *Americans at Play*, pp. 131–134, 1933.

[5] *The World Almanac*, 1937, p. 843.

boxing and tennis matches. The numbers of daily sport reviews bear witness to the extent to which persons who cannot even follow a game while it is being played get satisfaction out of hearing about it afterward. In addition to the radio commentators, we have the sports writers who fill pages of our newspapers every day reporting, anticipating, and otherwise discussing all sorts of sports for the benefit, no doubt, of participants, but chiefly with an appeal to those who enjoy these sports vicariously.

Pursuing this matter of passive enjoyment of sports a little further, Steiner estimates the annual attendance at professional baseball games to be in excess of 20 million. There was steady growth in the decade of the twenties, followed by some decline during the depression but an apparent recovery since 1935.[1] The attendance at football games has been less adequately reported, but it involves very large numbers, running admittedly into the millions. It happens, however, that college football games are often played in small towns rather than great cities (although the audience may be composed largely of visitors from neighboring cities). Professional football is definitely an urban phenomenon. The attendance at urban football games is not far from 10 million a year. Boxing and wrestling draw smaller crowds and bring them together less frequently than do baseball and football, but intermittently they are the occasion of very large gatherings, usually in large cities. However, the era of million-dollar "gates" seems to have passed. In the twenties there were five occasions on which the gate receipts for a boxing match exceeded $1 million. Whether the decline since that is due to a loss of prestige on the part of this so-called sport or whether it is bound up with a diffusion of following, in the course of which interested spectators scatter to many different matches instead of assembling at a few, we do not know. There is, however, clear evidence of the spread of boxing, both amateur and professional, in states that are largely rural.[2] Another attraction for urban spectators is horse racing. Originally associated with county fairs, horse racing is found now almost exclusively in metropolitan districts. We have very limited data

[1] Jesse F. Steiner, *Americans at Play*, pp. 83–86, 1933. Data used by permission of The President's Research Committee on Social Trends.

[2] *Ibid.*, pp. 94–97; *The World Almanac*, 1937, p. 840.

as to the attendance, but we are sure that the figures would run into the millions each year.

Other more or less passive forms of recreation, or ways of spending leisure time with a minimum of activity, include drinking, eating, and just plain loafing. Again, data are insufficient to warrant any sweeping generalizations, but it appears that city dwellers spend more of their leisure time in drinking than do country people. Eating for both is frequently associated with visiting and other sorts of sociability, hence no inference may fairly be drawn about it. Neither can we be sure about the relative amount of loafing in rural and urban districts. City visitors to villages are impressed with the men and boys leaning against lampposts and hitching rails along Main Street, but country visitors to the city can scarcely fail to be impressed with the "drugstore cowboys," poolroom idlers, and window-shoppers of the city.

All in all, it is clear that city people spend a great deal of their leisure time passively or vicariously enjoying other people's activities. The other side of the picture, however, must not be neglected.

The playing of golf, tennis, amateur baseball, handball, volleyball, and similar games is certainly activity! We have already noted the urban-rural diffusion of golf, but the great majority of golf courses are still in or on the edge of cities. Hence the increase from about 750 courses in 1916 to nearly 6,000 courses in 1930 indicates an increase in the active participation of city dwellers in this form of recreation.[1]

Yearbook numbers of *Recreation*, official organ of the National Recreation Association, give some notion of the extent to which city people use public recreation facilities. Unfortunately, they do not enable us to compare urban and rural districts or large and small cities. Table 26 shows that the number of such participants is very great.

Two facts make it hard for us to draw conclusions from Table 26. One is that many cities failed to report; the other is that we do not know how many different persons are included or the extent of each one's participation. However, in another part of its report the National Recreation Association furnishes some data about the number of different individuals taking part in

[1] Jesse F. Steiner, *Americans at Play*, p. 71, 1933.

"special recreational activities" included in the programs of cities. These figures do not appear to bear any consistent relation to those in Table 26, except that they are naturally very much smaller. Thus for baseball we have less than 300,000 participants, for basketball about the same number, for horseshoes about 375,000, for softball 400,000, for tennis 340,000, etc.[1] The sum total of all participants, assuming no duplicates, would be only about one-tenth of our urban population. But these figures come from only part of our public recreation departments. Hence we may fairly say that a surprisingly large number of city people engage in sports, but that they constitute a fairly small minority of all city dwellers.

TABLE 26.—CITIES REPORTING RECREATION FACILITIES AND PARTICIPANTS, 1935[a]

Facilities	Number	Cities reporting	Participants per season	Cities reporting
Athletic fields	1518	497	7,990,000	210
Baseball diamonds	3669	621	10,225,000	287
Bathing beaches	488	230	46,670,000	113
Golf courses	332	226	6,560,000	134
Handball courts	1336	162	1,350,000	76
Horseshoe courts	6760	493	1,965,000	257
Ice skating areas	2094	331	10,475,000	151
Shuffleboard courts	773	97	1,555,000	56
Softball diamonds	6896	616	9,345,000	329
Swimming pools:				
Indoor	328	117	4,835,000	71
Outdoor	710	318	18,045,000	180
Tennis courts	9313	610	8,015,000	275
Toboggan slides	280	93	575,000	48

[a] *Recreation*, 30 (1936) 104–105. By permission of the National Recreation Association.

So far we have confined ourselves to sports, principally outdoor. But there are many other kinds of recreation which involve active participation. One of the most widespread is dancing. No statistical data are available, but observation indicates that this is more common in cities than in rural districts. Lynd found dancing both in 1925 and in 1935 "a prominent feature of the leisure and social life of Middletown people of all

[1] *Recreation*, 30 (1936), 109–110.

classes under thirty."[1] Amateur dramatics and musical organizations do not include large percentages of city populations, but they are not to be ignored. Bowling, and the playing of pool, billiards, and cards are often associated with loafing, but for many people these represent active participation of a significant sort. Some reading might be classed as active rather than as passive recreation, for while it usually is a solitary form of entertainment, it does call for some mental alertness and effort on the part of the reader. Lundberg found that on the average Westchester County people (suburbanites) spent 13 per cent of their leisure time in reading. Lynd discovered in Middletown a great increase in circulation of library books during the depression but a falling off in magazine subscriptions and newsstand sales.[2] But these are only two limited studies. We have no means of determining how representative they are. Moreover, we cannot at present distinguish reading that is study, reading that is discriminating enjoyment of literature, and reading that is a mere "painkiller."

Because the data pertaining to passive and active uses of leisure time are quite incomparable we have offered no general conclusions except the impression that city people spend less time in active participation than they do in passive enjoyment. Until the use of urban leisure has actually been measured, this must remain an impression rather than an established conclusion.

Organized and Unorganized Recreation

From the preceding discussion it is evident that a great deal of urban recreation, whether classed as active or as passive, is more or less formally organized. Recreational programs of schools, municipal departments, social settlements, and churches are more or less carefully planned, staffed, and financed. Clubs of various sorts—luncheon clubs, country clubs, bridge clubs, and others which we shall discuss later—represent organization in a thoroughgoing sense. Even the commercial forms of recreation are organized, for while we may attend the movies or go to the baseball park as individuals, the provision of these forms of

[1] Robert S. Lynd and Helen M. Lynd, *Middletown in Transition*, p. 269, 1937. By Permission of Harcourt, Brace & Company, Inc.

[2] Geo. A. Lundberg, *Leisure*, pp. 100–101, 1934; Lynd and Lynd, *op. cit.*, pp. 252–260.

recreation is organized as a network of business enterprises. On the other hand, visiting friends, having "pickup" parties, reading for pleasure, going for drives, and most loafing are informal and unorganized. What is the relative amount of urban leisure time spent in organized and in unorganized ways, we frankly do not know. Neither can we say with assurance whether the relation of the one to the other is different in city and in country. Our impression, however, is very definitely that an increasing share of urban leisure time is devoted to organized recreation as just defined, and that the same trend is apparent in rural America, though with some delay and to a lesser extent.

Most of the forms of organized recreation mentioned have developed fairly recently and in cities. It is important to inquire, therefore, how it has come about that this has happened, *i.e.*, why does organized recreation seem to be peculiarly a phenomenon of the modern city? The first clue we have is that there is an increased amount of leisure time. The President's Research Committee on Recent Social Trends found that the average hours of labor per week in 11 industries declined in the 30 years just preceding the depression from 6.5 per cent, in newspaper printing, to 29.3 per cent, in blast furnaces. In the latter instance this meant a drop from nearly 85 hours per week in 1890 to about 60 hours per week in 1928.[1] Steiner has assembled data from studies made by the National Industrial Conference Board showing that in 25 manufacturing industries the average weekly hours dropped from 51.5 in 1914 to 38.9 in 1936.[2] Lundberg shows graphically the growth of leisure time of American wage earners for nearly a century.[3] We do not have corresponding data concerning hours worked by farmers and other rural people. There are some reasons to believe that they, too, are putting in shorter time than a generation ago, but because the farmers' hours are controlled by weather and other natural conditions it seems reasonable to infer that the reduction in hours of labor has been less for country people than for those in cities.

A second clue to understanding the development of organized recreation in the modern city is the presence of large numbers of

[1] *Recent Social Trends*, vol. 2, p. 829.

[2] Jesse F. Steiner, *Research Memorandum on Recreation in the Depression*, p. 29, 1937.

[3] Lundberg, *op. cit.*, p. 5.

young unmarried people. We have already seen that the percentages of single, widowed, and divorced persons are greater in cities than in the country; on the other hand, there are more young folks in rural America than in our cities. But these young people in the country are more frequently married or still attached to their parental homes. Many of those in our cities are detached dwellers in rooming houses or participate rather superficially in the home life of their family.

A third lead is the apparent lack of personal acquaintance, the decline of neighboring, and the scattering of friends over a large metropolitan district. These are all matters concerning which statistical data are quite inadequate, but in our later discussion of neighborliness we shall present considerable evidence in support of these generalizations. Now if it be true that there has been a decline in primary relationships such as those of family, neighborhood, and intimate friends, this must be an important factor in causing the people of our cities, especially the young unmarried people, to look to more formal agencies for their recreation.

Attention might also be called to the relative lack of space in our cities for outdoor play, especially the rural types of spontaneous sport such as fishing and hunting. Perhaps no less importance should be attached to the lack of house space. We noted earlier the declining size of the average dwelling unit. This must evidently drive young people out of the house to seek their recreation elsewhere.

Some students lay great emphasis upon the monotony of industrial jobs, the machine-set pace, and the external control of the work, which they contrast with the varied tasks and greater personal control of work on farms and in villages. Again we lack measures of these aspects of rural and urban life, but our own observations support the impression just indicated.

Other economic aspects of the rise of organized recreation in modern cities include the fact that considerable capital outlay is required for land and equipment. Such capital is not available in rural districts, but it may be had in cities. In cities there is an economic surplus with which to pay for recreation. Hence there are profits to be made from commercial enterprises in this field. Perhaps what we ought to say is that city people may have no greater actual surplus, but they handle cash more than do country dwellers and hence may more easily divert their income from one form of expenditure to another. If they crave stimulation or relaxation they have money which can be used for this purpose. Country people, lacking the cash, are therefore more dependent upon what is naturally present or can be made available more informally for their entertainment.

What we have just said pertains especially to commercial recreation, but many city people entertain doubts as to the adequacy, the financial accessibility, and the wholesomeness of commercial recreation. Hence they have stimulated the development of semiphilanthropic agencies such as the Y.M.C.A., the Camp Fire Girls, and social settlements, which represent a substitution of one form of organized recreation for the other. This same movement has led not only to semiphilanthropic organizations but also to municipal recreation and other tax-supported agencies. Both these types of organized but noncommercial recreation rest not merely on a skepticism about that which is run as business but also upon belief in a relation between organized play on the one hand and health, conduct, and social solidarity on the other.

In short, it appears that the development of organized recreation in modern cities is the composite result of increased leisure time, increased numbers of unattached persons, limitations on space, and monotonous jobs, combined with the economic possibility of commercial recreation, adverse reactions to which have produced semiphilanthropic and municipal recreation.

Municipal Recreation

Recreational activities and agencies supported through taxation and administered by governmental units are almost unknown in rural America. To be sure, there are some county parks and some community buildings in villages and country districts, but on the whole these are so rare as to be for our purpose quite negligible. On the other hand there has been a tremendous growth of municipal recreational facilities in our larger cities. Some notion of their extent and variety may be had from Table 27. The data for two years are reported, not to show any particular change but because the numbers of cities reporting and the detailed facts vary enough from year to year to make it seem wise to do this. Two or three cautions should be offered in connection with this table. The materials are quite miscellaneous. In some instances it appears that recreation under organized private agencies has been included, and, as already noted, the number of cities reporting varies considerably. Nevertheless we have here a real basis for asserting that public recreation in cities has now reached proportions that are truly great.

It is a bit difficult to trace the growth of municipal recreation with anything approaching accuracy because reports have been made in such different ways at different times. Thus, Lundberg tells us that in the first half dozen years of this century only 20 cities made provision for recreation, but Davie reports that 100 cities had municipal parks by 1892.[1] Probably what Lundberg has in mind is supervised recreational activities, which are after all quite different from the mere provision of park space in which people may walk about and view the flowers and lawns. By 1910 some 55 cities had public playgrounds, buildings for recreational purposes, and school community centers. By 1921 there were over 350 cities expending public funds for recreational purposes. By 1931 this number had passed 800.[2] At this last date the value of public recreational property in cities was $2,405,000,000 and the per capita expenditure for tax-supported recreation had risen from $0.68 in 1915 to $1.44 in 1928.[3]

Until the middle of the nineteenth century there were practically no municipal parks. To be sure, there were village greens or commons, but these had been established either as grazing grounds or as places for military drill. In Europe there were a few parks, originally attached to ecclesiastical or royal institutions. Davie reports that in the late seventies there were not over 20 American cities with municipal parks. In the next 15 years the number rose to 100, and soon after 1900 nearly 800 cities had made some provision for park space.[4] The *Social Work Year Book* for 1937 reports nearly 900 cities maintaining nearly 12,000 parks. Steiner has measured the growth of municipal parks from 1907 to 1930 in relation to the population and size of cities. No comment will be made on his analysis at this point except to say that the best showing in many respects has been made by middle-

[1] Lundberg, *op. cit.*, p. 356; Maurice R. Davie, *Problems of City Life*, p. 694, 1932.

[2] Jesse F. Steiner, *Americans at Play*, p. 174, 1933.

[3] *Ibid.*, pp. 185, 173.

[4] Davie, *op. cit.*, p. 694.

TABLE 27.—SUMMARY OF COMMUNITY RECREATION, 1935 AND 1936[a]

	1935	1936
Number of cities with play leadership or supervised facilities	2,204	1,122
Total number of separate play areas reported (Including outdoor playgrounds, recreation buildings, indoor recreation centers, play streets, athletic fields, bathing beaches, golf courses, and summer camps)	18,799	17,443
New play areas opened for first time during year (Not including indoor centers)	1,790	1,275
Total number of play areas and special facilities reported:		
Outdoor playgrounds	9,650	9,490
Recreation buildings	1,149	1,347
Indoor recreation centers	4,949	3,947
Play streets	179	212
Archery ranges	199	270
Athletic fields	1,818	1,439
Baseball diamonds	4,197	3,568
Bathing beaches	605	516
Bowling greens	189	184
Golf courses	336	354
Handball courts	1,426	1,409
Horseshoe courts	7,497	7,445
Ice Skating areas	2,325	2,411
Shuffleboard courts	833	1,159
Ski jumps	136	114
Softball diamonds	7,696	7,369
Stadiums	145	155
Summer camps	113	
Camps—day		138
Swimming pools	1,098	1,148
Tennis courts	9,880	10,029
Toboggan slides	315	272
Wading pools	1,292	1,295
Total number of employed recreation leaders	43,976	46,550
Recreation workers paid from regular funds (Remainder paid from emergency funds)	20,052	18,496
Leaders employed full time year round	2,606	2,792
Volunteer leaders	10,346	8,579
Local expenditures	$21,500,000	$24,000,000
Emergency relief funds	16,000,000	32,000,000
Total expenditures for public recreation in cities	$37,500,000	$56,000,000

[a] *Recreation*, 30 (1936), 99; 31 (1937), 123. By permission of The National Recreation Association.

sized cities. Thus, among the cities with the largest park area in relation to their population are Denver, Dallas, Minneapolis, and Kansas City.[1] One particularly important aspect of municipal parks is the changing conception of their purpose and the changing facilities provided in them. In the nineteenth century most municipal parks were intended to be quiet and beautiful places in the midst of otherwise noisy and unattractive urban landscapes. Such parks are still offered as places of beauty and rest, but increasingly they provide for active recreation. They contain football fields, baseball diamonds, tennis courts, golf courses, swimming pools, boating facilities, and children's playgrounds.

Playgrounds as distinguished from parks are newer and if anything more completely urban. During the last quarter of the nineteenth century some philanthropic citizens in Boston and other eastern cities established, under organized private auspices, sand gardens and other experimental playgrounds for children in slum areas. On the basis of their demonstration, cities began to make similar provision, sometimes in connection with public schools, sometimes in municipal parks, and increasingly on separate small tracts of land scattered conveniently through the city. By 1910, 180 cities reported playgrounds, some tax-supported and some maintained by philanthropic effort. By 1936 the National Recreation Association reported 718 cities maintaining 9,490 playgrounds. The total average daily summer attendance of participants and spectators was estimated to be 3,160,000. Over 200 cities maintained 2,300 playgrounds throughout the year. Others operated only during the summer season. In addition to the outdoor playgrounds there were over 300 cities which maintained more than 1,300 recreation buildings in large or small parks. As in the case of parks, the middle-sized cities seem to have made the most progress in developing playgrounds. Small cities, *i.e.*, those under 25,000, have a smaller number of playgrounds in relation to their population than do cities of 50,000 or over. The earlier playgrounds were usually small and were equipped with apparatus of the sort commonly found in a gymnasium. Recently there has been a decline in the use of gymnastic equipment. Instead there are swings, slides, seesaws, and facilities for playing all manner of games.

[1] Jesse F. Steiner, *Americans at Play*, pp. 25–29, 1933.

Schools as social centers have already been discussed in relation to the diffusion of urban recreational traits to rural areas. Their development grew out of the recognition that the board of education of every city had playgrounds, gymnasiums, auditoriums, and other facilities which were used only part of the time and which might easily be made available for club meetings, lectures, concerts, forums, and other recreational and educational events for old and young. In a study published by the United States Office of Education in 1927 it was reported that over 700 cities and towns were maintaining nearly 1,600 school social centers.

In addition to the facilities already described, some account should be taken also of municipal theaters, museums, zoos, and libraries. The first three types of institution are almost exclusively urban, and as a matter of fact are rarely found outside of large cities. Public libraries, however, have been established in smaller communities, although they remain overwhelmingly urban. In nine Midwestern states in 1935 nearly 90 per cent of the rural population was not served by any public library, while less than 5 per cent of the urban population in the same states was without public library facilities.[1] The general circulation of public libraries throughout the United States in 1934 was 367 books per 100 persons. In individual cities this varied from 175 in San Antonio to 1,095 in Cleveland.[2]

One of the most important aspects of the development of public recreation has been the appearance in increasing numbers of trained leaders. In 1936, 700 cities reported a total of over 20,000 recreation workers. Most of them were on duty only in the summertime, but about 2,800 were employed full time all the year round. Volunteers have been used a great deal in organized private recreational agencies, but not so much in the municipal service.[3]

The forms of municipal administration of recreation have varied from time to time and are even yet quite diverse. In 1936, 229 cities reported having playground and recreation commissions, boards, or departments; 210 cities administered their recreation through park commissions or boards; 199 put this in

[1] E. L. Morgan and M. W. Sneed, *The Libraries of Missouri*, p. 17, 1936.

[2] *The World Almanac*, 1937, p. 367.

[3] *Recreation*, 31 (1937), 126.

the hands of boards of education; 200 other cities distributed the responsibility variously among departments of public works, of public welfare, of public service, semiofficial committees and advisory commissions, and various other civic authorities. In many instances the responsibility for municipal recreation in one city is divided between two or more distinct offices. This is not only confusing but uneconomical, and interferes with the development of a unified program.

Semipublic and Semiphilanthropic Recreation

During the same period in which American cities were developing the conventionalized parks, various groups of private citizens were organizing to provide recreational and other facilities for their less advantaged fellow citizens. Sand gardens and model playgrounds we have already mentioned. More important in some respects than these were the social settlements which made their appearance in the eighties and nineties. The pattern of these institutions was directly borrowed from London, where it had been developed by university people interested in social service among the poor. This was a reaction against exclusively missionary effort and rested on the assumption that it was essential to have in every inhabited area educated persons with a capacity for leadership. Some Oxford and Cambridge students settled in a slum area, making themselves residents and developing their house so far as possible into a kind of headquarters for many sorts of civic, educational, and recreational activities. The full story of the settlement movement cannot be told here, but credit should be given to these pioneers for experimentation, demonstration, and continuous provision of recreation to many thousands of underprivileged city dwellers. In the United States the settlements which started along the Atlantic seaboard and later spread to Midwestern and other cities have been brought together in a national federation which includes about 150 of these agencies. It is interesting to note that their number has not changed greatly in the last 15 years, which may indicate that the period of their maximum usefulness is passing, with the rapid development of municipal social centers.

A host of other semipublic and semiphilanthropic agencies offer what are sometimes described as youth programs. That these are not exclusively urban is made plain through the widespread development of 4-H Clubs, the Y.M.C.A., the Y.W.C.A., the Boy Scouts, and the Camp Fire Girls. The Y.M.C.A. has already been discussed. The Y.W.C.A. started in London, made its first American appearance in Boston shortly after the Civil War, and grew to a total of 1,900 local associations in 1936. The great majority of these are still in cities of 25,000 or over.[1]

Quite separate from the Christian associations and from the social settlements have grown up boys' clubs and girls' clubs, the former united into a national federation. Their purpose is similar to that of the other organizations discussed, namely, to provide in congested areas of our cities places where boys and girls respectively may spend their leisure time profitably at a minimum cost. By 1930 there were over 250 boys' clubs affiliated with the federation, located in 130 cities and having a membership of nearly 240,000. The girls' clubs developed less rapidly and abandoned their national federation after a short-lived experiment.

Perhaps best known of all the agencies with youth programs is that of the Boy Scouts. Started in 1907, and chartered in the United States in 1910, this organization has expanded rapidly, until it now has over 1 million members. The general features of its program are too well known to necessitate further discussion here. It should be said, however, that, while we lack actual data, we know that the great majority of Scouts are city boys and we have the impression, subject to correction, that the bulk of them are drawn from the middle class. Other organizations for boys and girls, varying somewhat but having the same general purposes and programs, are the Girl Scouts, the Boy Rangers of America, the Camp Fire Girls, Pioneer Youth of America, etc. Commenting on this whole group of agencies and the public recreational departments which the private have helped to promote, Lynd remarks that the urban child's out-of-school life seems to be passing through a cycle. In an earlier period there were chores about the home. Cities grew, and dwellings and yards declined in size. The child's leisure was largely unorganized and random. More recently, with the development of these agencies just discussed, there is a tendency to organize, direct, and supervise the leisure time behavior of city boys and girls.

[1] Davie, *op. cit.*, p. 643; *Social Work Year Book*, 1937, p. 560.

Organized Private Recreation

We turn now to a very different group of private agencies, a group whose motivation is less that of philanthropy than of self-service. We have in mind clubs, fraternal orders, and associations of many kinds which might freely be described as mutual, cooperative, and self-supporting, and which are usually restricted to more or less limited groups. They include clubs devoted to golf, fishing, hunting, tennis, yachting, bicycling, hockey, bowling, bridge, politics, literature, dramatics, music, art, and many other special interests. Some of them are identified quite exclusively with leisure time activities pursued as ends in themselves. Many of them are only incidentally recreational in character, having as their major objective economic advantages, political favors, civic improvements, etc. Still others, like our fraternal orders, combine certain aspects of leisure and "utilitarian" groups. Many of them seem to have grown out of the great American game of competitive and conspicuous consumption. The membership of others is not unrelated to pressure and a feeling that one must join; yet Steiner holds that the vogue of the "joiner" is waning. His observation has been quite varied and wide, hence considerable importance should be attached to it although no statistical evidence is immediately available. Lynd, on the other hand, found in Middletown a "hardy persistence of the city's club life."

It should be observed that organizations of this type are neither new nor exclusively urban. There were some clubs in American villages of long ago—literary societies, music clubs, the Grange, athletic clubs, and others. Some of the fraternal orders were established early, but their greatest growth took place during the period of rapid urban expansion. Out of 190 fraternal societies, 72 were started before 1890; 73 between that date and 1900; only 45 after 1900. Nevertheless, the number of members increased in the 25 years ending 1930 from 5 million to 10 million.[1] Unfortunately, we are unable to report how many of these lodges and their members were located in cities and how many in villages and the open country. We are disposed to take the position that because of their early appearance, on the one hand, and their rapid growth in the twentieth century, on the

[1] Jesse F. Steiner, *Americans at Play*, pp. 127–129, 1933.

other, that these organizations are neither distinctively urban nor distinctively rural.

There is, however, another sort of private leisure time organization, which originated in cities and has continued to be essentially urban in character. Earlier in this chapter we commented upon the diffusion of luncheon clubs, or service clubs, from city to country. It might be well here to give a little further account of their development and character. Rotary dates from 1905. It was founded by an attorney who was seeking the fellowship of kindred spirits in a strange city. He gathered a few friends, who drew in others. The first meetings were held in members' offices in rotation, then as numbers increased they changed to hotels and restaurants. A member of the Chicago club carried the idea to San Francisco in 1908. In 1910, 16 Rotary Clubs met in convention and formed a national association.

Kiwanis was founded in 1914 by the promoter of a fraternal order which never materialized. He brought together some of the members of the unsuccessful fraternal order as a nucleus for a businessmen's club. This developed hopefully in Detroit and spread rather rapidly. At its second convention, in 1917, 52 clubs were reported.

The Lions originated somewhat differently—as the result of a planned effort to affiliate existing businessmen's luncheon clubs scattered over the country. In the course of this promotion, however, some new clubs were founded. Between 1914 and 1917, 150 groups were established or affiliated, and the International Association of Lions Clubs came into existence.

These organizations select their members in such fashion as to distribute them over a wide range of professions and businesses. Much is made of the prestige value of membership, though emphasis is also laid upon "service" activities. They lend their support and influence to various civic, patriotic, educational, economic, and "welfare" movements. Sometimes a good deal of enthusiasm is displayed and sometimes the effort to keep up the spirit is forced and not particularly successful. Lynd observed in Middletown in 1935 that these organizations were trying hard to build morale through the repetition of familiar slogans and the avoidance of divisive issues, that they were less spontaneous and more self-conscious, and that the members seemed tired, as though their ritual had been too long performed.

Despite such evidence of possible decline or at least interruption of enthusiastic growth, the 15 men's organizations of this general type had in 1931 over 9,500 clubs and about 415,000 members. Apparently they all declined slightly during the depression, but their losses were small enough to be regarded as probably only a temporary interruption of growth.

No description will be attempted here of the multifarious lodges and clubs ranging all the way from Elks and country clubs to petty organizations for the playing of bridge or stud poker. We will simply observe that in 1930 the taxes paid on the dues of social and athletic clubs amounted to $12,500,000, and that Steiner estimates that the total expenditures for such organizations amounted to over $300,000,000.[1]

Commercial Recreation

Until very recently commercial recreation has been almost wholly absent from rural communities in the United States, and even now it is represented in small towns by little besides the movies. In the city, however, we find theaters of all sorts—legitimate, vaudeville, burlesque, and motion picture—amusement parks, great amusement centers like the famous Play-Mor in Kansas City, dance halls of many kinds, cabarets, excursion steamers, billiard parlors, swimming pools, skating rinks, stadia where professional sports are displayed, race tracks, and many others. Some of these afford opportunity for participation, most of them for observation, and incidentally nearly all of them for gambling—not that gambling is essential or even approved by the management but that it seems inevitably to creep in wherever competition is in progress.

We have already commented on the spread of the movies from city to country. By 1930 there were 23,000 motion picture theaters, with a seating capacity of 11 million. As we observed earlier, it is hard to divide these between urban and rural because now it is a poor village indeed that does not maintain at least one little motion picture house with a weekly or biweekly showing. The attendance upon the movies in 1930 is estimated to have reached 100 million per week. During the depression this fell off considerably, but in 1933 it began to mount again. Two important changes during recent years are to be observed. One

[1] *Ibid.*, pp. 136–138.

is the introduction of sound equipment; the other is a decline in the total number of theaters, accompanied by an increase in their average size. Also, there is a tendency to adopt mid-city locations, which seem to be displacing both downtown and neighborhood theaters. What the movies mean to different people is a bit hard to say. "If the older generation takes its movies as an anodyne and small children as an exciting weekly event, adolescent Middletown goes to school to as well as enjoying the movies."[1] Many people have feared the movies and have charged them with contributing directly and seriously to the demoralization especially of youth. Some careful studies to determine the truth of these charges have been made, but the findings in most instances are rather inconclusive.[2]

Next to the movies it is probable that the most widely used commercial recreation facilities in our cities are dance halls. These are of several different sorts. There is the dance palace which is large, frequently rather attractive, and conveniently located. Admission is expensive if one includes the cost of tickets for individual dances. The patrons are a rather heterogeneous lot, and interest is largely in the dancing itself and in social contacts which are made. Another sort of dance place is the outdoor pavilion, usually on the edge of a city, though sometimes appearing as one of the attractions at an amusement park. Then there is dancing on excursion boats, in restaurants, and in hotels. There is a small number of dancing academies where instruction is given and some ballroom dancing is enjoyed as well. Cabarets, night clubs, and roadhouses will be discussed a little later. Perhaps the most distinctively urban of all is the taxi-dance hall, sometimes called the closed dance hall. This is an institution maintained for men customers only, couples not being admitted. The girls who dance with the patrons are employed by the management, usually on a commission basis. Cressey, who made a study of this institution in the city of Chicago,[3] found these girls passing through a life cycle somewhat

[1] Lynd and Lynd, *op. cit.*, p. 262. By permission of Harcourt, Brace & Company, Inc.

[2] Alice M. Mitchell, *Children and Movies*, 1929. See especially Tables in Appendix II.

[3] Paul G. Cressey, *The Taxi-Dance Hall*, 1932. Data used by permission of the University of Chicago Press.

as follows: Being dissatisfied with home, neighborhood, or job, or all three, they find their way to the taxi-dance hall. Here as newcomers they are at first "rushed" and enjoy the thrill of considerable popularity, but after a time they fall into the background as other new girls are employed. At this stage they may turn to Orientals or other minority groups for new prestige. Finally some of them either leave the dance hall or drift into a lower-class cabaret. There are various sorts of girls among these dance hall "hostesses." Some of them are really quite decent, possessing some personal charm and physical attractiveness. They have little difficulty in finding patrons without overstepping any of the conventional bounds of propriety, but there are others who find the going a little harder or for other reasons are interested in the exploitative possibilities. They engage in "fishing," sometimes known as "gold digging" and the "sex game." Then there are those who definitely go in for sensual dancing. All of them have the problem of maintaining sufficient respectability to keep their place in the dance hall while making themselves sufficiently attractive to the constant stream of strange men to earn the desired money.

Turning from the girls to the men patrons of the taxi-dance hall, we find a miscellaneous lot. First of all, there are Filipinos, Chinese, and others who do not find social acceptance elsewhere and only here can have opportunity for association with members of the opposite sex. A second type is the European immigrant who is detached from home and has limited opportunities to meet girls of his own nationality. A third variety is the older man, perhaps nearing fifty, who may be a widower, a divorcé, or a deserter. Another kind is the younger married man whose matrimonial venture has been unfortunate. A fifth is the lonely stranger in the city, a sixth is the worthless globe-trotter, and a seventh is the "slummer." Finally, there is a small number including such misfits as sufferers from physical abnormality and fugitives from justice.

From these descriptions of the hostesses and their patrons it is evident that the taxi-dance hall undertakes to serve a real need in providing interesting association between the sexes for individuals who are somehow handicapped or unfortunate, but at the same time that the dance hall makes a contribution to this genuine need it also seems to promote demoralization. The anonymity, the release from ordinary social restraints, the opportunity for living "double lives," the economic nexus, and the constant dilemmas involving casual familiarities both on the dance floor and after leaving the hall make this a situation in which wholesome adjustments cannot be counted upon with much assurance.

In listing the various types of dance halls found in our cities we mentioned cabarets, night clubs, and roadhouses. The cabaret is distinguished from the ordinary dine and dance establishment by some sort of floor show, as it is ordinarily called, and by showy though not necessarily expensive equipment and high costs. Cabarets were found by Reckless[1] to have grown out of the old-fashioned beer garden, public dance, and revue once associated with the saloon. These cabarets, in Chicago at least, are found in the same parts of the city as houses of prostitution and frequently fall under the same influence of politicians and gangsters. Night clubs, which perhaps are not really to be distinguished from cabarets, have been classified by Davie as follows: (*a*) respectable night clubs frequented by "smart society"; (*b*) near-respectable clubs with more boisterous drunkenness and with "hostesses" to stimulate the sale of drinks; (*c*) clubs with more "liberal" revues and with entertainers who circulate among the men customers as "gold diggers"; (*d*) clubs of a still lower type, variously called "sucker dives" and "gyp joints," which often solicit their customers through taxi drivers and bellboys (their "hostesses" not only stimulate trade and entertain the customers but also serve as prostitutes); (*e*) clubs which are definitely disguised houses of prostitution. In all of these the name "club" is a misnomer, for membership is at most nominal and is often nonexistent.[2]

A newer institution of this general character is the roadhouse. This may be little more than a filling station and "hot dog" stand, or it may be an elaborate establishment wherein are found liquor, gambling, and rooms for immoral purposes. Roadhouses are found, quite naturally, along the principal highways outside all of our larger cities. They are usually outside the limits of the municipality and frequently in areas where there

[1] W. R. Reckless, *Vice in Chicago*, Chap. 4, 1933. By permission of the University of Chicago Press.

[2] Davie, *op. cit.*, pp. 592–596. By permission of author and publisher.

is some doubt as to which law enforcement officials have jurisdiction. Their removal to the suburban area and beyond is related to two developments of the last 20 years. One is the increasing use of the automobile for joy rides and wild parties. The other is the reform movement which closed up many of our red-light districts and dubious places of amusement inside the city. New as they are, relatively speaking, the roadhouses have quickly fallen under the domination of vice syndicates and other racketeers. They are frequently forced to buy their liquor from particular dealers at excessive prices, must pay for "protection" and accept a certain allocation of territory, and are otherwise absorbed into a system of control quite at variance with that of governmental agencies. The unconventional behavior and the extralegal controls are alike facilitated by the fact that roadhouses occupy a jurisdictional frontier between city, county, and state. Our county police systems are not noted for their effectiveness. Suburban villages are sometimes glad to tolerate these establishments because of the income from legal licenses or from extralegal payments to officials. Sometimes those interested in this group of institutions carry to the suburban community the political methods found effective in the inner city. Intimidation from gangsters and controlled justices, peace officers, and local legislative bodies represent the means through which the "vice lords" may manage to have their own way.

Social Control of Leisure Time

The situations presented in connection with the taxi-dance hall and the roadhouse suggest why the problem of social control is especially urgent. In both these institutions we find an effort to meet a genuine and legitimate demand for association between the sexes, release from boredom, escape from the stress and strain of daily life. But the community as such, instead of setting out to supply the wants of its citizens, leaves the field more or less to those who see an opportunity to make money by catering to these natural desires. Since the interest of proprietors is primarily in securing a financial return, they are not over-squeamish about the kind of entertainment provided or the behavior of patrons. Furthermore, the proprietors in turn are subject to exploitation by racketeers, gangsters, politicians. Finally, the dance hall of any sort provides a setting for what someone has called "intimate behavior on the basis of casual association." That is, utter strangers meet under circumstances which lead quickly to the most intimate conduct. Lacking the informal social controls of old-fashioned neighborhood and community, these intimacies proceed in an atmosphere of irresponsibility. Boy and girl, man and woman, meet at the amusement park, cabaret, excursion steamer, or perhaps at the movies, skating rink, or race track. They chat, dance, dine, "neck," and possibly sleep together. Through all this they may not know each other's names, occupations, homes. In other words, they are amazingly intimate strangers. Of course this sort of thing does not happen in extreme form to every young person in the city. It is simply the exaggerated aspect of the urban-rural contrast in the uses of leisure time.

In addition to possible demoralization from the combining of intimacy and casualness, other factors have led to a demand for the control of commercial recreation. One is the possible influence of the movies, soft drink parlors, amusement parks, and the rest on impressionable youths and children. That there is some influence and that it is not all in the direction of making "wholesome citizens" we have no doubt, although we have yet to see any satisfactory measures of how these recreational agencies affect personality.

Davie has classified the possible means of social control of recreation under four heads: suppression, regulation by law, trade control, and public opinion.[1] Suppression has manifested itself in various attempts to restore the Puritan Sabbath, to eliminate racing, the saloon, the house of prostitution, gambling, and prize fighting. The limitations of suppression may be illustrated by the case of the old-fashioned saloon. Along with its abuses it served many useful purposes, especially for workingmen, and when it was closed without the provision of some substitute there was a tremendous reaction and a great deal of defiant violation of the law. In many cases the closing of vice areas has been similarly unsuccessful. In general it may be said that suppression and repression are likely to fail and to evoke behavior more troublesome than that associated with the condemned institutions and activities.

[1] *Ibid.*, pp. 586 ff. By permission of author and publisher.

Regulation by law has been rather more hopeful, though it, too, leaves much to be desired. Regulation, for example, of dance halls, billiard parlors, and other commercial recreation appears commonly as a system of licensing and inspection. In the case of dance halls, ordinances frequently fix a minimum age for patrons, specify hours of closing, and regulate lighting, the issuing of pass-out checks, types of dances, and conduct of dancers. Often the direct supervision of policemen or policewomen is required. When we come to the movies, official regulation more commonly involves some sort of censorship, sometimes by the state, sometimes by the municipality. It is hard to say whether official boards of censorship have, to date, accomplished enough for public morals to offset the damage they seem to have done to the aesthetic side of the cinema.

A third form of social control is undertaken by the trade, either through associations of promoters or producers or through the appointment of an arbiter or dictator, *e.g.*, Judge Landis for baseball and Will Hays for the movies. A very interesting case of cooperation between a social service organization and proprietors of commercial recreation establishments is reported from Chicago.[1] After attempting in various ways to secure public sentiment and legislation that might reduce undesirable features of commercial recreation, the Juvenile Protective Association of Chicago adopted the policy of cooperation with proprietors. It induced the Ballroom Managers Association to share in the salary of a social worker whose responsibility it was to study ways of controlling the behavior in public dance halls, in the interest both of better business and of the public morals. For one year the Illinois Billiard Association paid the salary of a member of the Juvenile Protective Association's staff to find and prosecute violations of the law and help to make poolrooms more attractive and wholesome recreation centers. Later, in collaboration with the Candy Jobbers Association, a program was developed for the elimination of candy gambling devices and machines which familiarize small children with games of chance. These cooperative ventures appear to have had rather more success than some other forms of control, but we are unready to say how practicable they may be for cities in general.

[1] *National Conference of Social Work*, 1924, pp. 185–186.

Finally, there is the method of control through public opinion. This obviously requires an initial arousal of interest, then the bringing to the attention of many people of significant facts involved, and finally the inducing of large numbers to act. Such action may take various forms, *e.g.*, publicity, the circulation of petitions, lobbying, boycotting, etc. How effective control through public opinion has been or may become is still in the realm of the unknown. Unquestionably, however, any sort of control, to be effective, must be founded upon an aroused public sentiment and an informed public opinion.

Summary

It appears that the leisure time of cityfolk, in contrast to that of countryfolk, is spent in ways that are more passive and more generally organized, not to say commercialized. However, the recreation of urban and rural people overlaps to a great extent, so that the greatest difference seems to lie in the frequency of indulgence rather than in the particular kinds of activity engaged in. In the past half century there has been a great development of commercial, philanthropic, and public recreation in our cities. Many of the new agencies and activities have been gradually diffused into rural areas, thus filling the leisure time of city and country people in ways that are more and more alike.

As already indicated, recreation in American cities is in one sense highly organized. That is, informal, casual gatherings and activities have been largely replaced by promoted, controlled, and formalized agencies and activities. But in another sense urban recreation is still unorganized. There is little coordination of public, semiphilanthropic, commercial, and private recreation. Also, some parts of each city seem to be well supplied with facilities for play of every kind, while other sections are relatively neglected. There is some attempt at central planning, which will be discussed in Chap. XXIV, but it has not made much headway.

Quite without systematic planning, recreational agencies tend to group themselves according to a fairly recognizable pattern. Downtown are some theaters, billiard parlors, and taxi-dance halls. In the mid-city are centralized most of the larger moving picture theaters, dance halls, billiard parlors, bowling alleys, social settlements, and young people's associations (*e.g.*, the

Y.M.C.A.). In the "better" residential sections and suburbs are found Scout troops, women's clubs, and neighborhood movies. Out on the fringe are golf clubs, roadhouses, amusement parks, and race tracks. Parks and playgrounds are now placed in widely scattered parts of the city.

Selected Readings

Steiner, Jesse F.: *Americans at Play*, The McGraw-Hill Book Company, Inc., 1933. One of the research monographs prepared under the direction of the President's Research Committee on Social Trends.

Lundberg, George A.: *Leisure: A Suburban Study*, Columbia University Press, 1934. A careful study of leisure time activities and facilities in Westchester County, New York.

Klein, Philip: *A Social Study of Pittsburgh*, Columbia University Press, 1938. Chapter 20 deals with leisure time activities and facilities in Pittsburgh and Allegheny County.

Lynd, Robert S. and Helen M. Lynd: *Middletown in Transition*, Harcourt, Brace & Company, Inc., 1937. Chapter 7 shows how leisure time is spent in a small American city.

Davie, Maurice R.: *Problems of City Life*, John Wiley & Sons, Inc., 1932. Part V is an excellent discussion of the significance of various types of recreation in our cities.

Muntz, Earl E.: *Urban Sociology*, The Macmillan Company, 1938. Part V deals with private nonprofit, commercial, and public recreation; a good description and discussion.

Cressey, Paul G.: *The Taxi-Dance Hall*, University of Chicago Press, 1932. An intimate study of a distinctively urban institution.

Mitchell, Alice M.: *Children and Movies*, University of Chicago Press, 1929. The movie experience of 10,000 city children.

Chapter X

RELIGIOUS INSTITUTIONS AND FOLKWAYS

Religion is one of the most difficult phases of life to define. Ames has identified it with "the most intimate and vital phase of the social consciousness."[1] But undoubtedly more people think of it as "the complex of man's interrelations with the superhuman forces."[2] For our present purpose we shall consider religion as a culture complex with characteristic activities, such as praying or assembling for the performance of ceremonies; characteristic attitudes, such as reverence, fear, devotion; characteristic symbols, such as cross, altar, hymn; characteristic traditions, beliefs, rules of conduct, and perhaps sacred books; characteristic physical equipment, such as church buildings and their furnishings. By a church we shall mean a fairly permanent local group of men, women, and children who engage in worship and religious instruction and who are usually affiliated with a more inclusive body, which we shall call a denomination or, in some cases, a sect. In framing these definitions we have deliberately avoided the mystical in order to confine our study to relatively objective data. We recognize that there is a mystical element in much, if not all, religion, but our concern is with religion as a complex of ideas, attitudes, and activities which can be studied. Moreover, we are not interested in the validity of beliefs or the efficacy of ceremonies in dealing with the unknown. We are trying to discover what religious traits have developed or survived in modern cities, particularly in the United States, and how they differ from those of rural districts. We should like to compare urban and rural religion in every aspect, but because of limitations on data we shall have to content ourselves largely with a comparison of city and country churches.

Religious Differences between City and Country

From their study of rural-urban differences in various lands, Sorokin and Zimmerman concluded that most of the people

[1] E. S. Ames, *The Psychology of Religious Experience*, p. 285, 1910.

[2] *Encyclopaedia of the Social Sciences*, vol. 13, p. 229.

affiliated with "native" religious groups would be found in the country, while most of those attached to "non-native" groups would be found in cities.[1] Obviously what they meant for the United States was that religions brought over by early settlers predominate in the country, while those introduced by more recent immigrants predominate in the city. We shall presently examine evidence indicating that this proposition is approximately correct, although it must be qualified in certain respects. Thus Protestants took possession of much of the territory which became the United States, but Catholics early occupied Maryland, Florida, Louisiana, and the Southwest. Because most Roman Catholic, Greek Orthodox, and Jewish folk have come to America in the last half century, they are found chiefly in cities, where they and similar groups constitute a large part of the church membership. But in rural America there is a predominance of Protestants, although many of the older denominations now have more members in cities than in the country. Sorokin and Zimmerman hold that religious innovations and the drifting away from established faiths occur first in cities and later spread to the country. Certain it is that Christian Science, spiritualism, the Foursquare Gospel, Theosophy, the Pillar of Fire Church, and many other sects and denominations originated in cities and are still predominantly urban. As to the falling away from established faiths, it is natural that this should occur more frequently in areas of cultural diffusion and conflict such as our great cities. Hence their second proposition appears to be sound. Their third hypothesis is less clear and less adequately supported. It is that religious practices and beliefs of city and country respectively are stamped with "stigmata" and "color" of divergent occupations and general environments. No doubt city people rarely pray for rain on growing crops and have generally forgotten the origin of Thanksgiving Day. Perhaps their leaders use the language of competing merchants and brokers rather than of neighborly agrarians. It would be reasonable to expect these things to be true. But they deserve further study. The fourth proposition in this group is the least convincing of all. It is that "man and man-made culture occupy a

[1] Pitirim Sorokin and C. C. Zimmerman, *Principles of Rural-Urban Sociology*, p. 420, 1929. Data in this section used by permission of Henry Holt & Company, Inc.

greater place in urban religion," taking today the forms of "mechanisticism," "materialism," and "determinism."[1] Until these terms have been translated into something more concrete and manageable, we do not see how the hypothesis can be either proven or denied. Finally, Sorokin and Zimmerman point to what they consider "greater rigidity and firmness in rural religious beliefs." No doubt evidence bearing on this can be assembled. For example, there are the antievolution laws of certain rural states; on the other hand we find dogmatic opposition to birth control clinics in churches that are largely urban. The issue cannot be settled without careful research.

Let us return to the question of which faiths are in the United States predominantly urban and which ones predominantly rural. Table 28 shows the Jewish congregations and the Salvation Army to be almost completely urban. Seven Eastern Orthodox

TABLE 28.—DENOMINATIONS PREDOMINANTLY URBAN, 1926[a]

	Churches			Members		
	Urban	Rural	Per cent urban	Urban	Rural	Per cent urban
Baptist Church, Northern Convention	2,860	4,751	38	1,290,000	885,000	59
Church of Christ Scientist	1,504	409	78	132,000	8,000	95
Congregational churches	1,923	3,105	38	611,000	271,000	65
Disciples of Christ	2,014	5,634	26	752,000	626,000	54
Eastern Orthodox churches (seven faiths)	384	62	83	242,000	17,000	93
Evangelical Churches (three faiths)	1,166	2,328	33	325,000	215,000	60
Jewish congregations	3,016	102	97	4,062,000	19,000	99.5
Lutheran, United Church in America	1,527	2,123	43	817,000	296,000	66
Methodist Episcopal Church	5,489	20,641	21	2,212,000	1,868,000	54
Presbyterian Church, U.S.A.	3,289	5,658	37	1,345,000	549,000	71
Protestant Episcopal Church	3,793	3,506	52	1,552,000	307,000	84
Roman Catholic Church	7,870	11,070	41	14,809,000	3,796,000	80
Salvation Army	1,030	22	98	74,000	1,000	99
Unitarian congregations	296	57	84	55,000	5,000	92

[a] Adapted from U.S. Census, *Religious Bodies*, 1926, vol. 1, pp. 82–91.

churches, the Christian Scientists, and the Unitarians also were more than 90 per cent urban in 1926, the time of the last census of religious bodies. Close on their heels was the Protestant Epis-

[1] *Ibid.*, p. 437.

copal Church. All the other denominations, with over 50 per cent of their members in cities, had more than 50 per cent of their local churches in rural districts. While the Roman Catholic and Jewish groups, which contain great numbers of recent arrivals in America, together constitute over half of the urban church members, it should not be overlooked that some of the predominantly urban denominations date from colonial days. Also, the urban religious groups include some new sects and denominations.

TABLE 29.—DENOMINATIONS PREDOMINANTLY RURAL, 1926[a]

	Churches			Members		
	Urban	Rural	Per cent urban	Urban	Rural	Per cent urban
Baptist, Southern Convention	1859	21,515	8	986,000	2,538,000	28
Baptists, Negro	4409	17,672	20	1,246,000	1,950,000	39
Churches of Christ	896	5,330	14	105,000	329,000	24
Friends	200	684	23	41,000	68,000	38
Lutheran, Norwegian	327	2,227	13	122,000	375,000	25
Methodist Episcopal Church South	1680	16,416	9	887,000	1,601,000	36
African Methodist Episcopal Zion	650	1,816	36	194,000	263,000	42
United Brethren	537	2,838	16	158,000	236,000	40

[a] Adapted from U.S. Census, *Religious Bodies*, 1926, vol. 1, pp. 82–91.

Table 29 contains a list of representative denominations that are largely rural. In addition to these there are many small sects and denominations whose members live almost entirely in the country. These include Freewill Baptists, the Church of the Brethren, the Mennonites, the Apostolic Christian Church, and the Cumberland Presbyterian Church. In contrast to some of the smaller city groups, these are mostly old and well established. Not only most of their churches but most of their members are found outside of cities. We note that these denominations are especially strong in parts of the United States whose urbanization has been delayed.

Table 30 shows that in 35 of the 50 largest cities the Roman Catholics had the largest number of churches and that in 44 cities they had the largest number of members. It is interesting to note that the Negro Baptists, with 80 per cent of their churches and 61 per cent of their members rural, had the largest number of churches in each of seven large cities and the largest number of members in two such cities.

TABLE 30.—RANK OF DENOMINATIONS IN THE FIFTY LARGEST CITIES, 1926

First	Cities	Second	Cities	Third	Cities
A. Denominations Ranking First, Second, and Third According to the Number of Churches in Each of the 50 Largest Cities[a]					
Roman Catholic	35	Roman Catholic	6	Roman Catholic	2
Methodist Episcopal	5	Methodist Episcopal	18	Methodist Episcopal	5
Negro Baptists	7	Methodist Episcopal South	4	Jewish	8
Jewish	1	Negro Baptists	5	Negro Baptists	4
Southern Baptist Convention	1	Jewish	2	Southern Baptist Convention	5
Christian Reformed	1	Southern Baptist Convention	2		
B. Rank According to Number of Members[b]					
Roman Catholic	44	Roman Catholic	1	Roman Catholic	1
Southern Baptist Convention	3	Southern Baptist Convention	3	Southern Baptist Convention	2
Negro Baptists	2	Negro Baptists	3	Negro Baptists	4
Jewish	1	Jewish	32	Jewish	5
		Methodist Episcopal South	4	Methodist Episcopal South	2
		Methodist Episcopal	3	Methodist Episcopal	13
				Protestant Episcopal	12

[a] Adapted from U.S. Census, *Religious Bodies*, 1926, vol. 1, pp. 64–65.
[b] *Ibid.*, pp. 66–67.

TABLE 31.—URBAN AND RURAL CHURCHES IN THE UNITED STATES, 1926[a]

	Rural	Urban	Cities of 25,000 and over
Number of churches	167,864	64,290	
Number of members	19,386,734	35,126,927	
Average number of members per church	115	546	762
Average number of Sunday scholars per church	76	210	242
Males per 100 females	78.7	80.3	81.6
Average value of church edifices	$6,198	$53,538	$77,397
Average expenditures per church	$1,400	$10,011	$13,850

[a] U.S. Census, *Religious Bodies*, 1926, vol. 1, pp. 82–83, 97, 102, 112, 117, 123, 348–349.

As a warning to the student it should be pointed out that the definition of "member" differs greatly from denomination to denomination. Hence the data presented must not be accepted too literally. Thus the Roman Catholic Church reports all persons baptized, including small children, while most of the Protestant Evangelical churches count only those who have formally joined the church, thus omitting nearly all children. However, we may tentatively accept the figures of the 1926 census of religious bodies as indicating the approximate facts about rural-urban differences.

One of the most important differences to be noted is between rural and urban clergy. Among Protestants four-fifths of the urban white clergy are reported to be graduates of colleges or theological seminaries or both, while in rural districts less than half have had this much training.[1] Catholic clergy on the average have had more formal education than Protestant; since they are principally located in cities, this accentuates the rural-urban difference. Negro clergy on the average have had less formal education than white; since they are mostly country dwellers, this emphasizes the rural-urban difference still more. Country ministers often are nonresident circuit riders, irregularly and poorly paid, with relatively short tenure.[2] The average pastorate of country ministers was two years in 1924 and less than three years in 1930, while the urban average was four years. Very few city pastors serve more than one church and very few are nonresident. As to salaries, it is impossible to secure satisfactory data, but there seems to be no doubt about the financial advantage of the urban clergy.[3] The larger city churches have staffs that include not only ordained ministers but also paid secretaries, visitors, musicians, specialists in religious education, recreation, and social case work, and maintenance workers. Thus, on the whole, professional leadership of city churches differs greatly from that of country churches. However, if we were to distinguish between village and open country churches, we should find fewer differences between city and village clergy than between urban and rural in general.

[1] *Recent Social Trends*, vol. 2, p. 1032.

[2] J. H. Kolb and E. de S. Brunner, *A Study of Rural Society*, pp. 474–475, 1935.

[3] H. Paul Douglass and Edmund de S. Brunner, *The Protestant Church as a Social Institution.*, Chap. 6, 1935.

The programs and activities of city and country churches differ in striking fashion. Kolb and Brunner found about seven out of eight village churches having at least one service every Sunday, while less than two-fifths of open country churches reached this goal. The great majority of both groups maintained Sunday schools, usually under the leadership of untrained laymen.[1] About two-fifths had some sort of women's organization and one-fourth had a young people's society. Village churches more frequently had subsidiary organizations. Town churches maintained them still more regularly and in greater numbers and variety. Douglass and Brunner have compared town and city churches with reference to several kinds of parish organizations.

Other aspects of organized religion in cities have been mentioned by Gist and Halbert:[2] specialization, cooperation, and stratification. Specialization refers to the carrying on of religious activities through various departments and under the direction of specialists. Cooperation is brought about through interdenominational agreements, church federations, and ministerial associations. Such teamwork, among Protestants at least, seems to be much more frequent in cities than in smaller communities, but there is a great deal of rural cooperation brought about through state church federations, home mission councils, and informal conferences between state officers of separate denominations. In both city and country the practice of comity means that given denominations agree not to duplicate work or to locate new churches without regard to those already occupying the field. In spite of the limited teamwork between Protestants and Catholics, Christians and Jews, we have the impression that cooperation of this and other sorts is more frequently urban than rural and that it is increasing; but both assumptions need to be checked by further study. By stratification Gist and Halbert mean that city churches tend to conform to class lines. So far as ethnic groups are concerned, we do not know whether this is more common in city or in country. Negro churches are separate in both urban and rural areas; Dutch Reformed, Norwegian Lutheran, and other nationality churches are found in the country; hence this remains for the moment an open question.

[1] Kolb and Brunner, *op. cit.*, p. 472.

[2] Noel P. Gist and L. A. Halbert, *Urban Society*, p. 550, 1933.

The same difficulty confronts us with reference to economic levels. Some city churches are attended chiefly by working people, while others of the same faith draw their clientele from business and professional folk. Some denominations in the city attract chiefly middle- and upper-class folk, *e.g.*, the Protestant Episcopal, Christian Science, Unitarian. To a considerable degree this appears to be true of Presbyterian, Congregational, and Reformed Jewish denominations. It is less evident in the case of Methodist and Baptist. Although the Roman Catholic Church has a large membership among the middle and upper classes, it draws most heavily from the working class. Minor sects—*e.g.*, the Pentecostal, the Apostolic Faith, and Holiness—attract chiefly persons of low income and limited education.

TABLE 32.—FREQUENCY OF CERTAIN SUBSIDIARY CHURCH ORGANIZATIONS IN TOWN CHURCHES AND IN MODAL CHURCHES OF LARGE CITIES[a]

Organizations	Per cent frequency	
	Town church	Modal city church
Some subsidiary organizations besides Sunday school	93	100
Women's organization	87	99
More than one women's organization	44	81
Mixed-sex organizations (usually young people's)	67	77
More than one mixed-sex organization	37	8
Men's organization	10	53
Boy's organization	15	52
Girl's organization	20	34

[a] H. Paul Douglass and Edmund de S. Brunner, *The Protestant Church as a Social Institution*, p. 137, 1935. By permission of Harper & Brothers, publishers.

TYPES OF CITY CHURCHES

We have been accustomed to classify city churches as metropolitan, neighborhood, mission, and "fly-by-night." By metropolitan church we have meant a parish with a large membership scattered throughout the city, an imposing edifice near the downtown business district or some subcenter, a widely known clergyman, and departmentalized activities. By neighborhood church we mean a smaller group of members, most of them living within a radius of one mile in a residential district, a less pretentious building, usually a less famous minister, and fewer subsidiary organizations and activities. The mission is commonly a branch or outpost of some larger and more opulent church or of a whole denomination, located in an area of deterioration or among newcomers to the city; its membership is small and usually localized, and its financial support comes from outside the parish. Finally, there is a type of church for which we have no satisfactory name. It is often called a mission, whether attached to any recognized denomination or not. The Negroes call it a "store front," because it often occupies an otherwise unused store building. It may be connected with some minor sect or it may be an independent venture. It usually does not remain long at one address; indeed its whole span of life may be short. The minister or leader commonly depends on some other occupation for his means of existence, since contributions are small and irregular. The clientele is made up largely of unskilled wage earners, many of them recently from rural America.

Douglass has developed a much more satisfactory basis of classification,[1] which is based, however, on the study of Protestant churches only. It is concerned with the number and character of subsidiary organizations and activities. First he classified churches according to the number of activities he found actually carried on: smallest (1–4), small (5–8), medium (9–12), large (13–16), and largest (17–20). Then he considered the character of the activities. From his study of 1,044 Protestant city churches he discovered the relative frequency of 33 different organizations and activities. Four of them—preaching and Sunday school, ladies' aid or guild, women's missionary society, and young people's society—were found in nearly all the churches, 81 to 100 per cent. Two more—chorus choir and general social events—appeared in 61 to 80 per cent of the churches studied. Three more—men's organization, Boy Scouts, and mission study classes—were present in 41 to 60 per cent of the churches. Then there were eight activities found in only 21 to 40 per cent; five in 11 to 20 per cent; and eleven in 1 to 10 per cent of the churches studied. Churches having only those activities and organizations found in 61 to 100 per cent, *i.e.*, quite general and conventional features, were classed as having

[1] H. Paul Douglass, *One Thousand City Churches*, 1926. Data used by permission of Harper & Brothers.

the narrowest range of activities. Those having features present in 41 to 60 per cent were considered narrow; those with features present in 21 to 40 per cent were called medium; those with features present in 11 to 20 per cent were rated broad; and those with features so rare as to be found in only 1 to 10 per cent of all churches were considered broadest. Figure 6 is the chart Douglass devised for combining the two aspects of number and range of activities. The cross classification yielded 17 subvarieties of

Scale of Number of Activities		Scale of Range of Activities: Per Cent Frequency				
		61–100 % Narrowest	41–60 % Narrow	21–40 % Medium	11–20 % Broad	1–10 % Broadest
	1–4 Smallest	A I	A II	A III	A IV	A V
	5–8 Small		B I	B II	B III	B IV
	9–12 Medium			C I	C II	C III
	13–16 Large			D I	D II	D III
	17–20 Largest				E I	E II

Fig. 6.—Chart for classification of churches. (*H. Paul Douglass, One Thousand City Churches*, 1926. *By permission of Harper & Brothers, publishers*).

city churches, each of which was given a symbol consisting of a letter and a Roman numeral.

The 1,044 churches under study were then assigned to the appropriate categories, whereupon it appeared that the mode, or most frequent subtype, was B-II, *i.e.*, churches with a small number and a medium range of activities. With this as a point of departure, he undertook to group the 17 subtypes into five major varieties. He added to the modal subtype the churches having the same number but a somewhat broader range of activities (B-III) and those with medium range but a somewhat larger number of activities (C-I). The combined modal type (type one) included one-third of all the churches studied and was regarded as the "core," or "center," about which other city churches varied. A review of the individual churches assigned to this major category showed that they really had many features in common and were different in important respects from the other subtypes. Their median membership was about 400, median age of the church about 40 years, median length of time in their present location 25 years; less than half of them had more than one paid religious worker. Most of their pastors (83.5 per cent) had full college and seminary preparation; two-thirds had been with the particular church less than 5 years, but nearly three-fourths had over 10 years' experience; over half received salaries between $1,000 and $3,000 in 1922. Current expenses averaged about $10,000 per year (median between $6,000 and $7,000); median value of church plant was $39,000. The median Sunday school had about 300 pupils, whose average attendance was about 180; nearly half of them were between 6 and 14 years of age. More than half of the churches of this type had at least three-fourths of their members living within one mile. For reasons elsewhere presented, Douglass designated this modal type of city church as "moderately developed and slightly adapted to urban environment."

Moving in the direction of a smaller number and a narrower range of activities, Douglass selected A-II as the center of a second type and added to it A-I, A-III and B-I. Their combined total was nearly one-fourth of all the churches studied. In comparison with the first type, this one is properly characterized as relatively undeveloped and unadapted, for these churches had less extensive and less diversified programs. These churches were definitely smaller than those of type one, averaging about 300 members each. Two-fifths were less than 25 years old and nearly two-thirds had been less than 25 years in their present location. More than four-fifths had only a single religious worker, namely, the pastor. The ministers of these churches had the poorest education, the shortest experience, and the briefest tenure of any group of city clergymen. There were more old men among them, and their salaries were low, 70 per cent receiving $2,000 or less. The general budget of these churches averaged about $3,000, and the median value of their church property was $20,000, or about half that of churches of type one. The Sunday school enrollment averaged about 220, which bears a relatively high ratio to the church membership. In fact, many of these churches had recently developed out of Sunday schools. Only half of them appeared to be well located with reference to the people they were undertaking to serve, and almost none were found in high-grade neighborhoods. Compared with type one, the parishes were less compact, only one-third having three-fourths of the members within one mile. However, they were not widely scattered, for two-thirds of the churches had at least half of their members within one mile.

Turning to the other side of the mode, Douglass sought to identify a type of church with a larger number and a broader range of activities. The statistical category C-II met these requirements and was also second to the most numerous subtype. To this he would naturally have added C-III and D-II, but an individual study of the small number of churches in the former subgroup showed them to be very unlike those of C-II in spite of their statistical nearness. However, C-II and D-II were found to be fairly homogeneous; hence they were combined as type three, designated as more developed and internally adapted. Their programs were so rounded as to provide in a special way for every age and sex group and cater to a wide range of human interests. Nearly three-fourths of these churches had over 500 members. More than half of them were over 50 years old; one-seventh were over a century old. They had moved more frequently than churches of any other type. Three-fourths had more than one paid religious worker; half of them had more than two. The clergy were highly educated men in the prime of life who tended to stay longer in the same parish than did those of other types. Their median salary was about $4,000, one-tenth receiving more than $7,000. The median budget was not far from $15,000, but the per capita cost was not much above the average for all city churches studied. Median value of church property was $120,000. The median Sunday school enrollment was about 400, attendance 250; it differed from the first two types in having a strong adolescent and adult participation. Because so many of these churches were located near the central business district, they tended to have scattered memberships. These "internally adapted" churches of type three constituted nearly one-fifth of all the churches studied.

The fourth major type was called "socially adapted," because of the extreme complexity of its development. It included only one-tenth of the entire group of churches, and was made up of the statistical categories D-III and E-II. Some of the distinctive elements in the programs of these churches were kindergartens and day nurseries, clinics, classes in English, civics, home economics, art, music, and dramatics, vocational advice, and employment services. These churches were usually large, nearly half of them having 1,000 members or more. They were old, having a median age of 55 years, and only one-seventh were under 25 years old. While the median length of time at the present site was only 36 years, nearly one-third had never moved; as to location, they were more stable than the churches of any other type. The median number of paid religious workers was four. Professional equipment of the clergy often included graduate study beyond college and seminary. These churches kept more elderly men and retained them longer in a given pastorate than did other types. Salaries showed considerable variation, one-fourth being under $3,000 and one-fourth over $6,000. The median budget was over $15,000; for nearly one-third of these churches it was over $25,000. Church property was valued on the average at $240,000. The median Sunday school enrolled less than 500 and was small as compared with the church membership. However, no other type of church had so large a proportion of adolescents in its Sunday school enrollment. Half of these churches were centrally located, many of them being in the heart of the downtown section. The remainder were located in quite varied districts, ranging from high-class residential neighborhoods to slums. The membership was often quite scattered. Only type two, "unadapted," had so few compact parishes.

These four types included seven-eighths of the churches studied, leaving a scattering of variants. Subtypes A-IV and A-V represented a small number of churches with rather unusual, but not very numerous, organizations and activities. On the other hand, those of D-I had a large number of activities that were fairly conventional. That is, some of these churches varied in the direction of novelty, others in the direction of conservatism.

To make sure that important features of Douglass's classification are not lost amid the details, let us recapitulate. *Type one:* At the center he found a "core" of churches moderately developed as to size, finances, plant, number and range of activities. Their parishes were fairly compact. Their leadership was in the hands of men well trained, moderately experienced, and fairly stable. *Type two:* In the upper left-hand corner of the chart he located a type of churches smaller, poorer (as to finance), with fewer and more conventional activities. Their clergy had the least education, shortest experience, and briefest tenure of all the groups studied. *Type three:* To the right and below the modal type was identified a class of churches that were larger, older, better financed, with a greater number and broader range of activities. Their membership was usually scattered. Their clergy were highly educated men in the prime of life who stayed longer than those in other types of churches. *Type four:* In the lower right-hand corner was established another class of churches—largest, oldest, best financed, with the greatest number and broadest range of activities. They were located in varied districts, but half of them were downtown churches. Their membership was often quite scattered. They had several paid religious workers besides the pastors, who were the best educated, most experienced, and stayed longest of all the clergy. *Type five:* Finally there was a fringe of widely variant churches representing no particular group of characteristics.

By comparing these city churches with those of the village and open country and by studying the history of the city churches Douglass reached the conclusion that "the city church is an evolved rural church."[1] In terms of the chart, churches belong-

[1] Douglass, *op. cit.*, p. 83.

ing in the upper left-hand corner, type two, were most like country churches and unadapted to city life. They were newer and had had less time to develop a program suited to the urban community. Those of the central class, type one, were less like rural churches, more developed, and somewhat adapted to city life. Types three and four were much further removed from the rural churches in age and in character; their organization was more complex and their accommodation to city life much more adequate. In still other ways city churches are evolved rural churches. Some of them have continued since the city was a village, and have never outgrown their rural traditions and practices. Others developed in villages that were later annexed to the city. Still others have been established in the city for the benefit of recent arrivals from the country. Finally, some "reflect the transplanted rural ideals of their denominations."

It should be repeated that this study is important both for the facts it reveals and for the methods employed. It is unfortunate that we do not have equally objective studies of Catholic and Jewish churches. These latter groups would doubtless display both similarities and differences. In the case of the Catholic churches, distribution and development probably differ greatly from the Protestant churches, because the former are under a centralized authority which carefully plans locations and interrelations.

The Ecology of Protestant Churches

The foregoing analysis of types of city churches has indicated that they are related to their environmental setting and that different kinds of churches may be found in different parts of the city. Another study made by the Institute of Social and Religious Research attempted to discover more precisely what relations may exist between church growth or decline and socio-economic factors in the vicinity.[1] Sanderson studied nearly 2,000 Protestant churches in selected "sectors" of 16 representative large cities. In each district he assembled data of eight sorts. First he asked whether in the decade under consideration there was growth or loss of general population. It was assumed that areas of declining population would be unfavorable for the

[1] Ross W. Sanderson, *The Strategy of City Church Planning*, 1932. Data used by permission of Harper & Brothers, publishers.

development of any institution like the church. Second, since he was concerned with Protestant churches, he asked whether there was an increase or decrease of elements likely to affiliate with a Protestant church. Obviously, if Catholics or Jews dominated a district, or were increasing in numbers, it would not be a favorable location for a Protestant church. The third question pertained to changes in the characteristic economic status. We assume that these were measured by rentals paid, assessed valuation of homes, occupations, automobiles, etc. The fourth issue had to do with desirability of residence, single dwellings being rated highest and converted tenements lowest, strictly residential areas being rated higher than those partially occupied by business and industry. Fifth was a question of mobility versus stability, measured by the number of rooming houses, changes in telephones and utility meters, movers' records, school transfers, and the like. The remaining questions had to do with dependency (persons on relief), juvenile delinquency (juvenile court cases), and health (infant mortality). In all these it was expected, subject to check, that districts of declining economic status, desirability of housing, or stability, and of increasing dependency, delinquency, and mortality would be unfavorable for the development of Protestant churches.

Next, each city or "sector" of a city being studied was divided into districts which corresponded to census tracts or groups of adjacent tracts. Each district was ranked on each of the eight points. The ranks were added and the sum was divided by eight, thus giving a combined rank indicating the direction of social change, or rather the relative nature of social change, during one decade, 1917–1919 to 1927–1929. Districts were then grouped into quartiles: the "best" fourth, the "better-than-average," the "below-average," and the "worst." It should be noted that this scheme, based on change, does not indicate the status of a district at any particular time. Thus a district that might be considered "good" may show little development or even deterioration during a decade; while a "poor" district may show considerable improvement and still remain on a low level.

So much for the social setting of the churches. Next the churches themselves were studied as to increase or decrease in membership, Sunday school enrollment, and total expenditure.

The differences between the figures of the earlier and the later date were stated as percentages of the earlier figures. On the basis of these percentages each church was ranked on each point, after which the churches were grouped into quintiles (fifths), instead of quartiles, and lettered from A (highest fifth) to E (lowest fifth). It was then possible to determine the proportion of churches of each class in each type of district. This was done separately with reference to membership, Sunday school, and expenditures, and with reference to all three combined. The results are shown in Tables 33, 34, and 35.

A study of this sort emphasizes the fact that churches, like all social institutions, do not exist in a vacuum but are involved in larger social situations. They vary with the whole social complex of the area in which they are located. When we come in Part III to fix our attention more intensively on selective and distributive aspects of the city, the significance of all this will be more evident.

TABLE 33.—PERCENTAGE OF CHURCHES IN EACH TYPE OF TERRITORY RANKING A, B, C, D, E[a]

Type of territory	A	B	C	D	E	Total
Best	41.0	23.0	16.4	10.4	9.2	100.0
Above average	25.0	23.0	20.7	18.3	13.0	100.0
Below average	14.0	18.6	21.4	22.0	24.0	100.0
Worst	10.0	14.0	19.6	24.0	32.4	100.0

[a] Ross W. Sanderson, *The Strategy of City Church Planning*, p. 88, 1932. By permission of Harper & Brothers, publishers.

TABLE 34.—PERCENTAGE OF A, B, C, D, E RANKINGS IN EACH TYPE OF TERRITORY[a]

Type of Territory	A	B	C	D	E
Better:					
Best	36.1	21.9	15.2	9.9	8.4
Above average	32.7	32.2	28.6	25.9	17.7
Poorer:					
Below average	19.3	28.1	31.7	33.7	34.7
Worst	11.9	17.8	24.5	30.5	39.2
Total	100.0	100.0	100.0	100.0	100.0

[a] Ross W. Sanderson, *The Strategy of City Church Planning*, p. 91, 1932. By permission of Harper & Brothers, publishers.

What Religion Means to City Dwellers

It would be very interesting and important to learn just what religion means to the mass of cityfolk, or to different kinds of cityfolk, and whether that meaning is substantially the same as its significance to country people. But unfortunately the data are not at hand to warrant much confidence in generalizations which might be made. It appears that the church is, more often in the city than in the country, a sort of prestige-giving club, an escape from the hard reality of everyday living, and a device for maintaining the *status quo*. But for the present these must remain hypotheses rather than settled conclusions.

Table 35.—Most Frequent Rankings on Each of Three Indices of Church Progress[a]
(All sixteen sectors)

Type of territory	Church membership	Sunday school enrollment	Total expenditures
Best	A	A	A
Above average	A	AB	ABCD
Below average	BCDE	DE	E
Worst	E	E	E

[a] Ross W. Sanderson, *The Strategy of City Church Planning*, p. 98, 1932. By permission of Harper & Brothers, publishers. Where more than one letter occurs the rankings indicated are of almost equal frequency.

In their restudy of Middletown in 1935[1] the Lynds found a great deal of doubt and questioning as to what is the function of organized religion. They believed that the depression had aggravated this situation acutely. They found the clergy "harried, overworked, perplexed," and relying heavily upon old theological terminology while avoiding controversial issues.

To such controversial issues as internationalism, disarmament, pacifism, labor organization, social planning in the interest of the masses and the re-distribution of wealth, civil liberty, the amendment of the Constitution, socialized medicine, and birth control, the great majority of the churches of Middletown present the negative face of the community, or are silent, or talk such generalities that their position is equivocal.[2]

[1] Robert S. Lynd and Helen M. Lynd, *Middletown in Transition*, 1937.
[2] *Ibid.*, p. 312. By permission of Harcourt, Brace & Company, Inc.

Certainly the city church differs from the church in the country by being more immediately confronted with culture conflicts and acute problems of social disorganization, though these are by no means absent from rural districts. It faces more competition from commercial recreation, civic organizations, and business for the time and loyalty of the populace. If it deals with issues of graft in politics, wage scales, social insurance, taxation, race relations, the R.O.T.C., and the C.I.O., it cannot escape bitter dissension. If it avoids these living problems of the world about it, little seems to be left for it except mysticism and a more or less comfortable respectability. However, we offer these statements not as established facts but as problems for investigation. Data will be elusive and inferences will be threatened by bias, but the most important work in this field remains to be done. Structure we are beginning to understand. As to function we have little but opinions and sentiments.

Selected Readings

DOUGLASS, H. PAUL, and EDMUND DE S. BRUNNER: *The Protestant Church as a Social Institution*, Harper & Brothers, 1935. A study made under the auspices of the Institute of Social and Religious Research, covering the development, activities, facilities, conditioning factors, and prospects of Protestant churches in American cities.

DOUGLASS, H. P.: *One Thousand City Churches*, Harper & Brothers, 1926. Presents an objective method of classifying Protestant city churches. With slight adaptations should be usable for Catholic and Jewish. A study made under the auspices of the Institute of Social and Religious Research.

SANDERSON, ROSS W.: *The Strategy of City Church Planning*, Harper & Brothers, 1932. A study made under the auspices of the Institute of Social and Religious Research, dealing with the relation between church growth or decline and changes in socioeconomic features of the immediate vicinity.

CHAPIN, F. STUART: *Contemporary American Institutions*, Harper & Brothers, 1935. Chapters 11 and 12 summarize methods of studying city churches.

SOROKIN, PITIRIM, and C. C. ZIMMERMAN: *Principles of Rural-Urban Sociology*, Henry Holt & Company, Inc., 1929. Chapter 18 deals with rural-urban contrasts in religious affiliations and beliefs.

LYND, ROBERT S., and HELEN M. LYND: *Middletown in Transition*, Harcourt, Brace & Company, Inc., 1937. Chapter 8 deals with religion in a small American city.

Chapter XI

POLITICAL INSTITUTIONS AND FOLKWAYS

The history, structure, functions, and problems of municipal government have been so long the objects of intensive study by political scientists that any discussion on our part must seem presumptuous. We shall not attempt a comprehensive or detailed analysis of the political aspects of city life. But municipal government is so involved in every phase of urbanism that we cannot avoid its consideration. Its first appearance was due to the necessities of life. Whenever large numbers of people began to live near together there had to be joint or centralized action to provide water, drainage, defense, markets, thoroughfares, and other communal necessities. Such action often had to be more prompt and more accurately adjusted to local conditions than it was likely to be if directed from a distant capital. Hence some degree of local autonomy was sought and secured by Roman provincial cities, medieval towns, and modern cities. The struggle for home rule is not over. But with improved means of transportation and communication the interests of cities are less narrowly localized. They are shared with whole regions, so that the problem of how best to divide authority and responsibility between local and central government is becoming more rather than less urgent.

The problems of municipal government have become complicated in still another way. With the development of great metropolitan areas we find a multiplicity of governmental units which overlap and interfere with one another. This situation represents one of the most striking culture lags in contemporary America. When the country was being settled, the area now occupied by any great city may have included many villages and incorporated towns and several counties. But as the central city expanded, it spread across township, municipal, county, and sometimes state lines. Some of these smaller units were annexed, but others remained politically independent, even though they were economically and socially one with the rest of the metropolitan area. When new needs arose, cutting across political boundaries, new governmental agencies of a special sort were created—drainage districts, park districts, port authorities, and the like. The result is a very complicated, confusing, and not very efficient administrative structure. Thus Greater New York includes parts of 3 states, 22 counties, 290 incorporated places, and a large number of school districts and special administrative units. A detailed study of local government in metropolitan Chicago[1] showed that this area possessed more than 1,600 separate units of administration and finance. Inside the city of Chicago alone were found 27 independent taxing bodies. Within Cook County there were over 400 separate local governments. In the metropolitan area as a whole were over 200 cities and villages, 15 counties, 165 townships, nearly 1,000 school districts, 70 park districts, 4 forest preserve districts, 11 sanitary districts, 190 drainage districts, 4 mosquito abatement districts. It is difficult to conceive of such an amount of separation, overlapping, and confusion. Some of these units, of course, were brought into existence before the population and area in question were absorbed into the metropolis. Others were set up for the performance of specific functions which overlapped the functions of several existing units. Some were created apparently because of distrust of existing governmental machinery, and it is suspected that others resulted from political jockeying. It is hard to see how order can be maintained in a metropolitan area which contains 350 different police forces, nearly as many public health agencies, and over 550 independent courts.

The Chicago situation is perhaps an extreme case, but the plurality of local governments in many, if not most, of our metropolitan districts has come about naturally through the expansion of our cities. However, with a few exceptions, it is a recent problem with which we are confronted. Before the nineteenth century only a few cities spread out over a large number of administrative areas. Even the satellite cities which grew up after the coming of the railways presented no serious problem of metropolitan government because they were usually

[1] Charles E. Merriam, S. D. Parratt, and A. Lepawsky, *The Government of the Metropolitan Region of Chicago*, 1933. The conclusions of this study are summarized on pp. xv–xx.

quite separate from the central city. But with the coming of the automobile the centrifugal flight has gone on at such a pace as to render the whole situation one of acute disorganization.

Before considering the efforts that have been made to overcome the culture lag in metropolitan government, we shall present brief accounts of the scope of city government, important steps in its development, and some current problems other than the one just outlined, which is the object of our chief concern in this chapter.

The Scope of Municipal Government in the United States[1]

City government has become not only an instrument of social control but also a form of big business. In 1900 our cities of over 30,000 population spent $500 million; in 1915 they spent $1 billion, and in 1930 they spent $3½ billion. In 1934, cities of more than 100,000 inhabitants spent $2½ billion. These figures include costs of operation and maintenance, outlays for permanent improvements, and interest on debts. Omitting outlays, the per capita cost of government in 146 cities rose from $16.40 in 1903 to nearly $60 in 1931. Including outlays, but correcting for the diminished purchasing power of the dollar, the costs of city government increased 35 per cent in the 15 years ending 1929. However, the rate of increase was less for municipal than for any other unit of government, local, state, or federal. Classifying cities according to size, we find that the per cent increase was highest in those of 50,000 to 100,000 and lowest in those of 300,000 to 500,000. What this means we are not sure, but perhaps cities approaching metropolitan dimensions find it necessary to add many new activities, while those which have "found themselves" and are not yet "overgrown" may require less supplementing of established services. In general the functions whose cost has expanded most are, in order, education, recreation, and health. Of course, since 1929 there has been a tremendous increase in the costs of relief and medical care. In 1934 the per capita expenditures for "charities, hospitals, and corrections" in cities over 100,000 were $9.20, compared with $3.15 in 1929. Roughly this means that munici-

[1] Fifteenth Census, *Financial Statistics of Cities; Encyclopaedia of the Social Sciences*, vol. 11, pp. 98–104; *Recent Social Trends*, vol. 2, pp. 1307–1315; *Statistical Abstract of the United States*, 1936, pp. 208–224.

pal expenditures for relief and social service were trebled in five years, despite the assumption of a major part of the relief burden by other units of government, county, state, and federal. One other measure of the growing expensiveness of city government is the increasing volume of debts. In 1903 the per capita net debt for all cities over 30,000 was about $45; in 1931 it had risen to $160. In 1934 in cities over 100,000 it was $170. We are not presenting these data for the purpose of adding to the hysteria about taxpayers' burdens, but simply to have the facts in hand. Presently we shall see that expanding functions, rather than bureaucratic waste, are largely responsible for increased expenditures.

Another measure of the extent to which municipal government has become a great business enterprise is the number of employees. Omitting teachers and others in the school systems, 746 cities in 1935 had 445,000 full-time employees. This means that 94 out of every 10,000 city dwellers were on municipal pay rolls. The larger the city the higher the ratio; in cities under 30,000 it was only 61, while in those over 500,000 it was 117.[1] In Minneapolis in 1930 the corresponding figure was 184. While no general reports are available, it appears that the numbers of municipal employees have been increasing both absolutely and relatively. Thus in New York City they grew from 30,000 (88 per 10,000) in 1900 to 86,000 (124 per 10,000) in 1930. This may be due in part to politicians' success in getting their supporters on the public pay roll, but it represents even more the expansion of services to the inhabitants of our cities.

The functions performed by city governments may be grouped into 10 or 12 categories. Table 36 presents a common classification and the percentage of municipal expenditures allotted to each in 1930. The many services included under these heads have made their appearance gradually over a long period of time. This development can be well illustrated by the case of Detroit.[2] In 1830, when Detroit was a town of 2,000 inhabitants, its government was carrying on 23 distinct activities. These included legislation, assessment and collection of revenues,

[1] *Municipal Year Book*, 1936, p. 192. These and other data in this chapter used by permission of the International City Managers' Association.

[2] Lent D. Upson, *The Growth of a City Government*, Detroit Bureau of Governmental Research, 1931.

enforcement of ordinances, maintenance and operation of public buildings, and fire prevention. By 1870 a population of 80,000 was served through 59 governmental activities. Some of the new functions provided for the construction of sidewalks and street pavements, sewage disposal, water supply, street lighting, elementary and high schools, a general library, an organized police patrol, and fire fighting. In 1900 the population was 285,000 and municipal activities numbered 132. Some of the additions were parks, art exhibits, evening classes, food and milk inspection, a general hospital, a system of quarantine, poor relief, garbage collection, and band concerts. By 1930 the population had increased to 1,575,000 and the activities to 306. A few of the twentieth-century developments were playgrounds, community centers, clinics, public health nurses, a probation system, women police, an employment bureau, water filtration, mosquito control, bus transportation, an airport, a lodging house, and zoning. These and many other municipal services represent an enormous expansion of governmental functions, not only in Detroit, but in all American cities. Whether they have developed organization and personnel adequate for carrying on such varied, important, and expensive activities will be considered later.

TABLE 36.—PERCENTAGE DISTRIBUTION OF MUNICIPAL EXPENDITURES, UNITED STATES, 1930[a]

Function	Per Cent
General government—administrative, legislative, and judicial	8.6
Protection—fire, police, etc	19.6
Health	2.5
Sanitation	7.2
Highways	8.4
Charities, hospital, correction	7.0
Education	36.6
Libraries	1.4
Recreation	3.6
Miscellaneous	5.1

[a] Fifteenth Census, *Financial Statistics of Cities*, p. 410.

THE DEVELOPMENT OF MUNICIPAL GOVERNMENT

In the preceding section we pointed out that the functions now performed by municipal government in the United States have accumulated over a considerable period of time. In this section we shall show that the very nature of municipal government has undergone change. The earliest cities, those of Egypt and Mesopotamia, were not municipalities in our sense of the word. They were urban centers ruled by kings and emperors either directly or through personal representatives. Self-government was almost wholly absent. The Greek city-states were autonomous, but they combined—from our standpoint—national with municipal functions. But under the Roman law provincial cities came to be treated as corporations with certain privileges and obligations. No doubt a major purpose behind their creation was to fix the responsibility of their inhabitants to the central government. At all events, these municipia were authorized by the state to regulate their own affairs within specified limits. They were "legal persons," who could acquire and dispose of property, administer their own business, and be held responsible for meeting their obligations. This was a new idea; it became the legal basis of municipal government in the Western world.

In the late Empire, municipalities were reduced to little more than administrative districts governed by imperial officials appointed from Rome. With the collapse of Roman power in the fifth century, municipal government declined still further. As we noted in Chap. II, the few towns that remained were neither units of a central power nor self-governing; they were often little more than the headquarters of some feudal lord, lay or ecclesiastical. However, with the revival of commerce came a struggle for local autonomy, which had varying degrees of success but made considerable headway in northern Italy, along the coasts of the Baltic and North seas, in France, and in England. Charters were won by force from feudal nobles, purchased from kings, or otherwise acquired. In England most of them were obtained from the king by free grant or purchase. Under these charters the cities were permitted to collect their own taxes and spend their revenues, though they were required to make periodical payments in money or services. There was great lack of uniformity, but all possessed some local legislative power, limited in the main to "the preservation of their ancient customs," the maintenance of their commercial privileges, and the administration of their property. It is also important to remember that the governing bodies in these English boroughs were "small, inefficient, self-continuing and self-serving bodies."[1] The Municipal Corporations Act of 1835 and that of 1882 undertook to establish uniformity in charters and responsible local governments based on popular suffrage.

The English colonists in America of course brought their old customs and institutions with them. So in New England and New York, town governments were set up under charters granted by the royal governors. These towns were at once subordinate agencies of the colonial administration and relatively independent local units. After the Revolution the state legislatures took over the granting of charters, which came to display not only a wide variety but considerable arbitrariness as well. In the southern and middle colonies there were already established counties and townships, subordinate agents of the state. The creation of municipalities brought no little confusion. As a result of the chaos many states sought by constitutional amendments and general statutes to make municipal charters uniform and somewhat in harmony with laws regulating coexisting local units, *i.e.*, counties, townships, etc. These efforts seem to have been partly successful, but through the device of classifying cities, legislatures were still able to regulate the affairs of individual cities rather arbitrarily.

As a reaction to the interference of rural-minded legislatures in the details of city government, a home rule movement developed. In 1875 the Missouri constitution provided that the voters of a city might elect freeholders to draft their own charter. When such a charter was ratified by popular vote it became the controlling instrument of government in all matters of strictly local concern, provided, of course, that it was consistent with the constitution and general laws of the state. Fifteen other states adopted similar provisions, but the issue remained far from solution. It is not easy to determine what matters are strictly local in significance. New inventions and new organizations, especially in the field of business, necessitate new regulations. It is natural that there should be some competition between state and municipality for exercise of the new powers.

During the nineteenth century most American cities developed rather complicated schemes of government, which were small-

[1] *Encyclopaedia of the Social Sciences*, vol. 11, p. 88. By permission of The Macmillan Company.

scale imitations of the federal system. The voters elected a mayor, a bicameral council, and various other officials. Committees of the council had charge of the administration of various departments. Later special boards, either elected or appointed by the mayor, undertook the management of public works, schools, police, parks, and the like. Inefficiency and waste were notorious. City officials were elected on the basis of their place in state and national party organizations. Franchises were practically given away. Debts mounted. Intermittently there were reform movements to "throw the rascals out." Usually they failed to win an election. If the "good government" party did elect its candidates, they were hampered by the systems of checks and balances, they sometimes proved inexperienced, "good" citizens often failed to stand by them—and at the next election the "gang" came back into power. It appeared that there was need of something more fundamental than putting "good" men into office.

There was more talk of home rule, of separating local elections from state politics, of simplifying city government, and of introducing business methods. But it was a catastrophe that furnished the occasion for initiating a new type of municipal government. In 1900 the city of Galveston was partially destroyed by a hurricane. In the confusion that followed the old type of administration proved utterly incompetent to meet the urgent needs of the people. So a new form, called the commission plan, was invented. A commission of five men, elected at large, was given all executive and legislative powers. It had authority to adopt ordinances, levy taxes, vote appropriations, and make all appointments. Each individual commissioner took charge of a division, or of a group of related divisions, of the municipal activities. The idea spread rapidly, and by 1914 several hundred cities had adopted the scheme. Then the movement slowed down, and one after another cities gave up the commission form of government. It had concentrated responsibility, introduced business methods, and drawn able and honest men into public office. But it lacked administrative unity. A commission of five was too small as a legislative body and too large as an executive authority. Dissensions often arose among the members and the city's business was delayed.

Still another type of municipal government—the city manager, or council-manager, plan—made its appearance in Staunton, Virginia, in 1908, in Dayton, Ohio, in 1914, and during the next 20 years in 435 other cities, large and small. Under this scheme an elected council chooses a single administrative officer, called the city manager, presumably without reference to political affiliation or local residence. He in turn appoints department heads and, sometimes with a civil service commission, subordinate employees. He plans and directs the operations of the city government, supervises the personnel, prepares the budget, and recommends policies and programs to the council, which also enacts ordinances, makes appropriations, chooses and discharges the manager. The mayor is the presiding officer of the council, the ceremonial head of the city, and sometimes political leader. Managers are more and more being trained specifically for this position; they often go from small to large cities. Thus they are becoming a group of professional city administrators. However, this form of government has not solved all problems. Much depends on the competence of the individual manager and on the alertness of the citizenry. Cincinnati, with an organized body of citizens determined to maintain good government and with an exceptionally able manager, has a noteworthy record. Kansas City, in the grip of a notorious political machine, has given a much poorer account of itself under the council-manager form of government.

The present state of affairs in the forms of municipal government is indicated in a report of 959 American cities for 1935.[1] Five hundred and forty-six cities continued with the old-fashioned mayor and council; 186 were governed by commissions, 190 had city managers, and 37 conducted their business in town meeting. The fact that over half of the cities reporting clung to the outworn forms suggests ignorance, indifference, or lack of constitutional means for adapting municipal government to present-day needs.

In the preceding section we noted the growth of the functions of city government. But we did not emphasize the fact that more and more cities have undertaken the ownership and operation of public utilities. Of 930 cities over 10,000 population

[1] *Municipal Year Book*, 1936, p. 166.

which reported in 1936, 70 per cent reported owning waterworks, 28 per cent airports, 14 per cent electric light plants, and 12 per cent markets. Smaller numbers reported municipal gas plants, street railways, and abattoirs. Only 20 per cent reported owning no utilities at all.[1]

Thus both the structure and the functions of municipal government have developed gradually over long periods of time. They have undergone some profound changes, and it is likely that they will continue to change. Already new developments are appearing in metropolitan areas, but of those we shall have more to say a little later.

Some Current Problems

It may be assumed that the modifications in city government which we have just reviewed did not arise out of vague desires to perfect a reasonably effective mechanism. On the contrary, it is obvious that some innovations, perhaps most, were deliberate efforts to solve urgent problems.

One of the perennial problems of city government is its expensiveness. Citizens demand more and more services from their municipality, but at the same time they complain about high taxes. In part because of this unwillingness to pay for desired improvements and additions, cities have accumulated a very great bonded indebtedness. So long as cities were growing rapidly in population and wealth, this did not seem serious. But when rates of growth began to slow down, when the expanding areas of blight reduced assessed valuations, when a prolonged depression further reduced the value of taxable property and the ability of owners to pay their taxes, there was real trouble. To maintain their credit, cities often curtailed important services in order to pay interest on the debt. They made short-time loans in anticipation of tax receipts. At the same time the relief burden was mounting to undreamed-of figures. In some cases the situation approximated that of bankruptcy. Creditors dictated terms. The municipality appealed for state and federal aid. The problem is one not merely of poor business practice but of popular attitudes. The citizens want services for which they are unwilling to pay; they mortgage their city's future; and

[1] *Ibid.*, pp. 169–170.

often they turn the management over to persons who are incompetent, dishonest, or both.

A second problem involves the issue of state control versus home rule. As we have seen, most city charters have been granted by legislatures, though there is a trend away from this practice. In some states, notably Massachusetts and Missouri, metropolitan police commissions are appointed by the governor. Legislative districts are so arranged as frequently to discriminate against large cities.[1] Candidates for municipal office often run on party tickets which confuse local issues with those of state and nation. Running through all this is a rural-urban antagonism which makes it difficult to secure rational consideration of the problem.

Another difficulty lies in the complexity of local government. We have noted the growing number and variety of activities. In most cities there are many separately elected officials whose relative independence makes unified administration almost impossible. Even the commission form of government has not brought about complete integration. Often the voter is called upon to choose from dozens or even hundreds of candidates on a long ballot. He cannot possibly know much about them, and after they are elected he has difficulty in fixing responsibility upon them. As a result he often despairs of making democratic processes effective, develops a low regard for officeholders generally, or becomes quite indifferent. Frequently his apathy is so great that he does not even go to the polls. In the 1934 elections in 760 cities only 42 per cent of the population over 21 years of age exercised the privilege of voting.[2] Another aspect of the same situation is the difficulty of finding competent persons to run for municipal office. Even if such a candidate appears, it is hard to arouse the "good" citizens to support him; and if he is elected, it is hard amid the complexities of municipal government and the opposition of groups with vested interests for him to give the city an effective administration. Behind the apathetic and fatalistic attitudes so often displayed toward urban politics and government we seem to see three factors: our preoccupation with money-making, our heterogeneous population, and our lack of a tradition of good government.

[1] *Recent Social Trends*, vol. 2, p. 1493.

[2] *Municipal Year Book*, 1936, p. 169.

By the time Lincoln Steffens wrote *The Shame of the Cities* in 1904 American municipal government was commonly identified with the spoils system and machine politics. The spoils system manifests itself in the selection of city employees, the adoption of ordinances, and the administration of various departments. It is natural for the leaders of political parties to reward friends and supporters by appointment to positions of various sorts. Such rewards to those who voted "right" and otherwise supported a party or faction help to keep a given group in power. Other opportunities come when a city council is confronted with a request for a franchise, for zoning, or for an appropriation. By voting one way rather than another, members of the council may further strengthen the party in power and handicap their opponents. In return for legislative advantages, aldermen receive cash bribes, business credits, fees as attorneys, and other advantages. The municipal courts play their part in the spoils system, especially through the "fixing" of traffic tickets and other cases involving the violation of municipal ordinances. But the most lucrative opportunities are found in administrative offices. Cities have many loosely drawn laws, and even some carefully drawn ones, which have to be interpreted in the course of their enforcement. Such interpretation may promote equity or may be a means of rewarding friends and punishing foes. Thus a building code may be utilized to stimulate the business of a friendly contractor or to ruin that of a man who is "uncooperative." Likewise the levying of assessments affords great opportunities for punishment, reward, and personal profit. Other systems of revenue and support are found in purchases and contracts for institutional supplies, buildings, pavements, sewers, and the like. Sometimes there is no call for bids at all. Sometimes bidding is "arranged" beforehand. Sometimes specifications are so drawn as to eliminate certain competitors. At other times rigid stipulations are published but there is a private understanding with an unscrupulous low bidder that he will not have to conform to them in fact. Still another area in which the spoils system operates involves relations between the city government and the underworld. Prostitutes, bootleggers, gamblers, pickpockets, pawnbrokers who handle stolen goods, drug peddlers, and others have been known to make deals with police departments whereby they offer political support and financial compensation in return for "protection."

Behind the spoils system is usually found not only a formal city government but also what we might call an informal or hidden government. There may be one powerful individual, sometimes called "the boss." Usually there is a strong organization which is designated "the machine." The revelations of Lincoln Steffens 35 years ago showed how generally the elected city officials were little more than "front" for men behind the scenes who really wielded the authority. There has been no general study of such situations in American cities recently, but every newspaper reader knows about Mayor Hague in Jersey City and Tom Pendergast in Kansas City. The extent to which bosses and their machines may go in the effort to gain and keep control of a city is suggested in the statement of a federal judge made at the time he sentenced four persons for participation in election frauds.

There is a reign of terror in Kansas City, Judge Reeves said before passing sentences on the forty-seventh, forty-eighth, forty-ninth, and fiftieth persons to be convicted in the 1936 election scandals.

A score of business men have mentioned to me that in Kansas City they do not dare take an attitude against conditions. They tell me there are secret influences that will militate against their business. They say there is a system of espionage and they dare not vote their sentiments.

The espionage of Kansas City is such if it were known they voted "wrong" there would be a secret boycott against their businesses, their tax assessments would be raised and their businesses would be driven out of the city.

This is not Red Russia, yet there is espionage there. In Fascist Italy there is an espionage system; likewise in Nazi Germany. Who is it that carries on such a reign of terror? Is it possible a reign of terror exists here that causes judges and clerks of election to certify false returns, that drives a business man to do what he does not desire to do and renders him quiescent, daring not to speak.

Judges are subjected to a reign of terrorism. We are threatened almost daily and are victims of outrageous abuse and profanity. How long will this reign of terror continue in Kansas City, that forces business men to go on like mummies? How long? This terror that drives business men to secrecy and seals their lips. These floods and tides of abuse that sweep into the judges' homes.

It seems to me the time has come for business men and citizens to stand up against this reign of terrorism, to stand against these things that have brought shame to our city. Difficulty is experienced in putting a finger on these secret influences. Yet persons come whining, whimpering and wheedling to the judges and say these poor puppets of theirs violated the instructions of the masters. How grossly unfair this is: One of the defendants was quoted as saying he had his orders from "higher up." Who gave these orders? Who is responsible?[1]

Limitations of time and space forbid our discussion of the many interesting devices employed by political machines in the exercising of their power. We must, however, guard against the notions that political corruption is peculiar to our cities, that it is altogether different from what happens in business, and that it has recently appeared on the scene. Lincoln Steffens found that the graft and incompetence he uncovered 35 years ago had been long in existence. He arrived at the conclusion that the morals of politicians are not worse than those of businessmen, and he might have added that municipal government in great cities was perhaps no worse than county government in rural areas. As a matter of fact, it is impossible, even now, to say definitely that the practices of city officials and employees are more to be condemned than those of many people of the business world, that municipal government is less effective and less honest than that of our rural sections.

Metropolitan Government

Earlier in this chapter we indicated that one of the greatest problems in the field of city government involves the coexistence and overlapping of many different units of government in every metropolitan area. We showed that this confusing and expensive structure is related to the expansion of great cities, their economic and social absorption of suburbs and satellities, and the creation of special authorities to meet new needs. We might also have mentioned the vested interests of officeholders, the inertia of voters, and the struggles of property owners to secure or preserve advantageous tax rates. In some suburbs there is great wealth coupled with small expenditures for government; there taxes are low. In others, poverty coexists with many needs calling for

[1] *St. Louis Post Dispatch*, February 2, 1938.

public action; there taxes are high. In the central city are found both wealth and poverty; usually taxes are high. Because local government is supported primarily through the general property tax, and because needs and ability to pay are very unevenly distributed over a metropolitan area, there is an acute problem of public finance. This seems clearly to call for some measure of unification.

There are many other matters which apparently can be dealt with only through some kind of centralization. There are the planning of major thoroughfares, the creation of building zones, the provision of drainage, and the control of smoke, to mention only a few items involved in metropolitan planning. The provision of such necessities as water, sewage disposal, gas, electricity, and telephone has to be made on an inclusive basis rather than in terms of separate governmental areas. Perhaps the whole thing can be more easily visualized in terms of police and fire protection, public health services, and other provisions for the public safety. Obviously, lawbreakers can operate more easily when their enemies, the police, are divided and restricted to various limited territories. As to fire protection, the story is told of a house on the line between two urban municipalities which burned to the ground while the two fire departments argued whose responsibility it was. Finally, communicable diseases can scarcely be expected to respect political boundaries. Their control must be in the hands of officials who are free to operate over an entire metropolitan area. These are only some of the more prominent issues involved in the evident need for some sort of coordination or unification.

Several methods have been devised for attacking these problems and developing a measure of metropolitan government. One of the most widely used is annexation. From time to time our cities have taken in large parts of the surrounding territories, but most annexations are of very small districts. McKenzie has found the trend to be toward more frequent annexation but of smaller parcels of land.[1] A second, but less generally used, plan is that of city-county separation or consolidation. Obviously the separation of a city from the county which might include it simplifies matters, although it does not bring about unification. It ordinarily involves the consolidation of municipal and county

[1] R. D. McKenzie, *The Metropolitan Community*, p. 196, 1933.

functions within the city limits, and the restriction of county government to what is left of the former county. This device was first employed in Baltimore in 1851. It has also been used in San Francisco, St. Louis, and Denver. Unification of city and county governments involves making the boundaries of the municipality and the county coterminous and combining the governments of the two. This was first accomplished in Philadelphia in 1854 and subsequently in New Orleans and Brooklyn. In a few instances, notably in New York City and Boston, some of the functions of city and county have been combined without a complete merger of legal or territorial identities. When city and county remain separate, some advantages have been gained through the expansion of county government to meet some of the metropolitan needs. Thus under a home rule charter Los Angeles County since 1930 has developed many of the features of a municipal government and has been enabled to serve its inhabitants to much greater advantage than it could under the usual form of county government. It assesses and collects taxes for the city of Los Angeles as well as the county, carries on regional planning, attends to sanitation, flood control, fire and police protection, health services, poor relief, street improvements, and maintains a county library and art institute. However, the relation between the county and city governments still presents some problems. The two have not been thoroughly coordinated or integrated. Similar expansions of county government have developed in Cook County (Chicago), Wayne County (Detroit), Cuyahoga County (Cleveland), and Multnomah County (Portland).

Some metropolitan problems have been attacked through intermunicipal agreements. Thus the Brooklyn Bridge was a joint undertaking between the then separate municipalities of New York and Brooklyn. The cities of Newark, Elizabeth, and the Oranges developed a joint sewer system. Detroit and Highland Park jointly established bus routes. However, the instances of such joint undertakings are few, perhaps because municipalities do not have sufficient faith in each other. Another type of intermunicipal arrangement is that in which one city furnishes services to its neighbors. Thus Baltimore, Detroit, Denver, and Seattle furnish water to neighboring municipalities. St. Louis provides high school education for Negroes, and hospitalization for mental patients, from suburban communities. The efforts of a city to control its water and milk supply may incidentally prove useful to other municipalities in the same metropolitan area.

In discussing the Chicago situation we spoke of numerous special districts set up for the performance of particular functions, which overlap several or many governmental units in a metropolitan area. Sometimes these districts are created by the state governments and function as its divisions. Sometimes they are agents of the municipalities and thus represent a limited degree of federation. Sometimes they are quite distinct local governments operating independently of others in the area. As long ago as 1850 there were ten special authorities in the Philadelphia district. In Greater New York the first one was created in 1857. From then on they have become increasingly numerous in many of our metropolitan centers. Their functions include the provision of a water supply, sewage disposal, local transportation, bridges, tunnels, parks, seaports, and health services. Perhaps these special districts represent about as near an approach to metropolitan government as we have in the United States, but there have been proposals looking toward much more completely federated government. Boston in 1896, Oakland in 1922, Pittsburgh in 1928, and Cleveland in 1929 were some of the battlegrounds on which this issue has been fought. The schemes have varied, but all had in mind a far-reaching measure of unification. Some of them propose making the county a central government for the metropolitan area. Some would preserve the existing municipality divisions much as they are, while others would abolish them in favor of new and larger subdivisions. In some plans the central metropolitan government is to be one of specific delegated powers, leaving all other powers to the separate localities. In other plans the exact reverse of this is proposed. We are in no position to pass on the relative merits of these, but have no hesitation in insisting upon the importance of a coordinated and a unified system of government for every metropolitan district.

Summary

We have traced in rough outline the rise of municipal government in response to the increasing number of specialized problems in urban centers. The people of cities wanted to manage some of their own affairs, and central governments often found it convenient to deal with cities as corporations. On the other hand, some state and national governments have been loath to give up direct control of municipal affairs. In America this tendency has been accentuated by rural-urban antagonisms and by party politics. On the whole, the trend has been in the direction of home rule.

The management of cities has become a matter of big business requiring more and more business methods of the best type. Yet most municipalities in the United States cling to outworn forms of government, quite unsuited to the performance of many functions for large populations. Municipal government has become very complex and expensive. With voters indifferent and spoilsmen alert, political machines have often dominated our cities. Efforts to promote the short ballot, proportional representation, nonpartisan elections, the council-manager form of government, civil service, and the like have made headway in many places but have been unsuccessful in others.

A major problem in political structure is how to coordinate or unify the agencies and activities of the many governmental units in some of our metropolitan areas. Annexation, consolidation, special districts, federation—all have advantages and disadvantages. Resistance comes from politicians who fear loss of patronage, suburbanites who fear rising taxes, and all who hesitate to risk change.

Selected Readings

Studenski, P.: *Government of Metropolitan Areas in the United States*, National Municipal League, 1930. Presents the need for integration of governmental machinery in metropolitan areas and attempts that have been made.

Merriam, Charles E., S. D. Parratt, and A. Lepawsky: *The Government of the Metropolitan Region of Chicago*, University of Chicago Press, 1933. Displays the chaotic condition of local government in metropolitan Chicago.

McKenzie, R. D.: *The Metropolitan Community*, McGraw-Hill Book Company, Inc., 1933. Chapter 22 deals briefly with the problems of metropolitan government.

Encyclopaedia of the Social Sciences: See articles on "Municipal Government," "Municipal Corporation," "Municipal Finance," "Home

Rule," "Civil Service," "Political Machines," "Political Corruption," "City Manager," "County-City Consolidation."

WOOLSTON, HOWARD B.: *Metropolis: A Study of Urban Communities*, D. Appleton-Century Company, Inc., 1938. Chapters 7–10 deal with some of the issues of municipal government.

STEFFENS, LINCOLN: *The Autobiography of Lincoln Steffens*, Harcourt, Brace & Company, Inc., 1931. Reveals the inside story of American city politics in the last generation.

CHAPTER XII

SOCIAL WORK AND PUBLIC HEALTH IN AMERICAN CITIES

Like organized recreation, which was discussed in Chap. X, professional social work is distinctively an urban phenomenon, and for similar reasons. The same congestion, heterogeneity, anonymity, and mobility which have rendered simple sports and sociability difficult in the city have also made it hard for old-fashioned neighborliness and mutual aid to function. But again it is possible that we may exaggerate the rural-urban difference; hence a word of caution is in order.

In colonial days families and individuals in need of food, shelter, nursing, guidance, or other goods or services received them most often from kinsmen or neighbors. But even in those days there were persons without friends or relatives near by, whose misfortune the town or church was called upon to relieve. Orphaned and illegitimate children, forsaken old folks, blind, deaf, crippled, insane, and feeble-minded persons were occasionally provided for by local government or, less often, by a religious order. But by and large the numbers not cared for by kinsmen were small; the costs were not great, and attention to them was an incidental responsibility of men busy with other affairs.[1] Specialization and professionalization were to come much later, and primarily in cities.

As towns developed into cities, spontaneous neighboring and mutual aid declined, relatively if not absolutely. There were too many people; they were too diverse in language and custom; they lived physically near but socially distant; they moved about

[1] Those interested in studying American social work in its pre-urban stage will find a number of monographs at their disposal, *e.g.*, Robert W. Kelso, *The History of Public Poor Relief in Massachusetts*, 1620–1920, 1922; Roy M. Brown, *Public Poor Relief in North Carolina*, 1928; Isabel C. Bruce and Edith Eickhoff, *The Michigan Poor Law*, 1936. They will also find valuable data in a collection of documents by Sophonisba P. Breckinridge, *Public Welfare Administration in the United States: Select Documents*, 1927.

too much. Primary social relations gave way to secondary. Hence when a person lost his job, fell ill, had an accident, or suffered other misfortune, he was likely to be stranded in the midst of strangers. Even if not socially isolated, he was often among friends who were little better off than himself and unable to render much assistance. At the other end of the economic ladder were nice ladies with leisure and gentlemen with money. They were shocked by mass poverty and unassimilated foreigners and were intrigued by the idea of doing something about it. What that something should be was not always clear. Certainly there was little notion of social and economic reorganization. But with a mixture of sympathy, fear, and self-importance the middle and upper classes undertook many sorts of philanthropic ventures.

Thus as cities grew there appeared increasing numbers of organizations designed to meet a great variety of human needs. Some provided food and shelter for the homeless; some gathered in street waifs; some taught English to foreigners, thrift to the impoverished, and religious doctrines to the wayward. Most of these agencies were established in slum districts near the centers of large cities. They were sponsored mainly by middle- and upper-class folk who lived in outlying residential sections. As the numbers of these organizations grew, problems of coordination appeared. Also, with mounting costs of charity and never-ending lines of applicants, interest turned somewhat toward the prevention of poverty, disease, and crime. In the twentieth century the movement took a definite professional turn. Gradually the activities we call social work were diffused into small towns and rural districts. But even yet professional work is predominantly urban both in character and in distribution.

Urban Concentration of Social Work

It is not easy to devise an exact measure of the relative urbanization of social work, but we have several series of data which may be made the basis of approximations. First of all, we find that the members of the American Association of Social Workers are located for the most part in large cities. In checking the directory of members for 1936 we counted 4,043 members in cities of over 500,000, and 2,932 in cities of 100,000 to 500,000. Since the total membership at that time was 9,552, this means that two-thirds of all professional social workers in the United States were in cities of 100,000 or over. While we believe this estimate to be approximately correct, there are some qualifications to be entered. Some of the persons whose addresses were in a large city merely made that city a headquarters for service rendered over a larger, and sometimes rural, area; such were traveling representatives of the American Red Cross and of state departments of public welfare. On the other hand, many social workers employed in large cities made their homes in small suburbs. Sometimes the business address was given and sometimes the home address. Still more important is the fact that many persons in similar activities, often employed by similar agencies, were not members of the professional organization at all. Many of these nonmembers were in the relief departments of rural counties. On the other hand, great numbers of nonmembers were similarly engaged in large cities. Hence we hold the distribution of members of the American Association of Social Workers to be one useful index of the urbanization of professional social work.

Another approach to the problem is through a study of the distribution of agencies of given types. We have chosen the member agencies of the Family Welfare Association of America and of the National Federation of Settlements. The former include private organizations and public departments which offer relief and service to family groups rather than to individuals and which meet certain requirements as to personnel and procedure. Social settlements are private agencies with nonsectarian programs of group work and other services for disadvantaged areas. There are many social centers which do not belong to the federation, just as there are many agencies dealing with families which do not belong to the national association in their field. Leaving more detailed description of both types till a little later, we are concerned here simply with the distribution of member agencies. In the 1936 directory we find 255 societies and departments members of the Family Welfare Association of America. Their classification is rendered difficult because for each agency there is stated the "population served," which in some cases occupies a fairly extensive area and in others represents only a part of a metropolitan district. However, on the basis indicated we find 40 agencies each serving a population of

500,000 or more, 98 serving populations of 100,000 to 500,000, 93 dealing with populations of 25,000 to 100,000, and only 24 concerned with populations of less than 25,000.[1] As might be anticipated, there are many more nonmember agencies, such as county relief offices and private charities, both in cities and in towns. If they were counted, the number and percentage of small-town and rural agencies would be greatly increased. Their omission is based either on their failure to measure up to standards set by the national association or on their lack of desire for affiliation. Turning to the National Federation of Settlements, we find in the 1936 membership list 95 settlements in cities of 500,000 or over, 40 in cities of 100,000 to 500,000, and only 15 in places of less than 100,000. The addition of social centers not members of the federation would probably increase the percentage in smaller cities, but would still show very few in rural America.

One other index of the urbanization of organized social service lies in the distribution of community chests. These are "overhead" devices for the joint financing of private social agencies. From the 1935 *Directory of Community Chests and Councils* we find that 138, one-third of the total, represented populations of less than 25,000 each; 110, a little less than one-third, "served" populations of 25,000 to 50,000; while 160, something over one-third, dealt with populations of 50,000 and over. This index is less significant than the others because ordinarily there is room for only one "chest" in a given urban area. However, some importance may be attached to the fact that of 93 cities having in 1930 a population of more than 100,000 there were only 9 in 1935 not reported as having a community chest or joint financing of a major group of social agencies. Moreover, 7 of the 9 were parts of a more inclusive metropolitan district in whose central city there was some measure of joint financing.[2]

Similar studies might be made of other types of social agencies and of other professional groups in the field; *e.g.*, member agencies of the Child Welfare League of America, individual members of the National Conference of Social Work, National Probation

[1] *Inter-agency Service of the Family Welfare Association of America* (1936).

[2] It is only fair to observe that joint financing in New York, Chicago, and some other cities pertained only to a minority of social work organizations in 1935.

Association, and American Association of Medical Social Workers. Although we have not analyzed them thoroughly, we are sure that they will all provide definite evidence of the urban concentration of social work.

Relief and Family Service

It would be interesting, if time permitted, to review the entire history of relief and family service to see what relation, if any, they have borne to the growth of cities. But that would be far beyond the scope of this work. We shall be content with reminding the reader that Christian charity may be said to have begun with the appointment of deacons in the Jerusalem church to care for widows and orphans in that large bilingual group. Jewish charity has a genuine rural background, but its organization took definite shape in the ghettos of medieval cities. Public relief began in the cities of northwestern Europe, becoming rather general in the fifteenth and sixteenth centuries. The idea of governmental responsibility for the needy was brought over from England by the colonists from that country, and poor laws were in operation long before the American Revolution. But life was hard in the colonies; there was no margin to warrant the toleration of loafers or any number of dependents of any sort. Hence both the laws and their administration were intended to discourage possible applicants for relief.

So long as the United States was predominantly a rural, agricultural nation the chief support of needy children, the aged, and other unfortunates appears to have come from relatives and neighbors. It was only the exceptional cases that became public burdens. But as cities grew, spontaneous neighborliness and mutual aid became less and less adequate. The mobility and anonymity of city life meant that masses of people did not know one another or sympathize with one another's need. Moreover, there were increasingly crowded together in slum areas great numbers of folk who had not the means to assist even when they knew and cared. Hence there developed formal machinery to make some provision for the most needy. In part this was an introduction of ecclesiastical charities, especially through the Roman Catholic Church. Especially after the Civil War and with the rise of the middle class it very often took the form of private, nonsectarian philanthropy. A host of petty, ill-managed organizations arose, whose functions appear to have been to occupy the leisure time of well-to-do folk and to save their souls even more than to feed, clothe, nurse, or discipline the "lower" classes.

Even before the Civil War there appeared a few larger organizations called Provident Association or Association for Improving the Condition of the Poor. These societies depended on volunteer visitors but insisted on investigation; they urged temperance and thrift; they sought the cooperation of other charitable organizations. But their success was limited. They neither rescued their clients from poverty nor won the affiliation of their fellow philanthropists. When the depression of 1873 came on, private charity was described as having "sunk into the sea of common almsgiving"; it was "profuse and chaotic, while still behind the demands made upon it, and was dispersed in tantalizing doles miserably inadequate for effectual succor where the need was genuine, and dealt out broadcast among the clamorous and impudent."[1]

It was during the depression of 1873 that the charity organization movement was brought over from London, where it had arisen in response to a similar situation. By 1880 there were 14 societies of this type. Their basic policies were (*a*) "mediating" between the "client" and possible sources of relief rather than giving directly, (*b*) abolition of public "outdoor" (home) relief on the ground of its hopeless immersion in partisan politics, (*c*) coordination of the work of other agencies, (*d*) central registration of persons helped, (*e*) "friendly visiting" among the poor, (*f*) district conferences to serve "as a popular school for teaching charity," (*g*) "provident schemes," (*h*) the repression of street begging, (*i*) housing reform. Later came intercity cooperation and a transportation agreement to eliminate "passing the buck." All this represented a rather ambitious program, although there were some who charged that it failed to get at the root of poverty. But it may be that the most important contribution of the charity organization movement was its development of a philosophy and a set of skills that have come to be called social case work. Gradually a professional literature came into being; formal training courses were established; and in 1904 the first professional school of social work was launched in New York.

[1] *Nat. Conf. Char. & Cor.*, 1893, p. 53.

Since the turn of the century the charity organization movement in American cities has become a family welfare movement. In this transition material relief has paradoxically become both less and more important. What we mean is this: Instead of concentrating on the physical needs of families in distress, agencies in this field have concerned themselves with the family as a social group, its unity and adaptability. They have used relief as a "tool in treatment," more or less incidental and subsidiary to other services, especially counseling. They have given particular attention to relations between husband and wife, parents and children, to family pride, loyalty, and "we-feeling" as against individualization, tension, and open conflict. On the other hand, during this same period these agencies have given up the policy of merely "mediating" and have given increasing amounts of direct relief. This trend was marked throughout the twenties and reached its climax in the early years of the depression. Originally an affair of private charity, the family welfare movement has come to include public departments that have adopted the principles under discussion and have employed a professionally trained personnel. The notion that public relief must be abolished has given way to cooperation between public and private agencies in the field. It is generally agreed that large-scale relief must be the responsibility of some governmental unit or units; it is less generally accepted that personal service of the sort called case work should accompany much relief; but it is not at all clear just what functions belong distinctively to private family welfare societies. Those variously urged include: supplementation of the relief and service of public agencies, development of new services and methods, public education.

Two episodes of the last quarter century involve rapid and extensive diffusion of family welfare work into rural areas. The first took place during the World War, when the American Red Cross organized chapters in many small towns and rural counties to aid in family adjustments necessitated by the sudden removal of many men to the army and navy. The sheer number of persons to be aided made it unlikely that spontaneous neighborliness and mutual aid among relatives would suffice. Also, there were technical matters requiring attention: soldiers' allotments, war risk insurance, and compensation. Many experienced social workers were drafted from the cities to organize and conduct the new "home service." The second episode occurred in 1933, when the Federal Emergency Relief Administration required the states, as a condition of participation in federal funds, to create suitable organizational machinery where such did not exist and to employ reasonably competent personnel. Again city-trained social workers invaded rural districts, and again some rural folk were given at least short courses in family case work. Since the liquidation of the F.E.R.A. there appears to have been some reversion to minimum relief administered by nonprofessional folk. But the urban influence is not likely to disappear entirely.

Child Welfare Work

It is difficult to measure the urbanization of child welfare work because many agencies, both public and private, serve both urban and rural areas. Thus in colonial days, before the rise of cities, orphans, illegitimates, and troublesome children were sometimes apprenticed or indentured by the local officials. About the middle of the nineteenth century, Massachusetts developed a state-wide system of boarding out needy children in foster homes. Several states authorized the establishment of "county homes" for dependent children, and half a dozen states set up "state public schools," as centers for distributing such children in foster homes. Nevertheless, it is correct to say that a large part of the child welfare movement has been urban.

The earliest orphanages were established in seaboard cities under religious or municipal auspices. The number of such institutions has grown to an estimated 1,400, and most of them are located in or near large cities. However, we have no data as to the number of young charges drawn from urban and from rural areas respectively.

Child placing received a great stimulus from the New York Children's Aid Society, which was established in 1853 to save the "young outcasts" from the "great lower class." The founder announced "emigration to be the best remedy for juvenile pauperism," and hoped to drain the city of these "vagrant children," placing them in "respectable country homes." After reaching the children through lodging houses and Sunday schools, he gathered together a carload lot and transported them to a small town in Michigan, where they were placed in farm and village homes recommended by clergymen and justices of the peace. Over a 40-year period more than 90,000 New York City children were scattered from Manitoba to Florida, and from New Jersey to California. From this wholesale shipment of boys and girls in the mid-nineteenth century to modern case work with needy children is a long road. But there has developed, first and chiefly in large cities, a program which includes careful inquiry into the physical health, intelligence, emotions, family ties, and other "resources and liabilities" of each child for whom care is asked. It involves similarly thorough study of each foster home that is discovered or offered. Great care is taken in the effort to fit home and child to each other. After placement there is continuing supervision and guidance. For some children board is paid; others are given free homes; a minority are adopted; and a small number work for their keep. Obviously the limited diagnostic facilities and the great distances make it hard to adapt such a program to the country, yet the diffusion is taking place through state-wide children's home societies and children's bureaus of the state government.

Humane societies and societies for the prevention of cruelty to children also had their origin in large cities. Apparently the first was the New York S.P.C.C., founded in 1874. "The society was formed to rescue children from vicious and immoral surroundings and to prosecute offenders, to prevent the employment of children for mendicant purposes or in theatrical or acrobatic performances, and for the enforcement of all laws for the protection of minors from abuse."[1] There followed juvenile protective associations and similar organizations to make investigations, issue publicity, and bring pressure to bear on legislative bodies and administrative officials. Among the problems to which they devoted considerable attention were those of child labor and irregular schooling. Most of these issues were approached as urban phenomena; the two just named, however, have subsequently proved to be primarily rural problems.

The protective work with and for children which began under private auspices has in many cities become largely a function of the juvenile court. This new type of social agency first

[1] H. H. Hart, *Preventive Treatment of Neglected Children*, p. 194, 1910. By permission of the Russell Sage Foundation.

appeared in 1899 in Chicago, whence it has spread pretty well over the nation. It deals not merely with children who have broken the law but with all sorts of children who are in need of special care and protection. Among its principal features are: (*a*) the holding of separate hearings for children's cases, (*b*) the substitution of informal or chancery proceedings for criminal proceedings, (*c*) making the child a ward of the court rather than finding him guilty and committing him to the custody of some institution, (*d*) making use of probation service both for investigation before the court hearing and for supervision after the child has been declared a ward of the court, (*e*) detention separate from adults, either in special institutions or in private families, (*f*) special court and probation records both legal and social, (*g*) provision for mental and physical examinations.

Another type of public child welfare work began with the mothers' pensions which first developed in Kansas City and Chicago in 1911. These spread very rapidly, until now all but two states have laws covering the matter, and aid to needy children with their mothers and elsewhere has been made a part of the Federal Social Security system.

One other type of social work with children might be mentioned here although it has not become very general. Visiting teachers, who are really social case workers attached to school systems, appeared first in New York, Boston, and a few other eastern cities. Their function is to study the whole personality and the home, school, and other environment of the pupils who present unusual problems in the school. Their usefulness was convincingly established in a series of demonstrations fostered by the Commonwealth Fund in the early 1920's, but for financial reasons and because competent visiting teachers have been few in number this type of service has not been widely established.

Social Settlements and Group Work

The social settlement, like the charity organization society, supposedly originated in London in the latter part of the nineteenth century. It may be said to have arisen in part out of the—to an Englishman—amazing discovery that in the metropolis there were great populations devoid of any "gentlemen" to assume leadership and responsibility in civic affairs. It was preceded by city missions and by a few ventures on the part of

Christian Socialists, but the settlement was an adventure of university men who wanted to make a contribution in service rather than in cash and in a secular rather than a religious fashion. A number of them settled in a slum area, seeking to participate as fully as possible in the lives of its inhabitants, promoting and conducting classes, recreational activities, semi-formal investigations, and participating sometimes in politics.

About 1890 the idea was transplanted to the United States, whose cities had not only slums but great immigrant populations whose lack of assimilation distressed many civic leaders. The early American settlements were established in New York, Chicago, Boston, and Philadelphia. As in England, they represented to a large degree the interest of college and university folk in the working classes of large cities. They were a true form of "bourgeois benevolence." Young college graduates of some means settled in slum districts and established centers of educational, recreational, and civic activities. They sought to make these settlements not merely "service stations" but also points for the development of contacts between social classes. It was hoped that a better understanding might be promoted and that each class might learn from the other. That is to say, there is a note of democracy in the settlement despite a seemingly contradictory note of condescension and uplift.

The social settlements were among the first, if not the first, agencies to develop the sort of thing that has come to be known as social group work. They concerned themselves not merely with teaching English to foreigners and home economics to young girls, not merely with supervising playgrounds for small children and dramatics for adults, but with the promotion of organized group activities as such. In other words, they wanted to give to their clientele experience in organized group life whereby they might learn to play their parts, "to lead and follow, to meet and handle propaganda, to integrate conflicting loyalties, to cooperate at certain points and to exert group pressure at others."[1] Social group work has not been developed as a systematized body of technical knowledge and skills to the extent that social case work has. But at least there have been built up informal, and sometimes quite formal, procedures for bringing

[1] Grace L. Coyle, "Group Work and Social Change," *National Conference of Social Work*, 1935, p. 395.

people together into groups, utilizing or developing common interests, discovering and training leaders, guiding the conduct of meetings and various kinds of projects. To this new and developing type of social work, contributions have been made not only by the settlements but also by various associations for youth—the Scouts and many others.

Other Varieties of Social Work

The types of social work discussed so far are by no means the only ones that deserve consideration, but limitations of space forbid more than passing mention of others. One of the important varieties of social case work that arose in large cities is medical social work, which is essentially the study of the social and economic situation of patients in hospitals and clinics and the carrying through of programs intended to help the patients recover and retain their health. It is based on the recognition of the fact that financial conditions, home responsibilities, working conditions, personal attitudes, religious beliefs, and many other social factors contribute both to health and to disease. Hence, starting in Boston and spreading throughout the nation, this has become one of the major varieties of American social case work.

Probation and parole, which are systems administered as forms of case work, are not exclusively urban, although to date their most successful development appears to have been in large cities. Vocational guidance, likewise, is essentially a form of social case work, although it has actually been developed by teachers and psychologists more than by social workers. Employment service, first developed on a commercial basis, then as an appendix to charitable organizations, has become a public function calling for specialized skills that are in part those of social case work.

Mention was made in the discussion of child welfare of orphanages and other kinds of institutions for the temporary or permanent housing and treatment of boys and girls. There are, of course, many other kinds of institutions in this limited sense, such as homes for the aged, convalescent homes, schools and colonies for the mentally defective, industrial schools and other correctional institutions for delinquents. These institutions may be regarded as specialties which have developed out of the undifferentiated institution which was the medieval hospital.

Some of them are maintained under governmental auspices, some by private contributions. They are by no means exclusively urban, but their greatest development, like that of other kinds of social work, is to be found in cities.

Coordination and Central Planning

In a small community where there is little if any organized social work there is correspondingly little need for joint planning, but as soon as a community is large enough to have a considerable number and variety of agencies there also appear overlapping, competition, mutual interference, and often gross neglect of given problems or areas. This is precisely what has occurred in all our large cities. Hence there have developed since about 1910 a great many councils of social agencies. Their purpose is not merely to overcome the grosser forms of overlapping and overlooking, but to promote the free discussion of common problems, the improvement of methods, the conducting of systematic studies, the assembling of service statistics, the development of city-wide plans for social work, the endorsement of responsible agencies, and the discouraging of those which seem to be incompetently managed or needless. Councils also carry on educational publicity and sometimes perform inter-agency services, such as purchasing supplies, recruiting volunteers, and operating a confidential exchange. In many cities public departments as well as private agencies join in the work of the councils for the purpose of better integrating their activities and developing a unified program of social service for the entire city.

Financing Social Work

In the typical rural community social services are supported either by taxes or by occasional collections in church, lodge, parent-teacher association, or some other local body. As a matter of fact, the principal income of urban social work is also derived from taxation, but personal donations and casual collections have come to be relatively unimportant in large cities. Instead there are some large endowments whose incomes maintain orphanages, traveler's aid societies, and many other kinds of social agencies. Some organizations have regular contributors whom they solicit from year to year. But since the World War the outstanding means of financing private social work in our cities has been the community chest. The system of joint finance which this represents is said to have originated in Liverpool, England, as long ago as 1873. Its first American appearance was in Denver in 1888, but the launching of the modern community chest movement is generally credited to Cleveland, in 1913. There are various types of organization, ranging from the semidemocratic plan of Cincinnati to the Chamber of Commerce dominated charity drive in Kansas City.

There are now more than 400 community chests in the United States and Canada; these in recent times have raised from $75 to $100 million each year. Major dependence is placed upon a whirlwind campaign, during which much pressure is brought to bear upon possible contributors. In fact, there is known to be a great deal of coercion applied to specially vulnerable groups such as policemen, street railway employees, schoolteachers, and industrial workers. So true is this that the charity aspect of private philanthropy is greatly reduced and contributions to a community chest are very much like the payment of taxes so far as the individual giver is concerned.

In addition to raising large sums of money, which they do more efficiently than individual agencies possibly could, community chests have introduced systematic budgeting, uniform accounting, centralized purchasing, and other features of businesslike administration in social work. It may be that these represent even more important contributions to this field than the securing of larger sums from more givers at a relatively lower cost.

Many problems raised by joint financing have yet to find satisfactory answers. The question of what agencies to include is always puzzling. Another problem confronts societies that have depended on individual memberships both for raising money and for developing popular understanding and support. Questions of the relation between local and national agencies, how to provide capital funds and what to do when the regular campaign falls short of its goal, constantly arise to plague the patrons and executives of community funds. But the most essential question of all, and the one furthest from solution, pertains to control—to what extent shall this be vested in the people who understand and carry on social work; to what extent in those who have large funds and are potentially, at least, large givers; to what extent in the beneficiaries of social work?

Medical Care in Cities

Like the history of social work, the history of medical care is associated with the development of cities. The physicians of antiquity and of medieval Europe were city men. The medieval hospital, though very unlike the modern institution of the same name, was nearly always located in a town or a city. So today in the United States we find medical facilities and services more common and more adequately developed in cities than in the country. Tables 37 and 38 indicate not only a concentration of physicians in cities but a greater concentration in 1931 than in 1906 and a greater concentration in large cities than in those of smaller size.

Table 37.—Percentage of Physicians Practicing in Communities of Specified Size, United States (Exclusive of New England)[a]

Size of place	Percentage distribution		
	1906	1923	1931
Under 1,000	29.5	20.1	13.4
1,000–2,500	11.6	9.4	7.7
2,500–5,000	7.3	6.8	5.9
5,000–10,000	5.9	6.2	5.9
10,000–25,000	6.7	8.2	8.7
25,000–50,000	5.0	5.5	5.8
50,000–100,000	4.2	5.9	6.4
Over 100,000	29.8	37.9	46.2

[a] Adapted from R. G. Leland, *Distribution of Physicians in the United States*, p. 51, 1936, by permission of the American Medical Association.

In 1931 the only cities that had about the same percentage of all physicians that they had of the total population were those of population between 25,000 and 50,000. There the ratio was 1.11, which means that the small cities of this class had a few more physicians than might be described as "their share." But in villages and the open country the ratio was 0.48, which means that rural America had less than half of its presumed share of medical men. On the other hand, in cities over 100,000 the ratio was 1.56, which shows clearly that they had attracted an undue proportion of the medical fraternity. Table 39 shows this discrepancy to be even more striking in selected urban and rural states. Otherwise stated, there was in 1936 one physician for every 526 persons in large cities, but only one physician for every 1,345 persons in towns with less than 5,000 population. Dentists are reported to be even more concentrated in cities than are physicians. The difference is still more marked in the matter of hospitals. Approximately 1,300 out of 3,100 counties in the United States had in 1936 no general hospital.[1] Now, this

TABLE 38.—POPULATION PER PHYSICIAN, UNITED STATES (EXCLUSIVE OF NEW ENGLAND)[a]

Size of community	Population per physician		
	1906	1923	1931
Under 1,000	997	1338	1602
1,000–2,500	590	910	1265
2,500–5,000	557	749	1023
5,000–10,000	604	688	927
10,000–25,000	571	721	774
25,000–50,000	530	647	714
50,000–100,000	597	628	661
100,000 and over	492	536	530
Average	675	763	823

[a] Adapted from R. G. Leland, *Distribution of Physicians in the United States*, p. 48, 1936, by permission of the American Medical Association.

centralization of health agencies in cities is not accidental. Most hospitals have had urban locations since the middle ages. Modern hospitals are so expensive to build, equip, and maintain that small communities cannot often afford them. Doctors like to be near hospitals, both to increase their own practice and to give their patients better care. Moreover, physicians and dentists fear that in the isolation of rural districts they may fail to keep up with their developing professions. The vogue of specialization attracts them to cities, and the difficulties of visiting patients via bad roads in bad weather drives them from the country.

Tables 40 and 41, based on a sample of over 8,600 families studied by the Committee on the Costs of Medical Care, show

[1] *Social Work Year Book*, 1937, p. 265.

TABLE 39.—PHYSICIANS, DENTISTS, AND HOSPITAL BEDS PER 100,000 OF THE POPULATION IN SELECTED STATES, 1927–1930[a]

	Physicians per 100,000	Dentists per 100,000	Hospital beds per 100,000
United States	126	56	730
Selected urban states:			
Massachusetts	147	80	1202
New York	163	63	994
District of Columbia	342	98	2016
Illinois	149	75	837
California	200	103	870
Rhode Island	111	55	950
Selected rural states:			
South Carolina	71	24	360
Mississippi	94	19	370
North Dakota	78	46	662
Arkansas	109	23	400
Wyoming	99	49	917
Arizona	86	27	940

[a] Robert I. Lee and L. W. Jones, *The Fundamentals of Good Medical Care*, p. 116, 1933. Data on physicians are for 1927, on dentists for 1928, on hospital beds for 1930. By permission of the University of Chicago Press.

TABLE 40.—PERCENTAGE OF FAMILIES RECEIVING CERTAIN MEDICAL CARE IN 12 CONSECUTIVE MONTHS[a]

	Cities over 100,000	Cities of 5,000 to 100,000	Towns and rural areas
Physicians	86.1	90.4	83.9
Surgery	23.8	23.0	18.6
Hospital	24.4	22.7	16.9
Nursing	18.0	21.1	15.1
Dentistry	60.9	54.2	44.1
Medicines	98.0	98.0	95.9
Refractions and glasses	15.6	13.8	11.8
Secondary practitioners and cultists	8.2	10.8	7.9

[a] I. S. Falk, M. C. Klem, and N. Sinai, *The Incidence of Illness* . . . , p. 92, 1933. A study of 8,639 families between 1928 and 1931. By permission of the University of Chicago Press.

how much more general are various kinds of medical care in cities than in towns and rural areas. In their report to the committee, Falk, Klem, and Sinai state that out of every 1,000 persons in large cities (over 100,000) 71 were hospitalized in one year; in small cities (5,000 to 100,000) the number was 66; while in towns and rural areas it was only 47. The average annual cost of all kinds of medical care for each person in large cities was $32.39, in small cities $23.89, in towns and rural areas only $15.80.[1] Since these data represent persons rather than institutions, they indicate clearly that even though some country people go to city hospitals, they are without such care more often than are city people. The combination of good roads and automobiles makes possible the taking of rural patients to small emergency hospitals in villages and from there, when necessary, to large hospitals in cities. Improved transportation also facilitates the calling of city doctors to small towns and the holding of traveling clinics. Nevertheless, there is a striking difference between rural and urban expenditures for medical care. This may be due in part to the lower fees charged by country doctors; but it should not be forgotten that many city people receive free medical attention.

TABLE 41.—PERCENTAGE OF PERSONS RECEIVING MEDICAL CARE[a]

	Cities over 100,000	Cities of 5,000 to 100,000	Towns and rural areas
Reporting illness and receiving care	44.5	46.2	40.7
Reporting illness but receiving no care	6.9	7.3	12.8
Reporting no illness	48.6	46.5	46.5

[a] I. S. Falk, M. C. Klem, and N. Sinai, *The Incidence of Illness* . . . , pp. 100, 279, 1933. By permission of the University of Chicago Press.

Dispensaries and clinics originated in London in the seventeenth century as a form of medical charity. The first American institutions of this type were established in Philadelphia, New York, and Boston for the dispensing of drugs to the poor of these

[1] I. S. Falk, M. C. Klem, and N. Sinai, *The Incidence of Illness* . . . , pp. 113, 146, 1933.

cities. Later the interest of physicians in broadening their experience and in teaching medical students promoted the development of these agencies into institutions for diagnosis and treatment; still later they became places for training nurses and social workers and for educating patients in habits conducive to health.[1] About 1887 the Mayo Clinic in Rochester, Minnesota, led the way in group practice of medicine for private, paying patients. There were in 1930 about 150 such private, group clinics, nearly all in large cities.[2] As early as 1923 over 500 industrial establishments had developed medical services for their employees. By 1927 there were about 1,000 health centers, cooperative ventures intended to bring about better teamwork and to lower expenses among health agencies serving urban districts. A characteristic combination includes Red Cross, visiting nurse association, antituberculosis society, agencies dealing with crippled children, heart disease, and maternity cases, and sometimes a branch of the local health department.[3] Pittsburgh, New York, Buffalo, Cleveland, and Boston were among the first cities to have health centers. A more specialized health agency is the maternal health or birth control clinic. In 1936 there were 280 contraceptive centers in the United States, mostly in large cities.[4] They operated under various auspices, but all functioned under medical direction.

Public Health Work

Cities have customarily differed from rural areas not only in the adequacy of medical care but also in the development of preventive measures and the positive promotion of health. This has been a natural result of the hazards of congestion. The necessity not only of providing but of safeguarding the purity of water, milk, and foodstuffs becomes greater as numbers increase, adding opportunities for pollution and spreading of disease. Quarantine, fumigation, extermination of rats and mosquitoes have all assumed special importance in cities. But urban health authorities have not stopped with preventive measures; they have undertaken constructive programs of health

[1] M. M. Davis and A. R. Warner, *Dispensaries* (1918), chap. 1.

[2] *Recent Social Trends*, vol. 2, p. 1076.

[3] *Ibid.*, p. 1079.

[4] *Social Work Year Book*, 1937, p. 38.

education, not merely to avoid disease but to make people stronger, more energetic, efficient, and happy. Since 1900 the public health movement has been best known through the efforts to reduce the incidence of and the fatalities from tuberculosis. It has also been effective in lowering the infant mortality rates, particularly in relation to diarrhea and enteritis. Today similar efforts are being directed against syphilis, cancer, heart diseases, and diabetes.

All this involves research which may reveal causal factors and possible means of control. It includes curative treatment of persons suffering from these various ailments, not merely those easily recognized and reporting of their own volition but those discovered through health surveys and periodic examinations. Then comes the use of specific preventive measures: immunization as against smallpox, diphtheria, and typhoid; isolation through hospitalization and quarantine. The testing of water, milk, and food supplies leads to the elimination or correction of those found to be unsafe. Abatement of nuisances includes the elimination of breeding places for mosquitoes, flies, and other carriers of germs. The disposal of sewage and garbage contribute their share to the reduction of sickness and the building of health. To guide those engaged in the administration of public health work, vital statistics bureaus and laboratories are essential. Thus the program requires the collaboration of physicians, nurses, laboratory technicians, and sanitary engineers. In some respects the most important part of all is that of educating the public, spreading the knowledge gained through scientific research and promoting use of tested procedures and facilities.

Until recently the public health movement was carried on in large measure by interested citizens through private, or semipublic, organizations. But increasingly its functions have been assumed by government, not least by municipal government. Cities now spend on the average about 75 cents per capita each year for public health. This type of organized activity, like professional social work, is being diffused from city to country, but in 1935 there were only 612 county health departments and local health units in the United States; the total number of counties being over 3,000.[1]

[1] *Ibid.*, p. 385.

Selected Readings

Social Work Year Book, 1937, Russell Sage Foundation. See classified list of topical articles.

National Conference of Social Work, University of Chicago Press. See annual proceedings and *Index* 1874–1933.

Warner, Amos G., Stuart A. Queen, and Ernest B. Harper: *American Charities and Social Work*. Thomas Y. Crowell Company, 1930. Covers changes in various types of social work from about 1890 to 1930.

Norton, William J.: *The Cooperative Movement in Social Work*, The Macmillan Company, 1927. The development of joint financing of private social work in American cities.

Falk, I. S., M. C. Klem, and N. Sinai: *The Incidence of Illness and the Receipt and Costs of Medical Care among Representative Families: Experiences in Twelve Consecutive Months during* 1928–1931, University of Chicago Press, 1933. A study made under the auspices of the Committee on the Costs of Medical Care.

Lee, Robert I., and L. W. Jones: *The Fundamentals of Good Medical Care*, University of Chicago Press, 1933. Another study made under the auspices of the Committee on the Costs of Medical Care.

Leland, R. G.: *Distribution of Physicians in the United States*, American Medical Association, 1936.

PART III

DISTRIBUTIVE AND SELECTIVE ASPECTS OF THE CITY

Chapter XIII

THE GENERAL PATTERN OF URBANISM

Thus far the discussion has focused attention on specific characteristics and functions of urbanism. It is now appropriate to consider the areal or spatial distribution or grouping of those specific characteristics and functions. If cities are far apart the significance of urbanism may be very slight. However, in many countries the distances between urban centers are so short that every part of the rural background feels the impact of urbanism more or less. It seems obvious that the maximum intensity of urbanism is concentrated in the core or heart of a central city. The relative degree of urbanism is in general inversely proportional to the distance from this central core. Enveloping each major city is a transition zone usually called suburban. In some regions the urban centers are so close together that their suburban zones merge and the country is almost wholly urbanized. Most countries, however, possess a pattern featured by urban nucleuses in the midst of rural areas of different shapes and sizes. These larger areas may be called urban or metropolitan regions. Each central core and suburban zone constitute a metropolitan district. We shall begin our discussion of this major pattern with the urban region.

The Urban Region

Various names have been applied to the area comprising an urban region, *e.g.*, hinterland, sphere of influence, and trade region. "Sphere of influence" is a good popular equivalent for the term "hinterland" and is rapidly gaining general acceptance. The urban region includes that area surrounding a city within which the city exercises economic and cultural dominance. Economically, within an urban region the given city has superior business advantages over adjacent centers. Obviously, the boundaries of such a region are statistically smoothed and hence more arbitrary than natural, although in many instances natural features tend to sharpen or narrow the zone of transition which rises between two competing urban centers. The overlapping of urban regions occurs because of the difference in significance of the various factors which are used to establish the boundary. From the point of view of commerce, certain businesses may have wider significance than others. Politically and culturally the same problem arises. It is only by weighting and combining the various factors into a composite index that the urban region's boundary can be finally determined.

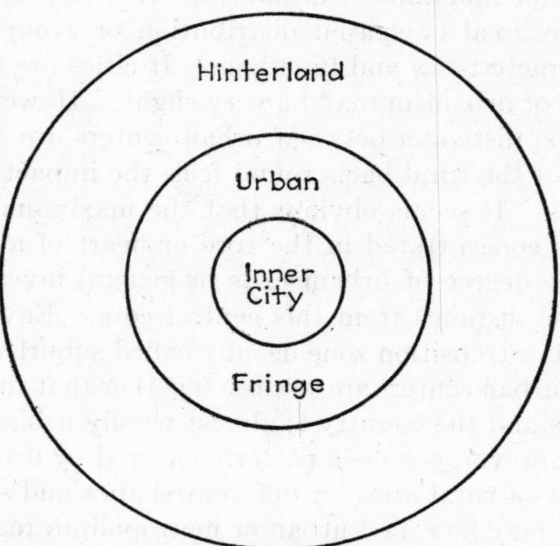

FIG. 7.—General pattern of an urban region.

One of the best measures of a city's influence is the circulation of its newspapers. If the newspapers from one city reach a larger part of the population of a given village, town, or other group than do those from another city, it is probably correct to consider the group as belonging to the hinterland of the first city. Here is the method of determining this. From the Audit Bureau of Circulation we learn the numbers of various metropolitan papers sold daily or on Sunday in a given area. We compare the total circulation of the papers from one city with that of the papers from any other cities involved and with the circulation of local papers, if any. Then, if we wish, we can compute the ratio of newspapers sold to the population of the area in question. Park used this method first in the Chicago region and later applied it to the United States.[1] Now the first advantage of this index of a city's dominance is that it is rather easy to compute. The second is that results of its use are very similar to those secured from studies of wholesale trade, marketing of milk and other farm products, telephone calls, sale of railroad and bus tickets, and highway traffic counts. The representative character of newspaper circulation is further supported by the importance of advertising. Merchants will not knowingly spend money for advertising among people who are not potential customers. But villagers and other people in the hinterlands do go occasionally to great cities to trade; they patronize mail-order houses, and their local dealers buy from urban wholesale stores. Hence the city whose newspapers have the largest circulation is likely to be the city that sells the most goods in an outlying district. But the newspaper, although a business enterprise, is more than that. It carries stories and editorial comments about politics, sports, "society," prominent persons, and a host of items about religious, civic, economic, artistic, and other interests and events. As readers of a metropolitan paper, country people share these interests.

All these facts indicate the usefulness of relative newspaper circulation as an index of urban dominance. But there are some difficulties to be encountered. Thus Park found that Chicago papers competed in Wisconsin with those of Milwaukee and in Indiana with those from Indianapolis on such even terms that the results were indecisive. We have found, however, in a region uncomplicated by near-by competing cities, that this index not only helps to determine the boundaries of a metropolitan region but also displays gradients. Thus the ratio of newspaper circulation to population in the "Forty-ninth State," of the St. Louis region, was 0.2321 within a 25-mile radius of the heart of the city, 0.0999 in the zone that lies from 25 to 50 miles out, 0.0482 in the 50 to 100 mile zone, and 0.0214 in the 100 to 150 mile zone.[2] McKenzie got similar results from a study of circulation

[1] R. E. Park and Charles Newcomb, "Newspaper Circulation and Metropolitan Regions," Chap. 8 in *The Metropolitan Community*, by R. D. McKenzie, 1933.

[2] This study was made by William Dee in 1934 under our direction. His data covered the morning paper and one afternoon paper but not the other afternoon paper. This omission was due to the limited time avail-

in the Detroit region,[1] and we have no doubt that corresponding gradients would be found in most urban regions. However, Park discovered in the Chicago area that the circulation of metropolitan papers in suburban places was more closely related to the number of commuters than to distance from the central city.

Urban regions assume tremendous significance in commercial distribution, particularly in wholesaling activities which are engaged in by companies having national scope. Such companies desire the most efficient distribution of their goods throughout the country and therefore scrutinize the urban regions of each trade center with great care. In response to the demand for study of national distribution, the United States Department of Commerce has issued maps and statistical studies based on a group of staple commodities of nation-wide consumption.[2]

Other methods of identifying the limits of metropolitan regions and various socioeconomic gradients may be described more briefly. One is an enumeration of telephone calls between the central city and various outlying places. When these were combined for successive 25-mile zones of the Detroit region, and their ratios to the population were computed, they showed a steady decrease from the center outward—1.479, 0.262, 0.070, 0.047.[3] Traffic counts have been made by state highway departments. As we proceed outward from a large city the traffic count drops fairly steadily. After an unpredictable "low" it rises again until another city is reached. The point at which the low count was taken may be regarded as a sort of "watershed" between two metropolitan regions. Another method utilizes the distribution of "country bank" services of metropolitan banks. In addition to the devices already suggested, attention may well be paid to the sale of railroad and bus tickets, the radio stations to which listeners tune in, the institutions of higher learning which young people attend, the cities which hinterlanders visit for shopping, recreation, or other purposes. Enough of these

able. However, we are sure that it did not affect the relative position of the ratios. For comparison with other regions it would be better to include all the metropolitan papers.

[1] R. D. McKenzie, *The Metropolitan Community*, p. 83, 1933.

[2] Paul W. Stewart, *Market Data Handbook of United States*, 1929, U. S. Department of Commerce, Domestic Commerce Series, No. 30.

[3] McKenzie, *op. cit.*, p. 83.

and other data might be secured by sampling the population along what appears to be the outer edge of an urban region to establish the limits more accurately than could be done with a single index such as newspaper circulation.

The reality of metropolitan regions has been increasingly apparent to administrators in recent years, even though they have not always been careful to discover their actual extent. In 1917, when the American Red Cross was suddenly confronted with the task of organizing the nation for "home service," it divided the country into 13 parts, each with headquarters in a large city. In other words, it found the whole United States too large to administer without subdivisions, the states too numerous, and large cities the logical centers. However, Red Cross divisions were merely groups of states, without reference to the now well-known fact that a part of a state may be more closely related to a part of another state than to the remainder of its own state. The 12 Federal Reserve districts, like the Red Cross divisions, are much larger than true metropolitan regions, but they do represent social and economic rather than political territories. Odum has assembled maps outlining 20 other administrative divisions of the United States.[1] Perhaps it is neither necessary nor wise that these should all correspond, but their wide variance suggests the importance of determining the natural limits of metropolitan, and possibly other, subregions as thoroughly as Odum has identified the 6 major regions of the United States.

The Metropolitan District

We turn now to the second of our two concentric circles, the metropolitan district, which includes a central city, a variety of suburbs, and a semiurban fringe. Several criteria have been employed to determine the area and population that may properly be considered those of a metropolitan district. Perhaps the first and most obvious is the presence of buildings near together. But a metropolitan district is more than a built-up area; in fact, parts of it may be devoid of buildings. It is an area within which people come and go daily to work, shop, play, study, and worship. Transportation facilities are such that it is feasible for a family to live in one part, derive its income from another, perhaps buy its food, clothing, and other goods in other parts, attend

[1] Howard W. Odum, *Southern Regions of the United States*, pp. 245 *ff.*, 1936.

church in still another, and amuse itself in various sections. Electric cars on the streets, in subways, or on elevated tracks have been supplemented in recent years by busses and privately owned automobiles. The telephone too is essential to people whose activities are scattered over a great metropolitan district. Other public utilities serve the people of such an area: gas, electricity, water, sewerage, and garbage disposal. To be sure, the territory in which some of them operate may be greater or smaller than a metropolitan district, but they tend to be identified with one city and its immediate environs. Other criteria include the daily delivery service from department stores, a central post office with branches and a two-cent rate for first-class mail, and solicitation for the community fund. All these can be established quite definitely and objectively. The various areas do not coincide exactly, but enough of them are very nearly the same to warrant using them as a group to identify a metropolitan district. After study of many cities in terms of the functions just discussed, the Bureau of the Census devised a simple quantitative definition which, in practice, identifies areas that correspond very closely to these determined by more involved procedures. Although it was quoted in Chap. I, we repeat it here.

Metropolitan districts for the census of 1930 . . . include, in addition to the central city or cities, all adjacent and contiguous civil divisions having a density of not less than 150 inhabitants per square mile, and also, as a rule, those civil divisions of less density that are *directly* contiguous to the central cities, or are entirely or nearly surrounded by minor civil divisions that have the required density.[1]

There are various differences that tend to obtain generally between central cities and the outlying part of their metropolitan districts. But for the moment we pass these over to consider the pattern of the metropolitan district or area as a whole. In approaching this we make use of two separate, but complementary, hypotheses; the geographic interpretation set forth in Chap. IV and a sociological interpretation several times hinted at, but not yet systematically presented, in this book.

Some years ago Burgess offered the hypothesis that a metropolitan area tends to resemble a number of concentric circles

[1] Fifteenth Census, *Metropolitan Districts*, pp. 5–6.

whose differences may be expressed as a series of progressive changes.[1] What this means will be illustrated presently. Figure 8 represents the conventionalized pattern of a metropolitan area. At its center is the main business district, dominated by stores, office buildings, and banks. Near by may be found passenger and freight terminals, wholesale houses, light industry,

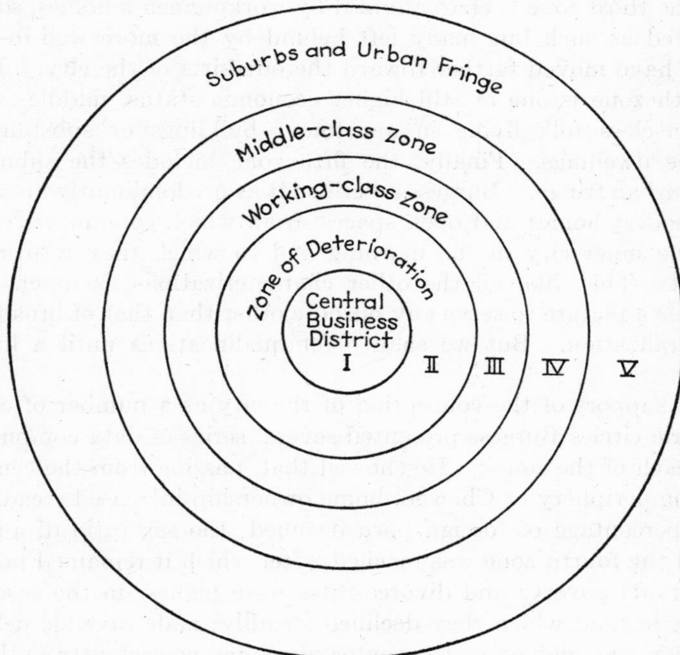

FIG. 8.—Conventionalized pattern of a metropolitan district. (*Adapted from E. W. Burgess.*)

theaters, and municipal buildings. Now admittedly the downtown business district is not circular in form; nor is it always at the geographic center of the metropolitan district. Generalized figures obviously cannot display individual variations. The second circle was called by Burgess "a zone of transition," because as the city grows the business district tends to push out into an adjoining area that was earlier residential in character.

[1] R. E. Park and E. W. Burgess, *The City*, Chap. 2, 1925. E. W. Burgess, "The Determination of Gradients in the Growth of the City," *Pub. Amer. Sociol. Soc.*, 21 (1927), 178–184.

We prefer to call this a zone of deterioration, for reasons which were suggested in the discussion of housing and which will be considered a little later. Again this circular form represents an unnatural simplification, but no one familiar with large cities—and most small ones—can doubt the existence of a deteriorated section, or belt, surrounding the central business district.

The third zone is characterized by workingmen's homes, some erected as such but many left behind by the more well-to-do, who have moved farther toward the outskirts of the city. The fourth zone is one of still higher economic status, middle- and upper-class folk living in apartment buildings or substantial single dwellings. Finally, the fifth zone includes the suburbs and urban fringe. Burgess described it as predominantly an area of modest homes and open spaces, from which commuters rush to the inner city in the morning and to which they return at night. This, like all the other characterizations, is much too simple a picture to serve any purpose other than that of broadest generalization. But we shall defer qualifications until a little later.

In support of the conception of the city as a number of concentric circles Burgess presented several series of data computed for each of the zones. He showed that, passing from the center to the periphery of Chicago, home ownership increased steadily; the percentage of foreign born declined; the sex ratio dropped until the fourth zone was reached, after which it remained fairly constant; poverty and divorce rates were highest in the second zone, beyond which they declined steadily; male juvenile delinquency was highest at the center, declining consistently until it practically disappeared in the fourth zone. Table 42 displays some corresponding series which have been computed for St. Louis.[1] For both Chicago and St. Louis, data pertain only to the central city.

[1] These series are parts of the cooperative research that has been carried on in St. Louis for several years. Net density was computed by Max Colodesch. Data on single dwellings, home ownership, and rentals, as well as population elements and sex ratios, were compiled by the United States Bureau of the Census. Vital statistics were secured from the Division of Health, rates being computed by Ralph C. Fletcher, Max Colodesch, and Harry L. Hornback. Dependency data were assembled from the Social Service Exchange. Those from the juvenile court were made available by Ralph Smith. The residential mobility study was made by Donald O.

In examining this table, note that density of population declines without a break from the second to the seventh mile, while the proportion of single dwellings rises steadily from the second to the seventh mile. Rentals rise only to the fifth mile, after which there is little change. Except for a slight drop in the sixth mile, the percentage of the population that is native white of native parents rises consistently as we pass from the center to the periphery. The sex ratio shows a remarkable drop from the first to the second mile, then a gradual decline to the fifth mile, and thereafter an increase toward equality. The death rates, both crude and corrected, show a steady decrease from the center to the periphery. The same is true of dependency and of juvenile court cases, except for slight deviations in the sixth and seventh miles. Finally, residential mobility displays the same characteristic direction of change throughout the seven miles. Now, it is admitted without hesitation that not all the other series show the same progressive changes. Thus the proportion of small children is highest in the second mile, but almost as high in the seventh. The relative number of elderly persons is highest in the first and lowest in the second, rising in the third and fourth, thereafter declining steadily but not greatly. In other words, the wavelike zones in terms of which the city may be viewed do not differ uniformly or in all respects; but there are enough consistent differences to warrant the use of this conventionalized scheme as one device for interpreting the distributive aspects of the great city.

This concept of concentric circles should be placed alongside, or superimposed upon, topographic and land-use maps of particular cities to emphasize the fact that geographic, economic, and social factors of various sorts are involved in the develop-

---

Cowgill. For each of these and more than 20 other series of data, ratios were computed, census tracts were assigned in whole or in part to the appropriate circle or zone, and weighted averages were calculated for each zone. The last steps were checked by Stuart A. Queen, Harry L. Hornback, and—for some of the series—students at Washington University. Despite the care taken, a margin of error remains, but the accuracy is sufficient to establish the hypothesis in question, so far as St. Louis proper is concerned. Unfortunately data are insufficient to test it for the entire metropolitan district. Many of the data and discussions of methods used may be found in Ralph C. Fletcher, Harry L. Hornback, and Stuart A. Queen, *Social Statistics of St. Louis by Census Tracts*, 1935.

ment of the pattern that finally emerges in any city. We illustrate this with the case of St. Louis again. Figures 9 and 10 show how much Burgess's scheme simplifies and distorts the actual pattern of a particular city. The central business district is located near the water front, somewhat east of the geographic center of the metropolitan area. But, as was shown in Chap. VII, there are subcenters and string streets, main thoroughfares

TABLE 42.—THE PATTERN OF ST. LOUIS AS IDENTIFIED THROUGH SERIES OF DATA COMPUTED FOR CONCENTRIC CIRCLES PLOTTED AT INTERVALS OF ONE MILE

	Indexes for each circle, zone, or mile						
	I	II	III	IV	V	VI	VII
Net density per 100,000 sq. ft. of residential property	71	150	130	115	83	70	41
Percentage of single dwellings	67	50	53	60	68	79	81
Percentage of homes owned	4	9	20	30	38	50	56
Median rental (dollars)	18	20	27	36	43	43	40
Percentage of native white of native parents	39	41	49	56	58	57	62
Adult males per 100 females	326	109	97	92	91	94	99
Deviations from normal death rate (specially computed)	27.6	15.5	10.4	9.3	9.0	9.0	8.8
Crude death rate per 1,000 population	25	16	13	12	10	10	8
Dependency cases per 1,000 families	147	91	50	20	12	11	12
Juvenile court cases per 10,000 families	125	103	56	42	20	16	18
Residential mobility (specially computed)	45.2	42.6	39.2	30.5	28.7	26.9	23.7

along which small businesses may be found for several miles. Light manufacturing, as might be expected, is mainly in the sections adjacent to the central business district. Heavy industry reaches north and south, occupying a narrow flood plain on the west side of the river; just south of the middle of the city it extends westward through a little valley; in the northwest and on the bottoms on the east side of the river similar developments occur. The distribution of heavy industry is evidently related to transportation facilities, whose location in turn is related to

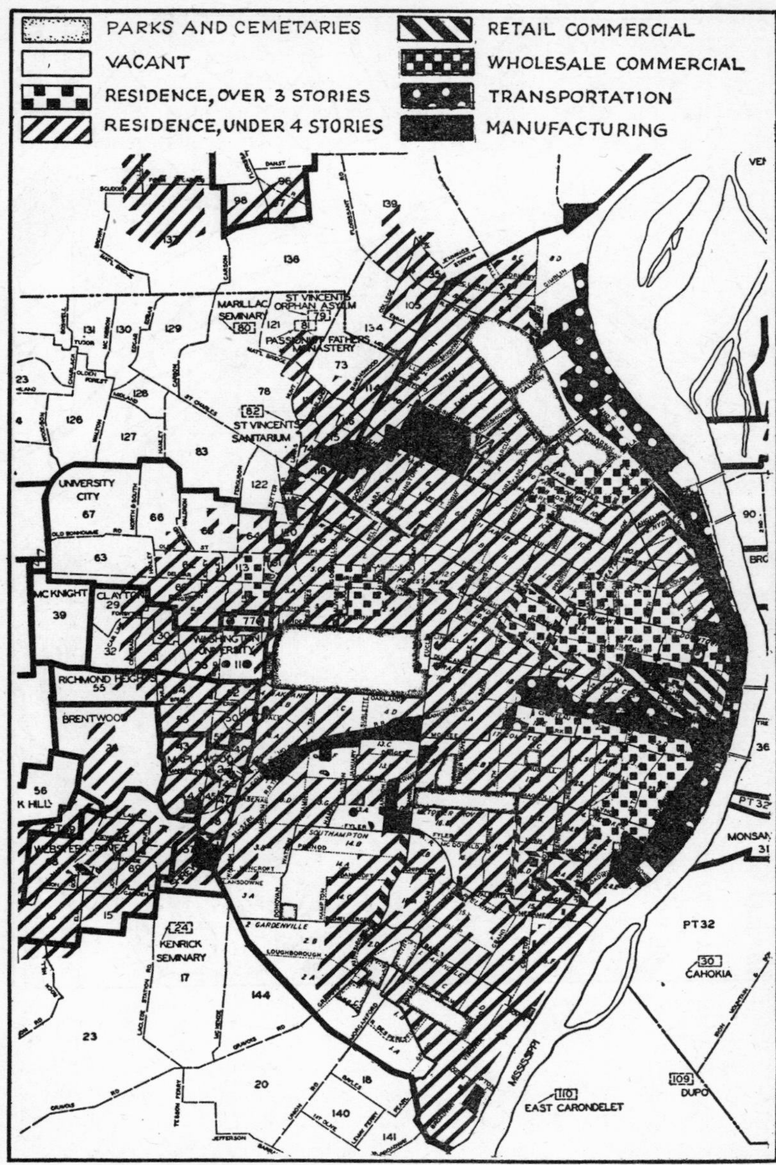

FIG. 9.—Distribution of land uses, St. Louis, 1935.

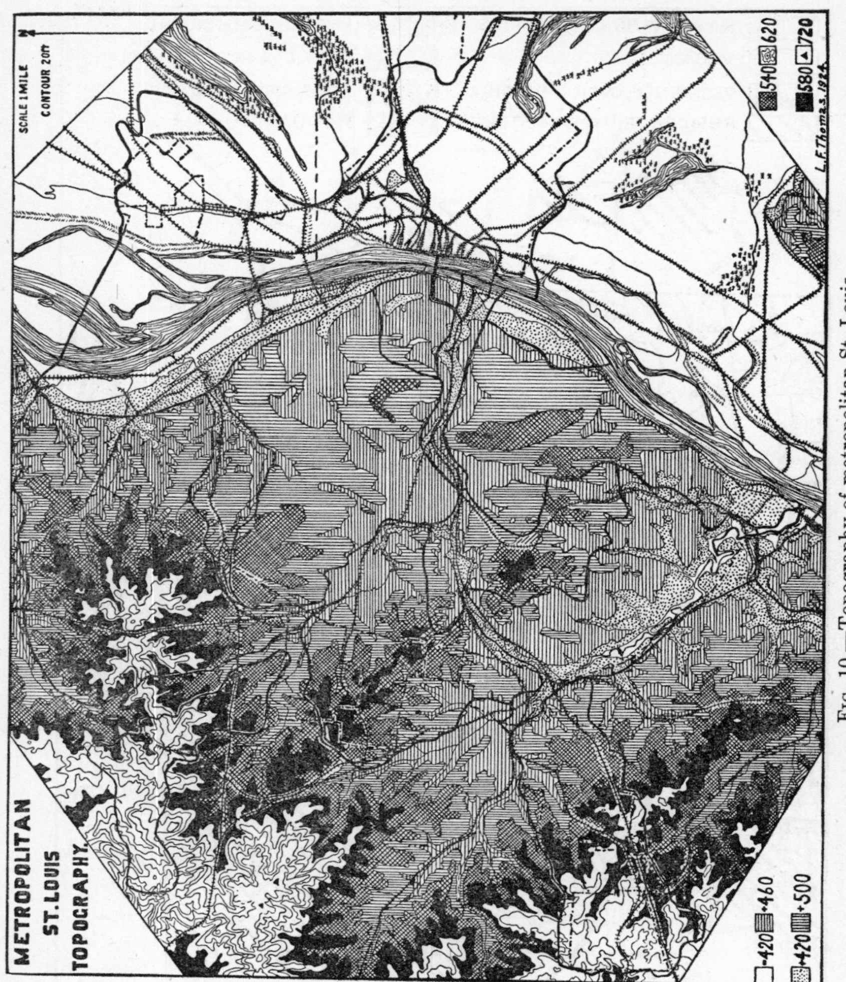

Fig. 10.—Topography of metropolitan St. Louis.

the physical setting. By referring to the maps in Chap. VI it can be seen that multiple dwellings and the cheaper residences of all kinds are most common just outside the central business district and in areas adjacent to factories. Parks, golf clubs, cemeteries, and other open spaces are distributed rather unevenly, though they are most numerous on the western fringe of the built-up area.

The Development of the Urban Pattern

As has been said several times, every American city has begun on a small scale. Often it has been merely a subsistence village or a trading post. Gradually there has developed retail trade for the local inhabitants, presently supplemented by the manufacture of certain articles for local use. Eventually, improved means of transportation bring in raw materials from the adjacent territories and distribute finished products through the metropolitan region. All these aspects of growth and development are reflected in the changing urban pattern. When the city begins, all these activities are concentrated in a small, compact area; as it grows, they not only occupy more space but also tend to segregate themselves. Presently the retail shopping district, the warehouses and wholesale establishments, the factories, and the residences become more or less separate each from the other. The commercial functions are likely to remain near the original site; the wholesale and manufacturing usually remain near by for a time at least. The residences tend to occupy the periphery of the growing city.

If the place is developing rapidly, stores, shops, etc., are now and again set down in the midst of a district that has been strictly residential. Thereupon some of the inhabitants, finding this undesirable, move farther out and establish a new residential section. However, it is not always possible to sell the old house without great loss; hence it frequently happens that the owner retains title to his property, hoping that without too long a delay the land may be needed for commercial or industrial purposes. When this occurs he expects to sell the lot for a high enough price to recoup the losses due to depreciation of the building and the expense incurred in the interim. Since he does not know how long he may have to wait, he undertakes to rent the old house. Now the people who could afford to pay an economic rent for such a dwelling are probably, like the owner, moving to the outskirts of the city. The only ones who are likely to accept the house are those who cannot possibly pay the rent the owner feels that he must receive. Hence he will probably make a few alterations and rent it in small units to several families. The advertisements will read, "Light Housekeeping," "Sleeping Rooms," "Apartments," or something of this general character. Thus what was once a nice residence for a single family of substance is converted into a tenement occupied by people of small means.

If the period between the first invasion of an old residential district and its complete occupation by commerce and industry is not too long, this general procedure serves a useful purpose for both landlord and tenant. But if the growth of the city is slower than was anticipated, or if the developing subcenters absorb some of the expansion which might otherwise have occurred near the central business district, then the delay may be very great. When the time runs to 20, 30, or 40 years, deterioration becomes quite marked. Naturally the owner hesitates to spend much money for repairs, since he is still hoping to be relieved of his property. Often the tenants who occupy such houses are careless of the property and hasten its general decline. Thus an area which might have been merely one of transition becomes a zone of deterioration. It is under these circumstances that the city slum characteristically develops.

However, whether the changes occur rapidly or slowly, this area comes to display certain well-recognized socioeconomic characteristics. It is likely to become the home of newcomers to the city, whether they arrive from Europe, Mexico, or the rural hinterland of the city in question. The reasons are simply that these people usually have little money, are strangers in the city, want to live near places of possible employment and near others of their own kind. Thus the zone of transition or deterioration becomes the area of first settlement of all kinds of migrants.

If the city continues to grow, business and industry continue, sometimes rapidly and sometimes slowly, to displace the occupants of this second zone. Being pushed out, or perhaps becoming adjusted to city life and economically more successful, they move farther out and are in turn probably regarded as a menace by the occupants of these outlying residential districts. This in turn stimulates another migration of the middle- and upper-class folk. Thus the various waves, or circles, press upon each other in what seems like a never-ending centrifugal movement. Obviously it cannot continue indefinitely, but in the development of American cities so far it has gone forward pretty continuously. One factor which tends to accelerate this outward movement is the activity of the realtors. Intermittently they open new subdivisions and conduct campaigns to lure residents of the inner city farther and farther toward the periphery of the metropolitan district. Moreover, the people respond to this pressure. Those with small children may want open spaces for them to play in or may wish to avoid the contact with children of strange tongues, strange faiths, and strange manners. Perhaps the pall of smoke that rises from factories, railroads, and other sources makes them long for the cleaner air of the suburbs. Last but not least is the prestige value of a home in an outlying district, which has certainly been an important attraction for many people.

Whatever the particular causes may be, one result is the marked decline in the population of the inner city. This has been demonstrated in numbers of cities—Pittsburgh, Cleveland, New York, Chicago, Detroit, and others. In the first 30 years of the present century, that part of St. Louis which lies east of Jefferson Avenue (about two miles from the Mississippi River) declined both relatively and absolutely in population. In 1900 this section contained 280,000 people, constituting 49 per cent of the city's total. In 1930 the district had only 190,000, who constituted 23 per cent of the total population. As a result of this general trend, we find that in the decade ending 1930 the central cities of our 96 metropolitan districts gained only 19 per cent in population, while the outlying parts of the metropolitan areas gained 39 per cent. The seriousness of this has become apparent to several kinds of people. Owners of residential property in the inner city are naturally distressed because the central business district has not absorbed their property as had been originally hoped. Proprietors of downtown retail stores worry lest their business decline owing to the absence of potential customers in near-by parts of the city and to the inclination of those in outlying sections to patronize stores in the various subcenters. The city government also is involved, because municipal revenue is based largely upon real estate taxes. If property values decline, assessments should be lowered; hence taxes will decrease. If on the other hand assessments remain high in order to maintain land values that are disappearing or perhaps never have appeared, then there is likely to be difficulty in collecting taxes.

It may be assumed from what has been said so far that the outermost circle represents consistently the highest economic levels and the most favorable living conditions. Sometimes this is true, but more often this outer zone includes a heterogeneous array of expensive estates, decentralized industrial establishments, belt lines of terminal railroads, golf clubs, and cemeteries. Because each new subdivision on the urban fringe may be laid out with little reference to those which are adjacent or to the metropolitan district as a whole, a detailed land-use map of such an area resembles nothing more than a crazy quilt. Then when some of the suburbs seek to incorporate as new municipalities, they too may take little account of adjacent sections, and ere long the political map likewise acquires a very curious design.

In the efforts to analyze and interpret the development of a large city a number of semitechnical terms have come into general use. Each of these represents a process or a phase of the inclusive processes of urban growth. First of all we note *concentration,* the drawing of population into a given area. This is measured by density or the ratio of population to land area. The opposite of concentration is *dispersion,* the scattering of the population, which is similarly measured. For some cities density maps have been prepared at various intervals, and from these it is possible to see the increasing density of certain parts of the metropolitan district and the concurrent decrease in density of other sections. In general we find the greatest concentration so far in residential sections close to the central business district. But these areas of greatest density, at least in St. Louis, and apparently in numbers of other cities, are losing population to outlying sections where the density is increasing.

A third process is *centralization,* the drawing together of institutions and activities, *i.e.,* the assembling of people to work rather than to reside in a given area. This is identified by buildings and other physical equipment, by the prices of land and by traffic counts. The downtown area is almost always the area of greatest centralization as indicated by these criteria. However, there are subcenters in various parts of every metropolitan district which display the same process, but on a smaller scale. In a sense they combine *decentralization* of certain functions, such as retail trade, with continued centralization of other functions, such as finance and administration.

The most obvious illustration of this is afforded by the chain stores, whose retail outlets are in subcenters and at scattered points, but are usually managed from a central office in the central business district. In the *Regional Survey of New York and Its Environs*[1] it was found that certain business activities tend to drift toward the periphery of the metropolitan district. Banks, brokerage houses, legal firms, commission merchants, and wholesalers are quite consistently found near the heart of the city. Until recently, department stores have been found almost exclusively in the downtown area; of late they have shown a tendency to remove to subcenters. Perhaps it would be more accurate to say that new department stores develop at subcenters rather than in old business districts.

Some of the so-called light industries tend to be drawn toward the center of a city and to remain there after other functions have started to move toward the periphery. Those which are more commonly found near the center are clothing, tobacco, job printing, and others which require relatively little ground space per worker, can operate on a small scale, can utilize obsolete buildings, need to be near their market, or in other ways find time and service an important factor. The heavy industries, on the contrary, which are relatively large and often have nuisance features, and in which the time and service factors are less urgent, seem to find their way toward the outlying parts of the metropolitan district. In recent years decentralization has extended far out into the metropolitan region, apparently as a consequence of employers' efforts to secure a cheap and docile labor supply.

A fifth process identified in the study of urban patterns and their changes is called *specialization*. By this is meant the clustering of particular types of institutions and activities. Thus

[1] R. M. Haig and R. C. McCrea, *Major Economic Factors in Metropolitan Growth and Arrangement in Regional Survey of New York and Its Environs*, vol. 1, 1927.

we sometimes find a "bright light" area occupied by numbers of theaters, dance halls, and other places of amusement. "Automobile rows," "petticoat lanes," Wall Streets, and medical centers are other examples of specialization. The drawing together of particular types of people is called *segregation*. This may occur either as a result of external pressure, such as that exerted upon the Negroes, or of relatively free choice, as in the case of the Italians. In Chap. XVI will be found maps illustrating the segregation of various ethnic groups in St. Louis at a particular time. The process of *invasion* has already been discussed. It is a convenient name for what happens when a new type of people, institution, or activity enters an area previously occupied by a different type. Thus when Negroes begin to come into a district previously occupied by whites or when business places appear in an area that had been exclusively residential, invasion may be said to be taking place. That is to say, it is a case either of group displacement or of change in land use. Finally, when an invasion has gone so far that the new population or new function dominates an area and the original occupants have moved out, we speak of *succession*.

Two other terms will be employed from time to time, although the activities to which they refer may be covered in whole or in part by terms already discussed. As the central city expands and as outlying towns grow toward the city, they come to exchange personnel and services to such a degree that ultimately the smaller community may be said to be absorbed into the larger. When this *absorption* involves political action we speak of *annexation*. However, it should be plain from earlier discussion that absorption may occur without annexation and that annexation might be forced without the smaller community's becoming fully identified with the larger in its economic and social life. Thus some years ago Los Angeles annexed almost the whole of the San Fernando Valley. In it were a number of small communities which gave up their political independence but remained economically and socially as separate from the central city as did other towns which were not annexed. The important thing to bear in mind throughout this discussion is not the names of particular ecological processes but the fact that changes such as we have described are constantly going on in our cities. There are superficial evidences of stability and permanence, but underneath the surface change is never ending. This change, moreover, seems to be bound up with what Park and Burgess describe as "competition."[1] By this they mean there is some sort of struggle going on—perhaps unplanned, possibly unrecognized. It is primarily a struggle for advantageous locations. When a real estate board deliberately seeks to limit Negro residence to a restricted area, competition has come into the open as conscious conflict. But when an area of homeowners gradually becomes one of tenants, and permanence yields to transience, there may be no recognized or open strife at all; it is a sort of subconscious tug of war. Many of the changes that take place in our cities are unplanned, unanticipated, and little noticed even after they have occurred; others are surprising and disturbing; still others are unquestionably the result of deliberate planning. It is our belief that much of the confusion in city life results from failure to recognize these processes of change and to deal with them in accordance with some well-defined program of action.

The Pattern in More Detail

The maps in Chap. VI show in some detail the distribution of various aspects of family living and housing in the city of St. Louis. Similar maps have been prepared for other cities, but for convenience we are drawing most of our illustrations from this one metropolitan district. As we noted in that earlier discussion, families tend to be small in old parts of the city and larger in the new, outlying sections. The sex ratio shows a predominance of males at the center and again on the extreme periphery, with a predominance of females toward the edge of the center city and the near-by suburbs. Throughout the middle of the city the percentage married is low, while in new residential districts the percentage married is high. As to housing, we noted the predominance of multiple dwellings in parts of the inner city, which gives way to a predominance of single dwellings as one moves toward the periphery. Obsolete houses are found, as might be expected, near the heart of the city, and it happens that the areas of oldest dwellings are also those of greatest density. These are just a few of the identifiable features of urban domestic institutions which show a clear relation to the general pattern.

[1] R. E. Park and E. W. Burgess, *Introduction to the Science of Sociology*, Chap. 8, 1924.

In later chapters we shall present tables and graphs showing that dependency, delinquency, vice, certain diseases, high death rates, illiteracy, and mobility tend to be concentrated near the heart of the city, while their opposites appear more commonly in outlying sections. In other places we shall also show the distribution of ethnic groups, neighborhoods, and communities. Suffice it here to say that Negroes, not only in St. Louis but very commonly, are located principally in the zone of deterioration and in the zone of workingmen's homes. Immigrants have usually been found in the zone of deterioration, but their children escape to better parts of the city. In St. Louis, the foreign born and their children are scattered rather more than in New York, Boston, Chicago, and some other cities. This is due possibly to the relatively small number of immigrants in this city and possibly to the fact that few of them are recent arrivals.

We have already noted in a general way that certain socioeconomic factors seem to occur together in particular parts of a city. To get at this relation more precisely, some of our associates have computed coefficients of rank correlation between various series of data. The method involved ranking census tracts according to various indexes and comparing a tract's rank in one series with its rank in another. Using a well-known formula, we determined the extent to which the ranking of all tracts in any series corresponded to the ranking in any other series. For example, in St. Louis the age of housing was found to display a high correlation with death rates, dependency, illiteracy, the employment of women, juvenile court cases, multiple dwellings, and Negroes. It showed a marked negative correlation with the size of family, home ownership, value of homes, and rentals paid.[1] This means that tracts in which houses were very old had high death rates and many families on relief, illiterates, employed women, delinquents, Negroes, and tenements. They had small families, few homeowners, cheap houses, and low rents. In another study, residential mobility was found to have a high correlation with relief and other social services, juvenile court cases, venereal disease, deaths from tuberculosis, employment of women, Negroes, multiple dwellings, and vacancies in residential property. It showed a marked negative correlation with size

[1] These correlations were computed by J. Bertram Black in connection with the Assessor's Survey, which was a 1936 W.P.A. project.

of family, percentage of males married, rentals, and the American-born children of immigrants.[1] A third group of correlations undertook to measure the relation between the percentage of males married and various other socioeconomic factors. It showed men to be most commonly married when living in areas of home ownership, where there is also a high percentage of women married. There is marked negative correlation with Negroes, density of population, illiteracy, relief and other social services, multiple dwellings, employment of women, venereal diseases among men, and tuberculosis deaths.[2]

Numerous other relations have been established, but these should be sufficient to demonstrate not merely that particular aspects of a city's life are different from section to section, but that certain changes seem to occur together. Thus mobility, obsolescence, poverty, disease, delinquency, illiteracy, and several other factors occur pretty regularly together in parts of the inner city, whereas a higher economic status, newer housing, lower density, lower death rates, and more stability are found together in certain outlying parts of the city. Howard Green found similar relationships in the city of Cleveland.[3] On the basis of rentals paid and values assigned to homes occupied by owners he divided the Cleveland metropolitan district into 14 types of economic areas. In the higher economic areas he found most single dwellings, home ownership, radios, increase in population, and births in hospitals. In the lower economic areas he found the highest density of population, most unemployment, illiteracy, juvenile delinquency, infant mortality, highest birth rates, and the largest percentage of males single. Since the lower economic areas are more frequently found near the heart of the city and the higher areas more frequently near the periphery, Green's findings and our own support the same general conclusions.

Some of the other cities in which similar ecological studies have been made are Boston, New York, Chicago, Kansas City, New Haven, Indianapolis, and Seattle.

[1] This study was made by Donald O. Cowgill in 1935.

[2] Ralph C. Fletcher, Harry L. Hornback, and Stuart A. Queen, *Social Statistics of St. Louis by Census Tracts*, 1935.

[3] Howard Green, *Population Characteristics by Census Tracts, Cleveland, Ohio*, 1930, pp. 64 *ff.*, 1931.

Methods Used in Ecological Studies

In the preceding discussions we have indicated in part the procedures employed in collecting the data which support our hypothesis concerning the pattern of an American city. However, for the benefit of readers who may want to undertake similar studies for themselves we shall present in a little more detail the methods that have been used. Before taking the 1930 census, 18 cities were divided into permanent statistical units. To illustrate with the case of St. Louis, the central city was divided into 26 census areas, some of which represent more or less well-defined communities or segregated districts. Each of these in turn was divided into tracts from 3 to 7 in number, yielding a total of 128 census tracts for the entire city. The tracts again were subdivided into enumeration districts, of which there is a total of 518. The outlying part of the metropolitan district was divided only into enumeration districts, of which there are approximately 275. It is intended that the boundaries of these various areas, tracts, and districts shall remain unchanged so that the data assembled from decade to decade and for various purposes may be legitimately compared. Formerly, enumeration was by wards, whose boundaries were frequently altered; thus comparative studies were very difficult. By the time the Sixteenth Census is taken there will probably be 50 or more cities so laid out for statistical purposes. In some of these cities administrative bodies and research organizations have been collecting data which have been classified according to these permanent census units. Thus in St. Louis cases which are cleared through the Social Service Exchange are classified each month by census tracts. This process is facilitated by a street and number index from which it is possible to assign any address immediately to the appropriate tract. Prior to the making of this index it was necessary to use a directory or to make spot maps as a basis for later calculations.

From data such as those recorded by the Social Service Exchange one can determine the distribution of families and individuals who apply for or receive relief, medical care, and various other services. For example, the number of clients of relief and family welfare agencies is known for every census tract. For the years close to the one in which the census is taken it is possible to compute a ratio of relief clients to the total number of families or to the total population of each tract. For earlier or later years this is not practicable because of unmeasured changes in population. When, let us say, the ratio of relief recipients to all families has been computed, it is possible to rank the census tracts from the one with the lowest ratio to the one with the highest ratio. When a similar ranking process has been carried out for another series of data it is then possible by the use of the formula $\rho = 1 - \frac{6\Sigma d^2}{n(n^2 - 1)}$ to compute the coefficient of rank correlation.

In some instances we have assembled data from firsthand studies. These obviously require a great deal more time, but the general principles involved are the same as those already indicated. In cities for which the Bureau of the Census has not established permanent census tracts, the problem of studying the distributive aspect of social and economic life is more complicated. In such cases it may be necessary to make spot maps and display relations graphically without attempting to work them out mathematically.

Summary

The purpose of this chapter has been to demonstrate the reality of the urban region, the metropolitan district, and the central city as parts of an integral pattern of social and economic life. The apparent crazy quilt which one sees on first examining the map of any large city and its environs is to a certain extent really there. The limited amount of planning that has gone into American cities is responsible for this. But actually, underneath the seeming confusion, there is some system and order, whether planned or not. Our assumption is that for the most part it has developed through the interrelation of many factors—geographic, economic, and social—mostly unrecognized or rather vaguely identified. Perhaps the first semblance of a pattern to emerge is the highway and street plan. The next is that of general land use. Closer examination then reveals economic and cultural segregation of various kinds.

The processes through which the urban pattern develops are constantly going on, hence the pattern is evidently undergoing constant change. These processes, to which have been given semitechnical names, are bound up with growth in numbers and area, new means of transportation, new industries, new types of buildings, and various other factors which have been discussed. The conventionalized concentric scheme which has been presented is therefore only a convenience for use in the study of the city and must not be accepted as representing its precise form, much less as a pattern that remains without change.

Selected Readings

GIST, NOEL P., and L. A. HALBERT: *Urban Society*, The Thomas Y. Crowell Company, 1933. Chapters 5–7 deal with the social ecology of the city.

DAWSON, CARL A., and W. E. GETTYS: *An Introduction to Sociology*, Ronald Press Company, 1929 and 1935. Chapter 5 in the first edition and Chap. 4 in the revised edition deal with selective distribution in metropolis and region.

PARK, ROBERT E., and E. W. BURGESS: *The City*, University of Chicago Press, 1925. Chapter 2 outlines the famous hypothesis of concentric circles.

MCKENZIE, R. D.: *The Metropolitan Community*, McGraw-Hill Book Company, Inc., 1935. Chapters 6–8, 13, and 17 describe various aspects of the structure of a metropolitan region.

HAIG, ROBERT M., and R. C. MCCREA: *Major Economic Factors in Metropolitan Growth and Arrangement in Regional Survey of New York and Its Environs*, vol. 1, 1927.

FLETCHER, RALPH C., HARRY L. HORNBACK, and STUART A. QUEEN: *Social Statistics of St. Louis by Census Tracts*, Washington University, 1935. Displays the pattern of the central city.

GREEN, HOWARD W.: *Population Characteristics by Census Tracts, Cleveland, Ohio*, 1930, Cleveland Plain Dealer, 1931. Displays the pattern of the metropolitan area.

DREIS, THELMA: *A Handbook of Social Statistics of New Haven, Connecticut*, Yale University Press, 1936.

Social Statistics by Census Tracts in Boston, Boston Council of Social Agencies, 1933.

Report of the Housing Survey of Kansas City, Missouri, 1934–1935, prepared by the Missouri Emergency Relief Administration Non-Manual Works Program, 1935.

Chapter XIV

URBAN COMMUNITIES

Against the background of a city's general pattern may be seen here and there nucleuses, or collections of people and institutions, more or less set apart from each other. There are subcenters of retail business with schools and churches which seem to belong to a particular area rather than to the city as a whole. There are sections occupied by people of fairly definite physical, economic, or cultural traits. Some such districts are rather clearly marked off by streams, hills, parks, cemeteries, major thoroughfares, railroad tracks, large industrial establishments, or other natural or artificial boundaries. Sometimes one of these areas, with its people and its institutions, has a name and history that further identifies it as a community, a neighborhood, or at least a distinctive section of the city. Thus Boston has its North End, Back Bay, Jamaica Plain, and West Roxbury. Chicago has its Rogers Park, Logan Square, Lawndale, Englewood, and South Shore. Within these districts may often be found smaller divisions indicated by the separation of apartment houses from single dwellings, middle-class residences from workingmen's homes, Jews from Christians, Poles from Italians, etc. These are sometimes called neighborhoods; whether properly or not we shall presently inquire.

The varied character of these local aggregations within cities may be illustrated by examples from St. Louis (see Fig. 11). Within the city limits is Carondelet, once a separate municipality, occupied successively by French, Germans, Irish, and a variety of other ethnic groups. It was originally set apart spatially as well as politically from St. Louis; it still has organizations and traditions of its own. Also inside the central city is an Italian colony, unceremoniously known as "Dago Hill," set apart by thoroughfares and mine property as well as by the differences between its inhabitants and those of immediately adjacent sections. Nearer the heart of St. Louis is a large district occupied

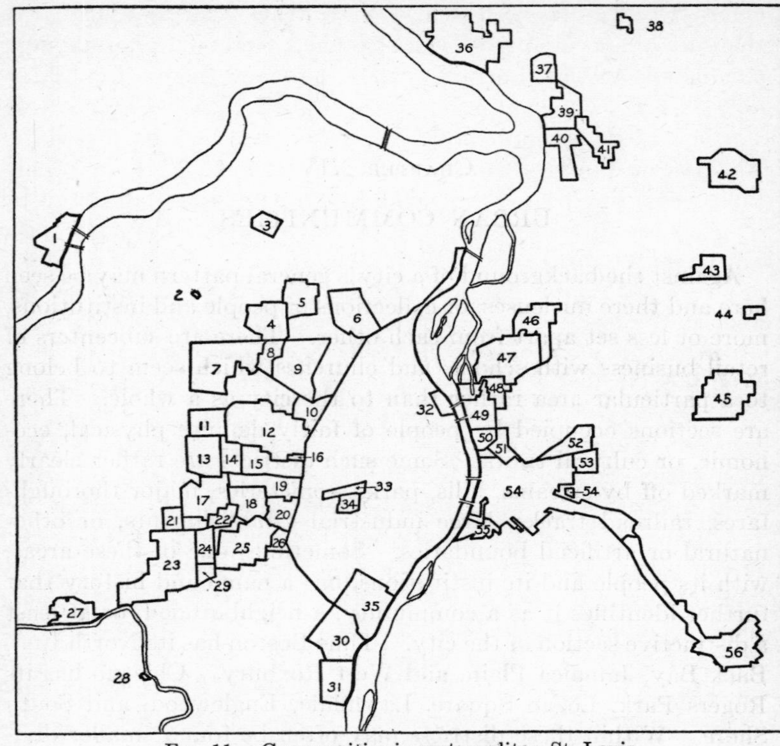

FIG. 11.—Communities in metropolitan St. Louis.

1, St. Charles
2, Bridgeton
*3, St. Ferdinand (Florissant)
4, Kinloch
*5, Ferguson
6, Jennings
7, Overland
8, Carsonville
9, Normandy
10, Wellston
11, Olivette
*12, University City
13, Ladue
14, McKnight
*15, Clayton
16, Washington University
17, Deer Creek
18, Brentwood
19, Richmond Heights
20, Maplewood
21, Huntleigh
22, Rock Hill
23, Kirkwood
24, Glendale
*25, Webster Groves
26, Shrewsbury
27, Valley Park
28, Fenton
29, Oakland
30, Luxemburg
31, Jefferson Barracks
32, Baden
*33, Cheltenham
34, Fairmount Heights
*35, Cardondelet
36, Alton
37, East Alton
38, Bethalto
39, Wood River
40, Hartford
41, Roxanna
42, Edwardsville
43, Glen Carbon
44, Maryville
45, Collinsville
46, Nameoki
47, Granite City
*48, Madison
49, Venice
50, Brooklyn
51, National City
52, Fairmount City
53, Washington Park
54, East St. Louis
55, Monsanto
56, Belleville

* Described in the text of this Chapter

chiefly by Negroes, with their own churches, schools allocated to their use, some commercial establishments and civic organizations conducted by colored people. Here, however, there is a considerable admixture of white persons and their business enterprises. The boundaries are quite artificial, having been set by the (white) Real Estate Board. Out toward the periphery of the metropolitan district are several independent municipalities, separated by open spaces from other local units. The names of some of these are Edwardsville, Collinsville, Valley Park, St. Charles. Closer in are other municipalities, not sharply marked off from one another or from the central city. Some of these were once quite distinct but have coalesced in recent years; others, such as Webster Groves, Ferguson, University City, and Richmond Heights, represent a pushing out from the central city. Then there are extensive built-up areas that are unincorporated. They have business districts, school systems, fire protection, and other local institutions. They bear definite names, *e.g.*, Normandy, Pine Lawn, Overland, Luxemburg. Both in the central city and in the suburbs are found private streets and places identified by gates, signs, and other marks of exclusiveness. These commonly have an administrative organization but no institutions in the physical sense of schools, churches, or stores. Whether these locality groupings are to be called communities, neighborhoods, or something else must depend on definitions and on further study.

For purposes of this discussion we shall define an *urban community* as a fairly large group of people (1,000 to 100,000) who occupy a relatively compact, contiguous territory and who are served to a considerable extent by the same set of local institutions, which perform a sufficient variety of functions to enable the residents to live a large part of their life within its confines. Put more concretely, an urban community usually has its own stores, schools, churches, clubs, movies, professional services, and other facilities which make it unnecessary for residents to go outside the local area. The chief exception to this is the employment of many persons in the central business district or other specialized sections of the city. Within such a community there may be smaller and more intimate groupings which we call *neighborhoods,* although this is not necessarily true. Often, perhaps always, an urban community has a name. Its inhabitants speak of themselves as belonging to this locality.

They utilize its institutions, follow its traditions, and possibly discuss common ambitions. They may display pride in local achievements, respond to local slogans, follow local leaders, rally in support of a local athletic team or in opposition to the invasion of alien elements. It is such manifestations of belonging together, the things that people have in common, that constitute them a community. It happens that in common parlance the word "community" is used very loosely, to mean any local area that is more or less distinguished from the surrounding territory, whether its people constitute a social group or not. This is confusing, and we must be on our guard against it. For districts that are set apart by physical features we may use the term *natural area.* For parts of a city that are not clearly defined physically or socially we prefer such colorless terms as *section, district,* and *area.* We shall not use the term "community" unless a territory is the home of a social group with its own local institutions, internally more or less united and externally more or less separated from the city as a whole.

By *urban neighborhood* we mean a local aggregation of families among which there is personal acquaintance, visiting, exchange of articles and services. The area occupied and the number of families are usually small, ranging from a dozen families in one block to several hundred families spread over a square mile. Formal organization and local institutions may or may not be present. Neighborhoods may lie within or apart from communities. In sociological terms a neighborhood is a primary group; a community is a secondary, or derivative, group. Both terms are carelessly used in everyday conversation. To the man on the street a neighborhood is a collection of houses or the district they occupy. But to us the people who just happen to live near together should be called "nigh dwellers"[1] rather than neighbors. The latter term will be restricted to persons who practice such folkways as visiting, borrowing and lending, granting favors, mutual aid, and doing things together. Further discussion of neighborhoods is deferred to the succeeding chapter.

Suburbs as Urban Communities

It is our thesis that the great majority of communities within our metropolitan districts are or have been suburbs. The

[1] This term was introduced by Bessie A. McClenahan in her monograph *The Changing Urban Neighborhood,* 1929.

principal exceptions are ethnic groups that have established themselves well inside the city. These will be discussed in Chap. XVI. The present chapter will be devoted to suburbs present and past, the stages and the processes involved in their absorption into the metropolis.

Suburbs are roughly defined as communities immediately surrounding a central city. They are characterized by less density of population than is found in the inner city but greater density than is characteristic of rural areas. They differ from independent towns of equal size because the city performs many functions for them. Also, they lack hinterlands or outlying trade areas of their own. Suburbs have close connections with the inner city through various means of transportation, whereby many of their inhabitants are enabled to be employed, to shop, and to carry on other activities outside the immediate community. They have many of the benefits of city life without the disadvantages of congestion, noise, and smoke. They belong to the city and yet they are separate from it.

For convenience, suburban communities are usually identified with outlying municipalities, yet they may not be incorporated and they may even be found inside the limits of a major city. We have already mentioned some of the unincorporated suburbs of St. Louis. The boundaries of this city do not now enclose any well-defined suburban community, although they did a few decades ago. However, the corporate limits of Detroit completely surround Highland Park and Hamtramck, which are independent municipalities; and the city of Los Angeles has annexed several communities that are still suburban in character, *e.g.*, Van Nuys, Owensmouth, Chatsworth, Wilmington. It is plain, therefore, that suburbs may be incorporated or unincorporated and may lie inside or outside the boundaries of a central city. Unfortunately for our purpose, statistical data are usually compiled for political units rather than for communities. This handicap will be recognized in the discussion which follows.

In our earlier consideration of the growth of cities we called attention to the fact that outlying parts of metropolitan districts are increasing in population more rapidly than the central cities. In the decade between 1920 and 1930 the central cities of 96 metropolitan districts increased 19.4 per cent, while the outlying portions increased 39.2 per cent. In particular cities the difference was very much greater than for the group as a whole.

Data for representative cities of this sort are displayed in the first part of Table 43. In the second part of the table are listed all the metropolitan districts whose central cities grew proportionately more than did their outlying sections. These 14 cities constitute only one-eighth of all the metropolitan districts reported in the Fifteenth Census. Moreover, 8 of the 14 central cities annexed part of the outlying district during the decade in question. Such annexations were particularly identified in the cases of Dallas, Fort Worth, Oklahoma City, and Tulsa, but they occurred also in Birmingham, El Paso, Erie, and Peoria.[1] Obviously, if in a given decade a city annexes a portion of the suburban fringe, part of the latter's population increase is transferred to the inner city. Even if there have been no recent annexations, the ratio of urban to suburban growth depends on where the city limits happen to be drawn. Hence our data must be regarded as approximate rather than exact measures of central and peripheral increase. Nevertheless, we are justified in asserting that to date an almost universal characteristic of our metropolitan districts is to grow more rapidly on the outskirts than at the center.

Other indications of the importance of suburban development are reported by McKenzie.[2] In Illinois, Michigan, and Ohio a majority of the new municipal incorporations in the decade just closed were in the four metropolitan districts of Chicago, St. Louis, Detroit, and Cleveland. In 1930 there were 1,566 incorporated places in 96 metropolitan districts. In general the suburban trend is most marked in the most highly urbanized regions, namely, New England and the Middle Atlantic states. As Douglass puts it, "Going out is proportionate to going up."[3] What he means is that, unless there are fixed barriers to restrict expansion or economic factors which promote it, the percentage of metropolitan population that is suburban varies with the percentage of families living in multiple dwellings in the inner city. He adds another generalization which should be apparent from data presented in the preceding chapter. It is that suburbs are bound to the city in the degree of their physical closeness, being more independent the farther away they are from the

[1] R. D. McKenzie, *The Metropolitan Community*, pp. 336–339, 1933.
[2] *Ibid.*, pp. 71–72.
[3] H. Paul Douglass, *The Suburban Trend*, p. 28, 1925.

central city. This statement requires some qualification, but it is approximately correct.

Classification of Urban Communities

In the classification of communities that are or have been suburbs we shall consider physical separation from the central city, economic status, and dominant social functions, but our chief concern will be with the degree of absorption into the metropolis. The types which we shall describe may be regarded as stages in the process whereby independent communities lose their identity and are merged in the life of a great city. But before presenting our own classification it may be profitable to examine briefly those of some other students of the city. Douglass, Gist, Halbert, and others speak of "suburbs of production"

Table 43.—Rate of Growth, 1920–1930, Central Cities and Outside Parts of Metropolitan Districts[a]

A: Some metropolitan districts with greater growth in outside parts			B: All metropolitan districts with greater growth in central cities		
City	Central city	Outside	City	Central city	Outside
Reading	3.1	61.6	Birmingham	45.2	40.0
Cleveland	11.8	125.8	Dallas	63.8	34.4
Richmond	6.6	61.8	Duluth	2.6	− 0.7
Rochester	10.9	112.4	El Paso	32.1	− 3.7
Baltimore	9.7	72.2	Erie	24.2	−16.1
Denver	12.2	79.9	Evansville	19.9	19.1
Atlantic City	30.6	151.2	Fort Worth	53.5	−52.2
Boston	4.4	21.2	Huntington	61.2	17.5
Buffalo	16.3	50.4	Louisville	31.0	1.6
Chicago	25.0	73.4	Norfolk	2.0	−31.3
Seattle	15.8	57.4	Oklahoma City	103.1	77.0
Indianapolis	15.9	80.4	Peoria	37.9	32.0
Toledo	19.6	75.0	Tulsa	93.7	33.3
Atlanta	34.8	68.1	Waterbury	8.9	8.4
Detroit	57.4	108.9			
St. Louis	6.7	71.3			

[a] Fifteenth Census, *Metropolitan Districts*, pp. 10–13.

and "suburbs of consumption."[1] By the latter they mean what are more commonly called residential suburbs. These have been further classified by Lundberg as wealthy, middle-class, and poor.[2] By the former they mean what are more generally called industrial suburbs, sometimes satellite cities. In addition we might call attention to suburbs whose major function is political (county seat towns), recreational (towns near parks, beaches, race tracks), educational (college or university towns), or institutional (towns dependent upon hospital, prison, or army post). We shall not ignore these features of suburbs, but in our judgment a "functional" classification of suburbs is less useful than one based on the degree of absorption into the great city. In the first place, all suburbs are residential, though they differ greatly in economic status. In the second place, no matter how much they may have been dominated at some time by a single institution (county government, amusement park, college, or army post), they presently come to serve a variety of purposes. They go at least part of the way toward a balanced community life, and then they are drawn more and more into a nexus of metropolitan relationships.

We present seven types of communities which are or have been suburbs and three series of stages through which they may be expected to pass. (1) The first type includes outlying communities whose social and economic life are relatively independent of the rest of the metropolitan area. Extreme isolation is rare, although some of these communities are really "cultural islands," little touched by the busy life about them. Usually they are separated in space from each other and from the central city. Often they are incorporated municipalities, but many of them are not. Their economic level is likely to be rather low. (2) In our second class are outlying communities with a measure of self-sufficiency but also with definite relations to the inner city. A significant number of men carry on their business or professional activities "in town." Economically they belong

[1] Noel P. Gist and L. A. Halbert, *Urban Society*, pp. 155–157, 1933; Douglass, *op. cit.*, pp. 84–86.

[2] George A. Lundberg, *Leisure: A Suburban Study* (1934), pp. 37–42. Strictly speaking, Lundberg's categories are "wealthy residential," "middle class and poor residential," and "mixed suburb or satellite city." This last corresponds approximately to the "suburb of production."

to the middle and upper classes. Usually such a community has its own government to provide necessary local services and to ward off the encroachments of "undesirable elements." (3) Less sharply defined are those parts of the continuous, built-up portion of the metropolitan area with local institutions and names. When set apart by natural or artificial barriers they are easily identified, but many times there are no distinguishing physical marks. Such a section may once have been like the first or second type described above; but with the increase of its own population and with the centrifugal drift from the inner city, suburb and central city have coalesced, or grown together. These suburbs are sometimes independent municipalities and sometimes unincorporated. When they lack a local government of their own there is usually limited social organization generally. (4) Another type of suburb adjacent to the major city is that which was created to attract or provide for the overflow of urban population. It too may or may not be incorporated. In fact, it may be established in otherwise unoccupied areas within the central city's limits. Because from the outset its inhabitants live an important part of their lives in the urban center, such a suburb may never develop into a well-integrated local community. (5) Quite different from the residential suburbs so far identified are industrial communities, or satellite cities. These are usually built around one or a group of large manufacturing establishments. Frequently marked physiographic features cut them off from the rest of the metropolitan area. Sometimes they are larger, and usually they are more congested, than other suburbs. Satellite cities live more to themselves because their people dwell, shop, worship, play, educate their children, earn their living, and spend most of their time within the cities. Their people read the metropolitan newspapers less than do the residents of other suburbs. However, the industries of the satellite city are dependent on the central city for financing, managing, sale of products, and extra labor supply, and the inhabitants go to the central city for some forms of recreation and for specialized shopping.

Types one, four, and five represent different ways in which a suburb may be started. Types two and three represent stages that tend to follow type one. Types six and seven are outgrowths of types three, four, or five. (6) As suburbs are drawn more and more into the orbit of the metropolis they tend to lose their identity. Through annexation they become politically a part of the central city. Their schools, libraries, playgrounds, police, fire, and health departments, each become part of a city-wide system. Many of their citizens hold membership in metropolitan churches and clubs. The decline of local community life may be slow, but eventual absorption appears to be inevitable. (7) Last of all, then, comes a stage which represents the almost complete disappearance of local unity and of separateness from surrounding groups. What was once the territory occupied by a distinct community is now merely a segment of a great city.

We offer now illustrations of each of the foregoing types of urban community, drawing upon metropolitan St. Louis as our source. While each account describes a particular stage in the development of a particular community, it also represents a point in the general process through which separate communities merge their life with that of a great city.

1. *An Isolated Community in a Metropolitan Area.*—In the northwest part of the St. Louis metropolitan area lies the little municipality of St. Ferdinand. This village of 1,000 inhabitants, seven miles from the St. Louis city limits, stands in interesting isolation from the rest of the metropolitan population. It was settled late in the eighteenth century by the French. After the Civil War many Germans came in, later a few Irish and a scattering of a few other nationalities. At first the French and the Germans were most hostile, as was indicated by their maintaining separate Catholic churches and carrying on Saturday night saloon brawls. In later years there has been much intermarriage, until the community is now very closely knit. Life is simple in St. Ferdinand. Houses are separate frame dwellings; there is no general water or sewerage system. An ancient charter limits the municipality's borrowing to a maximum of $1,000. A voluntary fire department serves those homeowners who have paid an annual fee and display an appropriate symbol on their premises. A sample study showed over one-half of the population to have been born in Florissant and one-third in other places in Missouri. Two-thirds were Catholic. Less than one-third owned either cars or radios; only a little over one-third of the families subscribed for a newspaper. Some years ago there

was an electric line through which connections could be made between St. Ferdinand and St. Louis. However, the route was quite roundabout and now the tracks have been taken out. At the present time there is occasional bus service to the city, but most of the people go to St. Louis rather infrequently. For a time a few of the men were employed at the near-by airport or at the Chevrolet plant in the city. Since 1930 there has been very little employment outside of St. Ferdinand. The town has a number of grocery stores, drugstores, saloons, garages, etc., which would seem to provide fairly adequately for the residents' needs along these lines. Some of the people, however, shop in Wellston, a suburb about seven or eight miles away. St. Ferdinand thus offers an illustration of the most extreme degree of separateness and isolation that is likely to be found in a metropolitan area.

2. *A Relatively Independent Community.*—An interesting contrast to St. Ferdinand is furnished by another outlying municipality, Ferguson, four miles nearer the central city and on a direct line between St. Ferdinand and St. Louis. Its fine old homes with wide lawns and friendly shade trees bespeak a different economic level. Its steam railroad, electric railway, and bus lines betoken a more intimate contact with the great city. Yet Ferguson too is a community apart, separated from the continuous, built-up area of Greater St. Louis by Maline Creek, and having its own local institutions.

Ferguson is a much newer settlement. Since 1855 it has had railroad connections. Indeed, until recent years two commuters' trains carried people from St. Charles, Ferguson, and other suburbs into the central city. Now, however, suburban service has been discontinued by the Wabash Railroad, giving way to busses and private automobiles. An electric railway line reached Ferguson in 1895, but since its route is north and south it serves to connect various suburbs rather than to take people from any of them to the inner city. Ferguson's telephone connections were established in 1902; previous to that, messages were telegraphed. At the present time there are two exchanges serving this suburb, one of which provides toll service, the other local service to St. Louis and many of the other suburbs. In the course of time various churches, schools, a moving picture theater, a park, and other facilities have been established.

Until 1870 Ferguson people are said to have done most of their trading in St. Ferdinand. Since then they have had an increasing number of retail stores which serve most of their needs. Today there are two industrial establishments in Ferguson—one a lumber company, the other a match factory. In general, however, the town is not dependent upon these industries but is essentially a residential suburb. Before the days of rapid transit Ferguson people were kept more closely at home and indulged in many activities which are now disappearing. The Fourth of July, for example, was the occasion of a celebration which brought together almost the entire community.

Unfortunately it has not been possible to take a census showing how many Ferguson people have employment and business in St. Louis. Neither do we know how much shopping is done in the central city, nor how often people go in to the theater, symphony, museum, zoo, or professional baseball games. Casual inquiry and observation make it plain that the life of Ferguson is much more closely bound up with that of St. Louis than is the case with St. Ferdinand, but Ferguson has a more marked individuality than some other suburbs which we are about to describe.

3. *Suburbs Coalescing with the Central City.*—Early in the history of the St. Louis area, settlements were established along the River des Peres and on the upland separating it from the Meramec River. Like a long tentacle this "string" of settlements reached out toward the southwest, being connected with the city since the 1850's by the Missouri Pacific and later by the Frisco Railroad. Cheltenham, Maplewood, Old Orchard, Webster Groves, and Kirkwood constitute the string. Cheltenham, as we shall see later, has been completely absorbed into St. Louis; Old Orchard has been annexed to Webster Groves; all of them have "run together," so that maps or traffic signs are necessary if one wishes to locate their boundaries.

Webster Groves is a "middle-class" residential suburb with a population of 16,000. It lies about 10 miles from downtown St. Louis and, as we have just noted, is not immediately adjacent to the central city. However, it is part of the continuous, built-up area. Webster Groves was settled about 1825 by a few families that moved out from St. Louis. The village grew slowly, as late as 1900 having less than 2,000 inhabitants. Early in its history it acquired a boarding school, later turned into an orphanage, and a Catholic college for women. Much later it became the seat of Evangelical and Catholic theological seminaries. For years the Missouri Pacific and Frisco railroads were the most satisfactory means of transportation between Webster Groves and St. Louis. Even yet the running of commuters' trains has not been wholly discontinued. In 1896 the street railway system reached this suburb; later a bus line ran to Maplewood; about 1930 jitneys or "service cars" came into use. But the increase in private automobiles is associated with the period of Webster's most rapid growth and with the closeness of its relations to the central city.

The residential character of Webster Groves is manifest in the overwhelming predominance of single dwellings, large lawns and trees, shopping districts of "neighborhood" stores, and almost complete absence of industries. Although middle-class in the popular sense, it is really well above the statistical average, and in its early days was considered "de luxe." The median value of homes occupied by owners was reported in 1930 as $9,000. The modal rent was between $50 and $75. The sex ratio was lower, 90 males per 100 females, and the population was older than in St. Louis. While the people were largely native white, there were nearly 1,000 Negroes along the northern edge.

The institutional life of Webster Groves is characteristic of middle- and upper-class residential suburbs. The stores are divided between two subcenters and two smaller groups. Among them chain stores are prominent and thriving. There are 10 churches with a combined membership of more than 5,000, and 10 smaller churches. Several have auditoriums seating 400 persons, pipe organs, dining rooms, separate rooms for educational and social activities. Their work is departmentalized, clergy are well trained, and budgets are relatively large. For leisure time activities there are a moving picture theater, buildings maintained by the Masons and the Knights of Columbus, several women's clubs, two dramatic clubs, Lions, Rotary, American Legion, Boy Scouts, a well-patronized public library, public school playgrounds, and various other organizations and facilities. It appears that informal gatherings and simple neighboring are very common. As to civic organizations, Webster Groves has a League of Women Voters, a Peace Council, the only suburban branch of the Red Cross in metropolitan St. Louis, and various improvement associations. There were once eight private places, and there are still several distinct neighborhoods.

As to stability, three-fourths of the families in 1930 owned the homes which they occupied; there were few multiple dwellings and few vacancies. The ethnic and economic homogeneity has already been mentioned. However, we must not overlook the 6 per cent constituted by Negro laborers and their families, or the moderate religious diversity. Webster Groves' separateness from St. Louis is partly a matter of habits and traditions established while transportation facilities were poor, partly a matter of governmental independence and the possession of other institutions of its own. Its close connection with the inner city is indicated by the estimate that 70 per cent of the gainfully occupied work or have their business in St. Louis. An uncounted number are members of clubs in the city; many consult professional men, shop for specialties, and attend musical and other events in St. Louis. The suburb and the central city are being drawn closer together in many respects, but Webster Groves continues to display a community life of its own.

Clayton is another suburb of the same general type, but with some quite different characteristics. In 1875, by act of the Missouri legislature, St. Louis City and St. Louis County were legally separated. After some delay a committee of prominent citizens selected 104 acres, donated by Mr. Clayton and Mrs. Hanley, to be their county seat. Previous to this, no town existed where Clayton now is. Trees, brush, and stumps had to be removed to make room for the new county buildings. By 1883 it was reported that "Clayton now includes twenty dwellings, three hotels, one grocery, three printing offices, three attorneys, one singing hall, and the County buildings." Up to 1892, the trip between the new town and St. Louis was slow and inconvenient. One might take a hack from the courthouse to Wells Station and from there a narrow-gauge steam railroad to Grand Avenue. Otherwise he might spend a half day traveling on horseback or by carriage. Not until 1904 was there a paved road connecting the two places. However, in 1892 an electric car line was extended out to Clayton. Although agitation for telephone connections began in 1881, service was not established until 1900. As late as 1905 there were less than 50 telephones in Clayton, but by 1930 the number had grown to nearly 3,000.

Clayton possesses its own city government with the usual municipal institutions, one of the important retail subcenters of metropolitan St. Louis, 10 churches, 3 of them metropolitan rather than local, and a variety of social, civic, and professional organizations. Throughout its history it has maintained one or more newspapers, usually published weekly, dealing with local politics, promoting trade with local merchants, and thriving on official advertising. The survival of its banks has doubtless been aided by the deposits of county funds.

Today Clayton is to the eye merely a part of Greater St. Louis. Apart from a small business district surrounding a dingy courthouse, there is little tangible evidence of its separate existence. We have no count of the residents whose employment and business activities take them to other parts of the metropolitan area, but casual observation indicates that the percentage is very high. The population appears to be fairly stable; but this matter too awaits enumeration. The age distribution of the population is about like that of St. Louis, but the sex ratio is lower, only 80 males per 100 females. The people are predominantly native white of native parents. Out of 10,000, only 350 are Negroes and 700 foreigners. Thus, like Webster Groves, Clayton has the homogeneity, stability, local institutions, loyalty, and pride which make it a community. Yet it too has intimate relations with St. Louis and no longer exists apart from the central city. Starting as a "political suburb," it has come to be much like an "overflow suburb."

4. *Overflow Suburbs: Residential.*—We turn now from the suburb which grew up as an independent town and was gradually drawn into the orbit of the metropolis to the suburb created *de novo* to provide for the surplus population of the inner city or at least to attract people from the center to an outlying section. St. Louis has a number of such suburbs along its western borders. Representative of this type is University City, a municipality of nearly 30,000 inhabitants created through a series of real estate subdivisions which began in 1904. It is commonly described as middle-class, but like Webster Groves and Clayton is really well above a statistical median. Most

of the homes are single dwellings whose characteristic value is about $15,000. They are of brick and often quite showy, suggesting the predominance of the *nouveaux riches*. In the eastern part of University City, close to the St. Louis line, are many apartment houses. Business is pretty well concentrated in the "Loop," which is one of the most important subcenters in the whole metropolitan area. It is the hub of transportation facilities east, west, north and south; streetcars, busses, and "service cars" carry passengers in all directions. In addition there are some business houses along Olive Street Road, a string street extending east and west through University City. All told, there are nearly 350 business houses in this suburb—garages, cleaning and dyeing establishments, restaurants, clothing stores, food stores, beauty shops, drugstores, and many others. In the northeast part of University City are a few small industries and large commercial yards, but most of the inhabitants of this suburb find their employment in other sections of the metropolitan district.

Additional light on the economic status and mobility of the population may be had from surveys made in 1933 and 1934. These showed that about one-half of the homes were occupied by their owners, that four-fifths had telephones, and that there were almost as many automobiles as families. However, in 1934 nearly one-tenth of the persons who might be expected to be gainfully employed reported themselves as without work.

The age distribution of the population is very similar to that of the inner city, but the sex ratio is distinctly lower, 81 males per 100 females. Most of the people are native white of native parents; there are no Negroes, but about one-tenth are foreign born and one-fourth are the children of immigrants. These latter groups are mostly Jewish people from eastern Europe. They are concentrated for the most part in the multiple dwellings which surround University City's principal business district. The diversity of religious organizations is another indication of the heterogeneity of the population in this, the largest of St. Louis's suburbs. Catholic, Lutheran, Christian Science, Presbyterian, Methodist, and Jewish are the principal faiths reported. Several of these churches are metropolitan in character, having moved out from the inner city and retaining a membership scattered through various sections of the metropolitan district.

University City is built up continuously with St. Louis, and only the street signs on main thoroughfares enable the stranger to know whether he is in St. Louis, University City, or Clayton. Some houses are actually divided by the lines between these municipalities. In a count taken in 1934 it was found that only one-ninth of the people going to work or to business were occupied in University City, that one-half went to downtown St. Louis, and that the remainder carried on their profession, business, or trade in other parts of the metropolitan area. We have no measure of residential mobility, but our impression is that this is considerably higher than in Webster Groves and Ferguson and probably somewhat higher than in Clayton. If this observation is correct, it suggests that an overflow suburb has little chance of developing a well-knit local community life. Not only do many of the residents of University City move in and out, but those who remain have so many interests identified with other parts of the metropolitan district that it is difficult to develop much loyalty and enthusiasm for University City. We mean to imply not that these traits are wholly lacking but that they are less developed than in suburbs which have had an independent life of their own. The integration of a suburban community, therefore, appears to be related in part to the distance from the central city and in part to the manner in which the suburb has developed.

5. *Overflow Suburbs: Industrial.*—On the east side of the Mississippi River, spreading over part of the American Bottoms is a number of municipalities dominated by large industrial establishments. A cluster of three—Granite City, Madison, and Venice—is just 15 minutes by streetcar from downtown St. Louis. Granite City has a population of 25,000, Madison 8,000, and Venice 5,000. Because the American Bottoms were, until recently, subject to frequent floods, the industrial overflow from St. Louis was greatly retarded. Also, for a long time the types of industries that might have made good use of such sites were poorly represented in the St. Louis region. But with the coming of several railroad lines and their terminal yards in the 1850's, utilization of the east side of the river began.

About 1892, the Niedringhaus interests decided to move their activities from St. Louis to the American Bottoms, where land was cheap and transportation was easily available. They laid out a rectangular townsite with the conventional grid pattern and a broad main street as the axis. On both sides the town, Granite City, was bordered by the large plants of stamping mills, rolling mills, and steel works. The residential districts developed in between, with contrasts which correspond to differences in types of jobs and wages. The north end is slightly higher than the southern and consequently less subject to damage from floods. Here are residences of the better type and a large community high school. One of the outstanding features of this school is the emphasis on technical and trade courses, given in well-equipped shops.

In Madison there are large steel works and car foundries. Near by are iron furnaces, tie yards, railroad yards and shops, and meat-packing plants. Venice is partially a Negro annex to Madison. It comprises a maze of wooden shacks. Madison and Venice literally grew between the railroad tracks.

The history of Madison involves attempted settlements as early as the eighteenth century, but no important development until the coming of the railroads in 1837 and few before the construction of the Merchants' Bridge in 1890. Immediately following the latter event, Madison was incorporated as a village, several industrial establishments were started, and a race track was opened just to the south. In 1903 the levee broke and there was a serious flood. Since then the river has been successfully kept in its own channel. There have been numerous labor conflicts, and politics have been quite involved. For some time Madison was the reputed "hide-out" of St. Louis gangsters.

Madison has a small business section in which food stores, garages, and filling stations predominate. Unlike the residents of many industrial suburbs, the people of Madison do a large part of their trading away from home. They are also somewhat dependent upon outside facilities for recreation. However, there are two unsupervised playgrounds, one motion picture theater, and some saloons with dance halls, and occasionally a Fourth of July celebration is held. The houses are for the most part poorly built, somewhat dilapidated frame buildings valued at $1,500 to $5,000 and renting usually for less than $30 per month. Certain streets are occupied by separate nationalities, but there is considerable acquaintance throughout the town, and rumors spread easily regardless of ethnic lines.

The heterogeneity of Madison's population is indicated by the list of churches. These include Bulgarian Orthodox, Roman Catholic, Independent Polish Catholic, Russian Orthodox, Greek Catholic, Christian Apostolic, Presbyterian, Methodist, Baptist, and Free Methodist institutions. It appears that most of the present inhabitants are the second generation of migrants from Indiana, the Ozarks, and southeastern Europe. Such a varied lot of folk cannot easily be assimilated into a united community. Neither can an independent local life develop readily when the people are so dependent upon employment in various east-side industries and the shopping facilities of the central city. This limited community life manifests itself in the lack of civic organizations. To be sure, there are a Boosters' Club and a Rotary Club, but several attempts to establish and maintain a commercial club and a community council have failed. Perhaps the most popular local institution is the public library.

From the foregoing description it is evident that Madison is not altogether typical of industrial suburbs. Gary, in metropolitan Chicago, and Argentine, in metropolitan Kansas City, appear to be much more complete local communities. Their self-sufficiency and the relatively limited coming and going of their inhabitants make them quite different from Madison.

6. *A Partially Absorbed Community.*—From the examples offered so far it may be inferred that the farther we go from the center of a great city the more likely we are to find well-integrated, relatively self-sufficing communities. As we turn back from the periphery we find local areas less well defined, their inhabitants more mobile and more heterogeneous, fewer and less adequate institutions. Suburbs that began as separate towns display more independence and retain it longer, whereas those that are merely extensions of the central city may never have an autonomous community life. But when any of the suburbs have been surrounded and annexed to the central city they tend gradually to lose their identity. Such is the history of Carondelet.

Founded a little before St. Louis, several miles to the south, Carondelet was for a long time merely another French village. From the beginning trade was centered in St. Louis, so that Carondelet grew very slowly. As late as 1865 it had less than 5,000 inhabitants, while St. Louis had grown to 200,000. In

1845, Germans began to settle in Carondelet, changing its dominant language and institutions as well as its physical appearance. They built frame and brick houses in place of the earlier log and stone dwellings. They opened stores, factories, and banks. About the same time Irish immigrants came to join the French and the German. With the opening of iron and zinc works in the sixties came Italians, Poles, Spaniards, and Negroes.

In early days the trip between Carondelet and St. Louis was arduous and time-consuming. One of the first German settlers started a bus line, but even then a full day was required for the round trip. Thus the two places remained quite separate. About 1875 a horsecar line was established. Now electric cars, busses, and private automobiles carry people back and forth easily and quickly. In 1870, on the initiative of its own citizens, Carondelet was annexed to St. Louis. The motivation seems to have been related to an empty treasury, rough streets, inadequate water supply and fire protection, and a chaotic school system. In respect to its early annexation to the central city Carondelet appears to be somewhat unusual. It is common to find more economic and social ties and less physical separation preceding political union.

Industrially Carondelet developed iron foundries, railroad shops, quarries, brickyards, and breweries. It also had its own commercial and financial institutions. But by the turn of the century iron ore had played out, and the furnaces and some of the foundries closed. Some of the people moved away, while others found employment in different parts of St. Louis. Improved means of transportation facilitated not only scattered employment but downtown shopping as well. Thus Carondelet has become economically a part of St. Louis, although it still has local stores handling food, drugs, and clothing. Much the same trend of events may be identified in other institutions. The first schools were maintained by Catholic sisters. Today, along with Catholic and Lutheran parochial schools, there are several public schools, integral parts of the St. Louis system. At first there was only one church, and sermons were preached in French. About 1850 a German priest arrived. By 1875 there were half a dozen Protestant churches, each more closely associated with other St. Louis churches of its own faith than with those of different denominations in Carondelet. Thus in religion, as in education and in business, we find increasing local diversity and ever closer ties with the city as a whole.

The story of leisure time agencies and activities is not very different. Up to 1840 there were cockfights, dances, drinking bouts, and card parties. During the next two decades Germans founded a lyceum, a debating club, a singing society, and a Turnverein. Until the World War this last was popular and influential. More recently have come the Y.M.C.A., the Y.W.C.A., Boy and Girl Scouts, and a public library, all of them parts of city-wide agencies. From the coming of the Germans until the last depression the Republican party was dominant in Carondelet, but in 1932 the Democrats carried this ward along with the rest of St. Louis.

In general we find Carondelet becoming more like the rest of the city, but in detail it is more and more diversified. Some of the indexes of this local heterogeneity are these: The sex ratio ranges from 92 to 108 in the various census tracts; the percentage of males married varies from 58 to 76; median rentals are as low as $18 in one tract and as high as $60 in another; multiple dwellings constitute from 4 to 37 per cent in different sections; dependency ranges from practically none to 26 cases per 1,000 population. Thus through increasing heterogeneity, mobility, and interdependence Carondelet has been gradually changing from a distinctive community into a section of St. Louis. However, the symbols of its identity are by no means gone. The name persists; people still mention with pride their German or French ancestry; most of the population lives in family groups, occupying single dwellings, which for the most part they own. Missouri Pacific Railroad shops still provide considerable employment. The process of absorption is far advanced but not yet complete.

7. *A Case of Complete Absorption.*—There is another section of St. Louis, Cheltenham,[1] which could by no stretch of the imagination be called a community today. It has run the whole gamut from pioneer conditions, through farming and village stages, to suburban mining and urban manufacturing. While its social life was apparently never as well integrated as that of

[1] L. F. Thomas, "The Sequence of Areal Occupance in a Section of St. Louis, Missouri," *Annals Assn. Amer. Geog.*, 21 (1931), 75–90.

Carondelet, there was a village community in the second quarter of the nineteenth century, and there is still an Italian colony, which will be described in Chap. XVI.

In 1785 Charles Gratiot secured a grant of land about three miles square lying about five miles southwest of the village of St. Louis along the River des Peres. During the next 45 years there was little tilling of the soil, the owners apparently concerning themselves only with firewood, lumber, and game. But between 1830 and 1839, as far as can be judged, the whole tract was gradually brought under cultivation. By 1840 the original area, called the Gratiot League, had been subdivided into 264 parcels. From that date to 1852 many subdivisions were platted, some for small farming and others for suburban residences. Village life developed.

In 1852 the Pacific Railroad (Missouri Pacific) was built through the district. This gave a needed stimulus to the manufacture of clay products. Fire clay had been discovered in Cheltenham in 1844, but for eight years lack of adequate transportation made fuel expensive and the distribution of products difficult. Now there was a steady increase in the output of firebrick, building brick, sewer pipe, and terra cotta. The clays were dug from shafts 60 to 100 feet deep, in drifts along the valley walls or in open pits on the hills and slopes. Factory buildings four and five stories high were erected and equipped with many kinds of clay-shaping machinery. Alongside were kilns and extensive acreages covered with piles of bricks and sewer pipe. Industrial development was further stimulated by the Frisco Railroad in 1883, street railway service, and improved highways. The city was growing out this way, and in 1876 Cheltenham became a part of St. Louis.

Because valley locations were damp, the villagers who could afford it had long ago moved to more healthful sites. But wage earners and others of small means continued to live in the lower parts of the district. Population grew with industry. In the 1850's came a French communistic society, which, however, disbanded within a few years. Later came Italians, who established a community on the heights to the south (see Chap. XVI for an account of Fairmount Heights, sometimes called "Dago Hill"). Some Negroes were employed, but none of them resided in the district. There were obstacles to the further increase of population. Subsurface workings in the clay beds created a hazard for dwellings, since the surface might sink or settle at any time. Smoke and dust were unattractive, to say the least. Hence many of the subdivisions laid out during previous stages were withdrawn from sale, and streets created on paper never took form on the ground. The surface of the greater part of the clay properties today lies idle, is covered with weeds, or is occupied by scattered squatters.

About 1925, signs of another set of changes began to appear. Because some of the clay beds were exhausted and others had become expensive to work, some companies dismantled their plants and sold their land. Others changed from firebrick to sewer pipe, suitable shales still being available; still others opened pits or mines elsewhere and brought their clay to Cheltenham by rail. In 1928 gigantic storm sewers eliminated the flood hazard. With modern excavating machinery it became feasible to create extensive terraces in the valley wall. New industries began to enter the district, and a promising new era seemed to be under way when the depression of 1929 interrupted the development.

Cheltenham has not been a community since the early mining stage of its evolution. Today it is just a part of a great city, occupied by railroad tracks, factories, mine properties, and the homes of wage earners and some middle-class folk. Many of the men who work in Cheltenham live elsewhere, and many of those who live in the district are employed in other parts of St. Louis.

The Life Cycle of Suburbs

We have now described several different types of suburbs, drawing most of our illustrations from a single metropolitan area. We have noted some of their differences in physical appearance, population, institutional life, origin and development, self-sufficiency, and relation to the central city. In general it may be said that the natural history of suburbs is a series of characteristic changes through which they become more completely parts of the city. The typical sequence, however, varies somewhat for the several kinds of suburbs.

An outlying town that later becomes a suburb may at first seem quite as important as the town which eventually becomes the central city. In any event, new means of transportation enable families with business or work in the city to live in what thus becomes a residential suburb. Also, dwellers in the outlying town work and shop in the city. Then intervening land is built up. Eventually annexation may take place, though some suburbs resist this for a long time. Finally there is complete absorption into the metropolis, with heterogeneity, mobility, scattering of activities and affiliations, and interdependence with the rest of the city.

An overflow suburb, on the contrary, may never have an independent existence. A subdivision is laid out, lots are sold, and houses are built. The section is occupied by a growing number of families of the same social class, often *nouveaux riches*, but sometimes old-established families, white-collar folk, or even Negroes. Local institutions appear—stores, churches, schools—which often fail to unite the people because they are from the start partly in and of the city, partly separate from it.

An industrial suburb more commonly has its origin in the erection of a factory, the opening of a mine, or the establishment of some other industrial project. Company houses may be erected. Subdividers and builders bring into being a residential district of shoddy dwellings. Stores, schools, churches, and other institutions develop. Transportation brings laborers from other parts of the metropolitan district to work in the satellite city, and carries local folk elsewhere to work, shop, play, etc. Gradually there is economic and social absorption into the larger city, though political independence may continue for a long time.

A political suburb may be either an old town or a new one created for the purpose. In either case it will be for a long time relatively independent and an important local community. However, through steps similar to those which appear in the life history of any old-town suburb it is sooner or later drawn into the life of the metropolis.

We have dwelt thus at length upon suburbs because it appears that a large number of the communities that may be found in American cities are or have been suburbs. However, there are some that arise inside the central city. Frequently these are immigrant colonies or Negro communities. Such ethnic groups will be discussed in Chap. XVI.

Selected Readings

Dawson, Carl A., and W. E. Gettys: *An Introduction to Sociology*, Ronald Press Company, rev. ed., 1935. Chapters 1 and 2 describe and contrast rural and urban communities.

Queen, Stuart A., W. B. Bodenhafer, and Ernest B. Harper: *Social Organization and Disorganization*, The Thomas Y. Crowell Company, 1935. Chapter 8 describes various types of urban communities and neighborhoods.

Lundberg, George A.: *Leisure: A Suburban Study*, Columbia University Press, 1934. Chapter 2 describes types of suburban communities.

Douglass, H. Paul: *The Suburban Trend*, D. Appleton Century Company, 1925. Important on the assumption that many urban communities are or have been suburbs.

Ogburn, William F.: *Social Characteristics of Cities*, International City Managers' Association, 1937. See Chap. 10, "Specialization and Suburban Development"; Chap. 11, "How Satellite Cities Differ from Others"; and Chap. 12, "Wealthy Suburbs and Industrial Suburbs."

Steiner, Jesse F.: *The American Community in Action*, Henry Holt and Company, 1928. The story of Roxbury and its absorption into Boston.

Ware, Caroline F.: *Greenwich Village*, Houghton Mifflin Company, 1935. The story of an independent village that became part of New York; special emphasis laid on the changes of recent years.

Zorbaugh, Harvey W.: *Gold Coast and Slum*, University of Chicago Press, 1929. A vivid description and history of Chicago's Near North Side.

Chapter XV

URBAN NEIGHBORHOODS

In the preceding chapter we discussed the relatively large local aggregations of people and institutions in metropolitan areas. We noted that their identity was revealed by various factors, such as a name, physical separation, a business or industrial center, a local government, or a group of people with common interests, traditions, and activities. Whenever we found a relatively stable, homogeneous population occupying a fairly well-defined, compact area, and utilizing a distinctively local set of institutions, we have been disposed to assume the existence of a community. But there are other, smaller, and more intimate groups of people, who occupy still more limited areas, which we call neighborhoods. It is to these that the present chapter is devoted.

To restate and elaborate our definition, we mean by *neighborhood* a local aggregation of families among which there is personal acquaintance, visiting, exchange of articles and services. The area occupied and the number of families are usually small, ranging from a dozen families in one block to several hundred spread over a square mile. We shall employ the participle *neighboring* to describe the practice of such folkways as visiting, borrowing and lending, granting favors, rendering mutual aid, and doing things together, *e.g.*, shopping, picnicking, petitioning, cleaning up. Then the noun *neighborliness* may stand for the attitude of being willing or ready to engage in the practices just mentioned. It may be displayed by people who live in non-neighborhood areas and who have little opportunity to practice neighboring. With these meanings in mind we may anticipate that detailed studies will reveal few neighborhoods in cities, but considerable neighborliness, and the practice of neighboring among people who often live some distance apart. In the country we would more frequently find the attitude and the practice among nigh dwellers, who thereby constitute a neighborhood.

Unfortunately we do not have at our disposal studies of neighborhoods which can be arranged so as to display an expected sequence of events or even well-defined types. We shall discover as we proceed that urban neighborhoods do tend to display a characteristic life cycle, but evidence of this will appear in each individual case more than in the series of descriptions we are about to present. An incidental difference between this and the preceding chapters is that here our illustrations are drawn from several different cities at several different dates instead of from one city and one period.

URBAN NEIGHBORHOODS: COLUMBUS, OHIO

Nearly 20 years ago, McKenzie studied a number of neighborhoods in the city of Columbus, Ohio.[1] Four of these he found to possess rather highly organized local life. Another was rather thoroughly disintegrated. He discovered some immigrant groups located near industrial areas or close to the central business district. In outlying sections of moderately high economic status and usually on high ground, he found what were known as organized streets. These were limited areas, usually along a single street, whose inhabitants had established formal organizations for various purposes. The disintegrated neighborhood McKenzie studied was located on low land near the heart of the city, an area of low economic status.

The organized streets, or well-integrated neighborhoods, were, as stated, usually on high ground in relatively new parts of the city. Sometimes the boundaries were marked by granite boulders. Characteristically, the lots were wide and houses were set uniformly back from the street. There were parkways and other evidences of programs to beautify the section. All houses were single dwellings. There were no apartments and no stores. Some of these organized neighborhoods carried on a variety of activities. They had meetings at various intervals, often at the public elementary school. At these meetings they conducted their business as neighborhood improvement associations; afterward they enjoyed a social hour. The program of

[1] R. D. McKenzie, *The Neighborhood: A Study of Local Life in the City of Columbus, Ohio*, 1923. Data used by permission of the University of Chicago Press.

street beautification has already been suggested. In addition, they sent floral tributes in cases of severe illness or death, published a local paper, organized a bowling team, conducted celebrations on such occasions as the Fourth of July, and held picnics. Many of the residents were close friends, some of them were kinsmen. Each of the successfully organized neighborhoods has given evidence of the work of competent leaders.

The disorganized neighborhood was in an old part of the city which went into further decline after the floods of 1913. Real estate prices dropped, and there was an influx of poor people, including some Negroes. Thus the population became more and more heterogeneous. At the time of the study, women outnumbered men, and children were quite numerous. Mobility was high, as evidenced by the number of boarders and lodgers, a low percentage of home ownership, and changes in the voting lists. The low economic status was indicated by the character of occupations, mostly unskilled, the employment of many married women, and the absence of modern conveniences in the houses. Limited social participation was shown by the small number belonging to voluntary organizations, by the sectarianism in the churches, and by the slight amount of mutual aid extended beyond the kinship group. School attendance was relatively poor, dependency and juvenile delinquency rates were high. Recreational facilities were quite restricted. One mark of the disorganized social life of the district was the "individualization" of leisure time activities. Thus older men tended to gather about near-by saloons. Young men were drawn to the poolrooms, cabarets, or cheap dance halls of the area. Young women more frequently went to the uptown dance halls and movies. Small children attended the neighborhood movies, while their mothers had very little recreational life of any sort except that associated with the churches. Thus economic necessity had forced people of unlike attitudes and tastes to dwell near together. They took little pride in their district, paid little attention to their nigh dwellers, united in few joint activities, and in general behaved as individuals rather than neighborhoods.

Thus McKenzie indicated in this study the significance for neighborhood life of a favorable site, stability, homogeneity, at least a moderate economic status, common activities, pride in the district, and leadership. He assumed, more than he demonstrated, the basic importance of intimate, face-to-face dealings, which sociologists call primary relationships.

Urban Neighborhoods: Chicago

More recently Roper has studied the neighborhoods in the part of Chicago known as Hyde Park.[1] This district is on the lake front, six or seven miles south of the central business district. It is bounded on the north by a wide boulevard, on the west by another main thoroughfare and a park, on the south by that wide parkway and trafficway known as the Midway, on the east by the lake and another park. Being thus well defined by natural and artificial barriers, it might be expected to possess a considerable measure of local community life. As a matter of fact, there is evidence that it was once a rather well-defined community. But today it is an apartment house area occupied by people whose business and other interests are scattered throughout the city. Roper estimated that 85 per cent carried on their business and professional activities outside of the Hyde Park area. Economically this was an upper-middle-class section. Nevertheless, it was far from being homogeneous. Roper found one-fourth of the population to be of foreign birth and a small number to be Negroes. Moreover, he found that Jewish people and other groups remained somewhat apart even when they lived in the same residential hotel. Considerable mobility was indicated by a relatively high turnover in the public schools. Rising land values also marked a steady change in the character of the occupants. This much information shall serve to characterize the area as a whole.

We turn now to consider the natural subdivisions which in popular language would doubtless be called neighborhoods. To begin with, these smaller areas were found to have no definite names, and some of them had no well-marked boundaries. However, railroad tracks, a business street, and a university campus served to divide the larger area rather naturally into seven smaller districts. They differed somewhat from each other as to the proportion of the population that was native white of native parents, and as to occupation. Only the two small districts close to the university showed any marks of a

[1] M. W. Roper, *The City and the Primary Group*, 1935. Data used by permission of the author.

well-knit local life. In these, Roper found considerable friendliness and social intercourse. People visited back and forth, borrowed from one another, and performed numerous minor services. However, those who were acquainted and carried on these practices which we call neighboring were very small, congenial groups living in a single apartment house or in the dwellings stretched along one block. Larger groups were brought together at some of the churches. Children associated at the schools, but this did not ordinarily bring their parents into direct contact. Sometimes homeowners united to prevent the erection of an apartment house. All in all, those areas near the university presented many of the earmarks of neighborhood life as we are accustomed to think of it, but in each district the inhabitants were too numerous and their natural contacts too few to make possible more than a rather vague sense of neighborhood.

Along Hyde Park Boulevard and in the hotel area on the lake front, neighboring was very much less in evidence than in the university districts. Such intimate contacts as were found seem to have been made outside this district, through a church or otherwise, and to have developed here when the families moved in. In these sections, moreover, the division between Jew and Gentile was especially marked. One resident stated, "The old type of neighborly intimacies is confined almost entirely to the flat and to the small apartment housing six families or less. Mobility increases with the size of the building."[1]

Two other so-called neighborhoods, each centering more or less about a public school, seemed to Roper to lie between the university districts and the boulevard and hotel areas. They were intermediate not only geographically but also in the character of the local life. There were old residents who complained about the strange new people who were coming in, and lamented the passing of neighborliness of bygone days. Parent-teacher associations were difficult to promote because of the heterogeneity of the folk and their unwillingness to accept one another. So far as adults were concerned, it seemed that no neighborly contacts extended over districts larger than a block. Often they were confined to a single building. Children, however, formed contacts over somewhat larger areas and of a more intimate character. They met at school or at play. They

[1] *Ibid.*, p. 62.

made friends and showed themselves to be the most real neighbors in the district. But even they found their associates within quite restricted areas. Sometimes a child would not go more than a couple of blocks to join his little friends. Children of the Kozminski school reported that over half of their best friends lived within a distance of two blocks.

Thus in all the subdivisions of this former community we see a diminution of neighboring and of locally organized activities. Large numbers of people living in close proximity have few personal contacts, know little about one another, and have their own diversified interests scattered throughout the city. Within the residential district children are likely to do more neighboring than their parents and to go a little farther to meet their friends. But for both young and old the range of primary relations is exceedingly limited. This is probably quite characteristic of apartment areas in the large cities of America.

The Columbus study revealed both well-integrated and almost wholly disorganized neighborhoods. The Chicago study shows the dissolution of neighborhood ties far advanced but not yet complete.

Exclusive Neighborhoods: Private Streets in St. Louis

In metropolitan St. Louis there are over 75 subdivisions in which not only the building lots but the streets themselves are, or have been, owned and controlled by the residents. Some of these date back to an earlier period. A few of the older ones have passed out of existence or at least gone into decline, but most of them appear to be thriving ventures in a certain kind of neighborliness. The characteristic sequence of events in the establishment, conduct, and decline of one of these private streets is somewhat as follows. An area which promises to be a desirable residential district is chosen, subdivided, and restricted. The restrictions, which are written into the deeds of the individual lots as sold, usually forbid the erection of any but single family residences, excluding all types of business, even boarding houses and physicians' offices. Often they stipulate minimum cost of building, materials, type of architecture, size of lot, distance from the street, etc. Commonly, ownership is restricted to the "Caucasian" race. The purposes of all these restrictions, indeed of the venture as a whole, are to maintain property values, ensure a certain exclusiveness, and make possible a kind of neighborhood protected from the encroachment of business or unwelcome types of people.

Whether the venture is promoted by a realtor or by a group of people already associated, it presently comes to be occupied by a homogeneous group of more or less congenial families. They are organized into an association for control of the area and its residents. Usually they elect a small board of trustees who carry on the business of the association. Their powers and duties include the collection of assessments which range from $0.50 per front foot to a flat rate of $400 per year for each lot owner. They make contracts with public utilities and with individuals to supply water, gas, and electricity, to collect garbage, and to afford police protection. Sometimes the members of the association hold annual or special meetings at which they vote on matters of importance. But in most instances no formal meetings are held at all. The law requires that gates to private streets be kept closed at least 30 days in the year lest the streets automatically become public property.

Gradually the surrounding area is filled with family residences. In time these begin to give way to apartment and business houses. Property values decline. For a time all this may have little effect upon the private place, but eventually its occupants are displeased with their surroundings and with the fact that many of their friends have moved much farther toward the periphery of the metropolitan district. From time to time, old families die out or suffer financial loss. Unable to maintain expensive establishments, as these usually are, owners wish to sell, rent, or remodel. Forbidden to do this, they may leave the house vacant or tear it down. Discussion of changing or dropping restrictions divides the occupants of the street and marks its decline as a neighborhood. Eventually the streets, *i.e.*, the actual pavements and sidewalks, are voluntarily dedicated to the city, and restrictions are withdrawn. Perhaps a court may set them aside on the ground that the area and its relation to surrounding districts are so changed that the restrictions are no longer valid.

Because some of these places have been in existence for three-quarters of a century and because some of them have ceased to exist, it is possible not only to identify their life cycle as we have just done, but also to consider some of the advantages and disadvantages to the residents. In the first place, these folk have succeeded in maintaining property values over long periods of time. In the end, however, they suffer great losses because of the inflexibility of their plan, which impedes their adjustment to changes in the districts about them. Also they are successful from the standpoint of exclusiveness, stability, and homogeneity of life. They make possible the escape from noise and traffic.

Like St. Louis's private streets in some respects is Chicago's Gold Coast.[1] Both represent high economic levels and social exclusiveness, both "go in" for philanthropy, civic reform, art, and music. However, the Gold Coast includes hotels and displays much more mobility than is characteristic of the private streets. One gets the impression of more conspicuous consumption, greater snobbery, and more social climbing on the Gold Coast, although this is obviously difficult to measure. But the greatest difference appears to be in the practice of neighboring. Zorbaugh's account emphasizes the absence of neighborly contacts on the Gold Coast despite the "localization of society," with its self-consciousness and common traditions. But in some of the private streets we have found much informal visiting as well as the previously mentioned marks of the true neighborhood.

From these two studies we are warranted in the inference that high economic status and superior physical conditions may facilitate, but do not guarantee, neighboring. Neighborhoods are essentially matters of folkways and traditions rather than of economics and architecture. The illustrations which follow indicate that neighborhoods may develop on any economic level, providing nigh dwellers have the willingness and the desire to share their experiences and actually behave as a group.

An Unfashionable Neighborhood: Hooverville

In complete contrast to the well-to-do groups just discussed are the shifting settlements of squatters in river bottoms and on other vacant land, usually at the edge of the city. Sometimes these settlements are spoken of as "jungles." The occupants, among whom are single men as well as families, may be quite transient, but during the depression of 1929 and afterward there developed in some cities more permanent neighborhoods

[1] Harvey W. Zorbaugh, *Gold Coast and Slum*, Chap. 3, 1929.

of the unemployed, settlements which were frequently called Hooverville.

In St. Louis, Hooverville started in 1929 with the erection of two shacks near the western end of the Municipal Bridge. The pioneer settlers were lone men, first white, later colored; finally whole families moved in. The land was unused public property. Settlers had to erect their own dwellings, which they did with the most miscellaneous collections of material that could be imagined. They gathered pieces of lumber, beaverboard, tar paper, tin, and almost anything that could be salvaged from scrap heaps. Shanties so erected were sometimes sold or traded and sometimes simply abandoned. It was a rule of the community that any house which remained vacant for 30 days should belong to the first who took possession. By 1932 the population was over 1,300, white and black, native and foreign born, most of them old residents of St. Louis. A few had irregular work. Most were wholly unemployed. One man sent out an appeal for help which brought such returns that it accomplished his "election" as "mayor." Sensational publicity continued to bring gifts, which were assembled in a rude headquarters building and doled out by the "mayor" until dissatisfaction forced him to abdicate in favor of another. Through this crude relief system, odd jobs, and freedom from rent, most Hooverville people managed to keep off the public relief rolls for some time.

For education, children were sent to the regular public schools. But the neighborhood developed a religious life of its own. First the Pentecostal Church, or Church of God, erected a structure in keeping with the local style of architecture. Then better-known denominations undertook to establish missions, but perhaps most active of all was a Gospel Center, whose doughnuts and coffee attracted good-sized congregations.

Twice Hooverville was visited by fire and once by flood. But C.W.A. and W.P.A. thinned the ranks more than any action of the elements. This particular settlement seems doomed to early extinction, but it represents a type that is neither new nor likely to disappear.

In contrast to St. Louis, Seattle developed a Hooverville occupied almost exclusively by men.[1] Otherwise the two were

[1] Donald F. Roy, "Hooverville: A Study of a Community of Homeless Men in Seattle," unpublished master's thesis, University of Washington, 1935.

much alike—in site, location, architecture, economic status, *modus vivendi,* and social organization. On a sandy waste, once the site of a shipyard, within easy walking distance of the central business district, arose Seattle's Hooverville. The bay was used for garbage and sewage disposal. Some of the premises were incredibly filthy. Naturally the city officials looked upon this new residential district as a menace to health, safety, and morals.

The population was surprisingly elderly, less than one-eighth being under thirty years, and fully one-eighth being over sixty. Ethnic groups were so mixed as to constitute a "racial rainbow." But except for the Filipinos, the settlers were "old-timers" in the Pacific Northwest.

The neighborhood was governed by a vigilance committee, which undertook to police the grounds and to settle minor disputes. It was chosen at an open-air caucus and made up of two white men, two Negroes, and two Filipinos. The "mayor," who seems to have been self-appointed, was an ex-cowpuncher. An important factor in his prestige and authority was his ability to secure a patrol wagon or ambulance by phoning from a near-by coalyard. The economic setup was various. Half of the population was on public relief. Others supported themselves by "rustling," *i.e.,* begging, stealing, and picking up discarded articles from alleys and dumps. Some found odd jobs, and many engaged in fishing. Recreation consisted principally in card playing and, when there was money, in drinking, attending cheap movies and burlesque shows, consorting with prostitutes, and engaging in homosexual amours.

The general atmosphere was one of friendliness and hospitality. Race prejudice was at low ebb. Eleven shanties were found to shelter groups including individuals of different colors. Curiously, there was little bitterness toward the established economic and political institutions. In general, there was an attitude of apathy concerning the future, expressed in such words as "I never expect to get work again anyhow. They say I'm too old."

Thus we find on the lowest economic level, as well as on the highest, genuine examples of neighboring. But the impression is inescapable that neither type of neighborhood has particularly good prospects of permanence.

The Rise and Decline of a Neighborhood: Los Angeles

About 1875 a woman named Mary Newman secured a federal land grant near the little town of Los Angeles.[1] After farming it for several years, she began to sell tracts. These too were cultivated, until, in 1887, their owners began to subdivide them into building lots. By 1903 this subdivision was completed. By this time the area had, moreover, become a part of the city. It was covered with bungalows and other single dwellings for middle-class homeowners. In the beginning it appears that "everyone knew everyone else" and "all were on an equal footing." In the years that followed, there was a steady increase in population of the original type. Fields and orchards disappeared; more houses were built. Ultimately the numbers and varieties of inhabitants became too great for widespread acquaintance.

About 1914 some rear houses were built and others were remodeled to accommodate more than one family. After the World War, the housing shortage and high rentals gave further impetus to the erection of multiple dwellings. But it was not until 1927 that the first real apartment house was built. During this period, as the population became more numerous, it also became more heterogeneous and more mobile. Home ownership declined and tenancy increased. Some old homes were turned into rooming houses. The character of the area was rapidly being changed. Presently, one street became a business thoroughfare with a growing number and variety of stores and populations. Soon divergent racial types invaded the area. Not only Europeans, but Negroes and Japanese, found their way here and there into the district. By this time the old residents were disappearing. Some had died, but others moved away. Some found opportunities to sell their property to advantage. Others left because they feared depreciation of property values or a loss of social status. As the homogeneous group of old residents departed and the heterogeneous types of newcomers established themselves in the district, the practices of neighboring showed marked decline. There was less and less participation in localized activities; there were fewer and

[1] Bessie A. McClenahan, *The Changing Urban Neighborhood*, 1929. Data used by permission of the University of Southern California Press.

fewer personal contacts. Interests were scattered over the city. Many persons displayed attitudes of superiority toward the district and apologized for having to live there. Conflicts developed between the residents. What was once a well-knit neighborhood had become just another part of the city.

Similar to the picture of this Los Angeles neighborhood after its sociological decline is Zorbaugh's account of a rooming-house district on the Near North Side of Chicago.[1] In a once fashionable residential district just west of the Gold Coast he found over 1,100 rooming houses. Fine old homes had been turned to this new use. Instead of old families who practiced all the folkways of neighboring, he discovered a predominance of single persons between the ages of twenty and thirty-five years and almost no children. Mobility was so great that every four months changes of address equaled the total population at any given date. Naturally, acquaintances were few and friendships fewer. Little interest was taken by the inhabitants in each other or in the district. It was an area of high mobility and general anonymity, almost wholly devoid of group life of any sort, "a world of atomized individuals, of spiritual nomads."[2]

The Life Cycle of an Urban Neighborhood

From the numerous studies that have been made and from the illustrations offered in this chapter it is possible to identify, tentatively at least, a typical life history or expected sequence of events in urban neighborhoods. (*a*) The first stage is the occupying of a district by homeseekers who wish pleasant, healthy, and otherwise acceptable surroundings in which to rear a family. They want congenial nigh dwellers who will become neighbors in the sense of people who visit back and forth, go shopping together, care for each other's children, and engage in the other practices associated with neighboring. (*b*) As time passes, the number of residents increases and personal acquaintance declines. The neighborhood is surrounded by various sorts of people and perhaps by business houses. It may be divided by a new thoroughfare. Some of the earlier settlers die or move away. Some of the newcomers are tenants instead of owners. Neighboring and neighborliness decline. (*c*) In a third stage,

[1] Zorbaugh, *op. cit.*, Chap. 4.

[2] *Ibid.*, p. 86.

there may be invasion of the neighborhood area itself by business or by strange ethnic groups. As single dwellings give way to converted tenements, apartments, and rooming houses, occupied increasingly by racial or other groups regarded as inferior, neighborhood pride and loyalty decline still further. (*d*) Finally, personal contacts practically disappear, neighboring ceases, and the district loses its identity in the general life of the city. It may continue as part of a respectable residential section; it may be taken over by business or industry; or it may deteriorate slowly while vice and crime get a foothold. In any case the life cycle of a neighborhood has been completed.

Now these events do not occur in identical sequence. Some of them may be absent from particular cases. But in general the shifts follow the approximate order that we have indicated: from residential home ownership, to tenancy, to business, to heterogeneity of inhabitants, sometimes to disorder, and to the final displacement of residents by other uses of the land.

The Measurement of Neighboring

In 1935 Jessie S. Bernard undertook the development of an instrument for measuring the relative amount of neighboring by different kinds of people in different parts of a city.[1] Indeed, it is our belief that her device might well be employed in a comparative study of neighboring in rural and in urban districts.

Through steps which are similar to those employed by psychologists in evolving schedules and scoring systems, Mrs. Bernard developed the instrument, part of which is reproduced below. This schedule was not mailed out as a questionnaire but was used by herself in interviewing persons whose responses were desired. Some of the questions pertain directly to neighborhood practices. Others have to do with matters which might be associated with neighboring or its absence. Here are some of the questions:

1. About how many of the people who live in your neighborhood would you recognize by sight if you saw them in a large crowd?
   Answer: None Few Some Many Most All

[1] Jessie S. Bernard, "An Instrument for the Measurement of Neighborhood with Experimental Application," unpublished doctoral dissertation, Washington University, 1935.

2. About how often do you chat or "visit with" your neighbors?
Answer: Never Rarely Sometimes Often
3. Do you and your neighbors exchange things, such as books, magazines, patterns, recipes, jellies, jams, preserves, suggestions, tools, dishes, seeds, plant clippings, or any other similar things?
Answer: Never Rarely Sometimes Often
4. Do you and your neighbors exchange favors or services, such as receiving parcels, telephone messages, or other similar favors?
Answer: Never Rarely Sometimes Often
5. Do you and your neighbors ever go to the movies together?
Answer: Never Rarely Sometimes Often
6. Do you and your neighbors ever go shopping together?
Answer: Never Rarely Sometimes Often
7. Do your neighbors ever talk over their problems with you when they are worried, or ask you for advice or help?
Answer: Never Rarely Sometimes Often
8. Do you and your neighbors ever take care of each other's children when the other one is sick or busy?
Answer: Never Rarely Sometimes Often
9. Do you and your neighbors ever have picnics or outings or parties together?
Answer: Never Rarely Sometimes Often
10. Is the church you usually attend in your present neighborhood?
Answer: Yes No Do not attend church usually
11. Do you belong to a church club, such as a Ladies' Aid, or a sewing club, or a mothers' club, or a church men's club of any kind *in your neighborhood?*
Answer: Yes No
12. Do you belong to a school club, such as a Parent-Teacher Association, or a mothers' club, or some similar school organization in your neighborhood?
Answer: Yes No
13. Do you belong to any social club or group, such as a bridge club, gymnasium class, dancing club, sewing club, or any similar organization in your neighborhood?
Answer: Yes No
14. Do you belong to a local improvement association (or Farmers' Grange, if you live in the country)?
Answer: Yes No
15. Do your best friends live in your present neighborhood?
Answer: None Few Some Many
16. Would you rather live in some other neighborhood?
Answer: Yes No Do not know

17. Are your neighbors of the same nationality as you?
Answer: None Few Some Many Most All Do not know
18. How many years have you lived in your present neighborhood?
______
19. Do you own your home? No Yes (This includes mortgaged homes)

We have included this much of Mrs. Bernard's schedule with the hope that it, or some modification thereof, may be employed in representative studies in many places.

As she developed her instrument, Mrs. Bernard tried it out in various parts of metropolitan St. Louis, scoring the rates and correlating them with other series of data pertaining to the same sections. As a result. she identified a negative correlation of neighborhood scores with mobility, median rentals, and multiple dwellings. She discovered a positive correlation of neighboring with single dwellings, home ownership, and percentage married. This means that wherever people moved frequently, paid low rents, and lived in tenements, flats, or apartments, there was little neighboring. But when they occupied single dwellings, which in most cases they owned, and when the great majority of adults were married couples, there was a great deal of neighboring. Mrs. Bernard also found that membership in local organizations, having a best friend in the vicinity, and having children were closely associated with high neighborhood scores. She ventured the tentative conclusion that some areas foster the practice of neighborhood folkways, while others do not. Perhaps some areas draw to themselves persons who are accustomed to neighboring and value it highly, while others attract persons given to transient and anonymous living.

Indexes and Trends

From the foregoing discussion it is plain that we do not have to content ourselves with casual observations and descriptive accounts in order to identify urban neighborhoods and discover trends in the practice of neighboring. From graphic displays of significant facts it is possible to locate quickly areas in which neighboring is most likely to occur and others from which it is almost certain to be absent. By correlating various series of data, including those derived from Mrs. Bernard's schedule, it is possible to identify rather definitely a number of social, economic, and demographic factors with the presence or absence of neighborhood life. From our own studies in St. Louis we have concluded that among the important criteria of neighborhoods are stability, homogeneity, standard age and sex distribution, family life, land use, and absence of the so-called pathologies.

First of all, it is apparent that unless the local population remains in the same vicinity for a reasonable length of time there cannot be personal acquaintance, familiarity with local traditions, behavior in accordance with local customs, or pride in local institutions. We shall see in a later chapter how stability and mobility may be measured. Second, it is believed that the integration of neighborhoods and communities requires a certain homogeneity of the population. We have not attempted to construct any index of homogeneity as such, but we do have rather definite indications of this in census data concerning color, nativity, and economic status. We ought to have data concerning religious affiliations as a further check on homogeneity or heterogeneity. In the third place, we assume that neighborhood and community life is most likely to be found in districts where the population pyramid conforms to that of a static or slow-growing population. That is, the sex ratio will approximate 100 and the number and percentage of persons in each age group will decrease steadily from youngest to oldest.[1] Fourth, it appears that family life and neighboring bear some relation to each other. That is, neighborhood and community organization may be expected in areas where a large percentage of the adult population is married, where families are above the city average in size, and where most of the residential units are single dwellings. A fifth criterion is land use. As just mentioned, when an area is occupied almost exclusively by single dwellings, neighborhood life seems more likely to develop, although its existence cannot be taken for granted. Multiple dwellings indicate that local organization is likely to be absent. A large number of rooming houses, hotels, or converted tenements almost guarantees the nonexistence of neighborhood and community. A mixture of residential with commercial and industrial property seems to interfere with the organization of local life.

[1] R. D. McKenzie, *The Metropolitan Community*, pp. 181, 246, 1933.

Negatively, such items as juvenile delinquency, adult crime, vice, poverty, and disease are believed to affect the integration or disintegration of local groups or institutions. For example, the occurrence of a relatively large amount of juvenile delinquency indicates that informal controls are breaking down or do not exist. If a small boy in a real neighborhood breaks a window, the chances are good that he will receive parental discipline and that some financial adjustment will be made with the owner of the damaged property. But in an area where people neither know nor trust one another such an event is more likely to be followed by a complaint to the police or the juvenile court. Thus a high juvenile court rate may indicate neighborhood disorganization rather than excessive delinquency; however, the latter may also occur.

As yet, it is too early to say with assurance that neighborhood groups and practices are disappearing from American cities, but such evidence as we possess indicates that they have been declining and may be expected to diminish further. Among the factors related to this apparent disintegration of neighborhood life is, first of all, mobility, which we shall discuss more fully in Chap. XVIII. Another aspect of the same phase of city life is the continuing invasions of residential districts. Few years pass without some new kinds of occupants or some new land use. The occurrence of these is doubtless related to immigration from rural America as well as from abroad, the centrifugal flight, obsolescence, and changing methods and routes of transportation. A third factor, related to the first two, is the dispersion of contacts and centers of activities. Many city dwellers have personal friends scattered over a metropolitan district rather than concentrated in a limited area. They work and shop away from the immediate vicinity. Their recreational and religious activities are carried on elsewhere. In the fourth place, it appears that special interest groups are increasing in number and in their demands on time, energy, and money, leaving less and less for local groups. Indeed it has come to such a pass that Park has held that "it is the incompetent persons, apparently, who still maintain an interest that could in any sense be called lively in the local communities of our great cities."[1]

[1] Robert E. Park and E. W. Burgess, *The City*, p. 113, 1925. By permission of the University of Chicago Press.

Some Rural-urban Contrasts

While we have as yet no comparable measurements of urban and rural neighboring, we do have some objective studies of country neighborhoods to place alongside of the urban data just presented. For example, Kolb studied Dane County, Wisconsin, beginning his search for neighborhoods by asking people the name by which they identified their immediate vicinity. On the basis of their replies, he mapped districts within which he expected to find more or less neighboring. Then he inquired where the people sent their children to school, where they attended church and Grange meetings, with whom they visited and exchanged services. He searched for topographic features that might separate one such area from others, and for additional factors in the development of a distinctive local group. He discovered a sharing of various experiences in the districts he studied. Sometimes the people were interrelated by blood and marriage, sometimes they were merely of the same nationality, sometimes they had a cooperative creamery or tobacco growers' association; but most frequently they maintained a district school or country church.[1]

Other such studies have been made in many different states. They show conclusively that there really are locality groups of the sort we think of as rural neighborhoods, although by no means all country people live in neighborhoods. Furthermore, these groups tend to persist, although there is also evidence of their decline and even disappearance.[2] Some country people go to a number of different centers for different purposes, some have friends of their own social class in scattered places but hold themselves aloof from their nigh dwellers. In these respects they are very like city people. There is more than superficial evidence that neighboring is declining in both city and country, but it seems to be more often vigorous and likely to continue longer in rural than in urban areas. Periodic studies of given districts, urban and rural, using a schedule such as Mrs. Bernard's, would afford a basis for much more dependable conclusions than are now possible.

[1] J. H. Kolb, *Rural Primary Groups*, 1921.

[2] J. H. Kolb and E. de S. Brunner, *A Study of Rural Society*, Chap. 5, 1935.

If such studies support our hypothesis that neighborhoods are disintegrating more rapidly in cities than in the country, we shall doubtless be warranted in attributing this fact to the greater mobility (also subject to future measurement), heterogeneity, and sheer numbers found in metropolitan districts. Another significant feature may be the individualistic method of buying and selling real estate, subdividing tracts, building houses, and selecting homes. Except in cases like the private streets, new subdivisions are rarely laid out and built up for the benefit of a homogeneous, congenial group of actual or potential neighbors. Houses and lots are usually planned for sale to individual families with a minimum of attention to their nigh dwellers. House hunters make some effort to assure themselves that there are no objectionable features about the property under inspection and its immediate vicinity. But such a negative approach gives little promise that the newcomers will respect local traditions, if any exist, join in local activities, or support local institutions.

But none of these features, except large numbers, are wholly absent from rural America. Farms have been sold to individuals without much reference to the occupants of adjoining lands. Farm tenants in some regions move rather frequently, farm laborers still oftener. The biracial complexion of the rural South and parts of the West interferes with the confidence, mutual aid, and cooperative effort which go to the building of communities. Hence we must conclude that the social integration of local aggregations of people is incomplete in both urban and rural districts. But from the information at our disposal we believe that neighborhoods and communities are disintegrating and disappearing more frequently and more rapidly in cities than in the country.

Selected Readings

McKenzie, R. D.: *The Neighborhood: A Study of Local Life in the City of Columbus, Ohio*, University of Chicago Press, 1923.

McClenahan, Bessie A.: *The Changing Urban Neighborhood*, University of Southern California Press, 1929. The rise and decline of a neighborhood in Los Angeles.

Roper, M. W.: *The City and the Primary Group*, University of Chicago Libraries, 1935. A study of neighborhoods in the Hyde Park section of Chicago.

Park, Robert E., and E. W. Burgess: *The City*, University of Chicago Press, 1925. See Chap. 8, "Can Neighborhood Work Have a Scientific Basis?"

Chapter XVI

ETHNIC GROUPS IN AMERICAN CITIES

In the two chapters just preceding we have discussed neighborhoods and communities without much reference to their ethnic composition. We assumed that most of them had native white populations. But there are in every city local groupings of immigrants and Negroes. Sometimes their physical appearance, more often their culture, marks them off from the people who live around them. Their separate neighborhoods and communities are maintained in part from choice and in part because of pressure from outside. Quantitatively these ethnic groups are important in American cities. In 1930 one-third of our urban population was of foreign birth or parentage. In addition, 7.5 per cent was Negro. Eighty per cent of our immigrants lived in cities, as did 73 per cent of their American-born children, and 44 per cent of the Negroes. Qualitatively too these ethnic groups are important. They introduce new culture traits; their lack of assimilation presents problems of social control; the diversity of their folkways and mores is a source of conflict. But what concerns us at the moment is the extent to which these groups are segregated in distinct neighborhoods or communities and the character of these local groups.

Immigrant Colonies

The segregation of Negroes is sufficiently recognized to warrant our temporarily taking it for granted; in the last part of this chapter we shall examine the matter in more detail. The segregation of immigrants from particular countries, and their descendants, is less uniform. "Everyone" knows that there are some immigrant colonies in our large cities. These more or less separate communities are identified superficially by foreign signs on stores, the Old World dress of people on the streets, and the sound of strange tongues. A more intimate view reveals distinctive goods in the shops, menus in restaurants, services in church and synagogue, and marriage customs, as well as the celebration of holidays not listed in any American calendar, foreign language newspapers, and neighborhood feuds. All these are symbols of the social distance that lies between the newcomers and those whose ancestors arrived long ago.

Comparing and contrasting three cities—Boston, Cleveland, and St. Louis[1]—we find some ethnic groups living pretty much apart while others are scattered over the metropolitan area. In general, representatives of the "old" immigration, *i.e.*, British and German, are mixed with the rest of the people. In St. Louis, where in 1930 one-fourth of the foreign born were natives of Germany and one-seventh of the total population was German (born in Germany or the children of German parents), there were two areas in which people of German stock predominated. Nevertheless, there was not a single census tract in which more than one-third of the population was German, as we are using the term. On the other hand, only 2 out of 128 census tracts were less than 1 per cent German. In Cleveland the English-speaking and German-speaking groups (including Austrians) were fairly evenly distributed throughout the city. In Boston substantially the same condition obtained. There natives of the Irish Free State comprised the largest group of foreigners. They were so widely distributed that they constituted one of the four most numerous national groups in 12 of the 14 census areas.

Turning to the non-English-speaking, "new" immigrants, we find Italians markedly segregated in all three cities. Other foreign colonies in Boston and St. Louis were small except for groups of Russian Jews.[2] But in Cleveland there were several fairly large and well-defined areas occupied predominately by Poles, Jugoslavs, Slovaks (natives of Czechoslovakia), Hungarians, and Jews (natives of Russia), as well as Italians. When data for other cities are examined, details are found to vary, but the general situation is much the same. In the Pacific Coast cities Japanese and Chinese have well-established colonies; in

[1] *Social Statistics by Census Tracts in Boston*, Boston Council of Social Agencies, 1933; Howard W. Green, *Population Characteristics by Census Tracts, Cleveland, Ohio, 1930*, 1931; Ralph C. Fletcher, Harry L. Hornback, and Stuart A. Queen, *Social Statistics of St. Louis by Census Tracts*, 1935.

[2] Incidentally the census data leave much to be desired, for they indicate country of birth but not language or cultural group. It is from other sources that we know a majority of the Russian and Polish born in Boston and St. Louis to be Jewish.

those of the Southwest this is true of Mexicans. On the whole we may say that immigrant groups from northwestern Europe, who have three or more generations in America, have practically

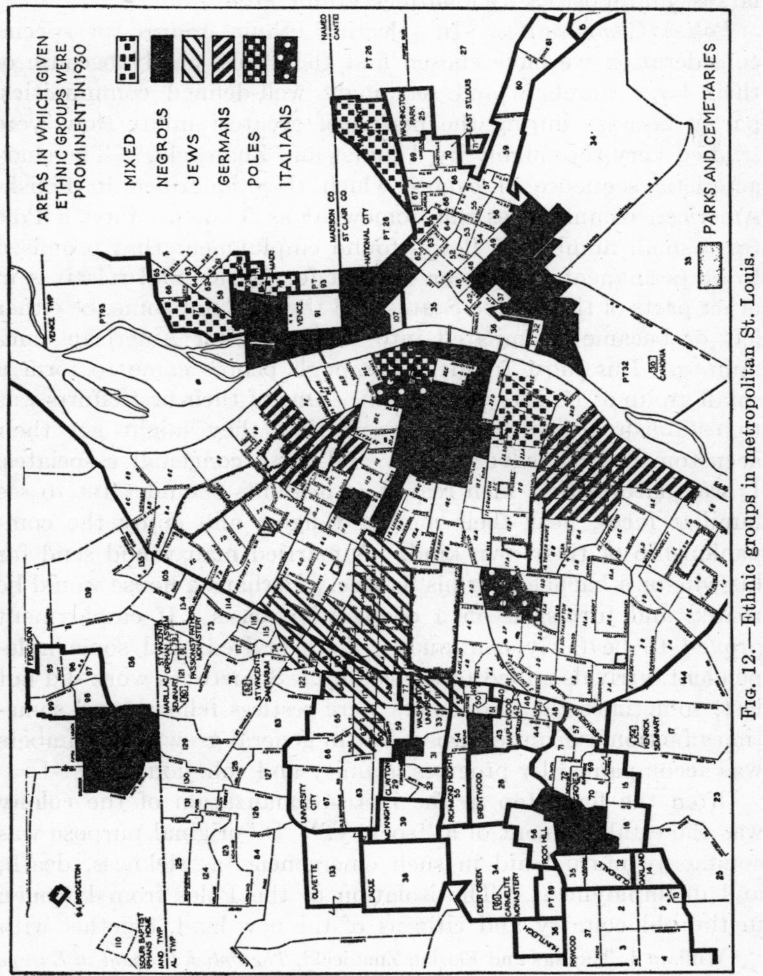

FIG. 12.—Ethnic groups in metropolitan St. Louis.

ceased to be separate communities, but newer groups from southeastern Europe, the Orient, and Latin America tend to be segregated in rather well-defined colonies. The newcomers are to be found near commercial and industrial districts; the older immigrants and their children are more commonly located in what Burgess calls the zone of workingmen's homes. Figure 12 shows approximately the parts of St. Louis occupied by the largest and most easily identified ethnic groups.

Polish Communities.—In selecting ethnic groups for special consideration we have chosen first the Poles, partly because of their large numbers and seemingly well-defined communities, partly because during the period of greatest influx they were studied very thoroughly by Thomas and Znaniecki.[1] The characteristic sequence of events which they identified in Polish-American communities was somewhat as follows. First a Pole (or a small number of Poles) found employment that promised to be permanent; very soon he sent for friends and relatives in other parts of the United States. If they did not come, he either left or became assimilated into the particular American community. But most frequently enough people came to form a small group of Polish workingmen. One of their first efforts was to establish a boarding house so that they might get their accustomed food, save money, and have congenial associates. It was natural that men reared as peasants should want to see familiar faces, hear their mother tongue, and enjoy the companionship of their own kind. A married man would send for his wife or a bachelor for his fiancée. Perhaps a house would be rented and furnished on a cooperative basis. If employment proved to be fairly continuous, more invited, and some independent, arrivals added to the colony. Sometimes work did not last, sometimes the newcomers were restless fellows, and sometimes factional disputes arose; but in general growth in numbers was accompanied by progress in unity and cohesion.

Often the first step in the institutionalization of the colony was the establishment of a "society." Its original purpose was commonly mutual aid in such emergencies as sickness, death, and unemployment. The isolation of the Poles from kinsmen in the old country and citizens of the new land, together with

[1] William I. Thomas and Florian Znaniecki, *The Polish Peasant in Europe and America.* This monograph was first published in 1918 in five volumes. Our own references are to the 1927 edition in two volumes. This is the classic study of an immigrant group. It occupied most of the time of Thomas, an American, and Znaniecki, a Pole, for several years. Each of them shared the research in both countries and in both languages. Data used by permission of the authors.

their economic insecurity, made this a logical step. To them public charity was a disgrace and the private charity of their own people was limited; hence cooperation was the more necessary. But such a mutual aid society was more than an economic institution. It brought the often scattered members of the colony together from time to time; it arranged dances and picnics, gave theatrical performances, invited lecturers, subscribed to periodicals, and arranged religious services. It was a center of information for newcomers and for the newspapers. It represented the colony in dealings with Polish nationalist societies and with American agencies—governmental, civic, philanthropic.

The second institution was commonly a church. Even though some of the immigrants were not devout Catholics, they felt the necessity of a minimum of religious ceremonies, such as christenings, weddings, and funerals. To be sure, they might have joined in Irish-American parishes, but these would not have been community centers, not really their own. The coming of a Polish priest brought new leadership to the group and a stimulus to develop the community in numbers, wealth, multiplicity of activities, and cohesion. In relation to the parish there appeared religious "fraternities" and lay associations. Presently a parochial school was established, using both the Polish and the English language. This last contributed vitally to the integration of the Polish-American community. First of all, it brought the folk physically near together; they found it desirable to be near the school which small children had to attend daily. Second, it acquainted the children with the language, religion, national history, traditions, and moral values of their parents. It fostered the understanding and respect between the generations which were so easily lost when the children attended American public schools.

Despite the conventional teaching of the Catholic Church, the Polish-American communities developed relatively few charities, and these few were largely devoted to the care of orphans, the aged, and the infirm. In contrast to Jewish communities, they have showed little interest in or provision for inefficient, disabled, maladjusted, and demoralized fellow countrymen. Thomas and Znaniecki attribute this to the difference between the Polish community in Europe and in America. In Poland the peasant community was a stable group of families, united by ties to the land, by kinship, and by long association. Over here it has been a collection of migrant individuals who associated themselves together more or less voluntarily. Hence if a person expected to reap the benefits of membership in the community, he must participate in its activities and contribute financially to its purposes. If he refused or was unable to do his share, he either was not accepted or was cut adrift; the local group assumed no responsibility for him. To some this may seem strange, but it was not very different from the behavior of New England colonists in the seventeenth century.[1]

Such elimination of burdensome individuals did not mean that the community was uninterested in extending its social control. It did this in other ways. First, it sought to engage as many persons as possible in public and semipublic activities. This was facilitated by the fact that some parishes had as many as 70 organizations, and each of these had from 6 to 20 officials. Thus everyone had some chance of recognition, and being chosen for some committee or office, he was then in the public eye and subject to general comment. The second mode of social control was the complement of the first, namely, the widespread institutionalization of activities. Thus public entertainments under the auspices of local associations or parish committees played a large part in the local life. The hours required for rehearsals and making arrangements were so many that the individual had a minimum of time for himself. This dual technique of social control—drawing individuals into group activities and institutionalizing these activities—was manifest especially in the immigrant press. There were commemorative pamphlets, published reports, programs of meetings, and ultimately a local Polish newspaper. This might be started by some political machine, by an advertiser, by an idealistic nationalist, or by someone seeking personal recognition. In any case it was likely to promote the unity and cohesion of the community.

Thomas and Znaniecki hold that the order of development in a Polish-American community tended to be unique in this respect, that social organization preceded and stimulated territorial concentration. However, when a large number of Poles occupied a limited, compact area, their proximity furthered their social inte-

[1] Robert W. Kelso, *The History of Public Poor Relief in Massachusetts, 1620–1920*, Chaps. 2, 3, 1922.

gration. Recognizing the reciprocal influence of physical nearness and social organization, priests took care to locate their churches as near as possible to places where Poles were employed, giving attention also to low rents and cheap real estate. The Poles did not wait for the original inhabitants of such districts to retire before their invasion, but systematically promoted the occupancy of houses by their own people. Polish real estate agencies, building and loan associations, and loan banks actively hastened the transition. When at last to church, school, and societies of various kinds were added Polish merchants and professional men, the occupation or succession was complete; the Polish-American community had reached its zenith. The story of its decline has not yet been so thoroughly studied. The period that Thomas and Znaniecki covered was essentially one of community building. We suspect that the postwar years have brought considerable disorganization. Factors which suggest this possibility include the practical stopping of immigration, the achieving of Polish independence, the aging and death of the first settlers, the "Americanization" of their children.

In certain respects we shall find the life cycle of a Polish immigrant community representative of all ethnic groups in American cities. In other respects we shall find it different. To bring out similarities and differences we shall describe two other kinds of foreign colonies, Jewish and Italian.

Jewish Communities.—The Jews, like the Poles, came to America in greatest numbers at the end of the nineteenth and the beginning of the twentieth century. But unlike the Poles, the Jews came with a long background of urban experience, training in business, a distinctive religion, a history of persecution, and an interest in learning. Also, as we shall see, the Jews are noted for their philanthropic work on behalf of the unfortunate members of their "race." Fortunately for our purposes a sociologist, who is himself a Jew, has prepared an objective account of the development of Jewish communities in European and American cities.[1] We take the liberty of summarizing and commenting on his narrative and interpretation.

After the Roman conquest of Palestine, the Jews were scattered through the Mediterranean world, forced to be mobile and

[1] Louis Wirth, *The Ghetto*, 1928. Data used by permission of the University of Chicago Press.

adaptable. Although they led a precarious existence, their lot was not so bad as it was in later centuries. With the opening of the Crusades, Jews were widely abused and frequently subjected to mob violence. Amid the general excitement, the crusading spirit, and the thwarting of remote and vague ideals, the Jewish people were regarded first as strangers, then as enemies; they were scapegoats. Against these new outbursts the Jews turned to popes and emperors for protection and status of a semifeudal sort. This was granted in return for financial contributions, and emperors often sold the privilege of "protecting," *i.e.*, taxing, the Jews.

Now there had already developed a kind of voluntary segregation. For the sake of religious practices, dietary laws, general customs and traditions, the use of their own language, neighborliness, and self-defense, Jews had begun to live apart in distinctive sections of medieval towns. Here they constituted a community within a community. This arrangement was congenial to them and convenient to their gentile rulers. As a united group they purchased the privilege of residing in a given city and carrying on business. But by the fifteenth century the ghetto, as the Jewish community was called, had become quite generally compulsory. It was commonly situated in an undesirable part of town, usually quite limited in area, and surrounded by a wall. At night its gates were locked, and all Jews had to be in by sundown or suffer severe penalties. Its boundaries were rarely extended, even though the Jewish population might increase greatly. Thus the ghetto became overcrowded; its buildings deteriorated; sometimes houses of prostitution (not Jewish) were moved into the ghetto; and in general it tended to become a slum. What the Christians most feared in the Jews is hard to tell; they mentioned heresy, "escape," and "nefarious practices." Thus voluntary gave way to compulsory segregation and tolerance to persecution. But even so the Christians needed and used the Jews—as traders, moneylenders, taxpayers.

Within the ghetto there grew up a vigorous community life. Family ties were strong; religious loyalty was marked; outstanding personalities appeared; self-reliance and mutual aid were highly developed. The most important institution in the ghetto was the synagogue, which was a house of prayer, house of study, and house of assembly, *i.e.*, a center of religious, educational, philanthropic, and recreational life. Indeed, it may be said to have been the administrative center of the ghetto, for the Jewish community was essentially self-governing, within the limits set by outside rulers. It was responsible as a unit for the behavior of its members; it was taxed as a unit. Thus the rabbis were not only religious functionaries but community leaders and officials. Besides the synagogue there were other communal institutions, such as a house for the poor and the sick, a public bath, a ritual bathhouse, a bakehouse, a slaughtering place, sometimes a guest house or a dance house. There was an elementary school (Cheder) and more advanced school (Yeshiba). "In the close life within ghetto walls, almost nothing was left to the devices of individuals. Life was well organized. . . . "[1]

Of course the reality was not so simple and uniform as this brief description may suggest. In western Europe the Jews gained citizenship under Napoleon, lost it after his fall, regained it in 1848, lost it again after 1850, received it again in the latter part of the nineteenth century, only to lose it once more in certain totalitarian states. In Russia the Jews lived "within the Pale," *i.e.*, they were permitted to reside only in certain districts, and within these districts they were restricted to specified cities and towns. Thus they had "a ghetto within a ghetto." They were culturally isolated, as compared with their much-traveled coreligionists of the West, and they were mainly villagers, whereas the latter were city dwellers.

Out of such backgrounds as we have just sketched, Jews began coming to America very early in small numbers. Some of the first were Sephardic Jews expelled from Spain. A few German Jews came after Napoleon went into exile. Following the revolutions of 1848, large numbers came from Germany and other central European countries; these were city people who belonged to "Reformed" congregations. But about the same time Russian Jews started coming to escape conscription. They were poverty-stricken villagers, Yiddish-speaking, and very orthodox. In the eighties many more Russian Jews came to escape pogroms, and after that their numbers increased rapidly. No accurate count has ever been made of the Jewish population in the United States, but it has been estimated that there were 1 million by 1900 and about 4½ million by 1930.[2] Of these about 2 million live in New York City, 300,000 in Chicago,

[1] Wirth, *op. cit.*, p. 61.

[2] *The World Almanac*, 1937, p. 259.

275,000 in Philadelphia, and smaller numbers in other cities. As we noted in the chapter on religious institutions, they are found almost entirely in urban centers.

Representative of Jewish communities in American cities is that of Chicago. First came an itinerant peddler, then a few merchants who lived over their stores. These early arrivals were from Bavaria. They founded a burial society, a synagogue, and a benevolent society. Later others came and founded their separate organizations. Even before 1860 Chicago Jews were engaged in bitter controversy over reform of the ritual. As the number of immigrants from eastern Europe increased, the community became more and more divided. These newcomers were inclined to settle by village groups and to cling to their old customs; they kept splitting off into "store front" congregations. But the real gulf was between the older, "Reformed" German Jews, who had acquired some wealth and status in the city, and the Latvian, Polish, and Russian Jews, who were poor, ignorant, rural, orthodox, and Yiddish-speaking newcomers. This breach in what might have been a united community was much in evidence during the efforts to raise money for the benefit of those who suffered from the fires of 1871 and 1874. Also after these disastrous fires the physical separation of the two main groups became more marked, the eastern Jews moving across the river toward Halsted Street, the western Jews invading the fashionable South Side residential district. The Reformed group began to substitute Sunday for Saturday services; it sought rabbis who were doctors of philosophy. The orthodox group drew apart and established a new (voluntary) ghetto. In the eighties, when more Russian Jews flocked into Chicago with their beards, long coats, and boots, the German Jews feared that the gentile public would associate them with the newcomers, that all would lose status, and that ground gained in breaking down "racial" barriers would be lost. So they were active in philanthropic measures for the Russian refugees, but their condescending ways made it plain that the newcomers were to keep their place. This proved an added stimulus to the eastern Jews to develop their own institutions and form a community apart.

In Chicago, as in other cities, the term "ghetto" has been commonly applied to the Jewish community or part of it which was found in the zone of deterioration near the heart of the city.

The district has been zoned for light manufacturing; no new dwellings have been erected for years; but land values have been rising in anticipation of the displacement of residences by factories. Meanwhile, however, rents for individual families remained low, and the district was near to places of employment. Now the Jews of this ghetto were poor, and were accustomed to living under crowded conditions; hence, being hemmed in by commercial and industrial establishments, the section became quite congested. Being an area of "first settlement," *i.e.*, of newly arrived immigrants, the ghetto was sharply distinguished from surrounding districts and from those occupied by Americanized Jews who were the children of immigrants. Particularly it tended to preserve the folkways, mores, and institutions of the European ghetto. Besides synagogues, kosher butcher shops, and outdoor markets, it had its own theater, bookstores, cafés, and newspapers. Despite conflict between village and national groups of Jews, the ghetto presented a united front to the gentile world. Wirth described it as rich in tradition and sentiment but "the slave of forms" and "out of touch with the world."

So far as possible it was a closed community. But children attended public schools, grownups worked for American employers, and other contacts were made with outsiders. With the increasing use of English, improved economic status, and stimulation of new wants, the younger generation began to chafe under the restraints of the ghetto. So certain families moved away, seeking freedom, recognition, and pleasanter surroundings. But others followed, and presently the new district became Jewish; some moved again into an area of "third settlement." This movement was not along continuous lines, but in jumps over considerable distances. It was a case of fleeing from the ghetto and being followed by the ghetto. Those who were succeeding in business or professional life wanted to be recognized as persons, not merely as Jews. They moved into residential hotels, they shifted from orthodox to "conservative," to "Reformed" synagogues, and sometimes to Christian Science or Ethical Culture, if indeed they did not give up all connection with organized religion.

But physical escape from the ghetto did not necessarily bring acceptance into the American community. Rebuffs and exclusion from certain districts and organizations wounded the Jew's pride. He had gained physical comfort at the expense of emotional peace. Within the ghetto life had been narrow but warm. Outside it was broad but cold. The hostility of gentiles plus the sensitivity of Jews caused some to return to the ghetto. However, others made places for themselves in the larger life of the city, in business, in professions, in civic organizations, even in politics.

We have probably overemphasized the divisive elements in the Jewish community. It is important for the non-Jew especially to realize that there is considerable cohesion within this group. Wirth considers the fact that outsiders treat the Jews as members of a community to be one of the strongest unifying forces. The revival of anti-Semitism has probably contributed largely to the reintegration of Jewish communities that seemed to be breaking up. The centralization of fund raising and the development of communal institutions, such as the Y.M.H.A., have also added to their solidarity. All in all, it may be anticipated that the Jews, having a long experience as city dwellers, having a well-developed set of institutions, considering themselves and being viewed by others as a community, will continue for many years to offer one of the best examples of local community life in our metropolitan centers.

Italian Communities.—As a result of their study, made shortly after the World War, Park and Miller reported that "among the more important immigrant groups the Italians show perhaps the strongest *wish* to remain in solitary communities. They settle here by villages and even by streets, neighbors in Italy tending to become neighbors here."[1] Certainly the studies that have been made of Italian colonies in American cities show them to be well knit, relatively isolated, and self-sufficient except in the matter of employment.[2] We offer as an illustration the case of an Italian community in St. Louis.

Reference has already been made to the section known variously as Fairmount Heights and "Dago Hill" on the southern

[1] Robert E. Park and H. A. Miller, *Old World Traits Transplanted*, p. 146, 1921. By permission of the Carnegie Corporation.

[2] See, *e.g.*, Park and Miller, *op. cit.*, pp. 147–159; Harvey W. Zorbaugh, *Gold Coast and Slum*, pp. 162–181, 1929; E. S. Wood, "Fairmount Heights: An Immigrant Colony in St. Louis," unpublished master's thesis, Washington University, 1936. The account which follows is based chiefly on the last of these.

ridge of the Des Peres Valley in the Cheltenham District. It may easily be identified on our maps. On the east this community area is bounded by a wide thoroughfare, Kingshighway; on the north and west are open fields of mine property which appear to the observer as dumps and goat pastures, leading to the railroad tracks of the Des Peres Valley. On the south are two busy streets. In appearance Fairmount Heights is identified by small, one-story frame houses, built close to the streets but having gardens in the rear. It has a small business district, most of the establishments being owned by Italians. It has a large Catholic church and a small Protestant church. One parochial school and one public elementary school are in Fairmount Heights, part of the children going across Kingshighway to another public school. Only recently has the district had direct transportation to other parts of the city, though for some years individuals have run trucks and small cars to places of employment outside the area.

The story of land use in this area has been told in the account of Cheltenham in Chap. XIV. It was about 1890, after the making of clay products was well developed, that northern Italians began to come in. How the first one happened along we do not know, but the word was passed around and soon there was a thriving colony. The reasons for settling at once in an outlying part of the city involved the location of heavy industries in Cheltenham, poor local transportation, and available space for home building. To be sure, the early residences were little better than shacks, streets were unpaved, and there were no sewers, but a stable community developed. In the years before the World War most of the folk were illiterate and unskilled. About 1900, southern Italians and Sicilians came in considerable numbers. At first they did not mingle freely with the folk from northern Italy, but no serious friction seems to have developed.

The making of terra cotta by hand, along with other clay products, furnished the principal employment. In the twenties the exhaustion of some clay pits and the closing of several plants caused unemployment. But prohibition, giving rise to "bootlegging," brought new prosperity to "the Hill." Small brick bungalows appeared, then larger and more modern houses. The Italians began to buy overstuffed furniture, floor lamps, stylish clothes, and automobiles. Trips were taken to the homeland.

A new Catholic church was built, at a cost of over $200,000. Then in 1933, repeal, coupled with the depression, brought disaster. Homes were lost; debts piled up; children stayed in school longer; their fathers got city jobs or went on relief.

The inner unity and cohesion of the community are indicated and promoted by a number of factors. First of all, 90 per cent of the local residents are Italian immigrants or their children. Family life is general and on the whole stable. High percentages of both men and women are married, children are numerous, and there is relatively little rebellion of the youth against parental authority and Old World customs. Women gossip with the neighbors; old men go to their halls to play cards and drink; young men join gangs or athletic clubs. In 1935 an enterprising man promoted a federation of such clubs, and other active members carried on agitation for a community center. The Catholic church has the usual array of subordinate organizations; the public schools maintain parents' associations. In earlier years there were fiestas, but these have largely been discontinued.

After rather long-continued isolation, contacts with outsiders are increasing. Illiteracy is still high, but the younger generation reads and writes English. Men who at first went nowhere outside the colony except to work came in contact with American politicians, who exchanged jobs and other favors for votes. The schools not only dealt with the children but gradually drew in their parents. During the depression of 1929 various educational and recreational projects were carried on for adults. Social workers were seldom seen before 1929, but from then on increasing numbers of Italians became clients of family welfare and child caring agencies. The International Institute of the Y.W.C.A. and a branch of the St. Louis Public Library also afforded new contacts and new ideas. Nevertheless old customs and traditions live on. A few of the young men are "dating" and even marrying outside the colony, but most of the girls continue to be "good" Italians. Fairmount Heights remains a community.

The Life Cycle and the Functions of Immigrant Communities

From the foregoing accounts there can be identified certain recurring events and sequences which justify us in seeking for generalized history of immigrant communities in American cities. They usually begin with the settling of a few individuals or families near the heart of a city or close to some outlying industrial section. If successful, these settlers send for relatives and friends; a neighborhood comes into being; local institutions are established. After a time the invasion of business or of newer immigrants drives them out; or possibly financial advancement and new ideas lure them into a somewhat better district. As numbers grow and status rises, the immigrant institutions develop; a community comes into being. But eventually the colony loses some of its members. The original settlers die out; second and third generation folk become partially Americanized and seek to escape the limitations of the ethnic community. In the zone of workingmen's homes, or perhaps in a middle-class area, the colony may disappear and merge into the general population. On the other hand, an area of third settlement, still noticeably foreign, may develop. Disappointed aspirants for Americanism, together with older and more conservative members of the group, plus newcomers who have acquired few American ways, unite to preserve the folkways, mores, ceremonials, institutions, and general integrity of the colony. Ultimately the original immigrants and their children pass from the scene. If there is no racial hallmark, and if prejudice is not too intense, the community will disintegrate. Especially with the stoppage of immigration, with education in American schools, employment in American industries, mobility, and intermarriage, the immigrant community seems doomed to disappear.

But during the period of its existence the colony serves a useful purpose in bridging the gap between the Old World and the New. It provides a place where the newcomer can be at least somewhat at home with people of his own kind. It enables him to adjust himself gradually to the strange life of America. It offers him assistance in time of trouble. It encourages and helps him to preserve culture traits which may enrich the life of his adopted country.[1] Its premature disruption would be a misfortune; but its perpetuation seems neither necessary nor probable.

[1] Fairmount Heights has produced a grand opera singer, and the Czech colony of St. Louis has given the city a painter of note. Both these and other groups have produced beautiful needlework.

Negro Communities

During the first half of our national history cities grew largely through drawing in native white people from farms and villages. Between the Civil War and the World War the largest part of our urban increase came through the immigration of Europeans—at first British, Irish, German, and Scandinavian; later Italians, Poles, and other peoples from southern and eastern Europe. But since then the most significant increments have been of Negroes from our own southern states. In fact, the cityward movement of colored people began about 1900. In that year only 2 million Negroes were counted as urban, while nearly 7 million were rural. Two-thirds of the city dwellers and 95 per cent of the country Negroes lived in the South. But by 1930 the urban population had grown to more than 5 million, while the rural population had declined about a quarter of a million. Of the former, nearly 3 million were in southern cities, while nearly 2¼ million were in northern cities. In the first decade of this century most of the increase in urban Negroes occurred in the South. Since 1910 it has taken place in the North. It is possible that this movement toward northern cities may have reached its peak, for industrial opportunities there are not expanding. But rural-urban migration may continue in the South because of what is happening to agriculture in that section and because urbanization there is still in its early stages. As yet not many Negroes have gone west; perhaps that will be their next great movement.

Nearly one-fourth of the total urban increase has taken place in four centers, New York, Philadelphia, Chicago, and Detroit; a second fourth has occurred in other northern cities; and most of the remainder in the South. This southern urbanization of Negroes has been relatively inconspicuous because of the numbers already living in southern cities and because the increase has been scattered over many rather small cities. There is another difference too. Cities in the South have drawn their Negroes largely from near-by rural sections, while northern cities have received them from many states and from urban as well as from country districts.

Factors involved in this great movement include discrimination in the rural South, the ravages of the boll weevil, the unusual demand for industrial workers due to the World War and to the restriction of immigration, the progressive mechanization of agriculture, crop limitation, and the dispossession of farm tenants and laborers. These and perhaps other factors are associated with the transfer of several million Negroes from the isolation and semifeudal character of plantations to the congestion and "individualism" of urban industrial centers.

The development and structure of Negro communities in American cities resemble those of immigrant colonies in some respects and differ in others. In the South Negroes had long occupied servants' quarters in the rear of the masters' houses. Hence they were scattered through the city, and few residential blocks were without a small number of colored inhabitants. In addition there developed, especially after the War between the States, sections devoted largely to Negro dwellings and institutions. In the North there were relatively few Negroes until the turn of the century. Chicago had less than 1,000 in 1860 and only 30,000 in 1900, but in 1930 its colored population was 235,000. In general there was a rapid increase in northern cities after 1910. During the decade ending 1930 the number of Negroes doubled in three cities and trebled in Detroit.

Community Organization: Limiting Factors.—Merely to provide physical accommodations—houses, transportation, schools, etc.—for so many newcomers was a problem of considerable magnitude. It was, of course, made more difficult by the usual attempts to keep Negroes within narrowly restricted boundaries. The result was that rents went up, houses were crowded, and new districts were invaded. As colored people spread out they often encountered strong opposition. White homeowners resented the approach of the dark-skinned folk. The latter looked strange, were considered inferior, usually had different habits and less money. White people did not want to be disturbed and they feared a lowering of property values. When they saw the invasion moving in their direction they often entered into agreements neither to sell nor to rent to Negroes. When surprised by the unexpected appearance of colored nigh dwellers they sometimes resorted to sterner measures—placing signs telling Negroes how unwelcome they were, bringing lawsuits, throwing bricks through windows, sending warnings through the mail, starting fires, bombing houses, and the like. Some years ago segregation ordinances were passed by a number of city councils, but these have been declared unconstitutional. The chief restraining influences today are agreements among property owners and realtors. Nevertheless, it seems inevitable that the increase in the number of Negroes and the centrifugal drift of the white population should be accompanied or followed by expansion of the Negro districts in most American cities.

Other conflicts with the white citizens have centered about jobs, schools, recreational facilities, and transportation. Negroes have sometimes been imported as strikebreakers. The 1917 race riot in East St. Louis grew in part out of this economic issue. Even those who came to fill vacancies in wartime were regarded as interlopers, and after the Armistice there was a struggle to see whether jobs should be returned to white men coming back from France or retained by Negroes who had replaced them. In general, it may be said that these open conflicts—together with more continuous, though less dramatic, pressures of racial discrimination—and poverty promote unity and cohesion.

On the positive side Negro leaders preach group integrity, pride of race, mutual aid, and insistence upon rights. The Negro community has its own institutions—churches, schools, lodges, civic associations, recreational agencies, and a few business houses. In St. Louis the 100,000 colored people maintain 140 churches. They are served by 22 public schools including 2 high schools and a teachers' college. A survey made by the Urban League in 1934 showed nearly 600 businesses owned and operated by Negroes. Most of these were very small. Food shops were by far the most numerous; the directory calls them "refreshments and culinary establishments." Personal service came next—barber and beauty shops, cleaners and dyers. Less numerous, but significant as indicating the economic development of the Negro community, were hotels, insurance companies, newspapers, garages, laundries, hospitals, florists, etc. But there was no retail clothing store, shoe store, bank, or pawnshop owned and operated by Negroes. In all large communities there are professional men—clergymen, physicians, dentists, attorneys, teachers, and musicians—but there is a marked tendency for colored people to pass by their own lawyers and physicians, patronizing white men instead. The greatest economic weakness of the urban Negroes is their dependence on white folk for their employment and their restriction in the main to unskilled, unpleasant, and poorly paid occupations.

Another weakness of Negro communities is the division and noncooperation of those who might be expected to act together for the defense and promotion of common interests. As we shall see presently, there is stratification, with social barriers between economic levels, between educated and illiterate persons, between old residents of the city and newcomers from the country, between religious sects and denominations, between those who seek cooperation between the races and those who want to fight for their rights, between mulattoes and blacks. But in general factional rivalry seems less serious than mass indifference and rapid increase of population. To be sure, the migrants have come to our cities hoping to better their condition, but without a pattern of joint effort. Moreover, the bringing together in a short time of thousands of rural Negroes unacquainted with each other, with city life, or with habits of cooperation creates a state of social disorganization or, more accurately, unorganization. As in the case of the Jews, the old city dwellers fear that the horde of unsophisticated newcomers may drag them all down together. They offer help, but in the form of charity rather than of comradeship. The net result is that, instead of forming a well-knit community, the Negroes in a large city are divided among a number of neighborhoods, perhaps two or three communities; but otherwise they constitute an unorganized mass of disadvantaged folk.

Spatial Patterns of Negro Communities.—Several years ago Woofter demonstrated that there are at least four major patterns of racial separation or segregation in American cities.[1] (*a*) In most northern cities the concentration of Negroes is very marked, but it affects only a small part of the whole urban area. That is, most of the Negroes are found in a very limited section devoted almost entirely to their own race and few of them are found in districts predominantly white. This is true, *e.g.*, of New York and Chicago. (*b*) In certain southern cities, such as Richmond, Negroes are highly concentrated in several large parts of the city besides being lightly scattered in other sections. (*c*) In some of the older cities in the deep South, like Charleston, South Carolina, the large Negro population is scattered throughout the

[1] T. J. Woofter, Jr., *Negro Problems in Cities*, Chap. 3, 1928.

city. This is due to the large number of servant houses and alley dwellings. (*d*) In a number of northern cities with rather few Negroes, these people are usually found in a small part of the city and somewhat scattered even within this area. Such is the case in Gary, Indiana.

Within the districts occupied largely by Negroes, interesting ecological patterns are displayed. Thus Frazier has shown that in Chicago characteristics of the Negro population correspond with those of whites in the same zones. But in New York the Negro community of Harlem has a pattern of its own which corresponds to that of the city as a whole.[1] In Chicago Frazier found the principal Negro district to be a segment reaching from the heart of the city to the south through seven fairly distinct zones. Proceeding from "the Loop" toward Seventy-third Street, certain characteristic changes occurred progressively and consistently. First of all, the percentage of family heads who were born in the South decreased. Second, the percentage of adults who were mulattoes increased. The relative number of illiterates decreased; the relative number of persons engaged in professional and white-collar occupations and skilled trades increased; while the proportion in semiskilled trades, domestic service, and unskilled labor decreased. The percentage of women gainfully employed decreased; the percentage of men married increased, but the relative number of married women remained about the same. In the succession of all seven zones, home ownership increased strikingly and the number of families and persons per dwelling decreased. The relative number of small children increased. The percentage of families on relief and receiving care from family welfare agencies decreased, as did the incidence of family desertion. There was likewise a decrease in illegitimacy and in juvenile delinquency. All in all, therefore, Frazier found the Negro community of Chicago, if such it may be called, conforming in its several zones to the characteristics displayed by the entire city. Close to the central business district, he found a section in which houses were dilapidated and occupied in the main by impoverished newcomers from the South. Next came the "bright light" area of the black belt, with its

[1] E. Franklin Frazier, *The Negro Family in Chicago*, Chap. 6, 1932; E. Franklin Frazier, "Negro Harlem: An Ecological Study," *Amer. Jour. Sociol.*, 43 (1937), 72–88.

theaters, cabarets, gambling places, and houses of prostitution. These were followed by districts of progressively better social and economic status.

In Harlem Frazier discovered quite a different pattern. Centering about One Hundred and Thirty-fifth Street and Seventh Avenue, he found a Negro community with its own system of concentric circles. This community had grown up first about the indicated center and then pushed out in all directions until it could be described as a series of five zones. The percentage of the population that was Negro was highest in the first, or central, zone, and lowest in the fifth. Buildings not devoted to residential uses were most numerous in the first zone and fewest in the fifth. There was a similar decline from the center to the periphery in the relative number of rooming houses and lodging houses. The relative number of children increased steadily from the first to the fifth zone, as did the percentage of adults who were married. In the first zone deaths exceeded births in number; in the second they were about equal; and in the next three zones there was a steady increase in the ratio of births to deaths. Delinquency showed an uneven distribution, but dependency declined consistently from the center to the outer edge of this Negro community. Thus the development in Chicago and New York has been rather different so far as the spatial distribution is concerned. The reasons for this are not altogether clear, but they are perhaps related to the fact that in Chicago, Negroes pushed out from the heart of the city, along with other ethnic groups, while in New York they were concentrated in a district at some distance from the center of the city as this is ordinarily conceived.

Social Patterns: Stratification.—We have already indicated that Negro communities are not uniformly well knit and that there are frequently divisions along economic, religious, color, and other lines. Many of these separate groups and their interrelations within the Negro community need to be studied. However, one bit of research conducted in St. Louis sheds light on the social levels recognized by the colored people themselves.[1] The method by which these were identified was very briefly this. Scattered members of the Negro community were interviewed with

[1] Edna Taborn, "Social Stratification among Negroes in St. Louis," unpublished master's thesis, Washington University, 1937.

reference to their judgment concerning the relative status of various occupations, incomes, places of residence, religious affiliation, and certain other matters. On the basis of these interviews a schedule was devised, and a number of presumably representative colored people were invited to indicate their opinions and attitudes on these matters. A rather simple rating or scoring device was invented, and with its use, four or five fairly distinct social levels were identified.

At the top were teachers, physicians, and mail clerks; people who held college degrees; those with fair skins; old St. Louis families with incomes of $300 a month, living west of Grand Avenue and belonging to a large church. The second level included such occupations as merchants, skilled laborers, hairdressers, and musicians; people who had been to college or at least to high school or vocational school; those with light brown skins; fairly old families with incomes of $100 to $300 a month, living west of Grand Avenue and attending fairly large churches. The third level was represented by Pullman porters, barbers, chauffeurs, domestic servants, and unskilled laborers; people who had been to elementary school and sometimes to high school; skin color ranging from light to dark brown; families that had come more recently from the South, with incomes of $50 to $200, belonging to rather small churches. Finally, the lowest level included such socially unacceptable people as "policy" sellers and prostitutes; those with less than an elementary school education; people with dark skins; families newly come from the South, living near the central business district, earning less than $100 a month, and attending "store front" churches or none.

It will be noted that there is some overlapping. These social classes are not sharply divided. Moreover it is obvious that not all persons on each level possess all of the characteristics suggested. These are simply composites which sum up the results of Miss Taborn's inquiry in the St. Louis Negro community. But her findings do seem to establish the facts that there are distinct social levels among Negroes and that social distance is quite as significant in the Negro community as outside.

Contrast of Negro and Immigrant Communities

In the discussion that has just preceded, there have been evident a number of interesting differences between Negro and immigrant communities in American cities. The immigrants, having come recently from distant lands, have to adjust themselves to a new cultural situation with different language, laws, customs, and traditions of many sorts. The Negroes, on the contrary, come to the city with a knowledge of English, some familiarity with American legal, political, religious, and other institutions. Their chief adjustment is one that they share with the immigrants, namely, that involved in the transition from rural to urban and from agricultural to industrial life. Both groups tend to settle near the heart of a city, but their outward movement is quite different. Immigrants frequently jump over intervening spaces, while the Negroes usually push along a continuous line. With immigrant communities segregation is largely voluntary, while with the Negroes it is largely compulsory. Members of immigrant communities tend, especially in the second and third generation, to withdraw from the ethnic group and lose themselves in the general population. Negroes occasionally "go white," but on the whole they have little escape from their own group. Some immigrant communities display marked solidarity; usually this is less developed among Negroes. Hence, while the communal institutions of some immigrant communities are well supported, most of the Negro institutions are relatively weak. The outlook is for the gradual disappearance of ethnic groups whose skin is light and against whom prejudice is not particularly marked. But it seems likely that the Negro populations will continue for an indefinite time as communities relatively distinct and yet very dependent upon the city as a whole, and particularly upon its white institutions and leaders.

Selected Readings

Park, Robert E., and H. A. Miller: *Old World Traits Transplanted,* Harper & Brothers, 1921. One of the Americanization studies sponsored by the Carnegie Corporation. Vivid descriptions and interpretation of immigrant communities, institutions, and personalities.

Thomas, William I., and Florian Znaniecki: *The Polish Peasant in Europe and America,* Alfred A. Knopf, Inc., 2d ed., 1927. Volume 2, pp. 1511–1574, deals with the Polish-American community.

Wirth, Louis: *The Ghetto,* University of Chicago Press, 1928. A study of Jewish communities in Europe and America, especially Frankfort and Chicago.

Young, Pauline V.: *The Pilgrims of Russian-Town,* University of Chicago Press, 1932. A study of a Russian sectarian community in Los Angeles.

WOOFTER, T. J., JR.: *Negro Problems in Cities*, Doubleday, Doran & Company, Inc., 1928. A study made under the auspices of the Institute of Social and Religious Research.

FRAZIER, E. FRANKLIN: *The Negro Family in Chicago*, University of Chicago Press, 1932. Part III includes a description of the Negro community in Chicago and its relation to the ecological structure of the city as a whole.

FRAZIER, E. FRANKLIN: "Negro Harlem: An Ecological Study," *Amer. Jour. Sociol.*, 43 (1937), 72–88. Shows a very different pattern in New York from that found in Chicago.

KENNEDY, LOUISE V.: *The Negro Peasant Turns Cityward*, Columbia University Press, 1930. Antecedents and sequelae of recent Negro migrations to American cities.

Chapter XVII

BLIGHTED AREAS

Blighted areas have been located and described in general terms in our presentation of the general pattern of the city. One aspect has been discussed in more detail in its relation to housing. In this chapter we propose to review the characteristics of blighted areas—physical, economic, demographic, and sociological—and to examine ways of determining how much of a liability they are.

Characteristics of Blighted Areas

Surrounding the central business district of the typical American city is a zone of deterioration. Its existence is due primarily to the expansion of commerce and industry and secondarily to the slowing down of this expansion. What we mean is this. As a town grows into a city its stores, shops, warehouses, and factories spread into the residence sections. But they do not push out evenly or in a straight line. Instead, we see here and there small shops established in old dwellings and other structures. Some of them develop into successful businesses and take over additional space. Still other shops are set up apparently at random—though not actually so—until the old residential section is dotted with light manufacturing and commercial establishments. Naturally, old residents move out as they are able, leaving their houses vacant or converting them into tenements, as described in Chap. VI. Now if the city is growing rapidly, business will probably occupy near-by residential sections within a few years. Houses will not have had time to deteriorate excessively, and slums will not develop. But the expansion of commerce and industry may slow down, because the city ceases to grow so fast, because vertical expansion in tall buildings displaces horizontal expansion into new blocks, or because subcenters absorb the new business which might otherwise flow downtown. When that happens, property is held a long time awaiting the delayed rise in land values supposed to accompany commercial and industrial demands. Over the years houses deteriorate excessively and come to be occupied by new sorts of people and groups with new folkways and institutions.

The most obvious physical traits of a blighted area are usually nearness to the business center and deteriorated buildings. Parenthetically, it should be remembered that blighted areas may also be found in outlying parts of a metropolitan district, near industries and along transportation routes. Their history and appearance are rather different from those of areas near the center. Both display a mixture of residential, commercial, and industrial land use. The dwellings are largely converted tenements, rooming houses, and alley dwellings. Visitors are impressed with dirt, smoke, rubbish, noise, odors, and other marks of confusion and disorder. Those with more intimate knowledge report a scarcity of gas, electricity, telephones, and running water. They can tell of basement apartments, stove heat, kerosene lamps, faucets in the hall, toilets in the yard, broken stairs and windows. Parts of such a blighted area may be cut off from the rest of the city, the narrow streets poorly paved and poorly lighted, being little used except by those who live or work in the district. Other parts may have widened streets that carry a large volume of traffic which has no relation to the district except to pass through.

Turning from the physical appearance to economic aspects of the blighted area, we find property held at high prices but bringing low returns. The high holding values are based in part on previous prices but principally on expected demand for commercial and industrial uses. The relatively low rents are due to the fact that few people live in such districts from choice. Most of those who dwell there are not able to pay much for their housing. They are people of low and irregular incomes. They are largely unskilled laborers, though some are ill-paid white-collar workers and others make their livings by unconventional means. These include "bookies," "policy" sellers, "dope" peddlers, prostitutes, pickpockets, gangsters, and racketeers. Some of these may have good-sized incomes and pay fairly high rents, while others lead a precarious existence. Employed women and unemployed men are relatively more numerous than

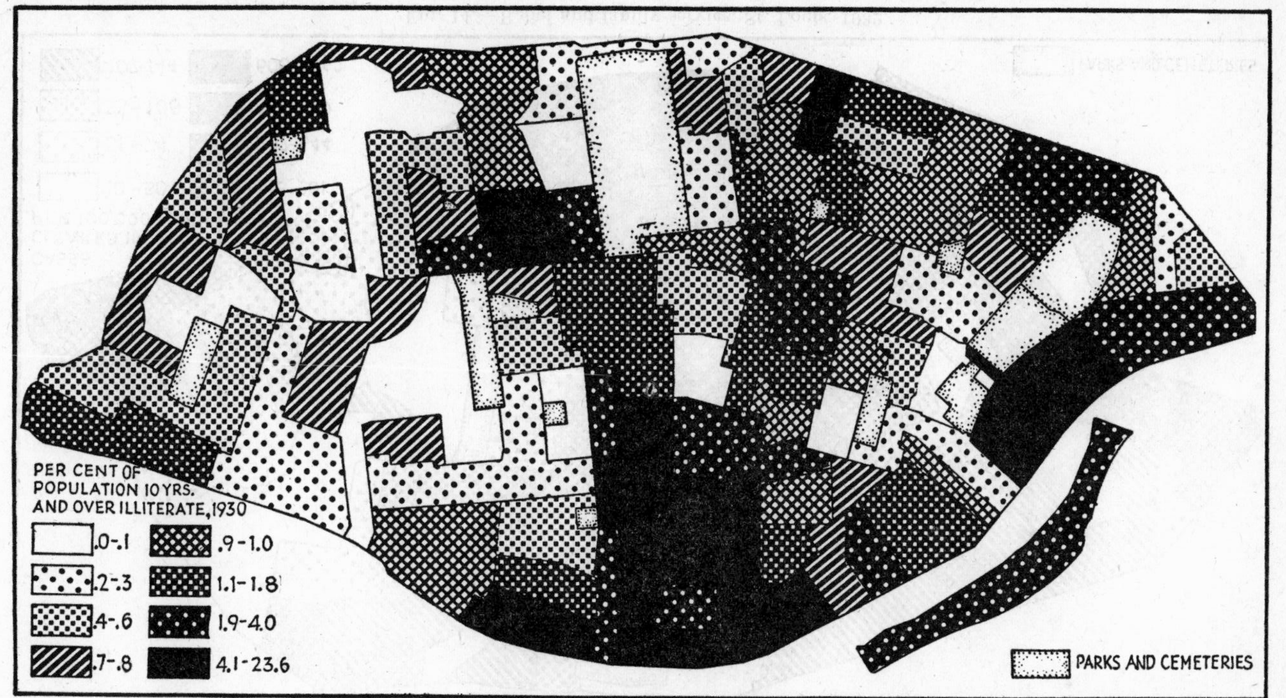

Fig. 13.—Illiteracy, St. Louis, 1930.

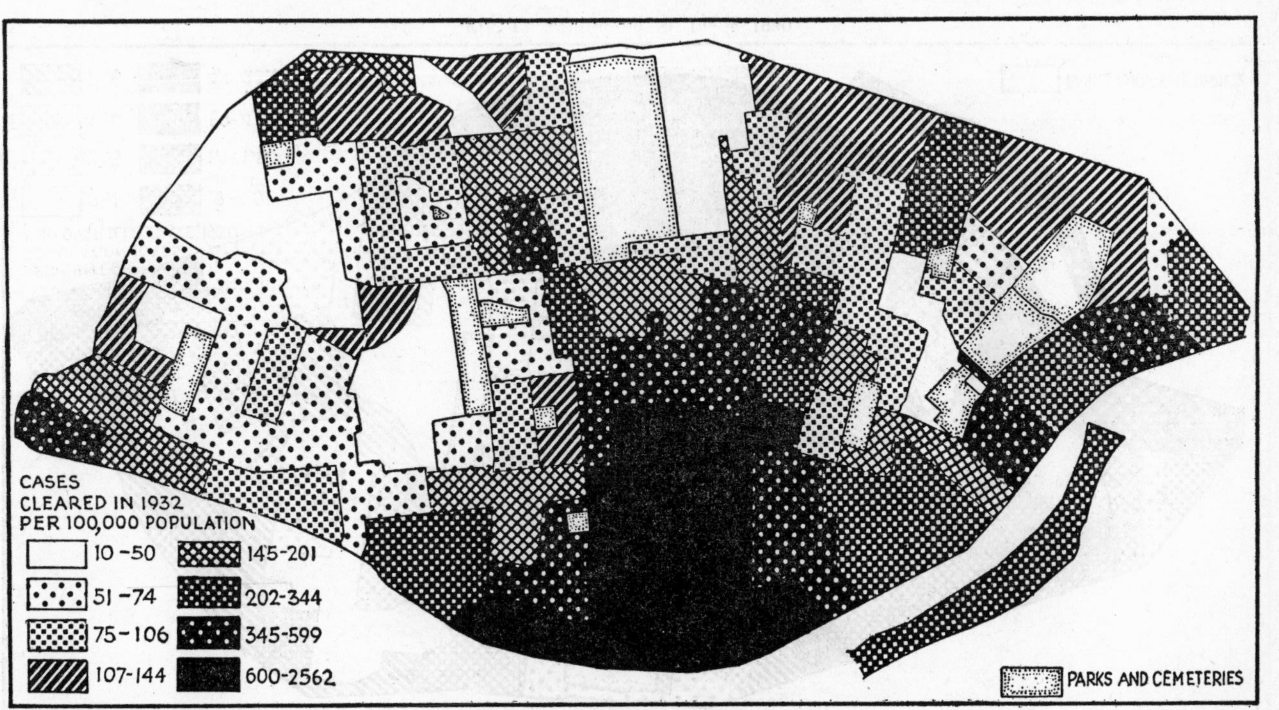

Fig. 14.—Relief and family service, St. Louis, 1932.

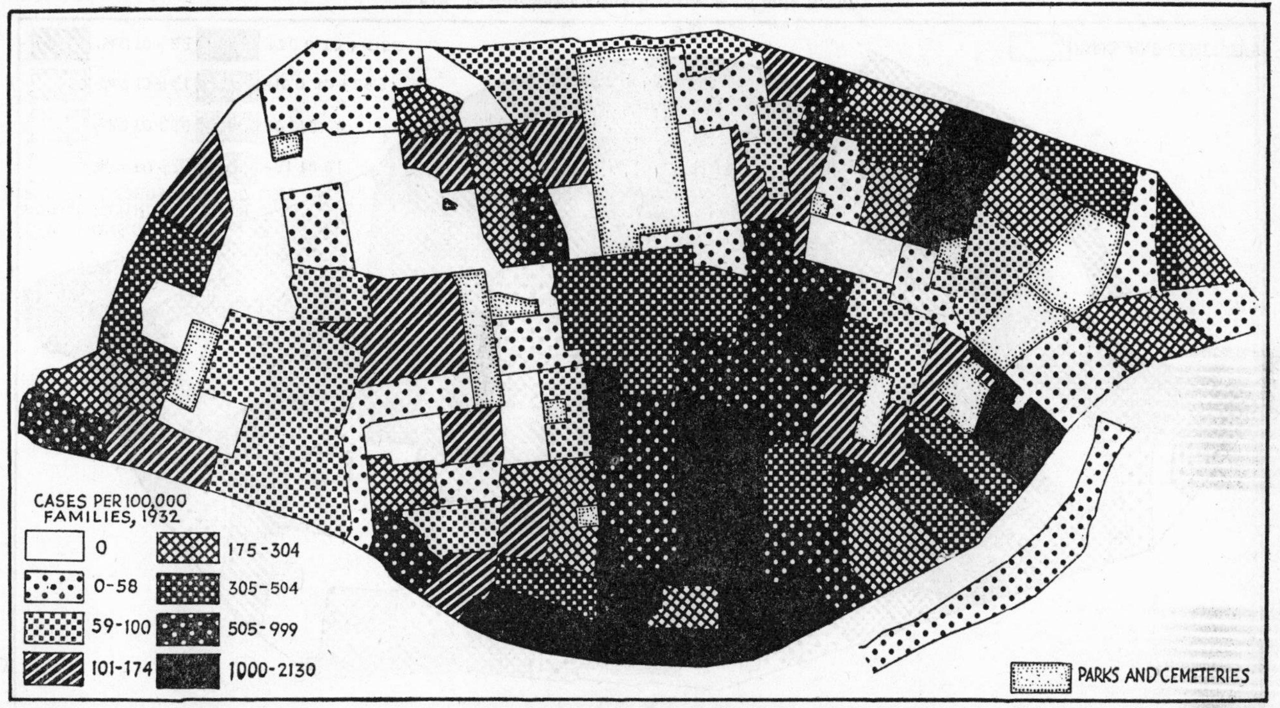

FIG. 15.—Juvenile court cases, St. Louis, 1932.

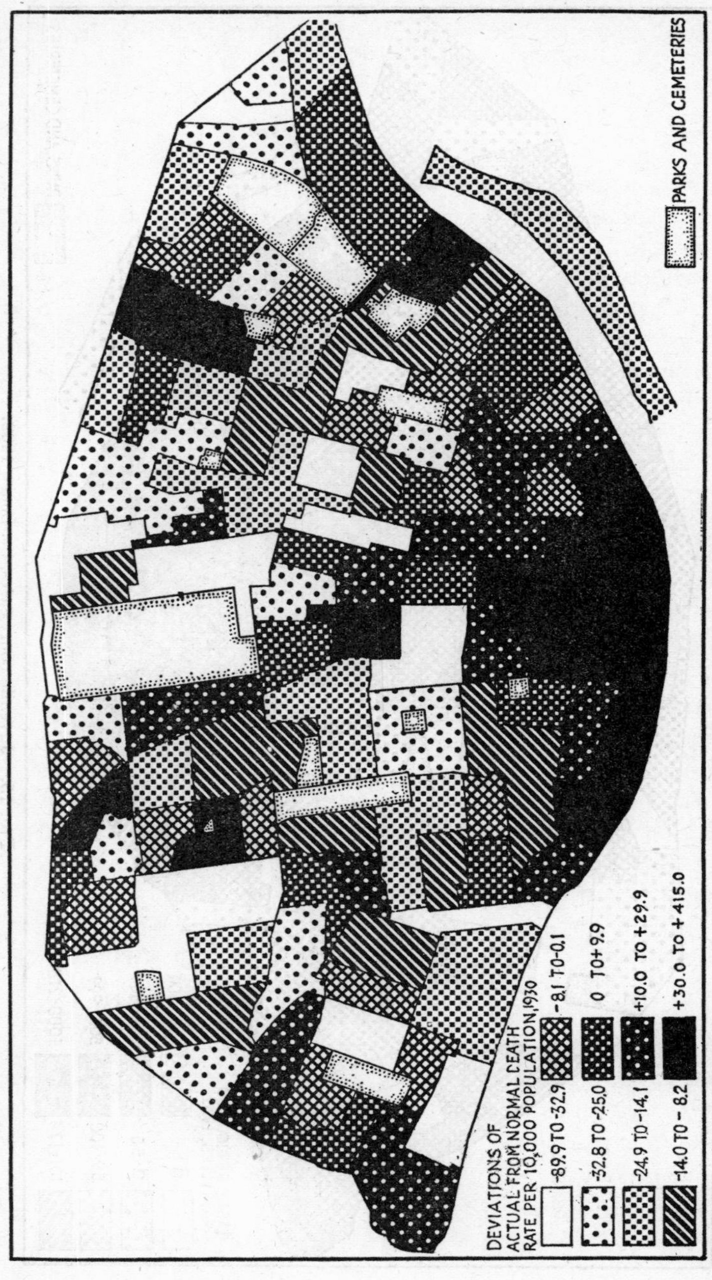

FIG. 16.—Relative death rates, St. Louis, 1930.

in most parts of the city. In general, dependency rates are high. Many families and single individuals are on relief; many children are receiving foster care; large numbers attend free clinics. A little later we shall show that this is an area from which the city receives a small income (taxes collected) but in which it spends very large sums.

Demographically this is an area of declining population, partly because some dwellings are demolished but chiefly because of the centrifugal flight. This evacuation is going on so steadily that some owners of slum property and some realtors are seriously worried. Downtown merchants, too, might well be concerned. However, despite the falling off in actual numbers, the density of population is still relatively high. Both lots and rooms are more crowded than in other sections. Heterogeneity also marks the blighted area. Zorbaugh found 29 nationalities on the Near North Side in Chicago. In such a section are found the stragglers from ethnic groups that have passed on and the vanguard of new invaders, as well as any larger bodies that may be having their day. Marooned old families and newcomers, members of dominant groups and stray individuals jostle one another on the street. Mingled with the others are those whose past or present lives render anonymity an asset. Such a population is highly mobile. There is constant movement, some of it in and out of the district, some of it within the area: a perpetual search for a better house that does not exist, flight from collectors or from "the law." In the Chicago rooming-house section which he studied, Zorbaugh found the turnover to be about 300 per cent a year. Other features that characterize the population of a blighted area are a high sex ratio (many more males than females); a small percentage of children; many old men but a predominance of young unmarried adults; high morbidity and mortality rates, especially high incidence of tuberculosis, venereal diseases, and suicide. In general it is an unbalanced population that is not perpetuating itself.

Sociologically the blighted area is characterized by large numbers of detached individuals. Whether from choice or from necessity, the inhabitants have few acquaintances and fewer friends. Some of them are very lonesome, while others seem to be quite satisfied with their isolation. Social distance (mingling with other people yet keeping them at arm's length), anonymity (telling no one your past or your business), and mobility ("here today and gone tomorrow") pretty well characterize the life of many people who dwell in the blighted area of an American city. The human types represented have been suggested in naming some of the occupations. They include day laborers, domestic servants, clerks, waitresses, artists, young men and women who are just starting out for themselves, perennial failures, those who have seen better days, hoboes (men who wander and work), bums (men who neither wander nor work), "Bohemians" (people who "like to wear bow ties and expose themselves to temptation"), prostitutes, drug addicts, homosexuals, "ward heelers," old residents in the city, and recent arrivals from rural America or Europe. Such terms as these suggest the variety of personalities to be found in the near-downtown sections of a city, but they do not constitute in any sense a classification.

As to social groups, families are relatively few, small, and quite varied. Immigrant families are apt to be patriarchal in character, above the city average in size, but frequently broken by desertion. Negro families are sometimes large, but usually small, and often broken. Native white families are of the kind that Mowrer called "emancipated," *i.e.*, husband and wife both work, there are few children or none, divorce and desertion are common. Thrasher has shown that gangs thrive in the blighted area, as in other districts which he describes as "interstitial" (in between well-defined sections of the city).[1] Some of these gangs are fairly harmless play groups, others are definitely criminal in character; some are much like athletic clubs, others are deeply involved in politics. They represent the most vigorous groups in the blighted area, yet even they do not long survive. In general, neighboring is at a low ebb in the blighted area, though neighborhoods may be found in the midst of immigrant colonies. An ethnic group may maintain a local community here for some time, but it too seems doomed to pass away.

In a blighted area may be found three types of local institutions: those left over from an earlier day, those that develop spontaneously in a slum, and those brought in to overcome some aspects of the blight. By way of analogy, and semi-facetiously, they might be called, respectively, vestigial, indigenous, and

[1] Frederic M. Thrasher, *The Gang*, Chap. 1 and map, 1927.

exotic. Those inherited from a more prosperous and more respectable past include metropolitan churches and public schools. The institutions that seem indigenous to the blighted area include secondhand stores, pawnshops, lodging houses, cheap restaurants, shabby motion picture theaters, burlesque shows, "store front" churches, poolrooms, barber "colleges," taxi-dance halls, and houses of prostitution. Institutions of another sort are imported usually for the purpose of "uplifting" or "saving" the local inhabitants; these include missions and social settlements. The public schools gather in the children of the district, but they are controlled from the office of the board of education and seem hardly to belong to the area. The functioning of relief agency, police department, and juvenile court seems likewise depersonalized and remote. The mores of various groups are in conflict, detached individuals are little affected by any moral code, vice and crime are rampant, social control is mechanical and weak.

Over against the statements which inevitably stigmatize the area, its inhabitants, and its institutions must be put the emphatic statement that none of the unpleasant features are inevitable. Indeed, there are some honest, industrious, thrifty citizens here. Slum clearance and rehousing are changing the physical character in some places. Social organization is not quite extinct and may someday be revived. But the blighted area does contain many of the city's problems in their most acute form.

Measuring the Cost of Blight

In recent years there have been some interesting attempts to determine what blighted areas cost the city. In part this is a characteristic American desire to reduce things to a dollars-and-cents statement; in part it is an effort to determine what slum clearance and social reform will actually cost. If they can be projected as self-liquidating business ventures, this is one thing; but if they must be subsidized, through either governmental bounty or private philanthropy, that is another. Without in any wise belittling the role of humanitarians, it can safely be asserted that, if it can be shown that slum clearance will pay in dollars and cents, this will be a great advantage. In the first place, it will be easier to secure adherents to such a program.

In the second place, it is hard to see how, in the long run, cities can afford projects which are not worth what they cost. This reduces our problem to one of method. How can we discover whether a city can better afford slums or slum clearance? Before answering, we must find out as nearly as possible just what a slum area costs, over and above what it contributes to the maintenance of a city. Fortunately we do not have to proceed altogether in the dark, for some attacks have already been made upon the problem.

The first effort in this direction, so far as we are aware, was made in Cleveland by the Reverend R. B. Navin and associates with the counsel of Howard W. Green.[1] They selected a slum area of some 300 acres, with 22,000 inhabitants, including 5,200 families. The area contained 2.5 per cent of the city's population and 0.75 per cent of its land area in 1930. In it were committed, over a 12-year period, 21 per cent of the murders. Eight undercover surveys located 26 per cent of the known houses of prostitution within its boundaries. During 4 years 7 per cent of the boys brought into juvenile court lived in this section. Ten per cent of reported unmarried mothers, 8 per cent of families on relief, 6 per cent of Class A jobless workers were identified within this district. It was the home of one-eighth of all Clevelanders who died of tuberculosis. Thus it was clearly a slum area. In general it was a liability to the city, but how could this be determined more precisely?

The investigators first enumerated the costs to the county of direct services rendered in this district in 1932. These included mothers' pensions, juvenile court cases, tuberculosis cases, child welfare, soldiers' and sailors' relief. The figure arrived at was $176,000. This evidently did not include administrative costs, but only care given directly to persons living in the area. Next the investigators calculated the costs of direct services rendered by the city in the same year. These items included fire department, police department, ash and rubbish collection, garbage collection, street cleaning, street lighting, sewer maintenance, library, bathhouse, playgrounds, milk fund, and health department. The estimated total was $818,000.

The report of this study does not set forth the details of cost accounting which would enable us to know just how this part

[1] R. B. Navin, *et al.*, *An Analysis of a Slum Area in Cleveland*, prepared for the Cleveland Metropolitan Housing Authority, 1934.

of the work was done. However, we are told that in computing the cost of fire protection, for example, there was a count of calls for fires, false alarms, unnecessary calls of other sorts, grass fires, emergency calls (presumably not for fires), rubbish fires, dumps, and some others. The cost per call was computed (apparently for the whole city), and then the cost of all calls in this section. The layman can hardly expect to understand all the steps that must have been taken by the accountants, but the results may be accepted as approximately correct.

The third major item in this study was the cost of direct services from the board of education. Presumably this was computed by adding to the cost of maintaining schools that served only this district, shares of the cost of other schools in proportion to the number of children from this area, and shares of the attendance and school health services on a per capita basis. Again it appears that general administrative costs were omitted. This item of education came to $362,000, bringing the total for tax-supported services to $1,357,000.

From this figure there should, of course, be deducted the taxes paid by residents of the district or on property located in the district. The investigators chose to consider only taxes on real estate in the area. They found the assessed value of land and buildings to be $8,153,000. The tax rates per $1,000 of assessed value for the following taxing authorities were added together: state, county, city, school board, library board. Perhaps the state was included on the ground that it was furnishing considerable sums for relief. The tax rate for 1931 and 1932 was $27.60. On this basis the tax-rate income was easily found to be $225,000. That was the amount of tax receipts which would have come in, had all real estate taxes levied been actually collected. But they were not all collected. Indeed, in 1932 the delinquent taxes had accumulated to the amount of $369,000, which is 164 per cent of the expected tax income for one year. This should be contrasted with a 97 per cent delinquency for the city as a whole. Green holds that "the tax-rate income is better than the actual income from taxes, since even though taxes become delinquent, they will have to be paid some time with accumulated interest."[1] Hence, if the district be credited with the tax-rate income of $225,000 the operating loss was $1,132,000.

[1] From a personal letter to one of the authors.

But this was really not the whole cost of public service in the district, for various semiprivate agencies carried on several kinds of social work among its residents. Omitting all except community fund agencies—which included neighborhood centers, visiting nurses, the Associated Charities and other family welfare societies—all together these rendered direct services estimated to have cost $362,000. This brings the total operating deficit for this district to approximately $1,500,000. This may be restated as a subsidy of $333 per family per year. In still another form, the net deficit, not counting community fund agencies, was 21 per cent of the appraised value of taxable land and buildings in the area. (Public and semipublic tax-exempt structures and land were omitted from the calculations.) This means that, if 1932 was a typical year, the governmental operating losses in and for the district would amount in five years to the total value of all privately owned property. This does not prove that the city could afford to buy and clear the area, but it brings us one step nearer to the question: What can the city best afford to do? As a matter of fact, Cleveland did decide to enter upon a program of slum clearance and rehousing, but this decision may have been affected by the possibility of securing federal funds.

In commenting on their own work the investigators say:

> After so careful an analysis of a section of the Slum Area it might have been well to have analyzed another section of the city far removed from such conditions. Lacking such an analysis, rates have been calculated for the more important elements of cost and compared with rates similarly calculated for some of the nearby suburbs.[1]

Thus were computed the cost of fire and police protection per capita, per family, per $1,000 appraised value of land and buildings, per $1,000 appraised value of buildings, per capita per square mile. As an example of what these calculations revealed, fire protection cost, per $1,000 appraised value of real estate, $49.81 in the district, but only $2.59 for the city as a whole, and only $0.63 for a residential suburb. Police protection cost, per family, $57.60 in the district, $18.12 for the whole city, but only $3.63 in one of the suburbs. Surely no municipal government can afford to ignore such wide variations as these.

[1] Navin, *et al.*, *op. cit.*, p. 15.

The Cleveland study has been described as fully as it has because it was a pioneer undertaking and because it illustrates many of the problems and methods of procedure that must be considered.

A St. Louis study[1] profited by the preceding work in Cleveland. Also, funds were made available whereby 13 separate districts of St. Louis were examined in a manner similar to that described. Three districts were in the blighted area just outside the downtown section; two were well-established mid-town residential districts; one was still in process of development; one included apartments, hotels, and rather expensive single dwellings; five were representative industrial districts with rather small populations; and the last was the central business district. Thus it is possible from the St. Louis data to compare various sorts of areas.

In computing costs the St. Louis City Plan Commission counted everything that enters into the municipality's budget, including general administration, debt service, courts, water department, art museum, zoo, and public schools. The inclusion or exclusion of some of these items would not affect the relative status of districts, but by taking account of them the commission was considering the total cost of local government. (St. Louis City is independent of St. Louis County.)

In apportioning the cost of various services to the several districts a number of devices were employed. Thus "the cost of Streets and Sewers Department was computed by multiplying the annual average cost for streets and sewers by the ratio of the area in streets and alleys within the district to the total area of the streets and alleys within the city."[2] The costs of library, art museum, and zoo, respectively, were computed by multiplying the population within the district by the average annual cost per capita. "The cost for debt service was determined by multiplying the average annual charge by the ratio of assessed valuation [land and improvements] of the district to the total assessed valuation of the entire city." "The cost of public schools was computed by multiplying the average annual cost for public schools by the ratio of the number of elementary school pupils enrolled in the city."

[1] *Urban Land Policy*, St. Louis City Plan Commission, 1936; *A Year of City Planning*, St. Louis City Plan Commission, 1937.

[2] This and following statements are taken from an unpublished document lent by the St. Louis City Plan Commission.

For parks and recreation a more complicated method was used:

> It was assumed that the unserved area of the city contributed ten per cent of the cost of parks; that the served area of the city contributed ninety per cent of the annual service cost for parks and recreation. It was also estimated that the served area comprises eighty per cent of the total city area and the unserved, the twenty per cent balance. With these assumptions, it was computed that the average cost per gross acre in the [un]served area was $12.00 per acre.

For areas assumed to be served by parks and playgrounds the figure was $26.99. Two districts considered to be half served were assigned a unit cost of $19.50 per acre.

In regard to income, the St. Louis study differed from that in Cleveland not only by taking a five-year average (1930–1935), but also by including taxes on personal property (money, notes, vehicles, household goods, locally assessed public utilities), water rates, and miscellaneous sources of income such as license fees, hospital and golf course charges. Perhaps this accounts for the fact that the deficits of St. Louis slum areas were much less than that computed in Cleveland. In none of the St. Louis districts studied were the costs of government, as computed, more than 250 per cent of the tax income credited to the district.

Instead of taking the tax-rate income, as in Cleveland, the St. Louis study considered the average yearly receipts from property taxes and meter readings made by the water department. The income from taxes on real estate was apportioned to each district by multiplying the annual average for the city by the ratio of the assessed value of land and improvements to the corresponding assessed value for the whole city. The assessed values used were those of 1932, which were the basis for taxes of 1933–1934; thus the high valuations of 1929 and the lower ones of later years were avoided. Income from taxes on personal property was apportioned to the districts studied in accordance with the ratio of the assessed valuation of real estate in the district to the corresponding assessed value for the whole city. This is admittedly not accurate but was considered to be a fair approximation. Actual plotting of the addresses of all personal taxes carried on the assessor's books would have been enormously expensive both in time and in money. As to the other miscellaneous items of municipal income, we do not have details. However, their total is relatively small, and we assume that the bases of estimate were appropriate to the particular items considered.

Studies more or less like those made in St. Louis and Cleveland have been carried on in Boston, Louisville, and Camden, N. J. By this time similar studies have doubtless been conducted in other cities.

In Boston, as in St. Louis, the effort was to determine what were the income and the expenditure of the city government for specified areas. Thus in Boston "some minor taxes and fees and also the City receipts from the Federal Government, the State and the County are not included under 'Income.' Some minor expenses and certain payments to the State and County and the deficit are not carried under 'Costs.'"[1] There are numerous differences in the details of cost accounting, but most of them may be ignored for our present purposes. One variant is noted because it displays vividly the complexity of the whole problem.

The Criminal Court Costs have been apportioned for the four Residential Districts using the proportion recommended by the Police and Court authorities, as follows: to cover the criminal work relative to automobiles, 25 per cent was apportioned on the basis of the total miles of streets and the density of population per mile;—50 per cent on the basis of the number of saloons, beer parlors, hotels, etc., and the density of population per acre;—to represent crimes against property, 5.5 per cent by assessed valuation;—to represent crimes against the person, 7 per cent by population;—12.5 per cent of criminal cases of numerous and varied types of crime has been allotted in the same proportion as the total of the other costs.[2]

In the report of the first Boston study, which covered six districts, the point is made that "as the Districts vary considerably in size, comparisons should be made, not by the total cost or income but by the ratios 'per capita' or 'per acre of gross area' or 'per acre of net area.'"[1] Since the true business and industrial districts contain few residents, their costs are reported "per acre" and not "per capita," which seems to us altogether

[1] *Report on the Income and Cost of Six Districts in the City of Boston*, Boston City Planning Board, p. 16, 1934.

[2] *Report on the Income and Cost Survey of the City of Boston*, Boston City Planning Board, p. 24, 1935.

sound. But the residential areas are reported both "per acre" and "per capita." Incidentally, the business, industrial, high-rent residential, and miscellaneous residential districts showed favorable balances, while the suburban and low-rent residential districts showed deficits.

In 1936 the Boston City Planning Board reported an analysis of income and cost for all 127 census tracts which go to make up the city proper. The general findings of this more complete survey were forecast by the first study, except that for the whole city industrial districts show a net loss instead of a favorable balance. However, industrial districts differ from each other.

There remain several important questions to consider. First, are we to concern ourselves with the various districts of a city as such or with their inhabitants? If we center attention on the physical areas, is it legitimate to charge them with the expense of schools for children who would have to be educated no matter where they lived, with pensions for handicapped persons who would be dependents no matter what their residence, with relief for unemployed men who might have difficulty in finding work anywhere, with prostitutes whose patrons come from "nice" districts, etc.? On the other hand, if we center attention on the people, is it fair to credit an area with the tax income from business properties or to debit it with the fire protection required by obsolete buildings? It must be confessed that the issue is very puzzling. All that seems clear is that industrial areas should be compared with other industrial areas as to costs per acre or per $1,000 assessed valuation, while residential districts should be compared with other residential districts as to costs per capita.

The second question is this: How great a deficit shall be considered excessive? It is unlikely that variations in income and standard of living will vanish. People will probably continue to group themselves somewhat according to economic levels; hence some areas will present great assets with few liabilities, while others will present great liabilities and few assets. In other words, some deviations in extent of needs and in capacity to pay for services may be considered normal. Furthermore, it seems to be generally accepted in America that the more fortunate should bear a large share of the costs of public and semipublic services. The question may be put in this form:

How great a deviation (negative in capacity to pay, positive in services needed) shall be considered normal, and beyond what point shall it be regarded as pathological? That is, at what point does a deficit become great enough to warrant a given program of reorganization or reconstruction? Perhaps we might consider the second and third quartiles "normal," the first "pathological," and the fourth "superior."

This brings us to the third question: How can we determine the possible financial benefits of a given program? If present assets and liabilities or costs and contributions have been computed, the next step is to estimate the probable initial outlay for renovation. If this is to include demolition, rehousing, revision of street plan, provision of open spaces, in whole or in part, there is a task primarily for engineers, architects, and accountants. The next step is to estimate the probable costs of public services over varying periods of time, contrasting how much they would probably be if the proposal were carried into effect and how much if it were not undertaken. Doubtless these can at best be only rough approximations and hence should be estimated conservatively. Then there must be an estimate of the relative costs of maintenance and depreciation, with and without the new program. Next is the calculation of probable changes in tax receipts. Finally there would be, we suppose, an attempt to work out an equation or two such as these: For the government, will Initial Outlay *plus* Public Services for x years *equal* y times the Tax Receipts for x years, y being that fraction of tax receipts which is now the proportionate cost of public services in areas considered "low normal," *e.g.*, the second quartile? For the private owner, will Initial Outlay *plus* Maintenance and Depreciation for x years *equal* the probable Earnings for x years plus inventory at the end of the period?

Is this group of problems capable of solution as it has been stated? Perhaps not. It may well be that a census tract or even a large section of a city is too small a unit of area and population. For schools and roads and relief we have deliberately enlarged units of taxation and administration from township to county, to state, and even to nation. The principle has been that of equalization. It has rested on the assumption that need and capacity to pay are very unlikely to be evenly distributed or to show a high correlation. In the light of this experience and of the difficulties inherent in the major problem of this chapter, the issue may have to be completely restated or even abandoned.

Perhaps all we can profitably do about social needs on an ecological basis is to discover their distribution and thus locate the areas in which effort may wisely be concentrated, without any assumptions as to the size of units that may be expected to pay their own way. This last becomes then a problem in public finance, which involves not only human ecology but also certain principles of relating responsibility for administration to responsibility for financial support. Hence we leave it to the political scientists and to the economists to determine the appropriate units of taxation and of administration. But questions which may well engage the attention of us all are these: Can cities afford to permit part of their people to live under the conditions which commonly obtain in blighted areas? Do we, the general run of citizens, know what is the long-time cost of tolerating these centers of disease, vice, and crime, of bringing up children in slums? Would it be cheaper to leave them alone, to engage in piecemeal reform, or to undertake comprehensive programs of physical reconstruction and social reorganization? Of course, this last question cannot be answered until we have before us definite plans. But in the last analysis it may prove impossible to reduce these matters to financial terms. Then the problem assumes this form: What are the demonstrated and other probable accompaniments and consequences of *laissez faire*, piecemeal reform, and thoroughgoing reorganization, respectively? Which of these combinations is most acceptable or least distasteful to us? The assumption underlying these questions is that it is better to go ahead with our eyes open than to drift into we know not what—in other words, that even *laissez faire* should be chosen deliberately and with some notion of what it involves.

Selected Readings

Navin, R. B., *et al.*: *An Analysis of a Slum Area in Cleveland*, prepared for the Cleveland Metropolitan Housing Authority, 1934. Identifies a "debtor area" in terms of income from taxes and expenditures by governmental departments and private charities.

Urban Land Policy, St. Louis City Plan Commission, 1936. A study of municipal receipts and expenditures for 13 selected districts.

A Year of City Planning, Works Progress Administration project under direction of the St. Louis City Plan Commission, 1937. Pages 43–92 describe methods employed in a study of the 13 selected districts.

Report on the Income and Cost Survey of the City of Boston, Emergency Relief Administration project under direction of the Boston City Planning Board, 1935. A study of the entire city divided into 127 census tracts.

ZORBAUGH, HARVEY W.: *Gold Coast and Slum*, University of Chicago Press, 1929. Chapter 7 describes the slum (in the narrow sense of the word), but most of the book is devoted to changes taking place in the blighted areas north of the Chicago River.

CHAPTER XVIII

PHYSICAL MOVEMENT AND SOCIAL MOBILITY

At numerous points in the preceding chapters we have had occasion to speak of the mobility of urban populations. Here we shall discuss more systematically and in greater detail what is meant by this term and how mobility can be measured. Unfortunately the word has been loosely applied to several different kinds of behavior. In its broadest sense physical mobility may include any movement through space. But when the coming and going is between relatively fixed terminals, as in commuting between a surburban residence and a downtown office, that is one thing; when restless or hard-pressed folk move from house to house or from city to city, that is quite another. The first is sometimes called fluidity, a term which we do not like, and it is a major factor in the traffic problem. The second is known as residential mobility; it involves a change of base. A change of job or of occupation requires in many instances a change of one or both bases or terminals, and in this sense it is a form of physical mobility. Very often it connotes a change in income, associates, and dominant activities. Hence occupational mobility is closely related to change of economic and social status. But change of status is commonly associated with change of physical setting. Thus the *nouveaux riches* may gravitate toward the Gold Coast or some exclusive subdivision; the "decayed aristocracy" may give up their fine old homes and move into a middle-class section or, clinging to the old district, find themselves surrounded by strange faces and strange tongues. Other changes in status, which are often accompanied by changes in locus, are those of immigrants who become "Americanized" and of light-colored mulattoes who pass for white.

Finally, the term "social mobility" has been applied to the making of contacts, their number, variety, intimacy, and permanence. Persons who meet many people of different types are described as more mobile than those who meet only a few or a limited variety of folk. Persons with a nucleus of fairly permanent intimates and a wide range of contacts are mobile in a manner different from that of persons whose relations are all superficial. It is maintained by some students of the city that no particular importance should be attached to physical mobility except as it provides a measure or explanation of social contacts and relations. But these depend on communication rather than on movement. The telephone, radio, newspaper, and other mediums of indirect communication are therefore important in the study of social mobility as just defined. Because this fifth kind of mobility is so different from the others, we shall leave further discussion of it to Chap. XX.

Returning to the first four varieties of physical movement and social change, we find change of economic or social status sometimes referred to as vertical mobility, the others being called horizontal. The distinction is suggestive, but the two are not mutually exclusive. As we have noted, change of status is often accompanied by change of residence or occupation. A more important distinction is that between occasionally moving from one house or city to another and being in the habit of shifting frequently, between occasional change of position or job and high labor turnover. Our emphasis therefore will be laid on relative frequency of movement as an indicator of habits and of social relations. Moreover, we shall pay particular attention to residential mobility, which has been more adequately studied than any other kind in our cities. The reason for this doubtless lies in the relative ease with which changes of residence can be identified and measured. If we had no ground for believing that social relations change with addresses, such studies might be dismissed as of little consequence except to realtors and landlords. It is because we can point to evidence that residential mobility and stability are associated with social standing and social organization that we attach importance to this phase of city life. We know definitely that people living in certain areas are stigmatized, whereas the occupants of other sections derive prestige from their place of residence. Obviously moves from areas rated "low" to areas rated "high" raise the social status of those making the change. Similarly, a move in the reverse direction lowers the mover's social standing. Also it is plain that the conduct of schools and churches is affected by the extent to which their clientele moves about. The management of business, too, must be different in the midst of a mobile population from its management in a stable area, for much moving disturbs credit, collections and deliveries. These are matters of common observation, but we shall present more systematic and objective data bearing on the interrelation of physical movement and social change.

Studies of Residential Mobility

Columbus, Ohio.—One of the early studies of residential mobility was made in Columbus, Ohio, by McKenzie.[1] His attention had been called to the weakness of churches, trade-unions, and other voluntary associations when their local membership did not remain long in a given area. He had observed the difficulty of creating interest in municipal affairs among people who move about a great deal. Hence he undertook to measure the residential mobility rates in different parts of the city and to discover their relation to various other social data.

The method he employed was the study of changes in lists of registered voters by precincts over a period of one year. Thus the 1917 list was checked against the 1918 list for each precinct. The percentage of names from the 1917 list that reappeared in 1918 was taken to represent the relative stability of one precinct as compared with another. This device obviously took no account of moves from house to house within a given precinct. Perhaps they are less important than changes covering a greater distance; nevertheless they may signify instability and lack of vital social connections. Furthermore, McKenzie's study took no account of persons ineligible to vote at all, or negligent about re-registering. There may have been many persons in both categories. Another possible criticism is that one year may not afford a fair test. Obviously the way to settle this issue is to study the changes in voters' lists for another year or for several years. However, the results of McKenzie's study correspond closely to those of common observation.

[1] R. D. McKenzie, *The Neighborhood: A Study of Local Life in the City of Columbus, Ohio,* 1923. Data used by permission of the University of Chicago Press.

In Columbus, mobility, as identified, was high in sections surrounding the central business district and low in outlying parts of the city. Its correlation with economic status was decisive and negative, economic status being measured by the ratio of tax returns on household furniture to the number of registered voters. In other words, where houses were well furnished mobility was low, and vice versa. Residential mobility showed a high positive correlation with dependency and delinquency. Where there was much moving about there were many people on relief or in court.

Seattle.—A quite different procedure was employed by Lind in his study of residential mobility in Seattle.[1] He used school records, autobiographical material, and, to a limited extent, addresses of newspaper subscribers and patrons of the telephone company and the municipal light department. From the school records he calculated the percentage of the annual enrollment that was in a given school at the end of the year. Thus in a mobile district he found that only 44 per cent of all the children who had been in the school at some time during the year were enrolled there in June; whereas in a stable district the percentage was 87. In general, districts with the highest mobility were near the downtown section and those of low mobility were outlying. However, there were some exceptions. One school near the center of the city and attended by Chinese and Japanese children showed little change in enrollment, while some schools in outlying districts where real estate was "active" showed a large number of transfers. It may be objected that this method of measuring mobility does not include single adults or families without children of school age. Nevertheless, it does cover a large part of the population.

A second device employed in the Seattle study was the autobiographical material provided by children of the upper grades in nine schools. This included information as to age, place of birth, changes of residence, and reasons for change. It would have been well if the number of different addresses had been reported separately for different age groups; but on the assumption that the age distribution in the several schools was approximately the same, Lind computed the median for each school.

[1] A. W. Lind, *A Study of Mobility of Population in Seattle*, 1925. Data used by permission of the University of Washington.

In schools near the center of the city the average child had lived at more different addresses than in schools near the periphery. Children in the near-downtown schools had more frequently lived in foreign countries and in other places in the United States, as well as at several addresses in Seattle.

Lind used the newspapers, telephone company, and city light department to estimate the relative amount of moving in the city as a whole, but did not break the data down into districts. His information from these sources indicated that telephone subscribers moved less frequently than users of electricity and that regular newspaper subscribers moved least of all. In other words, removal or sealing of electric meters provided a more adequate index of residential mobility than did either of the other sets of data.

Without collecting exact data, Lind gained the impression that family desertion and dependency were more common in districts of high mobility. He also estimated that high mobility (measured by changes in school enrollment) was associated with high rates of juvenile delinquency (ratio of juvenile court cases to children enumerated in the school census).

The reasons offered for changing residence were: advertising of the advantages of living in Seattle, mobile character of jobs (as of clergy, soldiers, lumbermen, and mining engineers), unemployment, high rents, unsatisfactory relations with landlords, undesirable districts, influence of relatives, and disruption of the home. While it is often impossible for individuals to tell just why they have moved, there is little doubt that these factors had some influence (not yet capable of measurement) on residential mobility.

Kansas City and Topeka.—An inquiry on a much smaller scale was made in Kansas City and Topeka.[1] Three pairs of precincts were studied to determine whether there was any relation between mobility and services requested of social work and public health agencies. In Kansas City, Mo., Kansas City, Kans., and Topeka pairs of precincts were chosen so that in each city one precinct was the residence of many clients of agencies, while the other contained very few. Their selection also involved the attempt to eliminate such variables as "race," nationality, education,

[1] Stuart A. Queen, "Segregation of Population Types in the Kansas City Area," *Pub. Amer. Sociol. Soc.*, 32 (1926), 230–232.

and economic status. This effort was not wholly successful, but the inhabitants of all six precincts were white and overwhelmingly native born. There were no Negroes at all, and the few foreigners had been long in this country and were naturalized. In two pairs of precincts the family incomes were approximately the same. The lists of occupations were similar except for a slightly larger percentage of white-collar jobs in the A precincts (those with few clients of social agencies). Also there were more employed women and children in the B precincts (those receiving many services from agencies). As to education, there was little difference either in the average age of leaving school or in the grade attained. However, among children still in school there was somewhat more retardation and less acceleration in the B precincts. These data, together with facts concerning mobility, were secured by a house-to-house canvass, and are important because of the definite effort to reduce the number of variables in the situation.

Physical mobility was measured in terms of length of residence in house, precinct, and city, re-registration of voters, ownership of homes and furniture, and continuity of employment. In general the people who lived in the A districts had lived longer in the same house, precinct, and city than had those who lived in B districts. The percentages that had lived in the same place less than one year were distinctly greater in the B districts. These results seem decisive provided that length of residence is really a good index of mobility. The criticism has been made that length of past residence in one place is not a measure of future prospects or of habits of moving about. The objection would be valid if other indexes of mobility did not yield the same results. In Kansas City, Mo., it was possible to check this in terms of the re-registration of voters in two successive years. In the A precinct 90 per cent of the 1924 voters were re-registered there in 1925, while in the B precinct the percentage was only 68. In the A precinct only 16 per cent of the 1925 voters were new to the district, while in the B precinct the percentage was 29. In all three pairs of districts the ownership of homes and of furniture was greater in the A precincts. These are indirect measures of mobility, but we know that people who own their furniture are less likely to move than those who live in furnished rooms, and homeowners are less likely to move than are tenants. Hence it seems to be established that residential mobility was greater in B districts than in A districts.

Occupational mobility corresponded rather closely to residential. Length of time in job and in type of work was markedly and consistently greater in A than in B precincts. Membership in local organizations differed in the same general fashion. That is, a larger percentage in the A precincts than in the B precincts belonged to church, lodge, or trade-union. Especially was there a larger percentage of those who were members of two or more organizations in the A districts. These items seem to us of even more significance than residential mobility, to which they are related. People who belong to local groups are believed to find in these organizations both material and moral support in time of trouble. Hence they do not have to turn so early or so frequently to the impersonal agencies of the city. This is as yet an unverified hypothesis, but we offer it as an important clue to the intimate relation between mobility and the services of social work and public health agencies.

Small Cities in Illinois.—Some differences both in method and in results appear in a study which Albig made of four Illinois cities of 30,000 to 40,000 inhabitants.[1] He made use of city directories in two successive years, school records, and questionnaires. From the city directories of Danville, Bloomington, Rock Island, and Moline he identified the families that remained for a year at the same address, moved into the city, out of the city, and within the city during that time. This was of necessity a minimum statement of changes of address, for it missed those who moved into the city and out again during the year and those who moved more than once. But it did differentiate single men, single women, married couples, and minors. The study showed that there was a smaller percentage of married persons and of minors among the mobile folk in small cities than in large cities. High mobility rates were not concentrated in sections near the central business district. Of moves within the city two-thirds were for less than one mile. How this would compare with a larger city we do not know, for no comparable data are at hand.

[1] William Albig, "The Mobility of Urban Population," *Social Forces*, 11 (1933), 351–367.

From the school records Albig learned the changes of residence of children from the sixth to the twelfth grade in Danville. Interestingly, these showed a slightly greater stability of families with children in high school. Also they confirmed the directory study in showing that near the business district there was a considerable number of families that had not recently changed their residence. In a larger city such folk would undoubtedly have moved to outlying sections as housing became obsolete and the area became more mixed as to land use and population types.

Finally, questionnaires were submitted to 200 children who had lived at only one address and to 200 who had moved more than seven times. From these it was learned that the mobile group lived more frequently in duplexes and multiple dwellings. The group was marked by such occupations as those of salesman, store manager, physician, and clergyman. Families had a smaller number of children but more dependent relatives living with them. There were fewer members of churches, lodges, and clubs, though the differences were not striking. Differences in frequency of voting over a five-year period were not great. Families with greatest mobility attended the movies more frequently, drew more books from the public library, and wrote more letters. They knew fewer of their nigh dwellers but were found more frequently borrowing and lending and shopping together. The exchange of articles, Albig thinks, may reflect scarcity, *e.g.*, of garden tools, rather than neighborliness. Visiting back and forth did not differ much as between the mobile and the stable groups. In the mobile families of high school students there was more giving of presents, sending of greeting cards, and caring for each other's children, but this was not true of the families of mobile grade school children. The latter being families of industrial and clerical workers, the important difference was apparently one of economic status.

These studies by Albig are of value because they display the usefulness of city directories in getting at relative mobility, because they indicate some differences between small and large cities, and because they raise some questions about the relation of mobility to neighboring. As to the last of these points, it is a bit surprising to note that mobile families in small Illinois cities indulged to a considerable extent in visiting, borrowing and lending, shopping together, exchange of gifts, and care of each other's children. Perhaps neighboring is more general in small than in large cities, regardless of mobility. Perhaps the samples studied in large cities have not been sufficiently large or representative. In any case the matter needs further study.

Cleveland.—In 1933 Howard W. Green made a detailed study of residential mobility in metropolitan Cleveland on the basis of public utility records.[1] Specifically he identified moves by the turning on or off of gas and electric meters. This had the advantage of counting all moves of families that changed their address more than once during the year, but it had the disadvantage of missing rooming-house and hotel families, for which individual meters were not provided, and those too poor to pay for gas or electricity. We do not know how many Cleveland families in 1933 were cooking on wood or coal stoves and lighting their quarters with kerosene lamps, but we suspect that many of the unemployed and underemployed were without modern conveniences. Nevertheless, this study must have identified the great majority of changes of residence. Furthermore, it reported for the entire metropolitan district families leaving and entering each census tract and civil division and families moving around within the tract.

With these and some additional data Green devised several indexes of instability. These included the percentage of increase or decrease in population 1920–1930, the percentage of change in families from April 1930 to October 1932, the percentage of change in families during 1933, the percentage of families owning their own homes, the percentage of residential units that were vacant in October 1932. Finally he constructed an "instability ratio," which was the sum of a year's moves from a location within a tract plus moves to a location within the same tract, divided by the number of families living in the tract at a given date.

The more general findings of Green's study were that 28 per cent of all families in metropolitan Cleveland moved somewhere during the year 1933. Almost nine-tenths of these migrants moved from one place to another within the metropolitan area.

[1] Howard W. Green, *Movements of Families within the Cleveland Metropolitan District*, 1933. Data used by permission of the Real Property Inventory of Metropolitan Cleveland.

Out of 91,722 moves only 3,288 were out of metropolitan Cleveland, despite the depression and unemployment; and moves into the metropolitan district numbered only 5,248. Within the metropolitan area about 2,000 more families moved from Cleveland into the suburbs than moved in the opposite direction, the actual numbers being 6,480 and 4,648. Over 24,000 migrant families did not leave the census tract in which they were residing. In general most of the moves were for short distances. Over 4,000 of the changes were made by families that were "undoubling," *e.g.*, children leaving the parental roof. The largest number of moves occurred in the month of September and the smallest number in December.

Instability ratios for the 321 census tracts showed that there was a definite segregation of mobile families in certain districts and of stable families in others. Ratios varied from 106 to 19, but tracts with high ratios were not concentrated in any one section. In fact, the highest 25 ratios pertained to tracts that were rather widely scattered. Nevertheless, it does appear from Green's maps that tracts near the central business district tended to have higher instability ratios than tracts near the periphery of the metropolitan area. Also there is evidence of a relation between residential mobility and economic status. In Chap. XIII we described the manner in which Cleveland census tracts were grouped on 14 economic levels. Here we note that the result of moving in and out of tracts on the five lowest levels was a net loss, while all the other levels showed a gain. As might be expected, families seldom fell from a high level to a low one and rarely climbed from low to high. Half of the families moved up one or two steps or down one; few changed more than one additional step in either direction. Contrary to expectation, there appeared to be no correlation between economic status and the amount of moving around within a tract. The percentages moving within a tract were lowest on the fourteenth (highest) economic level and highest in the eleventh; they were almost identical in the first, ninth, and thirteenth; they were practically the same in the second, eighth, and twelfth. This is surprising, because it is natural to assume that people on a low economic level move more frequently within a limited area than do people of larger means. We cannot help wondering whether if families without gas and electricity had been included the results might not have been different. Table 44 displays the relation between economic levels and residential mobility in Cleveland.

St. Louis.—In St. Louis a number of different sources have been tried out: reports of school transfers, For Rent advertisements in the newspapers, reports of bonded movers, and the city

TABLE 44.—RESIDENTIAL MOBILITY AND ECONOMIC LEVELS, CLEVELAND, 1933[a]

Economic level	Percentage of families living in metropolitan Cleveland in 1932 who moved into areas of higher, lower, or similar economic levels in 1933			
	Higher	Lower	Same	Total
Lowest	20.4	0	9.4	29.8
2	14.6	0.4	10.4	25.4
3	10.0	1.4	14.9	26.3
4	9.8	2.8	13.3	25.9
5	9.7	5.5	11.6	26.8
6	7.5	4.3	13.3	25.1
7	6.6	5.8	8.3	20.7
8	6.5	9.7	10.6	26.8
9	8.0	8.5	9.5	26.0
10	8.5	10.3	12.5	31.3
11	5.7	11.7	12.9	30.3
12	3.6	12.5	10.5	26.6
13	1.7	9.3	9.3	20.3
Highest	0	8.8	4.7	13.5

[a] Howard W. Green, *Movements of Families within the Cleveland Metropolitan District, 1933*, pp. 18–19, 1934. Adapted by permission of the Real Property Inventory of Metropolitan Cleveland.

directory. The use of school transfers was less satisfactory than in Seattle, because white and colored districts overlap but do not coincide and because there is a similar confusion in regard to elementary and high school districts. Furthermore, school districts are subject to change at uncertain intervals, and they rarely correspond to the permanent statistical units established by the United States Census Bureau. However, graphic methods of comparing these data with others, *i.e.*, spot and ratio maps, showed that mobility was high in sections of high dependency, delinquency, and death rates.

The second method involved classifying all For Rent advertisements for the month of November 1934. By means of a specially constructed index, described in Chap. XIII, these were sorted by census tracts. Duplicates were eliminated and individual units (rooms or room and board) were separated from family units (houses, flats, apartments, or light-housekeeping rooms). The capacity of each individual unit was counted as one. The capacity of family units for a given tract was assumed to be the product of the number of units multiplied by the average size of family in that tract. The total capacity of all units was then divided by the 1930 population, and the resulting ratios were ranked. The results of using this method were very inconclusive and did not correspond at all to those of the first method. The reasons are evidently that low-rent quarters are not often advertised in the papers and that high-rent property is frequently handled through agents who do not list it in the classified advertisements of the daily press.

The third method took advantage of a legal requirement in St. Louis that companies regularly moving household effects be bonded and report each month to the police department a record of every move including both the old and the new location. If everyone that moved had employed a bonded mover, this would provide an ideal index of residential mobility. But again the results were unsatisfactory, for it was evident that people of small means did not call on bonded novers. In fact, it is well known that many poor families move in a suitcase, wheelbarrow, or peddler's truck. However, there were probably other factors than the economic; for, even when the mobility index based on movers' records was weighted by the median rental for each tract, the correlation with other measures of mobility was low. What these other factors may be we do not know.

The method finally adopted by Cowgill for a city-wide study over a one-year period was that of comparing city directories for 1931 and 1932, classifying changes of address by census tracts, and computing the ratio of changes to the number of families enumerated in 1930.[1] While this method had the limitations pointed out in discussing the Illinois studies, it was deemed the most accurate device available. Furthermore, its validity was

[1] Donald O. Cowgill, "Residential Mobility of an Urban Population," unpublished master's thesis, Washington University, 1935.

partially tested in two ways. The ratings of certain middle-class tracts (*i.e.*, near the city median as to rentals paid and values of homes owned) on three scales were compared. The three scales were those based on newspaper advertisements, movers' reports, and the directories. The comparison showed that the relative standing of given tracts was the same or very nearly the same no matter which measure was used. The second test was based on a house-to-house survey directed by Dr. H. I. Spector, assistant health commissioner of St. Louis. In addition to questions about health matters his schedule included these: "How many times have you moved within the last two years?" "How long have you lived at the present address?" This survey was made in a low economic area inhabited largely by Negroes. The total number of moves reported by 2,700 families was divided by the total number of families, and that quotient was divided by 2 in order to get an annual rate. The result was 0.471, which is surprisingly close to the ratio 0.460 arrived at by the directory method for the same district. From answers to the second question a weighted average was computed. Assuming a constant turnover, or 100 per cent mobility in the time indicated as the average length of residence, we arrive at a mobility rate for one year of 0.445. This again is close to the ratio computed by the directory method.

Figure 17 shows graphically the results of Cowgill's study. Observe that most of the tracts with high mobility were near the central business district and that the ratios tend to decline as we proceed toward the periphery. In addition to this graphic display Cowgill computed rank correlations of mobility with several other series of data that have been assembled for St. Louis. These showed that mobility was high in areas of low economic status, measured by homeownership, value of homes, rentals, families on relief, and employment of women. They demonstrated that mobility was low in areas of well-established family life, indicated by percentage of males married, size of family, numerical equality of the sexes, and single dwellings. They displayed a positive relation between mobility and death rates, tuberculosis, venereal disease, suicide, illiteracy, and the presence of Negroes. Mrs. Bernard's study, described in Chap. XV, showed a negative correlation between mobility and the behavior we call neighboring. Cowgill also found that mobility

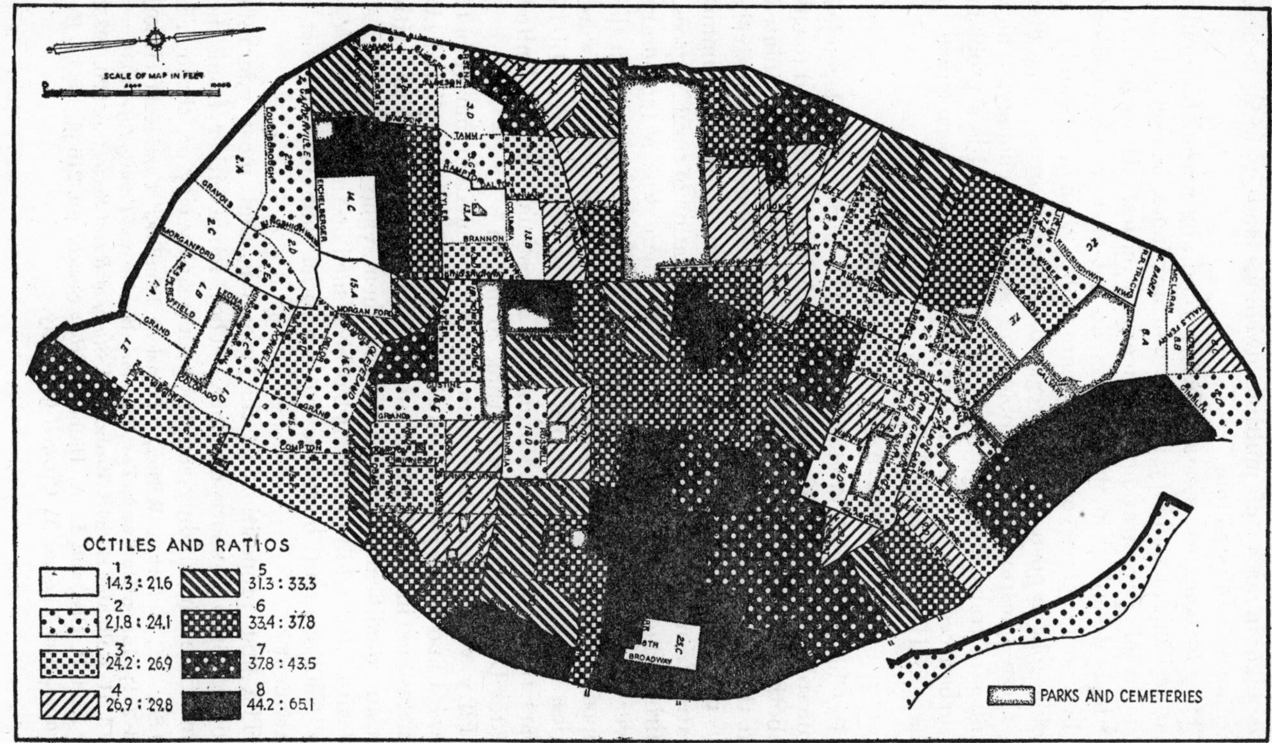

FIG. 17.—Residential mobility, St. Louis, 1931–1932.

was high in areas of multiple dwellings and in areas where vacancies were numerous.

Thus it seems to us established beyond any reasonable doubt that residential mobility is an important index of social status and social organization in American cities. However, the methods described in this chapter do not answer the questions of how some people come to be more mobile than others and how mobile folk happen to be segregated in certain areas. The first of these questions is a problem in social psychology, which studies of transients help to answer.[1] The second is a problem in urban ecology, to which a partial answer has been given in Chaps. XIII, XIV, and XV.

Other Aspects of Mobility

In Chap. III we showed that the growth of cities has depended primarily upon drawing in people from the countryside and towns in both the United States and Europe. In Chap. XVI we pointed out that three periods of our urban growth involved successively the movement of native white folk from rural America, immigration from abroad, and the cityward migration of rural Negroes. During the years 1930 through 1932, there was a temporary reversal, more people leaving cities for farms than moving in the opposite direction. But even when the net change is toward cities, there are many persons returning to the country. In 15 years they numbered, according to an estimate of the United States Department of Agriculture, 20 million.[2]

Fifty years ago, Ravenstein studied population movements toward and away from 64 British cities. Gist has reviewed his conclusions in the light of more recent American data; with certain qualifications, he considers them valid for our cities. Because little additional light has been shed on these hypotheses, we shall content ourselves with a brief summary of Gist's statement.[3]

The first proposition in this group is that most migrants proceed only a short distance. They move either from the immediate surrounding country to a near-by city or, through a

[1] See, *e.g.*, Robert S. Wilson, "Transient Families," *Family*, 11 (1930), 243–251; Marion Hathway, *The Migratory Worker and Family Life*, 1934.

[2] J. H. Kolb and E. de S. Brunner, *A Study of Rural Society*, p. 220, 1935.

[3] Noel P. Gist and L. A. Halbert, *Urban Society*, pp. 216 *ff.*, 1933. By permission of Thomas Y. Crowell Company.

series of moves, from village to town to city. The reasons for these short moves apparently lie in the facts that rural people know more about cities in their own region than about those which are farther away and that they frequently are not able or willing to bear the expense of long-distance moves. Two interesting exceptions to this general trend are the recent migrations of plantation Negroes to northern cities and the moves of Middle Western farmers to cities on the Pacific Coast. A second proposition is that the "pull" of a great city varies inversely with the distance and directly with the size of the city, the attraction in many cases being greatest for young adults. A third generalization contrasts intercity moves and rural-urban migrations. In contrast to the short distances usually involved in the latter, the former often involve long moves. Another difference is that people going from the country to the city are frequently limited in finances and in vocational skills, while those who transfer their residence from one city to another are apt to be of the professional and owning classes. Gist notes that cities attract women in larger numbers than men, but that the women go shorter distances. This varies somewhat, depending on the type of city involved. For example, when light manufacturing and commercial activities dominate, there are many vocational opportunities for women, but in cities devoted chiefly to heavy industries, the principal demand is for men. An exception to the general statement is that foreign-born men come earlier and in larger numbers than do their womenfolk.

Concerning the quality of rural-urban migrants, conflicting data[1] compel us to suspend judgment. Thus a Virginia study indicated that it was the superior countryfolk who were going to the city.[2] Of the samples studied, 46 per cent of the persons considered "upper-class" moved to the cities, 41 per cent of the "middle class," and 38 per cent of the "lower class." The three classes were identified with educational levels—college, high school, and elementary school, respectively. In contrast to the

[1] Gist and Halbert, *op. cit.*, pp. 243 *ff.*; Pitirim Sorokin and C. C. Zimmerman, *Principles of Rural-Urban Sociology*, Chap. 25, 1929; W. S. Thompson, *Research Memorandum on Internal Migration in the Depression*, selected bibliography, pp. 69–82, 1937.

[2] W. Gee and D. Runk, "Qualitative Selection in Cityward Migration," *Amer. Jour. Sociol.*, 37 (1931), 254–265.

Virginia study, one made in Minnesota appeared "to show that children of successful farm families stay on the farms more often, while those of the less successful families migrated to large industrial cities."[1] An Arkansas study contained within itself somewhat conflicting evidence.[2] It showed that, comparing different educational levels, the percentage of rural-urban migrants increased with the amount of schooling, but in absolute numbers persons with eighth-grade education or less constituted three-fifths of all those who moved to cities. These apparently conflicting reports come from states in widely different stages of economic development, both rural and urban. Within itself each state has both good and poor farming areas with somewhat diversified populations. The lure of cities and pressure to leave the farms may therefore be assumed to be of quite different kinds.

An unpublished study by Gist and Clark involved one of the most promising methods yet applied to the problem of the quality of rural-urban migrants. In 1922–1923, psychological tests were given to pupils in certain rural and village schools in Kansas. Starting with records of these tests, Gist and Clark undertook to discover the present residence of as many of the subjects as possible. They succeeded in locating 2,544, of whom 964 had moved to cities. Then the urban migrants were compared with those who remained in the country. The results showed an average intelligence quotient of 98.26 for those who had gone to the city and 94.78 for those who continued to be rural dwellers. At first glance the difference between the two seems slight, but it is statistically significant.[3] Gist and Clark also found that the average I.Q. of their subjects was higher in large than in small cities—99.31 in cities over 100,000, contrasted with 97.02 in cities under 10,000. Again the difference is small but statistically significant. Some question might be raised as

[1] C. C. Zimmerman, "The Migration to Towns and Cities," *Amer. Jour. Sociol.*, 33 (1927), 105–109.

[2] T. C. McCormick, "Urban Migration and Educational Selection," *Amer. Jour. Sociol.*, 39 (1933), 355–359.

[3] We are indebted to Gist and Clark for lending us a copy of their manuscript in advance of its publication. Throughout, their evidence seems thoroughly to justify their conclusions. In this particular item they found the probable error (0.316) of the difference between the means to be less than one-tenth of the computed difference (3.48).

to the meaning of intelligence tests and their value for sociological research. We do not need to assume that they measure innate or inherited capacity. We may accept the probability that what they measure is a composite of hereditary and environmental factors—of ability, opportunity, and incentive. But there is little doubt that this composite affects "the individual's later career, his choice of occupation, his success or failure in that occupation, his leisure time activities, in a word, the general character of his social adjustment."[1] The method used in this study commends itself to us especially because of its apparent freedom from bias. When the school children were tested, no one knew where any of them would be living 13 years later.

Summary

We have now reviewed, in this and other chapters, various forms of physical movement which have some relation to the social life of our cities. We have considered the coming of immigrants from other lands and their gradual dispersion. As they have moved out from the immigrant colonies frequently located in blighted areas and become scattered among the rest of the population, they have been undergoing "Americanization." That is, the physical movement and the cultural process of assimilation have gone hand in hand. The Negroes who have been coming to our cities have, like immigrants, needed to adjust themselves to urban life. They have had the advantage of already using the English language, but the handicap of race prejudice. Their rapid increase in numbers has caused them to overflow the bounds of districts in which they were segregated, thus frequently precipitating serious conflicts. Ordinarily they are not scattered throughout the city, nor are they merged with the general population as happens in the case of most immigrant groups. The white people coming from our own rural districts have many experiences like those of the immigrants and the Negroes, but they have the advantages of English-speaking American citizens and are spared the racial handicap of the Negroes. Like the other two groups, they tend to settle in blighted areas or near places of employment. As they raise their status economically and socially, they change their location too.

[1] From the manuscript of the study.

In other words, residential and occupational changes are paralleled by changes in status. Intercity migration seems to involve the fewest and simplest adjustments of all. Such habits as are acquired by driving in traffic, trading at chain stores, etc., enable experienced city dwellers to transplant themselves fairly easily even though there are noticeable differences between the manner of life in cities of different sizes and in different parts of the country. Intracity migration may be quite a routine affair, but often it is associated with flight from unacceptable nigh dwellers, changes in jobs, economic status, or social standing. Hence there are likely to be fairly difficult adjustments confronting people whose moves are confined to the same city.

Because our cities are poorly planned and because city dwellers arrange their affairs individually rather than cooperatively, they find their interests scattered in many parts of a metropolitan district. Hence they spend a considerable part of their time coming and going between places of residence, work, recreation, education, worship, etc. Because of this there is an enormous volume of traffic almost constantly moving on city streets. This type of movement differs from the others in that it is a routine shuffling back and forth between relatively fixed points, while the other type of mobility involves change of one or both terminals.

All these forms of mobility taken together necessitate the modification of social institutions so that they may effectively serve mobile populations. Churches, schools, social centers, stores, and other local institutions have developed in the past for the service of a presumably stable population. As our people take more and more to wheels, changing their place of abode and of work at frequent intervals, it becomes increasingly difficult to conduct or to carry on the processes of education, merchandising, and all the rest. We suspect, too, that the mobility of our population is a major factor in the apparent breakdown of social controls in American cities. The devices which were effective in rural neighborhoods and villages are not so effective in cities. Gossip and other expressions of neighborhood and community sentiment can more easily be escaped by the city dweller. Hence there is need for what are sometimes called secondary controls. With some of these we are familiar, namely, the police, trade associations, advertising, political parties, etc. But their weakness is evident to all who are familiar with city life.

Selected Readings

Green, Howard W.: *Movements of Families within the Cleveland Metropolitan District*, 1933, Real Property Inventory of Metropolitan Cleveland, 1934. During 1938 there is being published a similar study of movements during 1937.

Lind, A. W.: *A Study of Mobility of Population in Seattle*, University of Washington Press, 1925.

Albig, William: "The Mobility of Urban Population," *Social Forces*, 11 (1933), 351–367. Studies of Danville, Bloomington, Rock Island, and Moline, Illinois.

Gist, Noel P., and L. A. Halbert: *Urban Society*. Thomas Y. Crowell Company, 1933. Chapter 8 deals with urban migration and its selective aspects.

Sorokin, Pitirim, and C. C. Zimmerman: *Principles of Rural-Urban Sociology*, Henry Holt & Company, 1929. Part V deals with rural-urban migration in many lands.

PART IV

PEOPLE IN THE CITY

Chapter XIX

CHARACTERISTICS OF URBAN POPULATIONS

Having given some attention to how, when, and where cities came to be, we turn now to see what kinds of folk live in them. How are they distributed as to age, sex, marital status, ethnic origins, intelligence, and occupations? Are they like or different from rural people in these respects? By how much do they differ? In discussing these questions we shall consider chiefly American cities in recent years because it is for them that data are most accessible.

Heterogeneity of Origin

In our first chapter we presented the hypothesis that urban populations are more heterogeneous than rural ones. Now we have no generally accepted index of heterogeneity, but there are several ways in which we can attack this problem. First of all, in 1930 in our 96 metropolitan areas over 43.5 per cent of the population were native white of native parents, compared with 68.1 per cent outside these great centers. For the total urban population (living in places of 2,500 and over) the percentage was 48.6. Comparing urban as just defined with rural farm and rural nonfarm (chiefly villagers), we see in Table 45 that the urban folk are clearly most diverse in color and nativity. What makes the difference more emphatic is the fact that Negroes, who are more numerous in rural than in urban areas, often constitute the only important class other than native white of native parents; while the foreign born, who are more numerous in cities, are found along with Negroes. Furthermore, the rural Negroes are a fairly homogeneous group, while the urban immigrants come from many different lands. Thus in the South Atlantic and East South Central states, which are largely rural, 98 per cent or more of the people are native born—white or black. But in New England and the Middle Atlantic states, which are largely urban, over 20 per cent are foreign born. Observing in

Table 45 that 80 per cent of the foreign born were classed as urban, we note in Table 46 percentage distribution by country of birth.

TABLE 45.—COLOR AND NATIVITY OF URBAN AND RURAL POPULATIONS OF THE UNITED STATES, 1930, PERCENTAGE DISTRIBUTION[a]

	Urban	Rural farm	Rural nonfarm
Native white, native parents	48.6	68.0	68.2
Native white, foreign or mixed parents	27.0	11.0	14.6
Foreign born	15.6	3.6	6.6
Negro	7.5	15.5	8.5
Other	1.3	2.0	2.1
Total	100.0	100.0	100.0

	Urban	Rural farm	Rural nonfarm	Total
Native white, native parents	47.8	29.2	23.0	100.0
Native white, foreign or mixed parents	73.4	13.0	13.6	100.0
Foreign born	80.3	8.1	11.6	100.0
Negro	43.7	39.4	17.0	100.0
Other	45.8	29.3	24.9	100.0

[a] Fifteenth Census, *Population*, vol. 2, p. 34.

TABLE 46.—DIVERSITY OF THE FOREIGN BORN, 1930
Percentage of Foreigners Born in Certain Countries[a]

English-speaking countries:	
Ireland	6.5
Canada	6.4
England	5.7
Other	3.1
Other language groups:	
Italy	12.6
Germany	11.3
Poland	8.9
Russia	8.1
Mexico	4.5
Sweden	4.2

[a] Fifteenth Census, *Population*, vol. 2, p. 232.

This list includes only a few of the larger groups of immigrants. A complete list would be very long. Of course, even these facts are not conclusive proof of the heterogeneity of urban populations, for Italians might settle in one city, Germans in another, Poles in another, etc. The Census Bureau fortunately has listed the major foreign-born groups in all cities of 100,000 and over having at least 5,000 foreigners in 1930.[1] In nearly every case there were from 10 to 20 nationality groups, each furnishing from 1 to 20 per cent of the foreign-born population of the city. In 27 of these cities no group constituted over 20 per cent of the foreign population. In other words, the immigrants were well divided among various nationalities. In 50 cities only one group exceeded 20 per cent. In 5 cities two groups, and in 1 city three groups exceeded 20 per cent. In only 2 cities did a single nationality constitute over half of the foreign born—El Paso and San Antonio.

One other test of the relative heterogeneity of urban and rural populations may be applied. In 1930 only 59.8 per cent of the urban population born in the United States were residing in their native state. For the rural farm folk the corresponding percentage was 80.0, and for the rural nonfarm folk it was 70.9. Thus, so far as birthplace may be considered a criterion, even the American born are more heterogeneous in cities than in rural districts.

> Never before in the history of the world have great groups of people so diverse in social backgrounds been thrown together in such close contacts as in the cities of America. The typical American city, therefore, does not consist of a homogeneous body of citizens, but of human beings with the most diverse cultural backgrounds, often speaking different languages, following a great variety of customs, habituated to different modes and standards of living, and sharing only in varying degrees the tastes, the beliefs, and the ideals of their native fellow city dwellers.[2]

Sex Ratio

One of the outstanding differences between contemporary American cities and our rural districts is in the relative disparity of the sexes. In the whole urban population in 1930 there were 981 males to every 1,000 females. But among the rural farm folk the ratio was 1,110 and among the rural nonfarm people it

[1] Fifteenth Census, *Population*, vol. 2, pp. 251–259.

[2] *Our Cities: Their Role in the National Economy*, National Resources Committee, p. 10, 1937.

was 1,050. Thus today an excess of females marks our cities, while in the country there is an excess of males. In all regions cities show a lower ratio of males to females than do their rural districts. Nevertheless, there are still more males than females in the urban populations of the East North Central, Mountain, and Pacific states. Considering general categories of color and nativity, the lowest urban ratio is found among Negroes (913), the highest among the foreign born (1,110). Native white of native parents (973), and the children of immigrants (937) fall between. Substantially the same ranking, though of course higher ratios, appears in the rural population. We do not know what this means except that immigrants are predominantly males, while among American Negroes the sexes are nearly equal, with a tendency toward female dominance. Since immigrants are overwhelmingly urban, while Negroes are chiefly rural, these facts must be offset by some population movements not completely understood. Perhaps there are greater employment opportunities for men in young cities, while in older cities women may have the advantage. Thus it is possible that an increase in the Long Beach ratio from 871 in 1910 to 925 in 1930 may be a concomitant of Iowa farmers retiring and moving to the coast city. On the other hand, a decrease in the Birmingham ratio from 1,045 in 1900 to 940 in 1930 may follow naturally from enlarged opportunities for employment of women, drawing them in from the rural South. The decline in Seattle's ratio from 1,767 to 1,037 in the same period is obviously associated with the change from a frontier city of lumberjacks, miners, fishermen, longshoremen, and sailors to a more typical city—maturation, as McKenzie would call it.

This greater excess of males in rural America has been consistent since 1900 and apparently so since 1790. However, the excess of females in cities has not been consistent. In fact, in 1910 and 1920 there was a slight excess of males, though a much smaller ratio than in the country. The range of sex ratios (males per 1,000 females) in American cities in 1930 extended from 1,191 in Gary, a "steel town," to 878 in Nashville, a city of diversified industry and commerce. However, only 28 of 93 cities in the 100,000 class had more males than females.

Considering the 96 metropolitan districts, and putting ratios in terms of males per 100 females, we find for 1930 a ratio of 99 for all central cities and 101 for the outside portion of these metropolitan districts. The most extreme differences were 88

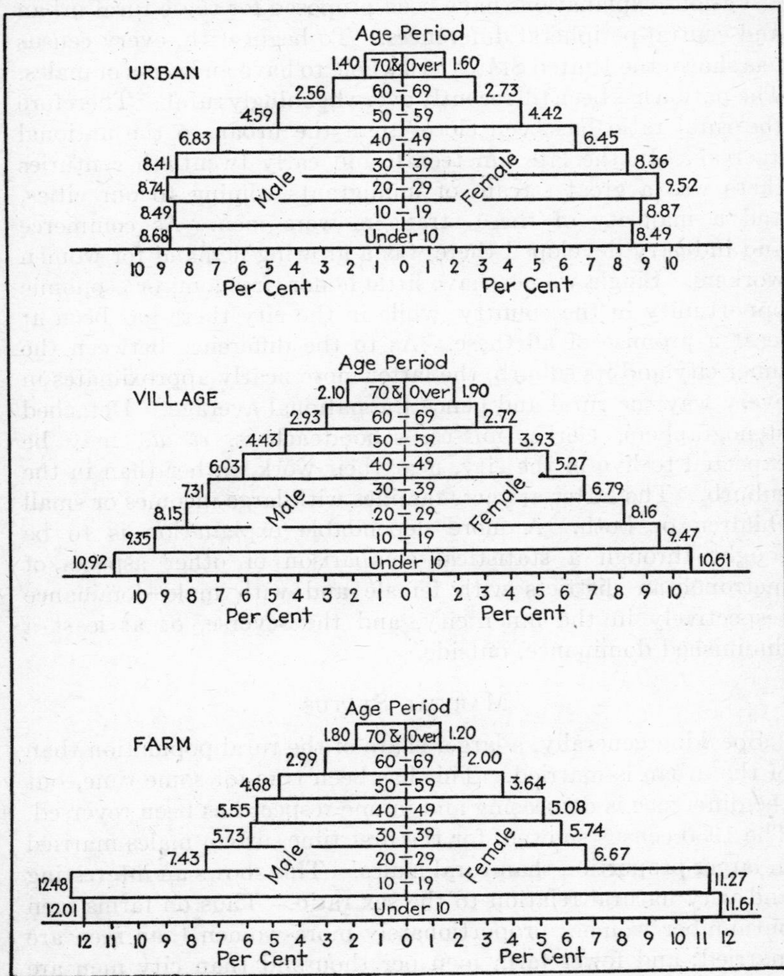

FIG. 18.—Urban, village, and farm populations contrasted as to sex and age, United States, 1930.

(central city) and 109 (outside) for Nashville; 100 and 120 for Spokane; Savannah, 87 and 103; Atlanta, 88 and 105; Baltimore, 97 and 112; Tacoma, 103 and 118. Exceptions to this general difference between the inner city and its environs were Cleveland,

103 and 93; San Francisco-Oakland, 110 and 107; New York, 101 and 99.

Various explanations have been proposed for these rural-urban and central-peripheral differences. To begin with, every census has shown the United States as a whole to have an excess of males. The nation has been till recently overwhelmingly rural. Therefore the rural ratio has been closer than the urban to the national average. In the late nineteenth and early twentieth centuries there was a great stream of immigrants coming to our cities, and a majority of these strangers were men. As commerce and industry developed there was a growing demand for women workers. Single women have little honor, freedom, or economic opportunity in the country, while in the city there has been at least a promise of all these. As to the difference between the inner city and its suburb, the latter more nearly approximates in every way the rural and hence the national average. Detached stenographers, clerks, nurses, schoolteachers, *et al.*, may be expected to live in the city, near their work, rather than in the suburb. The latter attracts families with large incomes or small children or both. A more dependable explanation is to be sought through a statistical comparison of other aspects of metropolitan districts with female and with male dominance respectively in the inner city, and the reverse, or at least a diminished dominance, outside.

Marital Status

Speaking generally, a larger share of the rural population than of the urban is married. This has been true for some time, but the difference is decreasing and in one respect has been reversed. The 1930 census showed, for the first time, urban males married in larger proportion than rural males. This shows an interesting and very natural relation to the sex ratio. Thus on farms men outnumber women; proportionately more women than men are married; and fewer farm men per thousand than city men are married. But in cities women outnumber men; proportionately more men than women are married; and fewer city women per thousand than farm women are married. Specifically the percentages married among men (males fifteen years of age and over) were: urban, 60.5; rural farm, 57.9. In the case of the women the relative proportions married were reversed: urban,

58.5; rural farm 66.0. The only major classes showing exceptions to the foregoing generalizations were native white males of foreign percentage (urban 51.1 per cent, rural 54.4 per cent married), and foreign-born females (69.1 per cent married, both urban and rural farm). The differential in favor of marriage for city men was greatest in the West North Central states, and least in the East South Central states. The differential in favor of marriage for farm women was greatest in the Pacific states and least in the South Atlantic states. Table 47 shows these differences in detail. It also displays the uniformity with which percentages of city men married exceeded those of city women. The only exceptions were the Mountain and Pacific divisions, where slightly higher percentages of urban women than of urban men were married. Ogburn has pointed out that differences of these kinds need to be corrected for age and "race."[1] Using 1920 data he corrected for age and found that urban-rural differences were increased in every geographical division except the Middle Atlantic and New England. Correcting for "race," he found the differences increased in the northeastern quarter of the United States and elsewhere reduced. We have not attempted to construct any corrected ratios, but we note from the published census data that while, generally speaking, urban males are married in larger proportion than are rural farm males, for native white of native parents this is true only in the age group twenty to twenty-nine. For native white of foreign or mixed parents it is true up to age forty-five, but not after that. For foreign born it is true except under age twenty. For Negroes it is not true of any age group. The reasons for these variations are not yet established. The general differences of marital status between urban and rural farm women are consistently maintained in each major "racial" and age classification.

Further light on the problem of how the differences in marital status of city and country folk came to be may be had from studying the changing percentages over a period of years and by examining the data for individual cities. Perhaps the 1940 Census will shed new light on this question. But the most promising procedure appears to be the study of various cities, noting any relation that may appear between sex ratios, ethnic groups, age dis-

[1] E. R. Groves and W. F. Ogburn, *American Marriage and Family Relationships*, pp. 308–310, 1928.

tribution, and other factors. It can hardly be "accidental" that in Minneapolis the percentage of males married rose from 47.9 in 1910 to 60.0 in 1930, while in Philadelphia it rose only from 55.3 to 57.6. It is unlikely that mere chance is involved in the drop in the percentage of females married in Birmingham from 59.1 in 1910 to 58.3 in 1930, while Albany showed an increase from 47.0 to 53.5.

TABLE 47.—PERCENTAGE MARRIED IN THE URBAN AND RURAL FARM POPULATION, BY GEOGRAPHIC DIVISIONS, 1930[a]

	Male		Female	
	Urban	Rural farm	Urban	Rural farm
United States	60.5	57.9	58.5	66.0
New England	58.6	54.3	54.3	63.7
Middle Atlantic	59.1	55.9	57.6	65.7
East North Central	61.6	57.2	61.4	68.0
West North Central	62.1	55.6	58.3	67.4
South Atlantic	61.7	58.0	56.7	61.4
East South Central	63.0	61.8	56.9	65.1
West South Central	62.6	60.5	59.9	67.5
Mountain	60.5	54.1	60.7	69.6
Pacific	58.8	52.8	59.7	70.1

[a] Fifteenth Census, *Population*, vol. 2, p. 934.

To summarize our discussion, we find that men are more likely to be married in cities than on farms, while with women the reverse is true. Many reasons have been suggested to account for these differences. They include greater economic opportunities and social privileges for single women in cities, drawing them from rural districts to urban areas, thus creating a lower sex ratio (males per 100 females) and reducing the probability of marriage. Other hypotheses refer to ethnic and age classifications and to the date of settlement. The exact significance of these and other factors is yet to be determined. But studies can profitably be made with the data now available, as suggested in this section.

AGE DISTRIBUTION

Another related aspect of population is its distribution among the various age classes. Where a large part of the inhabitants is married, we may expect to find many small children, as in rural

America. However, other relations between marital status and age distribution are not so clear.

In general, our age classes fall into three major divisions so far as urban-rural differences are concerned. Under twenty, rural folk show a larger proportion of their total. From twenty to sixty-four, cityfolk take the lead. Above sixty-five, there is little difference. These distinctions are manifest in Table 48. Reading from left to right, the first division yields an ascending scale, the middle division a descending scale, and the last division a rise and a corresponding decline. This suggests, subject to more

TABLE 48.—AGE DISTRIBUTION (PERCENTAGE) OF THE URBAN AND RURAL POPULATION, 1930[a]

Age period	Urban	Rural nonfarm	Rural farm
Under 5 years	8.2	10.5	11.1
5 to 9	9.0	11.1	12.5
10 to 14	8.6	9.8	12.4
15 to 19	8.7	8.9	11.3
20 to 24	9.3	8.5	8.1
25 to 29	9.0	7.8	6.0
30 to 34	8.4	7.1	5.5
35 to 44	15.5	12.9	11.4
45 to 54	11.2	9.9	9.8
55 to 64	6.9	6.9	6.6
65 to 74	3.7	4.5	3.7
75 to 84	1.2	1.8	1.3
85 and over	0.2	0.3	0.2
Unknown	0.1	0.1	0.0
All ages	100.0	100.0	100.0

[a] Fifteenth Census, *Population*, vol. 2, p. 570.

refined analysis, that the larger the place the smaller the relative numbers of children and youth and the larger the number of adults; also that there are relatively more really old people in villages than either on farms or in cities. Further study shows that these differences existed in 1920 as well as in 1930 and that they apply to both sexes. But while both Negroes and native whites of native parents follow the general trend, immigrants and their children do not. In both these groups, in both sexes, there is a higher proportion of children and youth in cities than in the country.

Table 49 shows that during the decade 1920–1930 the urban population was aging. The percentage of city dwellers under forty-five years of age decreased, and the percentage over forty-five increased. The same change was also taking place in rural districts. In fact, this has been the trend in the general population since 1850. But data are not immediately available to show

TABLE 49.—AGE DISTRIBUTION (PERCENTAGE) OF THE URBAN POPULATION, BY SEX, 1920 AND 1930[a]

Age period	1920	1930
Under 20 years:		
Total	35.8	34.5
Male	35.4	34.7
Female	36.1	34.5
20 to 44 years:		
Total	42.7	42.2
Male	42.9	42.1
Female	42.6	42.3
45 to 64 years:		
Total	17.0	18.1
Male	17.5	18.4
Female	16.5	17.7
65 years and over:		
Total	4.3	5.1
Male	4.0	4.7
Female	4.6	5.5
All ages:		
Total	100.0	100.0
Male	100.0	100.0
Female	100.0	100.0

[a] Fifteenth Census, *Population*, vol. 3, part 1, pp. 14–15.

whether the shift has always been more marked in cities than in the country. Our impression is that sanitation and medical service has improved so much more in urban than in rural areas that the urban span of life would naturally increase faster than the rural. Also, as we shall see, the urban birth rate has declined more than the rural. Hence cities have a declining percentage under forty-five. However, it is possible that as time passes and we approach a population equilibrium the differences in age distribution between urban and rural populations may diminish. Data from the 1940 census will be eagerly awaited on this point.

VITAL INDEXES

Birth Rates.—The predominance of children and youths in the country suggests that rural birth rates are higher than urban. As a matter of fact, the crude birth rates do not always bear out this expectation. By crude birth rate we mean the ratio of births in a year to the total population. More refined rates can be secured by computing the ratio of births to women between the ages of fifteen and forty-four, or by distinguishing ethnic or economic classes. Sorokin and Zimmerman found that in highly industrialized countries crude urban birth rates were as high as or higher than corresponding rural rates.[1] In countries predominantly agricultural they found the reverse to be true. In general they found progressive urbanization to be accompanied by declining birth rates, both urban and rural. When they corrected for sex and age they found these differences maintained and even accentuated. Also they discovered that for several decades urban birth rates have been dropping faster than rural.

Like most other countries, the United States has experienced a declining birth rate. Considering the registration area (that within which at least 90 per cent of all births and deaths are believed to be reported), the crude birth rate for the general population dropped from 25.1 (per 1,000 population) in 1915 to 17.1 in 1934. During these 20 years the registration area grew from one including less than a third to one including the entire population. Thus the figures for the two dates are not strictly comparable.[2] Hence it is wise to consider separately the original registration area. Fortunately data are available from 1915 to 1934 for Maine, New Hampshire, Vermont, Massachusetts, Connecticut, New York, Pennsylvania, Michigan, Minnesota, and the District of Columbia. These show a decline in birth rate greater than that apparent for the whole United States.

In these northeastern states, then, the expected facts are reversed. The rural birth rate has been for 20 years consistently

[1] Pitirim Sorokin and C. C. Zimmerman, *Principles of Rural-Urban Sociology*, pp. 206–208, 1929.

[2] These and other data concerning births and infant deaths are derived from *Birth, Stillbirth, and Infant Mortality Statistics*, 1934, U.S. Bureau of the Census.

TABLE 50.—CRUDE BIRTH RATES FOR URBAN AND RURAL DISTRICTS OF THE ORIGINAL REGISTRATION AREA, 1915–1934[a]

Year	Births per 1,000 population		
	Urban	Rural	Total
1915	26.0	23.8	25.1
1916	26.0	23.5	25.0
1917	26.4	23.3	25.2
1918	25.8	23.0	24.7
1919	22.7	23.8	21.1
1920	24.6	22.2	23.7
1921	24.5	23.1	24.0
1922	22.9	21.8	22.5
1923	22.9	21.1	22.2
1924	23.2	21.2	22.5
1925	22.2	20.3	21.5
1926	21.5	19.1	20.6
1927	21.3	19.0	20.5
1928	20.5	18.1	19.6
1929	19.7	16.8	18.6
1930	19.3	16.7	18.4
1931	17.8	16.3	17.3
1932	17.0	15.5	16.5
1933	15.8	14.8	15.4
1934	....	....	15.7

[a] *Birth, Stillbirth, and Infant Mortality Statistics*, 1934, U.S. Bureau of the Census, pp. 5–6. Urban is defined as including places of 10,000 and over. Rhode Island, though a part of the original registration area, is excluded from this table because it failed to provide satisfactory reports for two years.

TABLE 51.—CRUDE BIRTH RATES FOR URBAN AND RURAL DISTRICTS OF THE REGISTRATION AREA, 1927–1933[a]

Year	Births per 1,000 population		
	Urban	Rural	Total
1927	21.0	20.3	20.6
1928	20.1	19.5	19.8
1929	19.4	18.4	18.9
1930	19.1	18.7	18.9
1931	17.5	18.4	18.0
1932	16.7	18.1	17.4
1933	15.6	17.4	16.6

[a] *Statistical Abstract of the United States*, 1936, p. 87.

(except for 1919) lower than the urban. However, the urban rate has fallen faster than the rural rate, and the two appear to be approaching equality. Several possible explanations may be offered for this variation from what appears to be true in the United States and in most other countries. One is that cities in this area include in their populations many immigrant, low-income, Catholic people, while inhabitants of the rural districts are more generally native and Protestant. Another is that increasingly hospitals are being used for confinement; and since hospitals are usually in cities, urban births include rural residents.

When we take account of the entire registration area, from 1927 to 1933, we find urban rates higher for four years, then rural rates higher for three years. During the seven years 12 states were added to the registration area, but they included less than 15 per cent of the nation's inhabitants. On the other hand, they were all predominantly rural. Hence it may be that their earlier inclusion would have reversed the relative position of the rural and urban rates. Table 51 provides the details.

Again we are unable to offer an acceptable explanation. Perhaps the rapid diffusion of contraception in cities has caused their birth rate to fall faster than the rural rate. Perhaps a correction for sex and age will show that rural women have actually been more, rather than less, fertile than their city sisters. Also a comparative study of individual cities as cities and in relation to their hinterlands may help us to understand this situation. It may be that Table 51 does not really display a trend; the time series is short, and part of it preceded the financial collapse of 1929, part followed it.

Death Rates.—Up to the present, the average duration of life has been shorter and mortality rates have been higher in cities than in the country. Sorokin and Zimmerman have assembled from many lands and for various periods data which unquestionably justify this generalization.[1] However, there has been a general decline in death rates, so that urban rates, though higher than contemporary rural rates, are lower than rural rates of an earlier date. Table 52 shows this for the United States. Note that the urban death rate for 1933 was lower than the rural rate for 1920. Nevertheless, in every single year mortality was

[1] Sorokin and Zimmerman, *op. cit.*, pp. 182–204.

greater in cities than in the country. Negro rates were consistently higher than white, but among Negroes rural-urban differences correspond to those among whites.

For the original registration area, differences in crude general death rates correspond to those for the country as a whole, except that in 1932 and 1933 the rural rates were slightly higher than the urban. But infant mortality rates show considerable

TABLE 52.—DEATH RATES PER 1,000 ESTIMATED POPULATION OF CITIES AND RURAL DISTRICTS IN THE UNITED STATES REGISTRATION AREA, BY COLOR, 1920–1933[a]

Year	Cities			Rural districts		
	Total	White	Colored	Total	White	Colored
1920	14.2	13.6	22.7	11.9	11.5	15.2
1922	12.7	12.2	19.8	10.8	10.5	13.0
1923	13.2	12.6	21.4	11.2	10.9	13.9
1924	12.8	12.1	21.8	10.7	10.2	14.6
1925	13.0	12.3	21.9	10.8	10.3	14.9
1926	13.4	12.7	22.1	11.2	10.7	15.4
1927	12.5	11.9	20.6	10.4	10.0	14.1
1928	13.3	12.7	21.1	11.0	10.5	14.9
1929	13.1	12.4	20.5	10.9	10.4	14.9
1930	12.3	11.7	19.5	10.4	9.9	14.4
1931	11.9	11.4	18.5	10.2	9.8	13.5
1932	11.7	11.2	17.4	10.2	9.8	12.6
1933	11.5	11.0	17.2	9.9	9.6	12.2

[a] *Statistical Abstract of the United States*, 1936, p. 81.

variation. In 1915–1920, 1922, 1924, 1928, and 1933 the deaths of city babies in the original registration area were relatively more frequent than the deaths of country babies. That is, in 10 of the last 20 years the urban infant mortality rate was higher than the rural and in 10 years the rural rate was higher than the urban. Since the lower urban rates appear mostly in very recent years, it may be supposed that improvements in infant hygiene and in the control of communicable diseases have offset whatever natural advantages the country may have for babies. While these observations pertain only to certain northeastern states, census reports indicate the same thing to be true of the country as a whole.

We have some indication that the gains just referred to have been greater in large cities than in small cities and rural districts. Thus the infant mortality rate in 1934 was 58.1 for cities of 10,000 and over, 62.4 for cities of 2,500 to 10,000, and 61.5 for rural districts. Exactly comparable data are not at hand for other years. But in each of the 5 years 1930–1934 the rate was lower in cities of 10,000 and over than in all smaller cities and rural districts taken together. The rates for the so-called children's diseases have been dropping much more in cities than in the country, as shown in Table 53.

TABLE 53.—DEATH RATES PER 100,000 PERSONS FROM SPECIFIED CAUSES IN THE CURRENT REGISTRATION AREA, 1900–1929[a]

Period	Measles		Scarlet fever		Whooping cough		Diphtheria	
	Urban	Rural	Urban	Rural	Urban	Rural	Urban	Rural
1900–1904	11.9	7.6	15.6	7.0	12.0	9.0	43.0	20.1
1905–1909	12.3	7.5	12.0	6.3	11.5	11.2	28.5	16.9
1910–1914	10.9	8.9	10.1	5.8	9.8	11.4	21.9	15.0
1915–1920 (excluding 1918)	9.0	8.5	4.1	3.0	8.7	10.2	18.3	12.0
1921–1925	6.3	5.8	4.0	3.4	7.0	8.7	13.7	11.2
1926–1929	5.0	5.1	2.3	2.2	5.8	7.8	8.5	6.1

[a] Adapted from W. S. Thompson and P. K. Whelpton, *Population Trends in the United States*, p. 254, 1933, by permission of the President's Research Committee on Social Trends.

Fifty-six cities of 100,000 population or more had in 1934 an infant mortality rate lower than the national average (60.1 deaths under one year of age per 1,000 live births). Long Beach (31.3) was the lowest, other low rates being found in San Francisco (33.0), Lynn (33.5), and Portland, Ore., (35.5). It is curious that cities so diverse as these should have approximately the same infant death rates. Lynn is a manufacturing city with many immigrants and a harsh climate. The western cities named have mild climates, diversified business and industry, and fewer immigrants. Twenty-seven cities of the same class had in 1933 a general death rate lower than the national average (10.7 deaths per 1,000 estimated population). The lowest rate (7.5) was found in Detroit and Akron. Other low rates were in

Milwaukee (8.2) and Tulsa (8.4); Chicago (10.0) and New York (10.5) were just below the national average. This means that a majority of great cities had reduced their infant death rates below those for smaller cities and rural districts, but a much smaller number had made corresponding reductions in the general death rate. Among the cities with high general death rates in 1935 were Memphis (16.7), New Orleans (16.0), Washington (15.9), Wilmington (14.7), Albany (14.4), and Boston (14.1). Again we note similar death rates in quite different types of cities. However, we usually find high rates in southern cities with large Negro populations and in some northern cities with many

TABLE 54.—CRUDE BIRTH AND DEATH RATES OF URBAN AND RURAL DISTRICTS IN THE REGISTRATION AREA, 1920–1933[a]

Year	Urban			Rural		
	Birth rate	Death rate	Excess B − D	Birth rate	Death rate	Excess B − D
1920	23.9	14.0	9.9	23.5	12.2	11.3
1925	21.9	12.7	9.2	21.0	10.9	10.1
1927	21.0	12.4	8.6	20.3	10.4	9.9
1929	19.4	13.0	6.4	18.4	10.9	7.5
1931	17.5	11.9	5.6	18.4	10.3	8.1
1933	15.6	11.5	4.1	17.4	9.9	7.5

[a] *Statistical Abstract of the United States*, 1936, p. 87.

immigrants. Probably the low mortality rate in Detroit is a joint product of a young population and an effective health department. Perhaps the same is true oı Tulsa. In any case, much study may profitably be devoted to death rates and their concomitants.

Thompson and Whelpton[1] have assembled data indicating that urban death rates are higher than rural rates from some causes and lower than rural rates from others. Cities have shown consistently higher death rates from influenza, tuberculosis, syphilis, câncer, diabetes, cirrhosis of the liver, and diseases of the heart and arteries. Their rates are lower than those of country districts from typhoid, malaria, apoplexy, and senility.

[1] W. S. Thompson and P. K. Whelpton, *Population Trends in the United States*, p. 254, 1933.

Birth and Death Rates Compared.—This brings us to the very natural questions: Do cities have an excess of births over deaths, or have they a deficiency? Have they enough children to maintain themselves without migration? The first answer is that they do have in general an excess of births over deaths. The crude rates are shown in Table 54.

We see that while cities do have a margin, it is steadily decreasing and has been consistently smaller than the rural margin of births over deaths. But even this slight advantage is more apparent than real. The age distribution of cities is such as to make their death rate lower and their birth rate higher than they are likely to remain. As the urban population continues to grow older, we may expect a further decline in the birth rate and a rise in the death rate. Even now it appears that some cities are not really maintaining themselves apart from migration, and others would not be apparently self-maintaining were it not for their large percentage of women of child-bearing age.

> The present rate of urban production is below that required to maintain even a stationary population if the transitory favorable urban age composition (a large proportion of women of child-bearing age) is taken into account, and it is lower as the size of the city increases. Thus with unity (1.0) indicating that a community had enough children in 1930 to maintain its present numbers, it is found that the index for cities of over 100,000 is 0.76, that for cities of 25,000–100,000 is 0.88, that for cities of 10,000–25,000 is 0.97, and for the smallest cities 2,500–10,000 it is 1.04. For the rural communities, on the other hand, the index is 1.54.[1]

This analysis indicates that cities will be increasingly dependent on migration as a basis for growth and even for holding their own. But we have practically cut off immigration from abroad, and the internal migration from farm and village to city has recently slowed down. The net movement from farms to cities is estimated at about 6 million for the decade 1920–1929, and for the half decade 1930–1934 it is held to be about 600,000.[2] Of course this may be only a temporary reversal, but it should provide food for thought on the part of those who expect our cities to grow indefinitely.

[1] *Our Cities* . . . , National Resources Committee, p. 10, 1937.
[2] *Ibid.*, p. 34.

Occupations

In Chap. III we pointed out the great changes in occupational distribution of our working population from 1870 to 1930. Obviously a decline from over one-half to just over one-fifth in agriculture means a shift from country to city. But, contrary to what one might expect, the proportionate increase in factory workers was relatively small during that period. The marked changes were toward trade, transportation, clerical, and professional occupations. McKenzie has assembled data showing

Table 55.—Average Percentages of the Gainfully Employed in Certain Groups of Industries in 36 Cities of 250,000 and Over, 1930, and in the Same Cities, 1920[a]

Industry	Average percentage employed	
	1920	1930
Manufacturing and mechanical industries	47.5	37.5
Transportation	11.5	11.6
Trade	18.0	22.3
Public service	2.6	2.7
Professional service	7.3	8.2
Domestic and personal service	11.8	13.6

[a] R. D. McKenzie, *The Metropolitan Community*, p. 114, 1933. By permission of the President's Research Committee on Social Trends.

the general directions of occupational shifting in great cities during the last decade.

Table 55 shows that in our greatest cities the last decade was marked by a sharp decline in the relative numbers employed in manufacturing and by some gains in trade, the professions, domestic and personal service. Elsewhere and in a different way McKenzie has shown that the fraction of the urban population engaged in manufacturing has declined steadily from 191 per 1,000 inhabitants in 1890 to 128 in 1930.[1] In particular cities we have found this decrease very marked. Thus while New York City was growing by 25.7 per cent, the percentage of its population who were factory workers fell 11.3 per cent. In the Seattle-Tacoma area the corresponding figures were +17.6 and −29.6;

[1] R. D. McKenzie, *The Metropolitan Community*, p. 54, 1933.

in Mobile +18.2 and −36.7. Such data suggest diversification, expansion of the selling and financing functions, and increasing numbers of white-collar workers.

In general the rural-urban difference in occupational distribution is shown by the fact that nearly 80 per cent of all males gainfully employed in cities were found in manufacturing, trade, and transportation, while nearly 90 per cent of the strictly rural men (rural farm males, ten years of age and over) were engaged in agriculture. This does not, however, reveal anything new or striking. The amazing difference is in the number of separate occupations found in cities. We do not have truly comparable data, and much depends on the manner of classifying jobs, but in every large city the census lists several hundred kinds of employment. This matter has already been discussed in Chap. VII.

Summary

Other characteristics of urban populations might be discussed, such as intelligence, literacy, school attendance, anthropometric measures, and general bodily differences. But our information about intelligence and bodily differences is too limited to warrant any conclusions at present. Literacy and school attendance have been discussed in Chap. VIII.

To recapitulate, we have found city dwellers more heterogeneous than country people. In the city females predominate, while in the country males are a majority. In the city there is a larger proportion of males married than in the country, while the reverse is true of females. There are fewer children and more adults in urban populations. Crude urban birth and death rates have been higher until recently. Cities seem always to have depended on migration rather than on natural increase for survival and growth. Our largest cities are definitely not self-maintaining. City people are engaged in a growing diversity of occupations, with the emphasis shifting from factory work to white-collar jobs.

Selected Readings

Ogburn, William F.: *Social Characteristics of Cities*, International City Managers' Association, 1937. Chapters 1–3 analyze the make-up of urban populations in the United States.

McKenzie, R. D.: *The Metropolitan Community*, McGraw-Hill Book Company, Inc., 1933. Chapters 3, 13, and 18 are important in this connection.

Sorokin, Pitirim, and C. C. Zimmerman: *Principles of Rural-Urban Sociology*, Henry Holt & Company, Inc., 1929. Part II contrasts vital statistics of rural and urban districts in many countries.

Woolston, Howard B.: *Metropolis: A Study of Urban Communities*, D. Appleton-Century Company, Inc., 1938. Chapter 3 deals with urban populations.

Chapter XX

URBAN PERSONALITIES

Certain general characteristics of urban populations have now been identified. There remains a much more difficult task, namely, that of discovering whether cities tend to produce and maintain distinctive types of personalities. It is generally assumed that they do. In our culture there are quite different stereotypes of city and country folk. The latter are variously thought of as "hicks," "hillbillies," fruitgrowers, ranchers, plantation owners, cowboys, and croppers. In contrast, the former are referred to as "slickers," "dudes," "big shots," "bourgeois," "captains of industry," racketeers, and "society folks." These varied terms make it plain that unwittingly we acknowledge that there are different kinds of country people and different kinds of city people. They suggest, too, that comparisons of urban and rural dwellers may easily be confused through the symbolizing of all those in either category by a term applicable to only a part of the population, or through the pairing of types whose status is altogether different. Certainly it is stupid to assume that all country people are alike in economic status, education, daily work, and personal attitudes. It is equally stupid to assume similar identity among city people. Obviously it is unjust to contrast "the four hundred" with "sand-hillers," or gangsters with apple growers. Perhaps it would be fairer to compare plantation owners with large stockholders in corporations, ordinary farm owners with small businessmen, and share croppers with unskilled laborers.

Hypotheses concerning Rural-urban Differences

The foregoing remarks would be quite uncalled-for were it not for the fact that there are in print numerous generalizations whose supporting evidence is far from adequate. Some of them are merely the naming of surface differences that should not be taken too seriously. Thus we are told that country people are crude, while city people are urbane and sophisticated. Perhaps all this really means is that city dwellers wear the latest fashions, dance the latest steps, speak the latest slang, converse glibly about the latest movie star, debutante, or football players, attend the symphony or the dance palace, and play golf or badminton. But with the radio, the movies, the automobile, and the hard road leading to the city, country people are coming to share many of the experiences and to develop many of the habits popularly ascribed to their city cousins. Some countryfolk are undoubtedly crude when judged by the speech, ideas, dress, and manners of educated people of means. But so are many—perhaps most—of the people who live in cities. Either such comparisons are useless or they should be made systematically with the aid of objective tests. For example, the psychologists and educators have schemes for measuring vocabularies. Application of these tests to representative samples of rural and urban adults might reveal something of real importance. On the other hand, it might show merely that people talk about the things they do, and that differences within the urban population are quite as great as those between comparable elements in city and in country.

It is sometimes alleged that country people are more "superstitious," but we know many cityfolk who count on charms to protect them from harm, avoid seating 13 at dinner, refuse to walk under a ladder, etc. What is superstition anyway? Is it any belief that has been scientifically demonstrated to be false? If so, how about the city people who believe that a clean tooth never decays, that the quality of an article is measured by its market price, that a high tariff promotes national prosperity, that a large navy prevents war, etc., etc.? Perhaps it would be worth while to devise an information test that would check the erroneous beliefs (superstitions?) of both urban and rural folk. Then we might be able to make a definite statement supported by evidence, in place of the vague generalization that country people are more superstitious than city dwellers.

A variant of the preceding is a statement that countryfolk are more "emotional," while cityfolk are more "intellectual." In its present form this proposition means very little. We have no quantitative measure of emotionality. Perhaps the psychologists and the psychiatrists could put a satisfactory scale at our disposal, but so far as we are aware no such device has been applied to representative samples of urban and of rural dwellers. If by intellectuality is meant intelligence quotient, then the Terman revision of the Binet-Simon tests might serve our purpose. But if it is intended to imply that city people approach other persons and new situations with cool calculation, while country people come at them with more fear or anger or other excitement, a different kind of measure will have to be employed.

Again, it is claimed that country people are more "sympathetic." If this means that they know more about one another and can more easily understand one another's situations, that would appear to be a truism based on their small numbers, similar experiences, and face-to-face contacts. But if it means that city people do not care about each other, then it would be hard to explain the large sums raised for urban charities and the eager reading of human-interest stories in the newspapers. Nevertheless, it does appear that, in so far as country people still participate in stable, primary groups, they tend to regard others as intimates or as strangers. In so far as the life of city people is dominated by casual contacts, they tend to deal with others as representatives of categories—newsboy, salesgirl, conductor, policeman, etc. It would probably be possible to measure the relative number, variety, intimacy, and permanence of the contacts of urban and of rural folk. After giving such a test and scoring the returns we should be in a position to make statements whose meaning would be definite and whose supporting evidence would be convincing.

A rather different theory is that country people are "fatalistic," while cityfolk are determined to understand and control the conditions under which they live. It is true that in some rural districts disease and death are discussed in terms of God's will rather than of germs and habits. But that may be less the expression of an inherent trait than the result of limited medical service. Moreover, it can be matched by widespread "fatalism" with reference to bad city government. A related doctrine is that country people are retiring, while city people are self-assertive. Yet we have observed that whenever there is a rural-urban conflict in a state legislature, members of the farm group seem to hold their own quite successfully. Perhaps the notion that rural folk are shy arose in the minds of city people who found country dwellers unwilling to talk freely *to them;* and perhaps city people would be just as reticent in the presence of persons whom *they* regard with fear, awe, or admiration. Once again we are dealing with words when we need to study behavior.

Curiously, we have found the term "mechanistic" applied to both rural and urban folk: to the former because they work with material things rather than with people and are subject to the weather, which they cannot control; to the latter because they use machines so much. No doubt it would be practicable to learn the relative use made of specified machines in city and in country. Also it might be possible to measure the part of people's time that is taken up with nonmechanical efforts to control other people directly (selling, "bossing," propagandizing, etc.). We would not be likely to use the word "mechanistic" in reporting our findings, but would speak in terms of specific objects and acts.

Another word that has been used to describe both rural and urban folk is "independent." Farmers and village merchants are called independent because they are supposed to set their own hours of work, select the crops they will raise and the goods they will handle, and in general take orders from no one. They have vegetables from their own gardens, fruit from their own orchards, poultry and dairy supplies from their own barnyards. On the other hand, city people are independent in so far as they are free to choose the kind of work they will do, leave uncongenial employers, select a district and house in which to live, and pick their associates regardless of who their nigh dwellers may be. The whole difficulty is that one word has been given at least two rather different meanings; the argument has been over the word instead of the facts. A realistic study would examine the alternatives which are actually at the disposal of city and of country people, the variations in the behavior of each (indicating freedom from custom), the clashes with persons who give orders, the penalties or rewards of such rebellion, the use of goods passing through the hands of other persons, and the services received from others. Then we could talk about something concrete and compare city with country people in a manner that would carry meaning. Until then it is futile to discuss the independence or dependence of the two groups.

It has been said that country people are stable in locus, status, and habits, while city people are mobile, restless, and erratic.

As to residential and occupational mobility, we have reviewed the available evidence and methods of study in Chap. XVIII. Rural folk are more frequently owners of land, furniture, and machinery; they are tied by the growing of crops and the care of livestock. But increasing numbers of them are transient laborers and tenants. Whether they are emotionally more stable and inherently less prone to change than cityfolk we do not really know. Our guess is that things change more slowly in rural areas; there are fewer culture conflicts; hence the people find less to disturb their established habits and attitudes than in the city. But on the other hand we have heard it claimed that monotony and lonesomeness in some farming districts drive the women in particular literally to distraction. Moreover, we have made note of the millions of people who leave the country for the city. Obviously the problem requires further study.

Rural people are sometimes considered slow-moving, while city people are called more active, alert, and ready for change. Again the student must be cautious lest he confuse several different kinds of behavior. In general country people are probably much more active than city people in the sense of using major muscular systems in their work and in leisure time activities. The work of city people is more exactly scheduled. As someone has put it, they are "clock conscious." They suffer definite penalties for being late; hence they often have to hurry to catch a train, bus, or elevator. They often have short lunch periods; hence they eat in a hurry. They often live far from their work; hence they honk impatiently when the car ahead does not "jump" the traffic light. All this may create an impression of vigor, aggressiveness, "snap," and "pep," or it may leave the observer with an impression that city people have the "jitters" and are nervously rushing about. There do appear to be important differences, but they need to be examined in more detail and reduced to measurable units.

One of the most general observations is that rural folk are conservative in religion and politics, while urban folk more commonly attach themselves to new movements or lose interest altogether. In Chap. X we noted some evidence in support of the notion that country people do adhere more consistently than city people to established religious faiths. It is likely that similar studies would show that they are usually conservative in the matter of politics. But it should be remembered that most cityfolk belong to the Republican and Democratic parties, while the Farmer-Labor, Progressive, and Nonpartisan groups are found in rural states. Nevertheless, the Socialist, Communist, and American Labor parties are largely urban in their membership.

Following Allport's lead, Anderson and Lindeman have summed up their conception of rural-urban personal differences in terms of motility, temperament, self-expression, and sociality.[1] As to motility, they speak of city people as easily stimulated, having a vigorous positive tendency to action and relative freedom from inhibitions, showing, in a given line, persistence of activity, skill, and individuality of execution. As to temperament, they said they found urban folk experiencing a rapid succession of moods and a wide variety of emotional states, with definite sets toward suspiciousness, self-depreciation, cynicism, and snobbery. As to self-expression, they noted extroversion, domination, and drive. Finally they claimed to have found special sensitiveness to social stimulation. Of these, as of the other opinions we have examined, it should be said that they are suggestive hypotheses, possibly true but in need of study by methods that promise to yield quantitative findings about specific forms of behavior.

Approaches to the Study of Urban Personalities

In the preceding section we have reviewed a miscellaneous array of so-called personality traits. Here we shall consider more systematic ways of dealing with the problem of whether urbanism attracts or creates distinctive personality types.

Personality has been simply defined as "an integration of the individual's total responses to his total environment."[2] This suggests a study in terms of (*a*) the general situation in which city dwellers find themselves, (*b*) the specific stimuli to which they respond, and (*c*) the characteristic responses which they make. In the next section we shall review what is known of the urban situation or basis of social life. Here we shall merely note that it involves constant, or at least frequent, change; uncertainty; insecurity; speed; depersonalization; and large numbers.

[1] Nels Anderson and E. C. Lindeman, *Urban Sociology*, pp. 235–236, 1928.
[2] *Ibid.*, p. 221.

If these really are traits of urban environments and are absent from or less developed in rural environments, they are bound to do something to the persons who live in their midst. The specific stimuli which appear to be more frequently present in cities than in the country have never been systematically studied, but they include noises, artificial lights, smoke, moving objects (vehicles, signals, machinery), other persons. Not all of these are specific stimuli; some are groups, or configurations, which will probably have to be broken down into smaller units for research purposes. There are devices which the physical scientists have invented to study noises, lights, and smoke. These phenomena have been reduced to measurable terms, but their effects on the human organism are much harder to identify. The psychologists have done work on responses to moving objects, and the social psychologists have devoted much time—though little experimentation—to the interstimulation associated with different kinds of social contacts. But enough has been accomplished to encourage us to believe that objective studies can presently be undertaken on the specific stimuli to which human beings are subjected in urban and in rural environments.

The characteristic responses of city and of country people to given stimuli and situations are also ripe for investigation. How they will finally be identified and measured we do not know, but for the moment we suggest laboratory tests and observation under controlled conditions to see what habits develop and persist among urban and rural folk respectively. When they have been made we will no longer have to content ourselves with rather vague remarks about city people's "front," etiquette, selling, hurrying, joining, etc. Perhaps the anthropologists' techniques of observing and classifying behavior may be used to advantage. In addition to the study of habits, or regularly recurring forms of overt behavior, we propose the use of attitude tests to identify and measure general tendencies to behave in given ways. Particularly does it seem worth while to study attitudes toward time, distance, strangers, social change, family life, religion, government. In the third place, we would employ information tests to get at what is loosely called the "mental content" of country and of city folk. How much does each group know in each of several fields of knowledge? With what other factors are scores in these tests correlated? Finally, we would assemble, by interview and observation and from diaries, data concerning the social relations entered into and maintained by urban and rural dwellers. What are their relative numbers, diversity, continuity, and intimacy? All this means real work, but it should be attractive to those who are interested in substituting theories supported by objective data for speculation, however clever.

Park and Burgess offer an approach to the study of personality which overlaps and yet differs from the one just considered.[1] Starting with the conception that personality is "the sum and organization of those traits which determine the role of the individual in the group," they list half a dozen components which might be studied in order to determine their variations severally and in combination, in city and in country people. (1) Physical make-up, which includes vitality, appearance, defects or diseases, has not as yet been shown to be significantly different as between urban and rural folk. However, future studies may possibly reveal differences that affect the roles they play in various social groups. (2) Temperament is rather hard to identify and perhaps impossible to measure, but enough work has been done to lead us to hope for studies of possible differences in excitability, rapidity of response, fatiguability, and recuperation. While these are not the same as "feelings, emotions, moods, and sentiments," they are undoubtedly related to them, and appear to be more amenable to objective study. At present we would not even hazard a guess as to what temperamental differences, if any, may be found between city and country people. (3) Character, as "the sum and coordination of those mechanisms which we call habit," is being studied by laboratory tests and by the questionnaire method. However, we have not heard of any rural-urban comparisons. (4) Likewise, intelligence has been shown to be capable of at least approximate measurement. However, we must beware of assuming that an intelligence quotient represents innate capacity, uninfluenced by education and other experiences. Some studies seem to indicate that city people have higher I.Q.'s than country people. Larger samples may or may not support the initial findings, but even if they do, it should be remembered that most tests are based on urban

[1] Robert E. Park and E. W. Burgess, *Introduction to the Science of Sociology*, p. 70, 1924.

408
Park & Burgess

Robert E Park & E. W. Burgess
Introduction to the Science of Sociology p. 70, 1924

Personality is made up of
1. Physical make-up
2. Temperament
3. Character
4. Intelligence
5-7 Social expression, prestige & prejudice, conception of one's own role
p. 408-409

Not one urban environment, but many p. 409

Intro

"Personality has been simply defined as 'an integration of the individuals total responses to his total environment'"

– suggests study

(a) of the general situation in which ~~the~~ city dweller finds himself

(b) the specific stimuli to which they respond,

and (c) the characteristic responses which they make

P. 404

The City – Queen

p. (0?)

stimuli noises, artificial lights, smoke, moving objects, other persons experience and that I.Q.'s do sometimes change. (5–7) Park and Burgess list three other components of personality: social expression, prestige or prejudice, and conception of one's own role. The first might be studied through the use of vocabulary tests and written compositions. Perhaps moving pictures would reveal differences in facial expression and dress, but we are puzzled as to how these might be measured. Prestige and prejudice are matters of attitudes and should be studied as such. The conceptions which city and country people have of themselves would not be easy to get at. Even when individuals speak frankly it is difficult to reduce their statements to terms that can be manipulated statistically for the purpose of comparing a large number of urban and rural dwellers.

Urban Environments: Stimuli

As we stated in the preceding section, the behavior of city people cannot be understood apart from their environments, the situations of which they are parts, the stimuli which impinge upon them. A large part of this book has been devoted to describing various aspects of urban environments, and a complete recapitulation is hardly called for here. But it does seem profitable to restate some things in a slightly different manner.

In the first place, there is not one urban environment, but many. Both physical and social environments are different for the slum dweller and for the person who lives in a restricted residential district. They are different for apartment dwellers and for occupants of single houses. But in general, and in contrast to rural folk, city people live at a distance from their work and are conveyed back and forth in crowded vehicles or trafficways. Great numbers dwell, work, and go about in the midst of noise and hurry. All these might be called cosmopolitan experiences. The strictly human part of the environment may be summed up in terms of large numbers, heterogeneity, and mobility. Because of these, naturally, many contacts are fleeting, casual, and routine. In a sense stereotypes tend to replace persons. "Front" is encouraged, because first impressions are very important. One walks the streets with members of strange ethnic, religious, political, and economic groups; yet he may know very little about them. Some of them he may ignore, others he may despise, hate, or fear. A city man may live in a rooming house, work in an office, eat at a restaurant, and remain practically unknown, indeed almost unnoticed.

In the city the money economy rules, with many advantages, incidentally, in the way of flexibility, which is absent from barter and production for home consumption. So long as one has money he has a certain freedom to choose food, clothing, shelter, entertainment, associates. Of course, many people have little or no money; freedom is no part of their lives. But with money one is not only free to make some choices; he can secure goods and services without becoming personally involved with those who offer them for sale. He can buy a hat, a drink, a contraceptive, or a revolver, and no questions may be asked. When he consults a physician, social worker, or other professional person, he may have to tell a good deal about himself; but it is to someone with whom he is not otherwise associated. The warmth of personal relations may be lacking, but there are presumably expertness and specialization. The city person is very dependent on professional folk (*e.g.*, dentists and attorneys), skilled artisans (*e.g.*, plumbers and auto mechanics), unskilled laborers (*e.g.*, garbage collectors), purveyors of merchandise, entertainment, and personal service (*e. g.*, beauticians and cleaners). But he is rarely dependent on any particular person in a given employment. Hence he can insult and deceive without necessarily depriving himself of a given type of goods or service and usually without incurring popular ill will. The urban person may be said to be dependent on many specialized functions rather than on persons. He is not only dependent; he is manipulated and controlled by high-pressure salesmanship and advertising.

In his leisure time the city man can be almost, if not quite, anonymous—at movie, dance hall, or ball park. His politics, if any, may be known to a few or none. His religious beliefs or affiliations are "his own business," if he chooses to make them so. To be sure, if he falls into the hands of the law, applies for help from a social service agency, or sends a child to school, he is identified and may receive some individual attention. But even these relations may be rather impersonal.

The city is the scene of constant, rapid, and sometimes upsetting changes. The ebb and flow of employment, the invasion of old districts by new inhabitants and land uses, changing property values, and new styles, all symbolize urban change. Such experiences come to country people too, but not with the same frequency.

We might go on, but we refer the reader back to Parts II and III of this book. In so far as urban folkways and institutions are different from those of country life, they constitute a distinctive setting for cityfolk, a characteristic environment, a special set of stimuli. In so far as the distribution and localization of people and activities are different in city and in country, urban and rural folk live in different worlds. We cannot avoid the assumption that in response to these stimuli city people behave differently from country people. But we must repeat: Urban ways are being diffused into rural regions, and within every city are quite different culture areas. Urbanism is a reality, but its differences from that which we call rural are relative, *i.e.*, matters of degree. Moreover, urbanism itself takes many forms. Within any given city are quite different and contrasting features.

Newcomers to the City

One of the best ways that has been suggested for determining the impact of the city on personality is the study of migrants from rural districts. These are of three major types: native white, American Negro, and foreign born. Some work has been done on each of these, but less attention has been paid to the rural white Americans than to Negroes and immigrants in our cities. Nevertheless it is the native white migrants that should be studied most thoroughly, for their experiences are uncomplicated by race prejudice and culture changes that are international rather than rural-urban.

Methods of research and tentative findings are indicated in two studies of Ozarkians and other rural folk in St. Louis.[1] Personal visits were made to the homes, members of the families were interviewed, and records were read whenever such were available. Some data were assembled in statistical form, but some of the most revealing information appears in the statements of these country men and women. The Ozark families had left the country because of crop failure, low prices for farm products,

[1] Elsie Huseman, "The Adjustment of Rural Families in St. Louis," 1932; Lela Marshall, "Study of Rural Families," 1932. Both are unpublished master's theses at Washington University.

wartime experience in the army or industrial jobs, and rosy tales told by those who had previously migrated to the city. Hence their first concern was likely to be with the finding of employment.

They said that they were so worried and confused by the pressing need for subsistence that they were numb to other things about them. The tension was released when they were employed and as long as they worked they were quite satisfied. But often "on the job" it was hard to receive orders and work under "hard-boiled bosses."

The majority of the women described their first weeks in the city as a "terrible" period during which they almost went mad. Long hours "cooped up" with a group of children, who had been accustomed to spend most of their time outside, was far from pleasant. The mothers were too frightened to allow them to leave the crowded rooms. The smoke and dirt were stifling and the noise confusing. Lonesomeness, homesickness, and futile attempts to make friends with the neighbors who lived under the same roof marked the efforts to adjust. The church, which played a big part in country life, failed in the city.

The men who found work had little trouble "gettin' along" but leisure time was far from a pleasure. One man spent each Sunday and holiday at the Zoo when he could afford carfare. Another family rushed off to the country at every opportunity.

Some of the children had difficulty when they started to school. Not only were they frightened at seeing so many other children but they were timid and backward in their actions. Their dialect did not contribute to their acceptance among their schoolmates. Some turned belligerent and fought while others merely withdrew. The children, however, naturally began to make friends and brought them home; they soon went to the public libraries for books; they were invited to the mission Sunday schools and settlement houses, and soon the mothers and fathers were also becoming interested to a limited extent.[1]

Food habits were found to change. Corn bread, hot biscuits, fat pork, fried potatoes, string beans, eggs, and chickens gave way to canned goods, bakery sweets, lunch meats, and other foods which required little preparation. Storage space was so limited that some of the women gave up planning ahead and buying in quantity.

One explained that when she first came to the city she bought food in large quantities and at weekly intervals, since she thought "it was terrible to live out o' a poke," but now one of the children has to be sent

[1] Huseman, *op. cit.*, pp. 163–165.

to the store to buy "vittles" before they can even have a "snack." She used to "worry about" and "cook aroun'" but she has found it is much easier to run across to the store, come home and "pile things out ter eat without a mite of bother." "Living in the city is so different, but a person likes it when he gets on ter it."[1]

Care of health in the country had involved patent medicines, herbs, and occasional charms; a physician was rarely called. In the city corresponding habits continued, but presently these folk began to hear of clinics and visiting nurses; in time they came to use them. Schooling in the city was more regular and continued over a longer period of years. In time of sickness, unemployment, or other misfortune some families were referred to social work organizations, where they made their first acquaintance with interviewers, case records, and charitable relief. Religion, too, was a field in which adjustments had to be made.

The church has been the center of their social life in the hills and they go to it, thinking here to fill the void of which they are but half conscious only to find that "their church" in the country, although of the same denomination, has little in common with the city sister church. They are not warmly welcomed, in fact, their very appearance makes them feel conspicuous and ill at ease. Often after their first attendance they do not return. Only in two instances did families of this group continue to attend the denominational church of their choice. Six families of this group did not attend any church in the city after their first or second attempt. The reasons given were that they "did not feel at home" in the churches in the city, that they "couldn't dress fitten" or that the church was "too cold for poor folks." Some families did not attend a single service because they were advised by their friends, who had suffered the experience, not to go: "it would only make you feel bad because the church here isn't like it is at home." A majority of these families sooner or later became acquainted with the missions in the city and attend them occasionally. Often this contact was made through the mission worker, who invited the children to attend and called for them. Some of the families expressed their appreciation of the mission's aid, and said that they liked to attend because of the singing and the music and because every one was so friendly. Others felt aloof and possibly superior to the heterogeneous group who throng these places and therefore would not let their children go. Several of these parents sent their children to "church and Sunday School," although they would not go themselves. They felt that the children

[1] Huseman, *op. cit.*, p. 84.

should be "gettin' some religion" and did not wish to send them to the missions.[1]

In the typical Ozark family in St. Louis the man was definitely "head of the house" and "woman's place was in the home." Some of the women had served as domestics in country homes before marriage, but their employment in factories and stores after marriage was frequently the occasion of marital friction. Rebellion came more often from adolescent girls who sought to work outside the home, buy their own clothes, choose their own friends, use cosmetics lavishly, and smoke cigarettes. At this some of the older women were "plumb disgusted" and the men were even more disturbed. In general the rising generation became urbanized more rapidly and more completely than the parents who came from the country. The young folks sought to break away and live their own lives, while their parents expected respect and support in advancing years.

The Negro migrant to the city often has to make a double adjustment to urban conditions and to northern climate and ways. He is likely to face all the problems that confront the white migrant and some others. Both lose the intimate association of friends and relatives and the status they had in a small town or rural community. The Negro, apparently more often than the white, is released from the social control and moral support provided through the church. But a still greater difference is that the Negro in moving from South to North passes from a situation in which his status and role are well defined to a situation in which he does not know where he stands. Because of segregation he becomes part of a community within a community. The city Negroes view his coming with regret or resentment, for they fear that the ignorant, poverty-stricken newcomer may lower the status of the entire group. Thus the "culture shock" of rural-urban migration appears to be greater for the colored folk than for native whites.[2]

In the case of immigrants from other lands the transition is perhaps greatest of all. Since most of them have been peasants,

[1] Huseman, *op. cit.*, pp. 112–113.

[2] E. Franklin Frazier, *The Negro Family in Chicago*, Chap. 5, 1932; Chicago Commission on Race Relations, *The Negro in Chicago*, Chap. 3, 1922; T. J. Woofter, *Negro Problems in Cities*, Chaps. 2, 4, 5, 1928; Louise V. Kennedy, *The Negro Peasant Turns Cityward*, 1930.

they must adjust themselves to urban ways of life. But in addition they must commonly learn a new language, a new monetary system, new laws, and a wide range of new customs and traditions.

When the immigrant comes to America, not only must he leave behind the community which was the basis of his personality and self-respect, but here the very signs of his personality (dress, language, and so forth), which in his own country were the signs of his self-respect, are regarded with contempt and made the occasions of his humiliation. In Europe, the question of personality was not the subject of much reflection, because everything was habitual, but here the realization of incongruities between himself and American life makes the question of personality acute.

At home the immigrant was almost completely controlled by the community; in America this lifelong control is relaxed. Here the community of his people is at best far from complete, and, moreover, it is located within the American community, which lives by different and more individualistic standards, and shows, as we have seen, a contempt for all the characteristics of the newcomers. All the old habits of the immigrant consequently tend to break down. The new situation has the nature of a crisis, and in a crisis the individual tends either to reorganize his life positively, adopt new habits and standards to meet the new situation, or to repudiate the old habits and their restraints without reorganizing his life—which is demoralization.

The person who has been completely controlled by a group, whose behavior in a limited number of possible situations has been predetermined by his community, tends to behave in wild and incalculable ways, to act on any vagrant impulse that invades his mind, when withdrawn from the situations he knows and removed from the background of a permanent community. The result is behavior that is incomprehensible because it follows no known pattern.[1]

Of course it must not be supposed that a large percentage of immigrants or Negroes or rural whites become demoralized after migrating to cities. As a matter of fact, many of them seem to make relatively rapid and successful adjustments. It is precisely the changes in their habits and attitudes, whether well or ill adapted to urban conditions, that we are interested in discovering. Studies such as those to which we have referred here and in Chap.

[1] Robert E. Park and H. A. Miller, *Old World Traits Transplanted*, pp. 48, 61, 72, 1921. By permission of the Carnegie Corporation.

XVI shed some light on our problem and indicate both the importance and the possibility of further research in this field.

Summary: Is There an Urban Type?

If the question with which we opened this chapter be restated: Is there an urban type of personality, distinguished from the rural type?—the answer will have to be equivocal. We might say that there is at one extreme a thoroughly urban type and at the other one that is thoroughly rural. But most people, in both city and country, are at neither extreme. Most urban dwellers retain many rural heritages, and most countryfolk have acquired some urban traits. As a matter of fact, we have found many different kinds of personalities in both city and country. Nevertheless, some kinds of folk are relatively more numerous in cities than in rural districts; and there are more varieties of people in urban than in rural areas. Since occupation is one of the basic determiners of men's habits and attitudes, we note first the range of occupational types, which includes waitresses and realtors, taxi-dancers and policemen, garbage collectors and beauticians, artists and bankers. One's dwelling is also important; hence we may speak of types identified with rooming houses, hotels, and palatial residences as essentially urban. Roles played in various groups suggest as urban: "ward heelers," beggars, prostitutes, reformers, debutantes, feminists, clubmen, and many others. The question may fairly be raised as to whether these really constitute distinctive personality types. Certainly there is a great deal of overlapping in the lists we have presented. But there is no doubt about the fact that there are in cities a good many varieties of folk whose ideas, attitudes, habits, and social roles are infrequently or never reproduced in rural districts. The more exact determination of personality traits that are predominantly urban and rural respectively must, however, await further research.

Selected Readings

Park, Robert E., and E. W. Burgess: *The City*, University of Chicago Press, 1925. Chapter 1 contains suggestions for investigation of human behavior in the urban environment.

Thomas, William I.: "The Problem of Personality in the Urban Environment," pp. 38–47 in *The Urban Community*, edited by E. W. Burgess, University of Chicago Press, 1926.

WOOLSTON, HOWARD B.: *Metropolis: A Study of Urban Communities*, D. Appleton-Century Company, Inc., 1938. Chapter 4 is entitled "Urban Psychology."

GIST, NOEL P., and L. A. HALBERT: *Urban Society*, The Thomas Y. Crowell Company, 1933. Chapters 9 and 10 deal with the social basis of urban life, Chap. 11 with the urban personality, and Chap. 12 with urban social types.

ANDERSON, NELS, and E. C. LINDEMAN: *Urban Sociology*, Alfred A. Knopf, Inc., 1928. Part III deals with the city as dynamic stimulus, the urban personality, social types, occupational types, and the groups to which city persons belong.

SOROKIN, PITIRIM, and C. C. ZIMMERMAN: *Principles of Rural-Urban Sociology*, Henry Holt & Company, Inc., 1929. Chapter 14 deals with differences in psychosocial traits of city and country people.

Chapter XXI

PERSONAL CRISES AND MALADJUSTMENTS

In the preceding chapter we reviewed general notions about differences between the personalities of city and of country people. We also considered the available data concerning the impact of urbanism upon newcomers, the adjustments they must make, and the changes that occur in their habits and attitudes. We turn now to crises that occur in the lives of city and of country folk and to maladjustments that sometimes develop. We shall deal with the relative frequency and the general character of urban and rural poverty, disease, vice, crime, and suicide.

But first it may be wise to consider whether there are any reasons for expecting more or fewer personal crises and maladjustments in cities than in the country. Is it possible that city people are bombarded by a greater number of stimuli, which weary and bewilder them? It is well known that many of the present urban population are relatively new to the city and have not yet got over the initial "culture shock," as Carpenter calls it. Others may have become somewhat accustomed to the city but have not yet learned how to meet misfortune under urban conditions.

The operation of the money economy and direct dependence on others for an opportunity to earn a living increase the economic hazards of city life. Under the money economy, as we noted in the preceding chapter, one receives cash for his work and must have cash to pay for all manner of goods and services. Without money in hand or in the bank a city person finds himself very quickly in grave difficulty. Hence he is peculiarly subject to the irregularities of business, to various prejudices, to industrial conflicts, and to technological changes. The irregularities of business are not merely local in character; they are frequently bound up with the conditions of a world market. Prejudices which affect some urban workers are those against Negroes, against older men, and against married women. Industrial conflicts include strikes, boycotts, and struggles between hostile labor organizations. Technological changes include all sorts of inventions and innovations which replace men by machines.

A third circumstance which may increase the probability of personal crises and maladjustments is that the city itself is constantly changing. Its rapid growth often means that institutions are inadequate. The invasion of old neighborhoods and communities destroys the unity of local life and sometimes works havoc with property values. The whole set of factors involved in the development of blighted areas promotes the segregation of people who are least able to meet the burden of new misfortunes. But often in a slum people are not left undisturbed. There is constant shifting about of population, invasion of new elements, deterioration of buildings, and intervention by police and reformers.

Heterogeneity of the urban population involves greater conflicts. The city dwellers, especially in the nondescript areas of the inner city, must get along with all kinds of people. When their children go to school with members of different ethnic, religious, and other groups they usually acquire ideas and tastes that clash with those of their parents. Hence conflicts are most obvious among members of the second generation, who are often thrown into confusion. Instead of having a definite code of right and wrong, proper and improper conduct, they are frequently bewildered and behave erratically. This heterogeneity, together with mobility and the large numbers of people, produces a sort of anonymity. This means that when one is in trouble he lacks the material and moral assistance of friends and neighbors. Of course not everyone is a stranger to his nigh dwellers, but more frequently than in the country the game of life is sternly competitive and impersonal. It is more nearly a case of "Every man for himself."

Finally, there is the pressure under which city people live. There is the pressure of salesmen and promoters, organizations, agencies and causes, competing for his interest and support. There is constant pulling and hauling to induce him to join this, contribute to that, and buy something or other.

As a result of newness to the city, the hazards of unemployment involved in the money economy, changes in the city itself, heterogeneity, anonymity, and pressure, city dwellers may be expected to encounter more personal crises than countryfolk. Moreover, it should not be surprising if city people more frequently become maladjusted, involved in erratic conduct, vice, crime, and in extreme cases seek to escape through suicide.

Crises

Poverty in the City.—We have no adequate measure of the relative poverty in city and in country because we have no satisfactory measure of poverty itself. This is a relative thing which involves income, cost of living, size of family, and standard of living of the class to which a family belongs. In a narrower sense poverty is lack of the necessities for physical well-being. These have been measured with approximate accuracy by various students of home economics, but they have not been examined comparatively for rural and for urban populations. Hence relief statistics seem to be our best index of poverty, even though they have obvious limitations. For example, we do not know how many families, especially rural families, are destitute but receive help informally from neighbors and landlords. Moreover, relief agencies are more recent and less well developed in rural areas, hence their reports may minimize rural poverty and exaggerate that of cities. Furthermore, variations in the funds available for relief and in the administrative policies affect the number of persons helped and the amounts claimed for their aid. All vary so from time to time and place to place that it is difficult to draw conclusions from them. However, since we have no other general data we shall use relief statistics for what they are worth. The Unemployment Relief Census of October 1933 is the most complete count so far taken in the United States, hence we turn first to it.

From Table 56 it appears that the relief load was relatively heavier in cities than in the country, but the difference was much less than might have been expected. It may be urged that this just happened to be a time when drought, crop failure from other causes, and low prices for farm products created especially difficult situations for rural people. It may also be held that the relief program of the federal government made unusually large amounts available for the assistance of country people. Whether these circumstances made the relative number of needy people in rural and urban districts different from other times we do not know. It is, however, particularly interesting that the per-

TABLE 56.—PERCENTAGE OF UNITED STATES POPULATION ON RELIEF, OCTOBER 1933[a]

A. Urban and Rural Relief

	Total	Urban	Rural
United States	10.3	11.0	9.5
White	9.5	9.6	9.3
Negro	17.8	26.7	10.9

B. Relief by Size of City

Cities of 1,000,000 and over	10.6
Cities of 1,000,000 to 250,000	12.1
Cities of 250,000 to 100,000	11.7
Cities of 100,000 to 50,000	11.2
Cities of 50,000 to 25,000	10.8
Cities of 25,000 and under	10.2

C. Relief by Age Groups

	Per cent of all persons	Per cent of relief persons	Ratio of relief persons to total
Under 16 years:			
Urban	27.6	39.8	1.45
Rural	36.1	44.4	1.23
16–24 years:			
Urban	16.3	15.0	.92
Rural	16.4	16.4	1.00
25–44 years:			
Urban	32.9	26.9	.82
Rural	25.1	21.8	.87
45–64 years:			
Urban	18.1	14.9	.82
Rural	16.6	13.1	.79
65 years and over:			
Urban	5.1	3.4	.67
Rural	5.8	4.3	.74

[a] Federal Emergency Relief Administration, *Unemployment Relief Census, October 1933*, pp. 7–17.

centage of white people on relief was approximately the same in city and country, while among Negroes the urban ratio was two and a half times as great as the rural. This was doubtless due to several factors. Many of the Negroes in cities were newcomers. Most of them were living on a very narrow margin even when employed. In times of depression many employers discharge their Negro workmen first and take them on last; but in the country a good many Negroes have been tided over by their landlords. Also, it is likely that the policy of relief administrations has not favored the acceptance of rural Negroes as relief clients.

From the second part of the table we note that the percentage of the population on relief increased steadily from the smallest cities to those of 1 million inhabitants but that, for reasons which are not apparent, the percentage in cities of more than 1 million was lower than in any other class except cities under 25,000. The third part of the table is especially interesting with reference to the children and younger adolescents. In both city and country, persons under sixteen years of age were found on relief much more frequently than their numbers in the general population would lead one to expect. The discrepancy is particularly marked in cities where the percentage of persons under sixteen was one and a half times as great as the percentage of all persons in that age group.

For various periods since 1933 we have statistical data for representative urban and rural areas but not for the country as a whole. Publications of the Federal Emergency Relief Administration, the Works Progress Administration, and the Social Security Board show, however, that the trends in relief giving have been practically the same in urban and in rural districts. Recent public assistance statistics fail to differentiate urban and rural populations but are reported for the separate states.[1] The interesting feature of these factors is that rural states rank very high and very low while urban states are mostly intermediate with reference to the number of persons receiving old-age assistance, aid to dependent children, and aid to the blind.

Some characterization of the recipients of unemployment relief may be had from a study which the Works Progress Administration made of unemployed workers and their families in 79 representative cities. In this sample of nearly 200,000 families

[1] Social Security Board, Bureau of Research and Statistics, *Public Assistance, Monthly Statistics for the United States.*

it was estimated that one-fifth of the households had no employable member. However, there was an average of one person per family who was seeking work. The remainder of the persons who might have been expected to work were attending school, keeping house, or were actually unemployable.

> The typical unemployed person on urban relief rolls in May 1934 was a white man, 38 years of age who was the head of a household. He had not completed an elementary school education, but had had on the average ten years experience at the occupation he considered his customary or "usual" one. This occupation varied considerably with the type of community in which he lived but was most frequently a semi-skilled or unskilled occupation in the manufacturing or mechanical industries.[1]

In general, the impact of unemployment or other financial disaster upon city dwellers may be characterized thus: Destitution often comes suddenly and without warning. Because of his relative anonymity and mobility the city person has fewer friends, hence less material and moral support. Since the poor in cities are more or less segregated, their mass poverty is more dramatic than the isolated poverty of countryfolk. Perhaps this is one reason why there are so many agencies for relief in cities. However, it is not merely destitution that afflicts city people, but living below the standard set by advertising, salesmanship, and the "Joneses." Sometimes, perhaps more often than in rural areas, urban poverty is related to personality disorganization which may further manifest itself in mental disease, vice, crime, etc. This, however, is not definitely established and is offered only as a hypothesis.

In conclusion, we must not forget that there is stark poverty both in rural and in urban America. Millions of families are living without proper food, clothing, shelter, medical attention, and other necessities of decent living. Whether there are relatively more of them in cities or in country districts we do not really know, but the experience of being poor differs. For the country family poverty is something to be borne quietly and alone or with aid from relatives and neighbors. For the city family it is more apt to be a dramatic event. That is, it may come more

[1] Works Progress Administration, *Urban Workers on Relief*, part 1, pp. xxiii–xxiv, 1936.

suddenly and it may receive more attention from charitable folk, the government, and the press.

Sickness and Accidents.—In Chap. XIX we showed that up to the present the average duration of life has been shorter and mortality rates have been higher in urban than in rural areas. This means that fatal illnesses and accidents occur more frequently in the city than in the country. But in most cases neither sickness nor accident ends directly in death. We need to know the relative frequency of nonfatal physical defects and ailments in cities and in rural districts.

Sorokin and Zimmerman[1] reviewed the results of physical examinations of school children and of recruits for the armies of various countries. Data on comparative health of rural and urban children give "a very indefinite and contradictory picture." But among recruits and drafted men there were well-marked differences. Those from rural districts showed fewer physical defects than those from cities.

The Committee on Costs of Medical Care in the United States studied 9,000 families through observations by public health nurses and others, at various intervals over a period of one year. Hence the report is probably fairly complete as to the incidence of illness in comparable families. The study revealed a surprising similarity in large cities and in rural and semirural districts. In cities of 100,000 and over it indicated an average sickness rate of 79 cases per 1,000 white persons. In towns of 5,000 or less and in rural areas the rate was 83.[2] Turning from a general sickness rate to the incidence of specific diseases, Sydenstricker reports some significant differences between agricultural workers and men in urban occupations.[3] Using data concerning white male policyholders, he found that the agricultural workers more frequently than the others showed carious and septic teeth, pyorrhea, hernia, genito-urinary complaints, gastric disorders, and indications of affected gall bladder and appendix. Men in other occupations, mostly urban, more often displayed defective vision, enlarged and diseased tonsils, impairment of heart and circulatory system, nervousness, enlarged thyroid, chronic skin

[1] Pitirim Sorokin and C. C. Zimmerman, *Principles of Rural-Urban Sociology*, pp. 143–146, 1929.

[2] Edgar Sydenstricker. *Health and Environment*, pp. 68 *ff.*, 1933.

[3] *Ibid.*, pp. 62 *ff.*

affections, and constipation. Making a still more specific study, Sydenstricker reports the relative number of cases and of deaths from typhoid in rural Alabama and in cities of various sizes.[1] The frequency with which this disease was identified in rural districts was less than in cities of any size, possibly because of poor diagnostic facilities. However, typhoid was found to decrease as the size of city increased. Deaths from this disease were more frequent in rural districts than in large cities but less frequent than in cities under 25,000 inhabitants. The death rate from typhoid decreased as the size of city increased.

Since we have such limited data concerning the incidence of sickness and accident in urban and rural areas, we are practically compelled to use mortality statistics as a basis for whatever inferences we feel warranted in drawing. But these must be used with caution, because facilities for diagnosis are not equally good in city and in country. Country people sometimes go to city hospitals for diagnosis and treatment. City people sometimes acquire typhoid and other diseases in the country. They may go to small towns or rural districts in search of health. Therefore data need to be corrected for residence. Such correction has been made in Tables 57 and 58. Note that the rural-urban differences were of like character in New York and Ohio for tuberculosis but not for cancer or for fatal automobile accidents. Table 59 shows the relation of deaths from certain causes to size of city, no correction being made for residence. It is evident that for the year in question and for 1935 (whose data are not reproduced here) the death rates from tuberculosis, a communicable disease, and from cancer and diabetes, degenerative diseases, are in direct proportion to the size of cities. But there is no such relation in the case of appendicitis, an acute disease. Deaths from tuberculosis are relatively most frequent in southern cities and least frequent in those of New England. But for cancer the death rate is highest in cities of the Pacific Coast and New England, lowest in those of the South. Deaths from diabetes are relatively most numerous in the Middle Atlantic and New England cities, least numerous in southern cities. But the incidence of death from appendicitis is highest in cities of the mountain region and lowest in those of New England and Pacific Coast cities. What significance, if any, should be attached to

[1] *Ibid.*, p. 65.

these regional differences we do not know. Perhaps the high tuberculosis death rates in southern cities are associated with large Negro populations. Possibly the high cancer and diabetes rates in northern and Pacific Coast cities are related to their older populations.

TABLE 57.—MORTALITY FROM VARIOUS CAUSES, CORRECTED FOR RESIDENCE, NEW YORK STATE, 1930[a]

Cause of mortality	New York City	Rest of state	
		Urban	Rural
All causes	11.0	11.9	13.8 per 1,000
Tuberculosis	80.3	63.3	53.4 per 100,000
Cancer	116.9	130.3	136.3 per 100,000
Typhoid		1.3	2.1 per 100,000
Diphtheria		2.8	1.8 per 100,000
Auto accidents[b]	18.5	20.2	55.8 per 100,000

[a] Edgar Sydenstricker, *Health and Environment*, p. 80, 1933. By permission of the President's Research Committee on Social Trends.

[b] By place of occurrence instead of residence.

TABLE 58.—MORTALITY FROM VARIOUS CAUSES, CORRECTED FOR RESIDENCE, OHIO, 1930[a]

Cause of mortality	Urban	Rural
Influenza and pneumonia	90.5	98.7
Tuberculosis	63.6	48.1
Cancer	103.8	102.4
Diabetes mellitus	22.1	19.5
Heart disease	212.8	221.1
Diarrhea and enteritis	19.8	25.7
Appendicitis	16.5	11.5
Diseases of liver and gall bladder	11.8	14.2
Auto accidents	30.7	27.3
Other accidents	62.4	74.9

[a] Edgar Sydenstriker, *Health and Environment*, p. 80, 1933. By permission of the President's Research Committee on Social Trends.

It is generally known that the mortality from pulmonary tuberculosis has been greatly reduced during the present century. In 1900 the rate (United States Registration Area) was 180.5. In 1935 it was only 49.8. In 59 American cities it dropped from 174.4 in 1910 to 53.2 in 1935. But there was an enormous variation among the cities in 1935. Pontiac (6.0), Berkeley (7.3), Passaic (9.6), and Utica (9.7) demonstrated that some small cities had almost eliminated tuberculosis as a cause of death. But Lexington (166.2), Augusta (133.9), and Shreveport (106.2) showed that other small cities were very far from this goal. Note that the last three are old trading centers with a large percentage of Negroes, who are peculiarly susceptible to tuberculosis. Three of the first four are young industrial cities. Berkeley is a college town. No doubt such differences in age, "race," and economic base are partly responsible for differences in tuberculosis death rates.

TABLE 59.—DEATHS PER 100,000 FROM CERTAIN DISEASES IN CITIES OF DIFFERENT SIZES, 1936[a]

Population class	Pulmonary tuberculosis	Cancer	Diabetes	Appendicitis
25,000 to 100,000	33.6	123.8	22.7	15.5
100,000 to 250,000	41.3	125.6	23.6	14.8
250,000 to 500,000	53.6	131.3	25.0	15.9
500,000 and over	57.5	141.0	31.5	13.6

Adapted from tables compiled by Frederick L. Hoffman in *The Spectator*, June 10, 19, Oct. 28, and Dec. 23, 1937.

The medical profession knows what the general public does not, that while tuberculosis has been diminishing, cancer has been increasing. For the registration area the cancer death rate has grown from 82.1 in 1916 to 107.9 in 1935. This is probably due in part to better diagnosis, but it is unquestionably related to the aging of our population. Among cities with high cancer death rates in 1935 were Madison (286.8), Pasadena (235.8), Portland, Me. (229.4), and Fall River (213.5). Cities with notably low rates included Charlotte (60.6), Knoxville (64.0), Fresno (64.8), Tulsa (70.1), and Detroit (73.0). Again we have a variety of cities but, aside from age of their populations, we have no clues to the reasons for such divergent rates. In general the more extreme rates for cancer, as for tuberculosis, were found in small cities. But for both diseases the rates in most large cities were well above the national average.

Diabetes, like cancer, has been increasing in the frequency with which it is reported as a cause of death. From 17.1 in 1916 the rate has risen to 22.2 in 1935. Among the cities with high diabetes death rates in 1935 were Harrisburg (57.8), Paterson (47.4), Albany (44.1), and Shreveport (40.8). Unusually low rates were those of Pueblo (1.9), Davenport (3.3), Gary (4.6), and Fort Worth (7.5). No explanation of these differences has been brought to our attention.

Appendicitis we shall not discuss in detail, for there is no indication that it is related to urbanism. The national death rate from appendicitis in 1935 was 12.7. For 183 cities it was 14.7, and for the five largest cities it was 13.3. These differences are too small to warrant any conclusions. But the other three diseases we have discussed are predominantly urban. Tuberculosis is associated with living and working conditions found chiefly in cities. Cancer and diabetes are associated with the growing number of elderly persons; diabetes is also a matter of diet and perhaps of exercise.

In short, city people are more likely to incur certain ailments and eventually to die from them. But they have the advantage over country people in access to institutions and individuals that can provide medical care. Also the development of public health programs has greatly reduced the urban dweller's hazard in relation to certain diseases, such as typhoid, malaria, and influenza. No doubt in the future the situation for both city and country people will be improved.

Mental Disorders.—Such data as we possess indicate that mental breakdowns are more likely to occur in the experience of urban than of rural folk. Unfortunately, however, our information covers only commitments to hospitals and tells nothing about patients cared for at home or otherwise. Nevertheless, the differences between the rates of commitment in urban and in rural areas are so great as hardly to be considered the result of accident. Table 59 shows that for all classes (by nativity), for both sexes, and for each of the major psychoses the proportion of urban patients is much greater than of rural. Other data assembled by the Bureau of the Census show that the same thing is true for single, married, and widowed persons, for every age group, and for all but five states. The facts revealed for 1933 are substantially the same as those for 1923.

Now it is undoubtedly true that some patients who could be cared for in rural homes would require hospitalization if they lived in cities. Rural almshouses, or poor farms, shelter some who, if city dwellers, might be committed to hospitals for the insane. Country people probably have more antagonism to institutional care than do cityfolk. Probability of identification and diagnosis is undoubtedly greater in the city, for there are psychological and psychiatric services attached to dispensaries, courts, schools, and sometimes industries. Hence we may well doubt that the actual incidence of mental disorders is

TABLE 60.—FIRST ADMISSIONS TO STATE HOSPITALS, PER 100,000 POPULATION AGED FIFTEEN YEARS AND OVER[a]

	Male		Female	
	Urban	Rural	Urban	Rural
A. By Sex and Nativity				
All classes	106.0	60.7	75.8	41.2
Native white	103.1	59.2	71.9	40.1
Foreign-born white	107.9	69.2	85.6	41.0
Negro	130.9	67.2	89.8	49.5
B. By Diagnosis				
Cerebral arteriosclerosis	9.5	4.7	6.8	2.2
General paralysis	10.3	2.9	2.9	.9
Alcoholic psychoses	6.9	1.9	1.2	.1
Dementia praecox	14.8	6.9	13.3	5.6
Manic depressive	6.5	5.3	9.1	5.5
Senile	5.7	4.2	5.9	2.6
Paranoia	1.1	.5	1.1	.4

[a] U.S. Census, *Patients in Hospitals for Mental Disease*, 1933, pp. 48–49.

as much greater in cities than in rural districts as the statistics indicate. On the other hand, it would not be strange if the frequency of mental breakdown were actually greater under urban than under rural conditions. City people are subjected to noise, speed, competition, culture conflicts, and other forms of pressure which must in many cases make the difference between remaining fairly balanced and becoming psychopathic.

One other comment should be made at this point. We have presented mental disorders among the crises which may occur in the lives of individuals. In many cases it would be equally or more appropriate to consider them as maladjustments, *i.e.*, ineffective ways of meeting difficult circumstances. While a mental breakdown precipitates a crisis, it may be only one of a series of events following physical disability, economic collapse, interrupted love life, or other disturbance of the life organization. When a patient accuses "enemies" of causing his failure, hides behind an imaginary ailment, boasts of prowess he obviously does not possess, takes to the excessive use of alcohol or other drugs, and otherwise refuses to "face reality," his mental disorder is less a crisis than a maladjustment.

Maladjustments

Unemployment and other impoverishment, sickness and accident, and sometimes mental breakdowns may be considered crises in the lives of persons, as well as mass phenomena. Often, if not usually, they represent the disruption of one's scheme of life, his habits, and his relations to other people. Sometimes the disturbance is slight, sometimes it is quite devastating. Furthermore, crises differ as to the length of time they leave a person upset, detached, or otherwise unadjusted. A short period of unemployment or hospitalization may constitute a rather unimportant interruption of an individual's *curriculum vitae.* But prolonged unemployment or disability may eliminate him from certain groups and activities, bring him into conflicts, or make him a burden. He may lose his own "grip on things," "go to pieces," and become completely demoralized; or he may reorganize his life as a rebel against established codes of law and morals. In the former instance we may recognize him as an alcoholic, drug addict, aimless wanderer, chronic "kicker," or "insane person." In the latter case he is more likely to appear in the role of thief, gangster, grafter, prostitute, or perhaps simply as a "Bohemian." In the extreme case of social defeat the luckless one may commit suicide. Without attempting a thorough study of "social pathologies" in the city, we shall consider a few of them in so far as they manifest urban-rural contrasts and differ in cities of various kinds. We have chosen for illustrative material the fields of sexual irregularity, crimes reported to the Federal Bureau of Investigation, and suicide.

Sexual Irregularity.—It is quite impossible to get any quantitative data concerning the violation of sex mores in city or in country. On the basis of our general knowledge of social organization and social control we would expect to find stricter sex mores in the country and greater laxity in the city. The relative ease with which urban dwellers can lead "dual lives," the disproportionate number of unattached women, the sexual stimulation through advertisements, movies, and public dance halls, all furnish *a priori* grounds for believing sexual irregularities to occur more frequently in cities than in small towns and country

TABLE 61.—ILLEGITIMATE BIRTHS REPORTED PER 1,000 TOTAL BIRTHS, 1934[a]

	United States	Cities of 10,000 and over	Cities of 2,500 to 10,000	Rural
United States:				
Total illegitimate births	38.9	37.9	31.1	41.5
Native white mothers	21.1	26.2	17.5	17.4
Foreign white mothers	7.8	7.9	8.1	7.6
Colored (Negro, Indian, etc.)	151.5	156.3	145.4	149.7
Selected states:				
Alabama		101.6	77.0	85.8
Vermont		57.0	18.0	20.9
Missouri		52.5	24.3	18.0
Nebraska		33.3	12.1	9.7
Oregon		27.2	6.8	9.2
Utah		15.5	4.4	6.9
New York		17.9	19.8	22.3
Maryland		65.4	87.8	79.9

[a] *Birth, Stillbirth, and Infant Mortality Statistics*, 1934, U.S. Bureau of the Census, pp. 14–15. Note that California and Massachusetts are not included, because they require no record of legitimacy.

districts. Nevertheless it is quite possible that rural-urban differences are much less than is popularly supposed.

One possible index of extramarital sex relations is the percentage of births reported as illegitimate. Table 61 shows somewhat surprisingly that for the United States in 1934 the rural percentage was higher than the urban. Moreover, this difference has obtained for as long as we have reliable statistics, in spite of the fact that every year many cities have rates very much higher than those of rural areas. We are disposed to credit the low urban rates to widespread use of contraceptives rather than to continence. From Tables 61 and 62 it is plain that the difference between white and Negro rates is much more significant than that between urban and rural. Other factors must be studied before we can account satisfactorily for the wide variation between individual cities. The low rate in Salt Lake City may be the result of homogeneity, strong religious organization, and the absence of Negroes. But New York City has not a homogeneous population, nor is it noted as a stronghold of religion; it does have a considerable Negro population. Yet

TABLE 62.—ILLEGITIMATE BIRTHS REPORTED IN SELECTED CITIES PER 1,000 TOTAL BIRTHS, WHITE AND NEGRO, 1930[a]

City	Total	White	Negro
Richmond	97.5	41.7	207.6
Kansas City, Mo	94.5	85.9	177.1
New Orleans	68.6	25.9	152.0
Atlanta	63.4	24.9	137.7
Baltimore	59.2	16.1	213.8
St. Louis	37.5	23.3	132.9
Minneapolis	35.5	35.2	74.6
Portland, Ore	35.0	35.1	33.0
Philadelphia	32.7	15.6	139.2
Cleveland	27.4	22.5	81.9
Seattle	22.2	21.8	29.6
New York	12.7	9.9	56.1
Salt Lake City	10.6	10.4	29.4

[a] Adapted from Ruth Reed, *The Illegitimate Family in New York City*, pp. 242–244, 1934. By permission of Columbia University Press.

for years it has had a low illegitimacy rate. The large percentage of births out of wedlock in southern cities is clearly related to the large numbers of Negroes. Their apparent "immorality" is in part a heritage of slavery, in part a matter of present-day ignorance and exploitation. The high rate in Kansas City is partly affected by its racial composition, but the percentage of illegitimate white births is very large. This is due to the presence of well-advertised institutions which cater to unmarried mothers and attract girls from the rural areas of several states.

On the whole we are driven to conclude that illegitinacy rates are not satisfactory indexes of sexual irregularity, although they do indicate the presence of certain maladjusted folk. Unmarried mothers in our culture (excluding certain parts of the rural black belt) are stigmatized and their children are handicapped.

While we are unable to measure the relative amounts of sexual irregularity in city and in country, we do have some information about qualitative differences. In villages and rural neighborhoods that might be popularly characterized as "Puritan" or "strait-laced," extramarital sex relations are definitely taboo and persons found to be guilty of such behavior are penalized by public opinion if not otherwise. In fact, such pressure may be brought to bear that they find it necessary to leave the community. On the other hand, in parts of the rural South, Negroes engage much more freely in these relations and suffer very much less by way of penalties. In frontier communities prostitution, which is absent from both the other types of rural areas, is often quite general. Moreover, its indulgence is taken for granted, although a clear distinction is drawn between the small number of "decent women" and others. In cities there is a great deal of "intimacy on a basis of anonymity." That is to say, men and women may meet and engage in sex relations without ever having seen each other before or knowing each other's names. Cities also display the phenomenon of the mistress, or "kept woman." In cities there is known to be a great deal of "experimentation," perhaps better called "exploration," on the part of adolescents. Whether it is more or less common than in villages and country districts we do not know. Also we are in the dark as to the relative frequency in city and in country of premarital relations between lovers and engaged persons.

The significance of parenthood out of wedlock differs from city to country in ways that correspond to the contrasts just mentioned. It appears that rural mores more frequently than urban require "shotgun weddings," "to make the girl an honest woman," and "to give her child a name." The pregnant unmarried girl or woman in a small town or rural district is otherwise almost forced to go away to escape disgrace. These remarks, however, do not hold in parts of the black belt where Frazier has shown that unmarried mothers and their children are quite commonly accepted by their relatives and by the community as a whole.[1] In the city anonymity aids in the disposal of

[1] E. Franklin Frazier, "An Analysis of Statistics on Negro Illegitimacy in the United States," *Social Forces*, 11 (1932), 249–257.

illegitimate children if that is desired, or in enabling a girl to pass as a widow or divorcee if she so chooses. The unmarried father evades responsibility quite generally both in urban and in rural districts, but in the city his escape is even more easy than in the country.

Some irregular sexual behavior seems clearly to occur more frequently under urban than under rural conditions. Such is prostitution,[1] a special kind of sexual behavior involving promiscuity, emotional indifference, and some material compensation. The actual numbers of prostitutes are unknown, especially since the campaigns of 20 years ago, which resulted in the formal closing of all red-light districts. Widespread observation indicates that there are not many prostitutes in villages and almost none in the open country, although they are fairly common in towns devoted to mining and lumbering.

During the last quarter of a century there have been rather important changes in this institution. From 1910 to 1915 there was a series of investigations which resulted in "clamping on the lid" in nearly all the cities. Since then there have been repeated openings and closings but no return to the flagrant form of prewar days. During the time of most active suppression it was frequently predicted that vice resorts would invade good residential districts. As a matter of fact, they are more scattered than they were 25 years ago, but the sections invaded are those which were already declining in respectability. In the earlier period, houses of prostitution were rather permanent and generally recognized establishments. In recent years they have been impermanent, and very few of them persist long at one address. Likewise, there is evidence of a decline in the number of houses and in the number of girls per house. There is probably less streetwalking, and there may be less solicitation in public amusement places. On the other hand, there are more arrests from hotels, apartment houses, and furnished rooms. While there appears to have been a general decline, there has been a definite increase in Negro prostitution in our cities quite out of proportion to the increase in the Negro population. Another change is the narrowing of the gulf between prostitutes and other women.

[1] Walter C. Reckless, *Vice in Chicago*, 1933; W. C. Waterman, *Prostitution and Its Repression in New York City*, 1932; Geoffrey May, "Prostitution," *Encyclopaedia of the Social Sciences*, vol. 12, pp. 553–559.

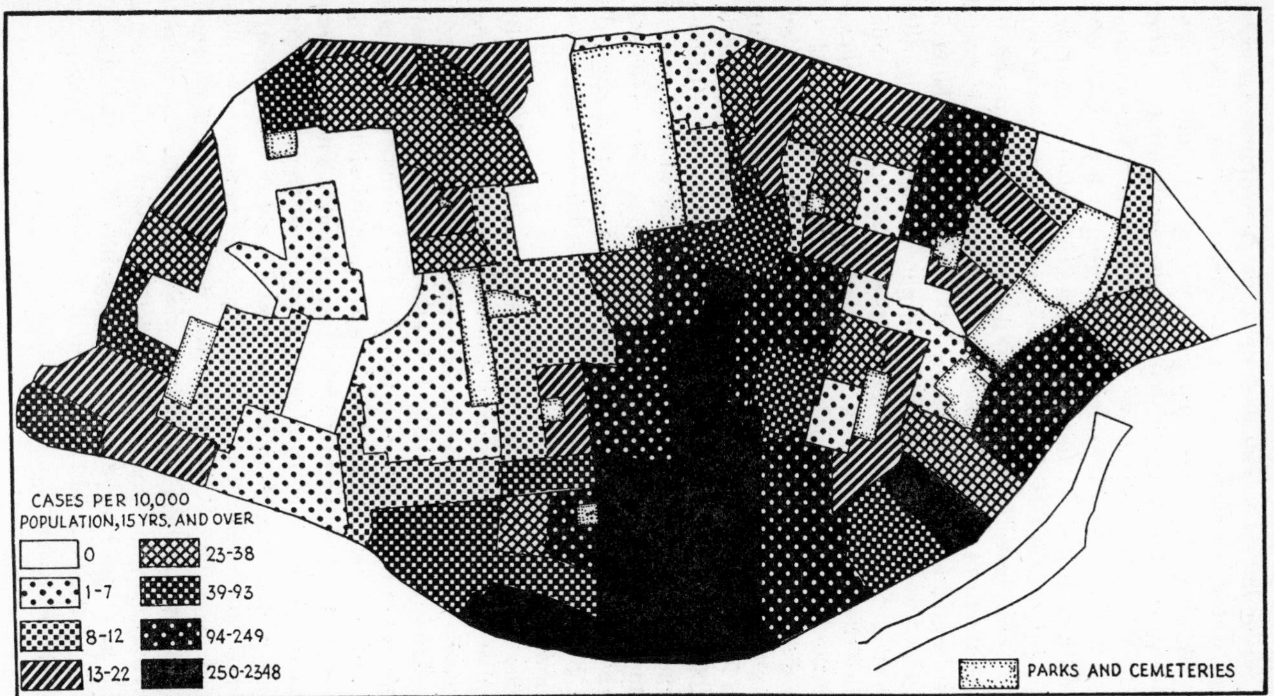

Fig. 19.—Venereal disease among St. Louis women, Municipal Clinic cases, 1932.

In an earlier day those who plied this trade were almost a separate caste. Today a number of circumstances combine to make it easier for them to adopt another mode of life and to evade identification while they are engaged in prostitution. White-slave traffic probably never was so extensive as it was imagined to be, and apparently it is even less general today. Girls often take up prostitution voluntarily and leave it after a temporary period, either to marry or to take up some other means of existence. Today much more is known about prophylaxis against and treatment of venereal disease. Whether quackery is more or less widespread we do not know, but there are more bona fide clinics for the control of syphilis and gonorrhea. Finally, there has been a development, in large cities at least, of what might be called syndicates. Numbers of vice resorts are linked together under the control of one individual or group operating with the aid of graft and blackmail. Their houses may be scattered over a city; sometimes they are attached to cabarets and night clubs. Not a few of them have left the inner city and are found in the form of roadhouses. Thus in a number of ways prostitution as an organized business has undergone considerable change; at all times it seems clear, however, that it has been essentially an urban institution. Sexual irregularities occur in rural districts, but for the most part they are on a different basis, as we have indicated.

Crime.—Sorokin and Zimmerman have assembled data from a number of different countries which show rather convincingly that most types of crime are committed more frequently in cities than in rural districts.[1] It is also indicated, although with less adequate data, that persons who have lived for the most part under urban conditions more frequently violate the law than do those whose life has been largely rural. There are some differences in the types of offenses found most frequently in city and in country, crimes against property being more common in cities and those against persons being sometimes more frequent in rural districts. Predominantly urban crimes include theft, fraud, forgery, embezzlement, and violations of laws pertaining to sex, drugs, traffic, etc. In rural districts arson, cattle stealing, assault, and infanticide appear with prominence, at least in some countries. Sorokin and Zimmerman remark that "cities are

[1] Sorokin and Zimmerman, *op. cit.*, Chap. 16.

marked by a technique of crime perpetration which requires a great deal of strategy, deceit, lies, and so on, while the country technique of crime perpetration is more direct, naive. . . ."[1]

We have no rural data for the United States, but for a number of years cities have been reporting to the Federal Bureau of Investigation offenses known to the police. Rates have been computed indicating the ratio of the various classes of offenses to the total population, and the data have been classified according to the size of cities. Table 63 shows the results of such computations for a period of four years. It is evident that criminal homicides, robbery, and auto theft bear a direct relation to the size of city, being relatively much more frequent in large cities than in small ones. Larceny and burglary seem to have been more common in cities of 100,000 to 250,000; thereafter they fell off, with the decline in size. Aggravated assault was reported most frequently in cities of 50,000 to 100,000 and least often in cities of less than 50,000. Studies are now being made to determine whether there is any relation between crime rates as reported and various other social and economic factors. For a small number of cities and for a single year there has been found a relatively high correlation between crime and rate of growth.

TABLE 63.—OFFENSES KNOWN TO THE POLICE AND REPORTED TO THE FEDERAL BUREAU OF INVESTIGATION, 1933–1936, ANNUAL AVERAGES PER 100,000 POPULATION[a]

Size of city	Offenses per 100,000 population					
	Criminal homicide	Aggravated assault	Robbery	Burglary	Larceny	Auto theft
Over 250,000..........	14.5	48.0	106.1	350.0	776.7	331.4
100,000 to 250,000.....	11.3	62.5	64.7	430.0	897.4	319.5
50,000 to 100,000......	10.5	65.8	63.0	370.4	835.7	248.0
25,000 to 50,000.......	8.0	42.7	44.9	315.6	752.9	199.9
10,000 to 25,000.......	7.5	34.5	34.4	242.3	594.7	144.0
Under 10,000..........	7.4	24.7	28.4	217.9	433.9	95.5

[a] Adapted from Federal Bureau of Investigation, "Uniform Crime Reports," *Quarterly Bulletins* for 1933–1936.

[1] *Ibid.*, p. 384. By permission of Henry Holt & Company, Inc.

This is probably to be expected on the assumption that newcomers to the city take some time to adjust themselves. Also they bring diverse folkways and mores, thus introducing cultural conflicts which have been shown to underlie some cases of delinquency. It is possible, moreover, that a rapidly growing city may have a less well-organized system of police and courts. Another correlation indicated by preliminary studies is that between crime rates and the percentage of the population that is native white of native parents. Curiously, we have found practically no correlation between crime rates and the percentage that is Negro. Further studies must be carried on before we can know just what is the significance of these data. In general it is evident that Negroes are arrested and convicted for crime more frequently than are whites, but in many cities they constitute so small a part of the total population that even a great deal of criminality among them may not produce a high rate for the city as a whole. When the reports have been analyzed for separate offenses and for separate cities we should be able to answer the questions involved in this apparent relation. Another finding is that crime rates vary with the percentage of the population between the ages of fifteen and forty-four. This is what one would expect, because most offenders are in their twenties and thirties. Also, there is a slight correlation with the sex ratio, which should be expected in view of the much greater frequency of crime among men than among women. There are some indications that crime rates and costs of relief bear a negative relation to each other. If this proves to be correct there will be a new argument for adequate relief as a crime preventive. Further studies should be made to see what relation there may be between various types of crime and heterogeneity of the population, dominant ethnic groups, the children of immigrants, and mobility. Concerning all of these matters we have some very plausible hypotheses but as yet inadequate data.

Suicide.—Persons who meet serious crises may undertake to deal with them, as we have pointed out, in several ways. They may, with careful study, persevering effort, and the assistance of others, find solutions to their problems that are satisfactory both to themselves and to their associates. If they are irritated, repressed, and rebellious, they may fight back, defying the world that seems to have "done them wrong." But if they are weak, discouraged, or lonely, they may seek to escape from their troubles—drowning them in drink, deadening them with narcotics, literally running away, or as a last resort committing suicide. In our culture suicide is usually the mark of complete defeat—disappointment in love, economic failure, disgrace, or broken health, accompanied by feelings of guilt, shame, or revenge. A few persons choose death rather than to become burdens on others who could care for them only at a great sacrifice. A minority of suicides are clearly psychotic.

In the United States and in most European countries suicide occurs more frequently in urban than in rural areas.[1] The suicide rate in American cities has ranged from one and one-third to one and three-fifths times the rural rate. In no year of the twentieth century has our rural rate been so great as our urban rate. At the opening of the century our national average (of suicides per 100,000 population) was low; it rose steadily until the depression year of 1908; thereafter it remained high until 1915; then it fell off to a point almost as low as that of 1900; but from 1920 to 1932 it climbed again to a new high figure; after which it dropped off slightly. Both rural and urban rates followed the same general trends. Regional differences are consistently great, suicides being relatively few in the East and increasing as one goes toward the Pacific Coast. In 1935 and 1936 the suicide rates in cities of the Far West averaged more than twice as great as those of New England. Among cities with very high rates in 1936 were Seattle (34.4), Omaha (32.6), San Francisco (30.4), Los Angeles (29.6), Denver (29.5), Galveston (28.1), Topeka (26.8), and Jacksonville, Fla., (24.2). These were mostly western cities, but at the opposite end of the scale there is no such concentration. However, the lowest rates were found in small industrial cities—Holyoke (0.0), McKeesport (1.7), Schenectady (4.1), Lawrence, Mass., (4.6), Decatur (5.0), and Kenosha (5.6). Table 64 confirms the belief that there is a correlation between size of city and frequency of suicide. How-

[1] Data used in this discussion are drawn from the following sources: Ruth Shonle Cavan, *Suicide*, 1928; Louis I. Dublin and Bessie Bunzel, *To Be or Not To Be: A Study of Suicide*, 1933; Frederick L. Hoffman, "The Suicide Record of 1936," *The Spectator*, June 24, 1937; Sorokin and Zimmerman, *op. cit.*, Chap. 7.

ever, it is worthy of note that the rate in our largest cities is somewhat less than in those of a quarter to a half million.

Some other facts shed further light on the significance of suicide. Men take their lives much more frequently than do women, in a ratio of about 3:1. The rate increases steadily with age. As to marital status, suicide is most common among divorced persons, next among the widowed, next among the married, and lowest of all among the single. White people commit suicide from four to six times as frequently as Negroes. Self-destruction is associated less with lack of money than with

TABLE 64.—SUICIDE RATES IN AMERICAN CITIES OF DIFFERENT SIZE 1935–1936[a]

Size of city	Suicides per 100,000 population	
	1935	1936
25,000 to 100,000	13.6	13.1
100,000 to 250,000	15.7	16.1
250,000 to 500,000	16.8	16.8
500,000 and over	16.4	15.7

[a] Frederick L. Hoffman, *The Spectator*, June 24, 1937, p. 7.

change in economic circumstances. In an unknown percentage of cases it follows arrest, incurable disease, pregnancy out of wedlock, and the rupture of intimate relations such as marriage, engagement, or liaison. In other words, it is apparently related to economic insecurity, the romantic complex, and loss of status. When a person has some strong desire and a fixed idea as to how it may be satisfied, failure to attain his wish may be so devastating as to lead him to self-destruction. When the persons or objects to which he has become accustomed and on which he depends for comfort and happiness are suddenly lost, the victim may not be able to withstand the shock; to him life may seem no longer worth while. All these crises and the attendant circumstances appear to be more common in the city than in the country, though this statement cannot be made with complete assurance.

SPATIAL DISTRIBUTION

In Part III we discussed the relation of various "social pathologies" to the general pattern of American cities. We noted that

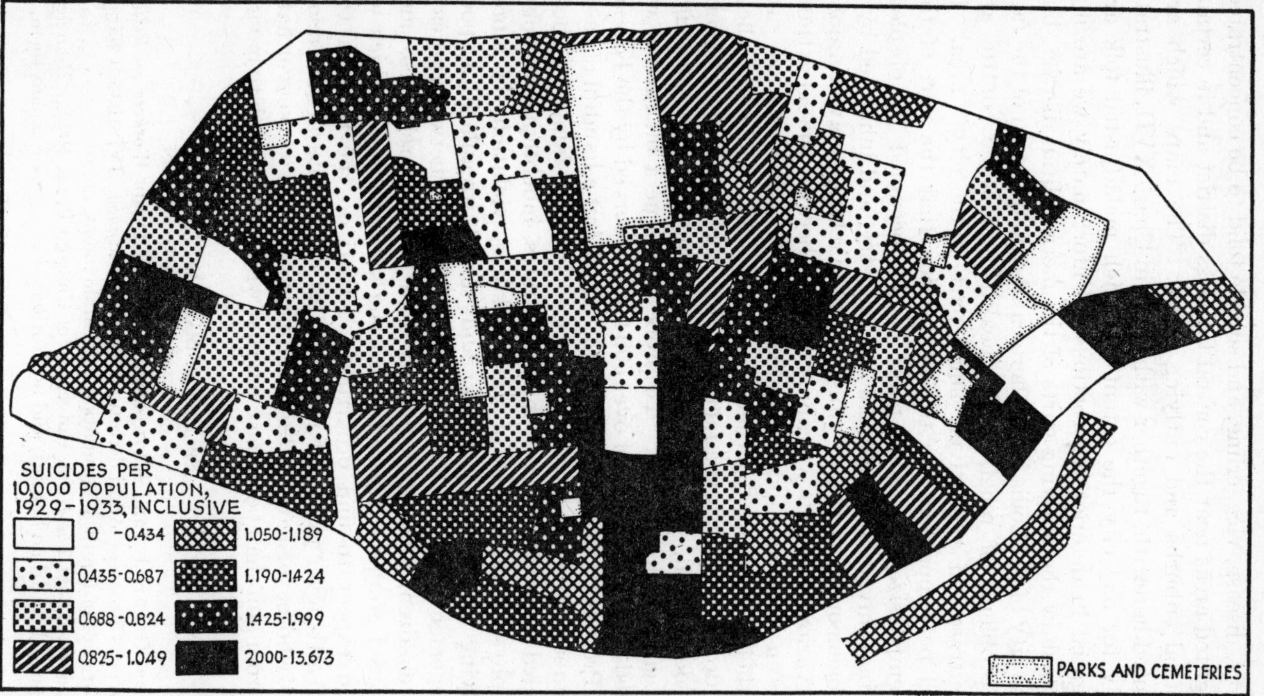

Fig. 20.—Suicides, St. Louis, 1929–1933.

poverty, disease, vice, crime, and suicide tend to be concentrated in blighted areas near the central business district and in certain industrial suburbs and outlying slums. The maps which are presented herewith, together with those in Chap. XVII, illustrate vividly for one city the extent to which maladjusted folk are segregated in deteriorated sections. Unfortunately we are not able to show the outlying parts of the metropolitan district, but for the city of St. Louis itself there can be no question of the fact that problems of relief, public health, and crime control are concentrated in a relatively small part of the city's area. It should be remembered in this connection that the part of the city emphasized on these maps is old, occupied by obsolete dwellings, invaded by business and industry, and inhabited by a heterogeneous population. Just what the relation may be among these various elements we cannot say, but because the same thing has been demonstrated in numbers of other cities we are sure that their occurrence together is not accidental. Of course, these data do not establish the fact that the same people may experience destitution, broken health, and demoralization, although often enough this is true. To probe this issue a bit further we studied statistical cards of over 500 families served by the Kansas City Provident Association in 1927. In all but a handful of cases a number of problems were presented by each family. These included unemployment or low wage rates, indebtedness, illness and physical difficulties of various kinds, violations of mores involving alcoholism, begging, and sexual irregularities, poor management, personal friction between mates or between parents and children, and detachment from friends, relatives, and organized groups. These are just the kinds of things which we should expect to find occurring together, on the basis of the adage "It never rains but it pours," or the scriptural statement that "whosoever hath, to him shall be given; and whosoever hath not, from him shall be taken even that which he seemeth to have."

Selected Readings

Palmer, Gladys L., and Katherine D. Wood: *Urban Workers on Relief*, Works Progress Administration, *Research Monog.* IV, 1936. Characteristics of families, occupations, unemployment, etc.

Anderson, Nels: *The Hobo*, University of Chicago Press, 1923. Homeless men, their urban habitat, and institutions that serve or exploit them.

SUTHERLAND, E. H., and HARVEY J. LOCKE: *Twenty Thousand Homeless Men*, J. B. Lippincott Company, 1936. A study of unemployed men in Chicago shelters.

THRASHER, FREDERIC M.: *The Gang*, University of Chicago Press, 1927. A study of 1,313 gangs in Chicago, their structure, life cycle, activities, habits, and general significance.

SHAW, CLIFFORD R., and H. D. MCKAY: *Social Factors in Juvenile Delinquency*, National Commission on Law Observance and Enforcement, Report on Causes of Crime, vol. 2 (1931).

SHAW, CLIFFORD R.: *Delinquency Areas*, University of Chicago Press, 1929. Spatial distribution of school truants, juvenile delinquents, and adult offenders in Chicago.

WATERMAN, W. C.: *Prostitution and Its Repression in New York City*, Columbia University Press, 1932.

RECKLESS, WALTER C.: *Vice in Chicago*, University of Chicago Press, 1933. Covers changes over a 20-year period.

REED, RUTH: *The Illegitimate Family in New York City*, Columbia University Press, 1934. A study of unmarried fathers and mothers and their children, agencies dealing with them, and the nature of their problems.

SYDENSTRICKER, EDGAR: *Health and Environment*, McGraw-Hill Book pany, Inc., 1933. One of the monographs prepared under direction of the President's Research Committee on Social Trends.

PART V

PREDICTION AND CONTROL

Chapter XXII

THE LIFE CYCLE OF AMERICAN CITIES

In the earlier parts of this book we have sketched the rise and development of cities and of urbanism; we have described some characteristic institutions and folkways of American cities; we have examined the selective and distributive aspects of their physical and social organization; finally, we have reviewed the evidence bearing on personality as it is affected by urbanism. In this chapter our problem is this: Is there a typical sequence of events in the life history of American cities? Do the same sorts of things happen in approximately the same order? Are there stages which might be identified as youth and maturity, perhaps even decline? We shall deal with this problem in terms of physical growth, relations to the surrounding area and to other cities, economic base, and social institutions.

The Physical Growth of Cities

From the data set forth in Chaps. III, V, XIII, and others it seems clear that our present great cities started as relatively self-sufficient villages, developed into towns which were small trading centers, then became genuine cities serving larger areas and involved in commercial relations with other cities, and finally expanded into metropolitan structures. Such a generalization as this must obviously ignore varied details, but it seems to be essentially sound. We know that St. Louis and San Francisco, *e.g.*, had widespread trade relations while they were yet quite small. But cities as diverse as Boston, Pittsburgh, Chicago, and Seattle followed substantially the sequence outlined above.

As to rates of growth, cities show great diversity. Thus St. Louis developed slowly for 75 years; it grew rapidly from 1840 to 1870, after which it settled down to a moderate rate of expansion. Detroit's development was fairly slow and steady until the automobile era began, about 1900, after which it grew at an amazing rate until the depression of 1929. Chicago started later than St. Louis and Detroit but since its first few years has maintained a rapid growth. Philadelphia's population has increased steadily at a moderate rate except during the 1850's, when it quadrupled. Seattle was an unimportant town until 1880; then it had 30 years of almost unbelievable development, from 3,500 to 237,000; since 1910 it has grown steadily but moderately. Until 1930 no American city of 100,000 showed an intercensal decline. But the Fifteenth Census showed that during the 1920's four such cities lost in population. They were Fall River, New Bedford, Lowell, and Wilmington. Perhaps the Sixteenth Census will show a decline in others. At all events, we can only conclude that different cities display varying sequences of rapid and slow growth, with a present tendency to slow down, *i.e.*, to become stabilized.

As to sources of population, our earliest cities were established by newcomers from Europe. They grew by attracting to themselves rural white Americans. From the Civil War to the World War their increase was chiefly due to European immigration. Since then the principal additions have been of rural American Negroes. Southern cities received fewer immigrants than did those of the North, and their Negro increase came earlier. Western cities have not yet acquired large Negro populations. Some cities, *e.g.*, Boston, New York, Chicago, and San Francisco, have depended longer and to a greater extent on immigration than have others, *e.g.*, Baltimore, Detroit, St. Louis, and Los Angeles. Los Angeles has attracted chiefly native whites; St. Louis, Detroit, and Baltimore have drawn Americans of both major "races." Thus while there are regional as well as individual differences, the typical sequence seems to be well established—European settlers, rural American whites, European immigrants, rural American Negroes.

As a city grows there are characteristic internal movements. Starting as a small, compact unit, it spreads out in arms and waves, occupying more and more territory. In time it approaches and surrounds outlying towns, which are gradually absorbed into the metropolis. As business and industry invade residential districts, old families move farther from the center. But factories and stores usually do not occupy the entire area evacuated by old residents. Single dwellings become converted tenements and house newcomers to the city. The centrifugal flight continues until the inner city begins to lose population. Then realtors, downtown merchants, and tax collectors manifest alarm. Perhaps new housing programs will rehabilitate the districts which have become blighted and draw population back toward the heart of the city. These characteristic internal movements have been more fully described in Chaps. VI, XIII, XVII, and XVIII.

The External Relations of Cities

As we pointed out in Chap. II, no real city can live unto itself. Also, urbanism as a characteristic way of life depends upon the existence of many cities between which there are various relations. Hence the dominant mode of transportation must be considered in its bearing on the life cycle of our cities. From the beginning of our history as a nation until the Civil War the principal mode of transportation was by water. As was perfectly natural, our earliest cities were along the Atlantic seaboard; later, cities grew up on the Ohio and Mississippi rivers. In view of this fact, cities not only appeared where there were good harbors or suitable river landings; they were in the nature of water-bound settlements, *i.e.*, business houses had to be near the water front. Trade was carried on for the most part with other places which could be reached by water. Trade consisted largely in the handling of goods which would not be damaged by slow transit.

About 1850 railroads began to be an important means of transportation. After the Civil War they spread over the country very rapidly. Railroads not only stimulated the growth of existing towns like Rochester and Chicago, but brought new towns and cities into existence, *e.g.*, Indianapolis, Wichita, and Oklahoma City. The railroads brought about a redistribution of business activities in individual cities. Terminals, warehouses, and factories no longer had to cluster about the water front; they could be located on any piece of ground conveniently reached by rail. The railroads also promoted suburban development and hastened the absorption of outlying communities by the growing city.

Since 1900 cities have been particularly affected by the enormous increase in the number of automobiles. These have still further stimulated suburban development and have caused it to take place in sections not easily reached by rail. The automobile has also created new traffic problems. It has facilitated outdoor recreation, particularly week-end trips into the country. The truck and bus have consolidated business relations between great cities and outlying towns.

Finally we have the airplane, the influence of which upon cities we cannot yet identify. It enables people to get back and forth very quickly from one city to another, but at present is too expensive for all but a favored few.

In keeping with the varied means of transportation there have been characteristic changes in the hinterland, or sphere of influence, belonging to each city. In most cases this was initially small, although there have been some exceptions, as in the cases of San Francisco and St. Louis. As transportation facilities developed, the trade area expanded until it overlapped that of some other city. Later, with the rise of additional urban centers and with changes in major lines of transportation, these trade areas, or spheres of influence, contracted, until they now seem to be approaching stabilization. The momentum of great cities is such that smaller places in the same region have long since ceased to be rivals of the metropolis. Instead, they take their place in a constellation centering about the great city. To a certain extent even metropolitan centers are ceasing to be rivals. Each has its own hinterland; each has certain major products which it distributes to the hinterlands of other cities. Hence the businessmen in each place tend to look somewhat tolerantly upon those of other centers. In other words, after expansion and contraction, after several changes in transportation facilities, and after the opening of all the more obvious natural resources, cities seem to be settling down to a fairly well-defined relation to each other and to their own hinterlands.

The Economic Bases of Cities

Another important aspect of the life cycle of a city is its changing economic base. However, the diversity here is so great that we find it very difficult to identify a characteristic sequence of events to which any large number of cities seem to conform. The few points which stand out are these. Initially the community is approximately a self-sufficient unit. There are local trade, handicraft, and agriculture. Then there develop gradually manufacturing on a larger scale and trade with a larger area. Sometimes wholesaling appears first and sometimes manufacturing, as we have seen in Chap. VII. Also, the manufacturing may be confined to a single industry or it may be diversified. This rise has been previously discussed and needs no elaboration here. Finally, as cities grow large they develop increasing financial and managerial functions.

In detail the economic base may change as one after another new natural resources are discovered and developed. Thus Duluth has developed in succession upon furs, lumber, iron, and wheat. Seattle started with lumber, later added fishing and mining, and subsequently became an important financial and administrative center. Los Angeles was initially a sleepy agricultural town. Then it became a booming tourist center. Presently oil, and later the movies, made their important contributions to its economic life. Such stories as these are a poor basis for generalization, but on the whole it appears that the economic life of our cities is becoming more and more diversified, so that in each metropolitan center there are manufacturing, wholesale and retail trade, banking, and in fact almost all the major types of business activity.

The Social Institutions of Cities

The Family.—Turning to what are sometimes called the social institutions, we find characteristic changes in the family, in recreation, in education, and in religion. Many of our cities were settled primarily by single men; others were settled at the very beginning by family groups. As family life developed it commonly took the patriarchal form, the family being large in size and paternal in control. However, with the coming of people of various cultural backgrounds the city came to display numerous forms, until today there is not only the patriarchal family of the immigrant and rural American groups but the so-called emancipated family, with few children and working wives, the equalitarian family on a somewhat higher economic level with few children and with wives engaged in "social" activities outside the home, and finally, the mother-dominated family from which the husband and father is absent most of the time in the conduct of his business or profession.

In general the changes that have taken place in American families, especially in cities, involve an increase in the number of married women working outside their homes, a decrease in the number of relatives, lodgers and servants, a declining birth rate, the diffusion of knowledge of contraception, an increase in divorce, and increased living in multiple dwellings. It is impossible to arrange these various changes in any particular order, but taken together they seem to represent a general direction of change in American city families. It is a change involving fewer functions, fewer members, more scattered activities, narrower quarters, and more democratic control. These changes have already been discussed in Chap. VI.

Recreation.—It is somewhat easier to identify a generalized sequence of events in the development of recreation in American cities. In an early day this was chiefly informal in character. There were dances, picnics, card parties, church socials, weddings, and funerals. During the nineteenth century there developed numerous recreational agencies on a commercial basis. These included the theater, public dance hall, skating rink, bowling alley, billiard parlor, and saloon. Perhaps to these should be added places with varied activities centering, however, about gambling and prostitution. Many of these commercial recreational institutions were condemned by thoughtful citizens; in fact, the condemnation sometimes extended not only to those more vulnerable ones like the saloon and the brothel, but also to others whose positive contribution to the common life was probably very important. Such were particularly the theater and well-conducted dance halls, billiard parlors, etc. In the last quarter of the nineteenth century there arose a number of semiphilanthropic recreational agencies which were in part attempts to offset the commercial agencies and in part efforts to provide recreation for people who previously had none. Among these semiphilanthropic agencies were the Young Men's and Young Women's Christian and Hebrew Associations, social settlements, institutional churches, and such organizations as Boy and Girl Scouts. Finally, and almost entirely since the beginning of the twentieth century, there have developed public tax-supported recreational facilities. These include parks, playgrounds, gymnasiums, bathing beaches, summer camps, and supervised sports of many kinds. The typical sequence, therefore, in the field of recreation is informal, commercial, semiphilanthropic, and public.

Education.—In early colonial days education was largely informal supplemented by some tutoring. But in New England there were early established public elementary schools. In the middle colonies there were parochial schools and in the South some private schools charging tuition. Later came public high schools and private academies, carrying education to what is now called the secondary level. Some of these academies developed into privately endowed colleges and universities. The next important development was that of vocational education, first in the trades and later in business. This developed under both private and public auspices. Still later came junior colleges and municipal universities, carrying public education to a higher level than any reached heretofore except in the city universities and teachers' colleges. Finally, there has been a significant development of adult education under both public and private auspices. Thus we find both public and private schools from colonial times until now, but there has been a steady increase in the relative importance of tax-supported education. Also, there has been a steady increase in the length of school terms, in the number of years attended, and in the variety of schools available. As in the case of the family, it is hard to specify a particular sequence except the very rough one indicated above, but the general trends seem to be quite clear.

Religion.—In colonial times it was common for a town to have only one type of church, although some places in the middle colonies early had several. As time passed and the population became more heterogeneous there was an increasing diversity of sects until, as we showed in Chap. X, the typical American city now contains a great variety of religious groups. These have become somewhat stratified, depending in part on the date of arrival and in part on the economic status of the communicants. Nevertheless, despite diversity and stratification there has developed, among Protestant churches at least, a fairly strong federation movement as a result of which more tolerance obtains and cooperation of several sorts is carried on. Finally, there is some indication that the churches may be suffering a decline in prestige in our cities. The evidence of these changes is circumstantial, hence subject to dispute.

The Life Cycle Only Partially Identified

We have observed now that in four types of social institutions there have been important changes. In recreation and in religion these can be reduced to a generalized sequence. This is less true of education and still less true of the family. Perhaps when our knowledge of all these is more adequate we may be able to recognize a typical institutional life cycle. For the present this is not possible.

Perhaps part of our difficulty arises from the fact that some of the changes noted are really very general changes in our culture which have affected both rural and urban life. Many of them have appeared first in cities, and some of them have appeared in many cities at about the same time. Other changes seem to be peculiar to our cities and less bound up with general cultural changes. In the first group, *i.e.*, general cultural developments, are changes in transportation and communication, changes in the sources from which urban population has been drawn, changes in such social institutions as the family, recreation, education, and religion. In the second group are the series of changes we identified with rate of growth, economic base, hinterland, internal movements, and we might have added the rise and decline of communities and neighborhoods within our cities. The only justification for considering the first group as involved in the life cycle of cities is that many of these cultural changes originated in cities and had their most complete development there.

Perhaps the most important and most valid generalization we can make in the face of our somewhat confusing data is that cities are losing those characteristics associated with pioneering and rapid growth. Urban populations are still highly mobile, as we noted in Chap. XVIII, but people are moving about within the same city and are moving from city to city so much that there appears to be less difference between our cities than in an earlier day. With the slowing down of the rate of growth, cities should be able to provide more adequately for the populations they have instead of struggling to build more schools, more churches, more stores, more transportation facilities, etc. They can now begin to concentrate on securing better schools and better facilities of every kind. It may not be amiss to call this a form of maturity. We may be justified in saying that our cities are getting over their youthful period of growth and excitement and settling down to a more quiet and more stable development.

Maturation and Standardization

McKenzie has made much of the point that our cities are becoming increasingly alike.[1] His evidence, however, is less convincing than one might desire. We shall examine it with some care in the order that he followed.

First of all, there is increasing occupational uniformity. Less and less frequently are the workers of a given city concentrated in one type of employment. More and more they are distributed among various kinds of gainful work. Moreover, the population in each major occupational group is more and more alike from city to city. This proposition is adequately supported so far as the decade 1920–1930 is concerned, but it is unfortunate that we do not have a long time series.

Next McKenzie calls attention to industrial diversification. Of 16 cities, 10 had a larger percentage of all types of manufacturing reported in 1927 than 1921. Three had a smaller percentage and three about the same. These six may possibly be explained by suburban movements and the decentralization of some industries. We should have studies of other cities and should have data covering the 10 years since the period reported by McKenzie. However, his generalization does accord with common observation.

The distribution of banking is another mark of what McKenzie calls maturation. In 1930 the 100 largest banks of the United States were more scattered than they were in 1923. At the earlier of these dates they were found in 25 cities in 19 metropolitan areas. In 1930 they were found in 30 cities in 27 metropolitan areas. In 1923 nearly one-half of the deposits in the 100 largest banks were in New York City. Including Brooklyn, Newark, Jersey City, and Hoboken, 55 per cent of the deposits in the nation's 100 largest banks were in 34 banks of Greater New York. In 1930 this metropolitan area had only 24 of the 100 largest banks and only 33.7 per cent of their deposits. Again we find the need of more data both for a given period and for a longer series of years.

[1] R. D. McKenzie, *The Metropolitan Community*, Chap. 9, 1933. Data used by permission of the President's Research Committee on Social Trends.

Two other changes have contributed greatly to the standardization of merchandise in American cities. One is the growth of chain stores. The other is the development of national advertising. In 1930 there were over 7,000 retail chains in the United States, operating more than 150,000 stores. For the most part their head offices were concentrated in a few great cities, but this development has spread so generally through the nation that one can buy the same kinds of goods from stores operated in almost identical fashion in many different cities. Similarly, national advertising, which is essentially "good will" advertising, has familiarized the people of the whole country with certain brands of goods and has unquestionably promoted uniformity in buying habits. However, it must not be forgotten that there are still regional and local differences in taste and fashion which neither advertising in magazines of national circulation nor the development of nation-wide chains seems likely to overcome in the near future. No exact measure of uniformities and differences of merchandise handled in different cities is at present available.

Newspaper circulation affords another means of measuring similarities and differences among cities. McKenzie found that over a 20-year period, ending 1929, not only was there an increase in the number of papers sold per 1,000 of the population, but differences between regions decreased. Unfortunately his data are presented according to regions only and not according to separate cities, hence they are indirect rather than direct evidence in support of this proposition.

In like manner McKenzie shows a decline in the average deviation from the mean of several other indexes of maturation or uniformity. These include post-office receipts, motor vehicle registration, telephones, health services, church membership and expenditures, and listing in *Who's Who*. Again our regret is that these indexes were computed for regions rather than for individual cities.

We have attempted to see what other evidence might be found to bear on this problem of uniformity, particularly in the realm of education, which McKenzie treated as he did communication, health, religion, and the others. We assembled data from the *Biennial Survey of Education* for 1930–1932 and for 1932–1934. These recapitulate certain material for a series of preceding years.

To test the general hypothesis that cities are becoming more alike we noted the difference between certain ratios in cities of the largest class (100,000 and over) and cities of the smallest class (2,500 to 10,000). For example, in 1932 the ratio of attendance to enrollment in cities of Class I was 0.863; in cities of Class IV it was 0.864, a difference of 0.001. In 1922 the difference was only 0.003. However, in 1928 it was 0.034, hence what we have here is a series of short-time changes and no well-defined trend. As to the number of days schools were in session, the difference between two classes of cities was 9 in 1921–1922 and 7 in 1933–1934—not an important change. The average number of days attended differed in the two classes of cities by 6 in 1921–1922 and again by 6 in 1931–1932, falling off to 3 in 1933–1934. The percentage of the term lost by nonattendance differed in the two classes of cities by 0.8 in 1921–1922, by −0.4 in 1931–1932, and by 1.7 in 1933–1934. Again we have short-time changes rather than a long-time trend. The percentage of men teachers in the public schools of cities in the two classes differed by 0.2 in 1933, −0.1 in 1930, and −1.9 in 1934. Incidentally, there was an increase in the percentage of men teachers in both large and small cities over the 12-year period. Finally, we consider the percentage of the school enrollment found in each of 13 grades in large and small cities in 1917–1918 and in 1931–1932. The average of the differences in 1917–1918 was 0.77; in 1931–1932 it was 0.67. On the whole we are compelled to conclude that for the period studied the evidence is inconclusive. However, it is our impression that study of a longer series reaching farther into the past would show a trend of the sort postulated by McKenzie.

Selected Readings

MUMFORD, LEWIS: *The Culture of Cities*, Harcourt, Brace & Company, Inc., 1938. Pages 283–292 present an interesting hypothesis concerning the urban cycle of growth and decay.

MCKENZIE, R. D.: *The Metropolitan Community*, McGraw-Hill Book Company, Inc., 1933. Chapter 1 outlines stages in the development of American cities; Chap. 9 discusses trends in terms of maturation.

WOOLSTON, HOWARD B.: *Metropolis: A Study of Urban Communities*, D. Appleton-Century Company, Inc., 1938. Chapter 14 deals with urban trends.

GIST, NOEL P., and L. A. HALBERT: *Urban Society*, The Thomas Y. Crowell Company, 1933. Chapter 23 discusses the future of urbanism.

CARPENTER, NILES: *The Sociology of City Life*, Longmans, Green & Company, 1931. Chapters 13 and 14 discuss the urban prospect.

Chapter XXIII

CITY AND REGIONAL PLANNING—PHYSICAL ASPECTS

We have seen, especially in Chap. XIII, that cities tend to develop according to some sort of pattern without formal planning or direction. More or less spontaneously commerce, industry, and residence seem to find separate and appropriate locations. In the first place, geographic features are largely influential in determining the sites of first settlement, of transportation routes and terminals, of major industries, etc. In the second place, the processes of expansion and succession tend to produce a pattern that resembles a series of concentric circles. Hence, without anyone having willed it in advance, we commonly find a central business district near the site of first settlement, railroads and heavy industries in the valleys, blighted areas near the heart of the city and adjacent to some outlying industries, good residential sections on high ground toward the periphery, a belt of suburban development surrounding the main city, and finally a hinterland that both supports and depends upon the urban center. All this may be called natural in the sense of being unpredicted and undirected. But planning is rarely wholly absent. The actual city of today is the result of a little planning and much spontaneous development.

The Nature and Purpose of City Planning

In the chapters that have gone before, the reader can hardly have avoided the growing impression that, despite the evidences of regularity and system in our cities, there is also a very great deal of confusion. This is made more vivid when he examines the map of almost any American city. Usually the streets represent approximations to a system but there are many curious arrangements and many instances in which there is a serious lack of alignment and integration. This lack is due probably to the separate adding of one subdivision after another, each laid out with little reference to the city as a whole. Upon examining a land-use map, or, if none is available, upon driving about a city, one is immediately impressed with the intermingling of commercial and industrial properties with residences. Often apartment houses and single dwellings are found in the same block. In other words, there is no orderly classification of districts or allocation to specific uses. Out toward the periphery one finds very uneven development. Some sections will be quite undeveloped, while others, farther out, will be closely built up. In general, there are about twice as many lots staked out as there are occupied by residences or other buildings.

Now all this crazy-quilt effect is bound up with a serious instability of property values. Sometimes a garage, a laundry, a beauty parlor, or an undertaking establishment is set down in the midst of a residential district. Because there is often danger that any of these may be located next door, homeowners feel rather insecure and frequently experience sharp declines in the value of their real estate. Also there is instability of neighborhood and community life. The invasion of commerce and industry may, as we have pointed out in Chaps. XIV and XV, quite disorganize, if not actually destroy, a previously well-developed neighborhood group.

Other aspects of the city which indicate a need of planning are the menaces to health. Some houses are built on lowlands which are damp and smoky. Others are near undrained marshes where mosquitoes breed. Others are close to streams which carry sewage and other waste material. The poor organization of residential, commercial, and industrial activities in a city compels people to spend much time coming and going over considerable distances. As a result streets are congested with automobiles. Electric cars and busses are crowded. Much time and energy is consumed and, in fact, a good many lives are lost by reason of the congested traffic in almost every American city. Those who drive downtown have, furthermore, the problem of finding a place to park. Usually they must spend a considerable sum or risk leaving the car some distance from their place of employment, thus using up still more time and encountering added inconvenience. In addition, the automobile owner runs the risk of theft and injury. When he wants to go out on a holiday he joins a long line of slow-moving cars and, in general, finds it hard to decide whether his ownership of a motor vehicle is more of an advantage than a nuisance.

One interesting aspect of the extent to which our cities are planned piecemeal is the way in which subways and tall buildings affect each other. Through the erection of skyscrapers and large apartment houses, means of transportation are crowded. But when more subways, elevated lines, and other facilities are provided, still more skyscrapers and apartment houses are built along the route. Thus everything that is done to relieve congestion seems to make it greater.

We have not mentioned numerous other facts which are further evidences that our cities are planned only to a limited extent. We might speak of the ugliness, the lawlessness, the multiplicity of governmental units, and many others.

In the face of such conditions as we have just enumerated, a growing number of people have been interested in the development of what has come to be called city planning. This has been defined as "the ordering of the physical elements of a region or a city so that each will serve most effectively in an economical, efficient, healthful, and agreeable development of the entire area."[1] Obviously this places the emphasis upon the physical structure of the city, but the objectives have to do with efficiency, safety, health, beauty, convenience, and order. City planning is made up of four fundamental parts. First, there is research into the situation as it exists and has developed. Second, is the civic design, the drawing up of plans and specifications for the urban layout. Third, there is regulation by law, which involves legislation and its enforcement in order to make possible the carrying out of a plan which may be devised. Finally, there is the influencing of public opinion: primarily, to secure necessary legislation; but also, to induce the owners of private property to do their part in achieving the purposes of a city plan. Stated a little more definitely, city planning may be said to have these six aspects: engineering, architectural, landscape architectural, economic, legal, and sociological.

When it comes to the actual practice of such planning, it is evident that there are some serious limitations. There are few chances to plan new cities from the start. For the most part we are restricted to the expensive task of remodeling existing cities. To be sure, there is bound to be some rebuilding and

[1] *Social Work Year Book*, 1937, p. 416. By permission of the Russell Sage Foundation.

some expansion, both of which afford opportunities for taking advantage of a definite plan. But because much of the land is already occupied, and because there are many vested interests, city planning in practice involves a multitude of compromises. There are other difficulties. Sometimes those who deal in real estate wish to have a plan which will aid them in their business but not do much else. Sometimes ambitious public officials promote the development of expensive ornamental features when there are many more urgent needs at hand. Because of the plurality of governmental units which we described in Chap. XI, there is usually no single authority with power to make and enforce plans for an entire metropolitan district. Finally, it is hard for people to visualize a master plan. They can conceive and understand the limited program of a drainage system, or a civic center, or a railroad terminal, but they find it difficult to think in terms of a comprehensive program.

Despite all the difficulties which have been encountered, the city planning movement has spread rather rapidly since the beginning of the twentieth century. There are now over 700 municipal planning agencies. There are 100 metropolitan and regional planning bodies, and recently there have been establised county and state planning boards or commissions. Only 2 cities over 300,000 and only 10 cities between 100,000 and 300,000 were without such official agencies in 1934.[1]

City Planning before 1900

Ancient, mediaeval, and renaissance cities had problems of congestion, of haphazard spreading of towns into rural environs, of excess of building bulk in relation to width of street, of blighted areas, and of defective housing of the common people. In some periods they showed extravagance in public buildings at the cost of human welfare, and in others parsimony in civic improvement in the interest of private gain.[2]

There are many indications that city planning was not wholly absent from the ancient world. Some cities of western Asia, like Babylon and Nineveh, were consciously designed. A number of Greek cities were constructed according to a thought-out

[1] *Ibid.*, p. 416.

[2] Thomas Adams, *Outline of Town and City Planning*, 1935, p. 132. By permission of the Russell Sage Foundation.

form in the fifth century B.C. In fact, throughout the ancient world the gridiron pattern, which has been widely used in this country, was very common. It was probably derived from the rectangular form of farm plots and military camps. The latter influence is especially apparent in provincial towns of the Roman Empire which were founded as colonies for soldiers. Ancient cities were usually crowded, but this compactness was due to the necessity of getting many buildings inside the walls. The best documentary evidence that the Romans were interested in city planning is found in the writings of the architect Vitruvius. He dealt with the city walls, public buildings, and streets. He emphasized the importance of symmetry, convenience, and economy.

In the middle ages there was not much city planning, although it appears that some towns were established by various rulers as fortresses. In order to hold conquered territory, rulers would build fortified places, in which they urged some of their subjects to live, assuming responsibility for their defense. Even those which were not constructed primarily as fortresses were laid out with definite reference to military considerations. That is, inside the walls there were circular streets from which radial streets ran toward the center.

In the Renaissance there were some cases of city planning which deserve attention. In 1607, Henry IV issued an edict setting up a major street system for Paris. Later, plans were made for improving the health of the inhabitants and adding to the dignity of the capital city. A series of half a dozen more or less comprehensive plans for Paris culminated in the famous project of Haussmann, which was initiated in 1853.

After the great fire of 1666, Christopher Wren prepared a plan for London, but it was not adopted. One hundred years later, John Gwynn made a comprehensive study and plan for London and Westminster, but it too seems to have fallen by the wayside.

Edinburgh adopted a plan drawn by James Craig in 1767. This was a rectangular layout which differed considerably from the early form of the city. Later plans supplemented this, so that in the end, Adams holds, "Edinburgh is one of the classic examples where good city planning and good architecture combined to create a high standard of civic design."[1] But after

[1] *Ibid.*, p. 113.

the coming of the railways, numerous unfinished projects were stopped, and "civic art in Edinburgh was neglected."

Other European cities were planned more or less comprehensively during the seventeenth, eighteenth, and nineteenth centuries. Among these were Berlin in 1646, Mannheim in 1699, St. Petersburg in 1703. In 1801 Vienna was rather well laid out, but Adams has not been able to find any record of comprehensive planning at any time in its history.

Town and city planning in America began in the seventeenth century. The Massachusetts Company engaged an engineer who drew up a plan for Charlestown; this, however, was early abandoned. Cambridge was planned, and building lines were enforced. Also, the location of slaughterhouses and distilleries was regulated here in the late seventeenth century. In the southern colonies, Williamsburg, Va., and Charleston, S. C., were systematically laid out. But the most comprehensive street plan devised in colonial times was William Penn's checkerboard scheme for Philadelphia in 1682.

In 1811 a street plan on the gridiron pattern was prepared for New York City. There was no provision for diagonal streets which might follow the lines of the island, except for Broadway. There was a lack of open spaces. Because most traffic was then from river to river, there were many narrow streets running east and west and a smaller number running north and south. The present street pattern of lower Manhattan, with its utter lack of adaptation to modern conditions, is our legacy from this 1811 plan.

In 1791, Pierre L'Enfant was invited to draw up a comprehensive plan for Washington, D. C. He took full advantage of his remarkable opportunity to lay out a new city unhampered by long-existent conditions and interests. His plan is marked by spaciousness, by the settings and approaches to buildings, and by their reciprocal relation. He used a rectangular scheme, on which he superimposed diagonal streets adjusted to the topography. At important intersections he provided large circles and squares. Later there were established building lines and regulations of material and height. According to Adams, "The plan remains as the one monumental example of comprehensive planning in the United States."[1]

[1] *Ibid.*, p. 127.

Other American cities which were planned in the early years of the republic included Paterson, Buffalo, and Detroit. L'Enfant prepared a plan for Paterson; it was not followed systematically, but it did influence the subsequent layout. Detroit was planned after a fire about 1807. This first plan was rather formal and grandiose. It presented such difficulties that it was only partly carried out. A second plan for Detroit, in 1831, omitted many of the previously proposed radial avenues, circles, and squares. In 1853 the same city was replanned in terms of a fairly rigid gridiron system with three radial streets.

On the whole, city planning received very little attention from nineteenth-century Americans. However, a number of influences which we have previously discussed were shaping our cities. Notable among these were the railroads, whose officials and engineers paid little attention to a city's appearance and local needs. Witness the way in which the Illinois Central occupied the lake front in Chicago. A second was the trolleys and elevated lines, which introduced noise, darkened windows, and increased congestion. In the latter part of the century the use of steel and concrete led to the erection of taller buildings. The expansion of business and industry, together with the waves of immigration, pushed the old residents farther and farther from the inner city, and apparently made them rather indifferent about the appearance, healthfulness, and safety of the growing areas of blight. Eventually there was, on the part of some persons, a growing concern for problems of sanitation, housing, the design of public buildings and places, transportation and traffic control, parks, and new subdivisions.

In 1893, the World's Fair at Chicago gave a great impetus to city planning in terms of beautification. There were already a few parks. There were some rather carefully planned industrial suburbs like Pullman (Chicago), Garden City (New York), Hershey (Philadelphia), and Sparrows Point (Baltimore). A few scattered reformers had attempted to lay out model towns, and there were some wealthy suburbs which were skillfully designed. But it was the World's Fair which brought architecture and landscaping together into a single project. To be sure, the emphasis was on monumental architecture, but the influence was strong and far-reaching.

Twentieth-century Developments

With the turn of the century came some new forces which had to be taken account of in the development of city planning. Among these were the motorcar, electrical power, and taller skyscrapers. There continued to be a rapid increase in urban population. The traffic problem was becoming more and more acute. Municipal government was adding to its functions and costs under the watchful eyes of bosses and their machines. Speculation in urban real estate was rampant and yet there was a demand for aesthetic, sanitary, and recreational features which gave a positive impetus to the movement for city planning.

In 1901, there was a revision of the original plan for Washington, D. C., designed to improve the parks, secure more appropriate settings for public buildings, and to provide a suitable railroad terminal. This plan was not adopted as a whole, but some of its features were put into effect. Other cities adopted plans for civic centers and transportation facilities. Among these were Cleveland, Harrisburg, and Denver. San Francisco in 1906 missed a wonderful opportunity to revise its street pattern and dominant architecture, just as Chicago had missed its great chance in 1871.

Chicago, however, in the twentieth century did make an important contribution to city planning. Under the leadership of Daniel Burnham, and with funds privately contributed, an elaborate city plan was drawn up and published by the Commercial Club in 1909. It dramatized architectural possibilities, but it paid little attention to such matters as street improvement, railroad rights of way and terminals, parks, playgrounds, piers, bridges, and lake-front reclamation. Its chief omission was lack of any proposals for controlling the development and use of private property. Although Burnham's plan was never formally accepted by the city, numerous major improvements have been carried out in conformity with it.

The Chicago plan and some less known ones which followed it emphasized the city beautiful. They were inspirational, but their costliness provoked a reaction against them. Nevertheless plans continued to be made for a number of cities, both large and small, in the years which followed. In their development, a small group of landscape architects was especially active.

Among the more important recent developments in city planning in the United States are the establishment of central authorities, the drawing of master plans, the extension of planning to metropolitan areas and whole regions. As was indicated earlier in this chapter, there are now hundreds of municipal planning boards and commissions. In 1913 the Massachusetts legislature passed a mandatory law requiring every city of 10,000 or over to set up a planning board. Master plans, to which we have referred, began to displace separate and unrelated programs for streets, railroads, recreational facilities, public buildings, and zoning. Sometimes these were prepared by private organizations and sometimes by public departments. Sometimes they were officially adopted, and sometimes they exerted only an indirect influence. The metropolitan and regional plans represented, as we have stated, extensions of city planning to larger and larger areas surrounding our cities. These will be discussed in more detail a little later. In the last few years there has begun to be some planning on a state-wide and even on a national basis. Since 1919 the Massachusetts department of public welfare has had a division of housing and town planning. In 1933 a National Planning Board was set up with the major object of interesting people throughout the nation in comprehensive planning. It urged each state government to appoint an official planning board, and as a matter of fact some of them did. In 1934 the National Planning Board was merged with the National Resources Board. The chief objective of the latter is the preparation of a plan for the development and use of natural resources; along with that, it is devoted to the promotion of regional planning.

Zoning and Other Details

There is one aspect of planning which has been so widely adopted and is so generally known that it is frequently mistaken for city planning as a whole. This is commonly known as zoning, and is the regulation of land use and buildings. It deals with such matters as height, building lines, the percentage of a lot which may be occupied, and the districting of a city with a view to specialization.

The need for zoning has been partly indicated in considering the need for city planning in general. But the factors which made city fathers most ready to adopt zoning ordinances were the unsettling of property values and premature depressions, the destruction of neighborhoods and communities, unsightliness due to the hodgepodge of all sorts of buildings of irregular building lines and heights. However, the early zoning was very far from solving these problems, for there was rather limited information available and there was much pressure from speculators in real estate. Hence there was very unsatisfactory distribution of land for various uses. Commonly too little was zoned for single dwellings and too much for multiple dwellings and commercial and industrial properties. Whenever a residential district was threatened with invasion, property owners who became panic-stricken wanted the district immediately zoned for business or industry in order that they might quickly realize hoped-for gains from the sale of land. Because this was overdone, many old residential sections were partly occupied by stores, factories, etc., instead of a few sections being completely taken over for these purposes.

The earliest case of anything like zoning which we have found in America was the Massachusetts legislation of 1692, which directed the selectmen of three towns to assign special places for slaughterhouses, distilleries, and other establishments which might easily be nuisances. Thereafter for nearly 200 years there was almost nothing of this sort so far as we have been able to discover. In 1885 the town of Modesto, Calif., excluded Chinese launderers from residential districts. Following this lead, San Francisco, Los Angeles, and Sacramento restricted the location not only of laundries but of dance halls, saloons, livery stables, and some other businesses. In 1899 Washington, D. C., regulated the heights of buildings, being followed in this by Baltimore, Indianapolis, and other cities. From 1909 to 1915 a number of separate ordinances divided Los Angeles into residential, commercial, and industrial districts, with regulations for each district. In 1916 New York adopted what seems to be the first comprehensive zoning of height, area, and use through a single ordinance. Now there are 1,200 municipalities with zoning ordinances and only seven cities of 100,000 or over which lack such legislation.

In addition to zoning there are several other detailed activities which may be carried on separately or as parts of a city plan.

These include the laying out of new suburbs, the establishment of civic centers, and the development of railway terminals, slum clearance, park systems, harbor facilities, airports, major thoroughfares, etc. One of the most interesting and perhaps the best-planned new suburb is Radburn, N. J., with its scheme of service drives to back doors, no streets in the front of houses, adequate and easily accessible play spaces for children, detached but easily reached garages and streets. Some of the most striking civic centers have been established or are still in the process of development in San Francisco, Denver, Cleveland, St. Louis. Slum clearance projects were discussed in Chap. VI. The other details have been already presented or will be taken up in another section.

Metropolitan Planning

Over and over again we have had occasion to emphasize the fact that a city rarely ends at its official limits. This is relevant to city planning as well as to other aspects of urbanism which we have considered. What we are interested in here is a master plan intended as a guide for the planning of separate municipalities within a metropolitan area and as a means of coordinating them so that there may be harmony, convenience, and efficiency in the whole. Metropolitan and regional planning are often confused. The latter term should be restricted to plans for the use of natural resources and the integration of rural and urban interests throughout an extended region; metropolitan planning is strictly urban in character.

The reason for metropolitan planning should by this time be obvious to any student of the city. Not only plural government and the common problems of traffic, police, fire, drainage, sanitation, and all the rest, but the necessity of having a well-devised system of through streets, the regulation of real estate subdivisions, the distribution of trading subcenters, all emphasize the importance of unified planning for a metropolitan area. Already the idea has spread so widely that there are something like 100 official boards and unofficial associations devoted to such metropolitan planning.

One of the earliest instances was the preparation of a plan for Greater Boston by Robert Copeland in 1872. Later in the same district there was set up a Metropolitan Improvement Commission responsible for the planning of parks, sanitation, and highways. Its work was not called metropolitan or regional planning and it was not actually that in a comprehensive sense, but it represented definite steps in that direction. Allegheny County (Pittsburgh) had an unofficial Planning Commission from 1918 on, and an official board from 1923. Los Angeles County created a Regional Planning Commission in 1922. An unofficial Regional Planning Association was set up in Chicago in 1923. This organization has agreements with the United States Bureau of Public Roads, the Illinois Division of Highways, and the Chicago Planning Commission that they will all adhere to the highway plan drawn up, unless it is modified after discussion. A similar privately supported organization was the Regional Planning Federation of the Philadelphia Tri-State District set up in 1924 and reporting in 1932. For the Buffalo region the Niagara Frontier Planning Board was established in 1925.

But by all means the most comprehensive and best known metropolitan plan is that which bears the title of *Regional Plan for New York and Its Environs.*[1] This venture was initiated by some private individuals and sponsored by the Russell Sage Foundation. A Regional Planning Association was set up on a unofficial basis but with the cooperation of public officials in and about metropolitan New York. The territory covered is about twice as large as that which the United States Census Bureau considers to be the metropolitan area of Greater New York, but it is smaller than what we would ordinarily consider to be the region dependent upon and tributary to a great city. Specifically, this plan has to do with an area of 5,500 square miles covering parts of 3 states, all or a part of 22 counties, 400 municipalities, and a population of over 11 million people. The survey conducted by the Regional Planning Association dealt with the geography, history, and population of the area. It included an especially careful study of the economic life with particular emphasis upon recent trends such as the gravitating of manufacturing to a belt about halfway between the central city and

[1] The committee which fostered this plan published eight volumes based on an extensive and intensive survey, and two volumes which set forth the plan which grew out of this research. The whole is interestingly and simply summarized by R. L. Duffus, *Mastering a Metropolis*, 1930.

the periphery of the area. The inquiry sought answers to such questions as these: What activities can be carried on at the center; what ones must be; what others would be more advantageously located farther out? The study of industries and their location was, of course, directly related to population trends and to traffic problems. Hence the study of trafficways and transportation was another significant part of the survey. Still others had to do with parks, housing, government.

The plan itself was similarly comprehensive. First of all it proposed a definite scheme of railroads, including trunk lines, outer and inner belt lines, commuters' lines, and terminals conveniently located in various sections of the city. It provided a system of highways and byways, broad through streets, express highways, either elevated or depressed loops or belt lines, and by-passes. It proposed several major north and south routes, a few diagonals and grade separations. Closely related to the general system of highways and streets was the program for parkways and boulevards which were intended to expedite traffic and to afford pleasure. A large part of the regional planning had to do, of course, with land use. It proposed that certain districts should be built up while others should be open. It proposed that certain sections should be residential, others industrial, still others commercial. It was based on the proposition, adequately demonstrated by the survey, that "there is ample room in our great regional apartment if we arrange the furniture sensibly."[1] The development which was indicated in the plan was for Manhattan to continue as the center of marketing, banking, finer manufacturing, and commercial recreation. Brooklyn, Queens, the Bronx, and Staten Island were to expand as centers of industry and residence. Heavy industry was to move gradually into New Jersey, where ocean and railroad terminals could be provided, where relatively inexpensive land was available. Residential sections were to be settled conveniently near, but unspoiled by, industries. For many of these projects, especially on the New Jersey side of the Hudson River, extensive reclamation projects were shown to be necessary. All through the area parks, parkways, golf courses, and other open spaces were to be carefully distributed. Land for these purposes was to be purchased in advance of close settlement

[1] Duffus, *op. cit.*, p. 186.

whenever possible, in order both to make sure of providing the needed open spaces and to avoid excessive cost. Other parts of the plan had to do with the development and protection of neighborhoods, civic centers, airports, and, in fact, nearly every aspect of the physical city.

Regional Planning

As was indicated above, there has been a tendency to confuse metropolitan and regional planning. In the case of New York this is perhaps forgivable because the territory dealt with is larger than the metropolitan area but smaller than the metropolitan region. But in general, regional planning involves the study and planning of the conservation, development, and utilization of natural resources, the coordination of rural and urban activities, the distribution of industries throughout the region, and the development of transportation facilities. Among the examples we have of regional planning bodies are the New England Regional Planning Commission, the Pacific Northwest Regional Planning Commission, and the Tennessee Valley Authority.

This last grew up in part out of the problems associated with the power plant and manufacturing of nitrates at Muscle Shoals. President Roosevelt realized that the production of electrical power and the manufacture of explosives and fertilizers represented only a small part of the possible development in the Tennessee Valley. There were also closely related problems of flood control, soil erosion, afforestation, withdrawal from agriculture of submarginal lands, distribution and diversification of industry. So in 1933 the Tennessee Valley Authority was established, with responsibility for 40,000 square miles, reaching into seven states. The belief behind this great project was that through the integration of work at these various tasks each of them could be more adequately carried out. Thus a series of coordinated dams and power sites could more effectively use water power in the development of electricity; unified transmission could more easily furnish power to all the people of the region and could make it available at a lower rate. Together with afforestation, the dams which made water power available could also help guard against floods. Flood control meant a reduction in soil erosion, which was bound to promote the prosperity of farmers. But there were already twice as many people in agriculture as were needed for its work. Hence the plan included the establishment of local industries with cheap power and producing a diversity of products. When some land was flooded, families had to be moved and highways had to be relocated. To provide for men working at the new construction and in the power plants and factories new towns were laid out in detail. This indicates only a few of the features of regional planning in the Tennessee Valley. It is intended to suggest the extent to which every phase of a people's life may be bound up with every other phase, and the necessity of considering their interrelations if the most effective solution is to be found for the separate problems involved. Regional planning is a relatively new thing in America. Its possibilities are as yet scarcely explored. It seems likely, however, to become a permanent and important aspect of our national life.

Summary

One of the major themes of this book has been that cities tend to develop rather well-defined patterns, both physical and cultural, without their having been anticipated or promoted. But these "natural" patterns frequently prove unsatisfactory, especially as they are affected by growth in numbers and by cultural changes. Congestion, disharmony, instability, hazards to health and safety, inconvenience, and mounting costs of living and of carrying on business—these are some of the major complaints against great cities which have created a demand for systematic planning.

Now city planning is not absolutely new. Indeed there are evidences of it in cities of the ancient world. But its systematic development as a deliberate combining of research, civic design, regulation by law, and molding of public opinion is quite recent. Through the nineteenth century there was some planning of details but rarely the projection of a master plan. The initiative for more comprehensive plans came largely from private persons and civic groups. But now more than 700 American cities have official planning boards and commissions. Only a dozen cities of 100,000 or over are without such agencies.

Zoning, slum clearance, and the development of suburban districts, civic centers, and terminals are important parts of city planning but not substitutes for a comprehensive program, as is mistakenly supposed.

In the last 15 or 20 years there has been a growing recognition of the fact that the separate planning of individual municipalities in metropolitan areas is also inadequate. Hence there have appeared a number of so-called regional plans. Although these are really metropolitan, there are a few cases of genuine regional planning, of which the Tennessee Valley Authority is the best known.

City and regional planning as discussed in this chapter have to do largely with physical aspects of cities. In the next chapter we shall consider the demand for and the development of planning in the realms of business, government, neighborhood and community life, recreation, religion, health, and social work.

Selected Readings

Adams, Thomas: *Outline of Town and City Planning*, Russell Sage Foundation, 1935. An excellent discussion of the history and principles of city planning.

Mumford, Lewis: *The Culture of Cities*, Harcourt, Brace & Company, Inc., 1938. Chapters 6 and 7 present a philosophy of regional and city planning. Physical and social aspects are intimately related. The whole is challengingly presented.

Bassett, Edward M.: *Zoning: The Laws, Administration and Court Decisions during the First Twenty Years*, Russell Sage Foundation, 1936.

Duffus, R. L.: *Mastering a Metropolis*, Harper & Brothers, 1930. A readable summary of the voluminous survey and plan for New York and its environs.

Regional Plan of New York and Its Environs, published by the organization of the same name, 1927–1930. Eight volumes report the regional survey; two volumes present the regional plan.

Chapter XXIV

SOCIAL PLANNING

In the preceding chapter we confined our attention almost entirely to the planning of a city's physical structure. However, we found it impossible to consider streets without reference to traffic, parks without reference to recreation, zoning without reference to mobility, etc. In other words, physical and social planning are inevitably bound up together. Hence there is an effort to integrate the specialized tasks, such as those of the architect, landscape architect, engineer, attorney, economist, and of specialists in the fields of government, education, religion, public health, and social work. Each of these represents a particular interest, and each possesses a particular body of knowledge and skill. But none of them can do his work effectively except as he collaborates with the others. City planning is of necessity a coordination of many interests. It is a comprehensive program of research, designing, construction, regulation, and education. It is inclusive in another sense, namely, that no municipality can be planned effectively except in relation to its environs. As was shown in Chap. XXIII, city planning leads inevitably to metropolitan and regional planning.

Now it happens that most of the urban planning recognized as such has dealt primarily with physical aspects of single municipalities. But there has been a great deal of unlabeled planning in the realms of business, government, social work, education, and religion. Chambers of commerce, bureaus of municipal research, councils of social agencies, boards of education, and church federations have been studying the city from the standpoints of their particular interests, have been outlining programs for the fulfillment of their purposes, and have been trying to "sell" their ideas to the public. But only to a very limited extent have these several groups worked together. Still less have they united people in various parts of a metropolitan area in comprehensive planning.

Economic Planning

We have seen that physical planning necessarily involves one phase of economic planning, namely, the location of various types of business and industry. The allocation of certain districts to heavy industry, others to light manufacturing and wholesaling, others to retail establishments, and still others to terminal facilities is well under way. But many errors have been committed, especially in the form of assigning too much space to commerce and industry, too little to exclusively residential uses. Much zoning has been based—not altogether unwisely—on present land uses and those anticipated on the basis of recent trends. But careful study, such as accompanied the making of a plan for New York and its environs, shows that business and industry are not always successful in finding the most appropriate sites. Separate efforts, even joint guesses, often lead business-men astray or leave them helpless in the face of forces beyond their individual control. The problem is very complicated, for the location of industrial and commercial establishments involves relations to other businesses, dwellings and transportation for employees, transportation of raw materials and finished products, accessibility to customers, and the possibility that they may be nuisances to the occupants of adjacent land.

In the United States economic planning for cities has not gone far beyond the attempt to direct the spatial distribution of economic activities over a metropolitan area or region. However, this does not mean that there has been no attention to the integration of supply services and disposal of waste, the provision of public utilities, the adaptation of urban commerce and industry to the region's needs, or the utilization of natural resources in the hinterland. What we mean is that there has been little evidence that these matters were viewed as integral parts of metropolitan planning.

Many cities have through one agency or another given attention to marketing facilities, both wholesale and retail. But this has been largely from the standpoint of promoting the sales of individual firms or groups of firms, rather than from the standpoint of consumer needs and a balanced economic life for the city and its region. In some instances municipalities have established public markets, but these are rarely distributed throughout the city; their location is determined with reference to their own success as business ventures rather than with reference to supplementing or supplanting existing stores. Zoning, which might be expected to control the distribution of marketing activities, has followed rather than guided the development of retail outlets along string streets and in subcenters.

In contrast to markets, the disposal of waste has come to be planned for an entire municipality, though not for a whole metropolitan area. Garbage, ashes, and trash are collected by municipal departments or by contractors who assume responsibility for the municipality. Sewage disposal is commonly a municipal function, not a metropolitan one.

The diversification of industry, which was discussed in Chap. VII, has been urged by businessmen's organizations and by newspapers, but it seems to be developing more spontaneously than under direction. The bringing in of a new industry is usually heralded not as an instance of diversification but as an increase in the number of customers of merchants, clients of professional men, members of churches, etc.

Likewise the adaptation of city and region goes forward more or less haphazardly. Individuals and corporations, of course, consider how they may secure raw materials cheaply and how they may sell finished products to advantage in their trade area. But there has been little joint effort to develop in an urban center industries that could make maximum use of regional resources and could offer maximum service to the region's population.

Such economic planning as we find has often been the work of chambers of commerce, although they are not, strictly speaking, planning bodies. Perhaps one reason why they have not devoted more attention to comprehensive planning is that their general pattern of activity was set long ago in an era of commercial and industrial expansion on a thoroughly competitive basis. The New York Chamber was founded in 1768. Before the Civil War there were 30 such bodies. However, their greatest development numerically has come in more recent years, reaching a total of about 2,000.

Chambers of commerce[1] are essentially businessmen's organizations, to which are sometimes attached professional men, public

[1] *Encyclopaedia of the Social Sciences*, vol. 3, pp. 325–328.

officials, and farmers. They are private organizations, built up by membership campaigns, supported by dues, and usually managed by paid secretaries. In general they perform two kinds of functions: (*a*) technical and administrative services for their members, (*b*) representation of business interests before governmental bodies. In the first group are included efforts to secure better transportation, provision of labor supply, advertising local products, attracting tourists and conventions, arranging sales days, etc. In the second group are included issuing publicity about pending legislation, calling on public officials, holding hearings, and otherwise seeking to exert pressure on government in the interest of merchants and manufacturers of the city or region.

Often members of chambers of commerce mistakenly imagine that they represent the entire populace. Frequently they undertake to act in the name of a whole community, metropolitan area, or region. They initiate or support civic programs which they regard as beneficial to everybody. Thus they "get behind" movements to reorganize municipal government, to construct express highways, to provide parking space, to develop parks, to increase the water supply, to get "chiselers" off relief, to balance the municipal budget. But it is reasonable to believe that such efforts are exerted primarily for the benefit of "business"—not in conscious opposition to the welfare of "labor," agriculture, or consumers, but with the somewhat dubious assumption that what is good for business is good for everybody. Further support for this belief may be drawn from the facts that chambers of commerce commonly oppose municipal ownership of gas, electricity, street railway, and other public utilities; that they seek to maintain or to establish the "open shop," or the so-called "American plan"; that they discourage consumers' cooperation. Sometimes they are identified with campaigns against "liberals" and "radicals." Thus it seems clear that chambers of commerce, though perfectly legitimate organizations of businessmen, have not functioned to any great extent as economic planning bodies; nor have the plans they project always been integrated into a more comprehensive program of social planning.

Perhaps it is inevitable that in a culture whose economic complex rests on the principles of private ownership and "free" competition economic planning should be undeveloped. One lesson of the "New Deal" seems to be that we may choose between individual competition and economic planning but that we cannot easily combine them—if at all. About all that has been accomplished so far is to unite the businessmen of one area against those in another, to unite employers against wage earners, to unite the makers and purveyors of one product (*e.g.*, cotton) against those dealing in another (*e.g.*, silk). This is hardly economic planning in any comprehensive sense.

Governmental Planning

In Chap. XI we pointed out the great need of replanning the governmental structure of metropolitan areas. We showed that political units have been brought into being one at a time, often with overlapping and even conflicting jurisdictions. This happened in part because previously separate communities were growing together, in part because citizens distrusted established authorities, in part because there were newcomers to the public "trough." We described in that chapter the partial development of metropolitan government and the struggles that are still going on.

Within individual municipalities, and sometimes extending throughout a state or the nation, there are voters' leagues, taxpayers' associations, bureaus of governmental research, and all sorts of good government movements. These are usually concerned with particular issues, such as civil service, the council-manager form of government, a balanced budget, or simply the ejection of a powerful "machine." Occasionally such a group may study the whole political structure of a metropolitan area and outline a plan for its reorganization. But most frequently its attention is confined to details and to segments of the metropolitan area. Such replanning of government as occurs is almost inevitably bound up with city planning in the physical sense. It also overlaps the planning of recreation, education, public health, social case work, neighborhoods, and communities.

One aspect of government in urban areas concerning which there has been much discussion and little action is the tax structure. The general property tax, special assessments, license fees, and fines do not constitute a satisfactory basis for the support of local government under urban conditions. They are particularly inadequate, confusing, and irritating when, as in

Chicago, there are numerous independent bodies with power to assess and levy taxes on the same group of citizens, and when a given person's taxable interests are divided among several municipalities in the same metropolitan area.

To us the need of an integrated metropolitan government seems obvious. But most people are bound by tradition, and those with vested interests are always ready to defend the *status quo*. Hence efforts to promote metropolitan government have been partial and halting. As we reported in Chap. XI, these programs have taken the forms of annexation, city-county consolidation, expansion of county functions, intermunicipal agreements and joint undertakings, special districts and authorities having to do with water, sewage, transportation, and health services. Such limited programs of coordination and unification have been put into effect in various places. No comprehensive plan has been adopted anywhere in the United States, although inclusive schemes of government have been seriously considered in Oakland, Pittsburgh, and Cleveland.

Educational Planning

The story of city planning for education is simply told. With the development of public school systems having governing boards and superintendents there was partial integration of urban education. But city boards of education have had little or no authority over private schools. Usually they enforce the attendance laws, sometimes they provide school health service. But compulsory aspects of the curriculum are usually set forth by state rather than municipal authorities. Thus there is little or no central planning that covers parochial, commercial, "progressive," "workers'" education. Furthermore, there are in every metropolitan area several, or many, independent school districts. Both within and without municipalities are found separate boards of education with separate taxing and spending powers, separate administrative officers, and separate programs of work. There is some informal consultation, but no comprehensive planning.

Religious Planning

In the field of urban religion there have been some definite efforts to bring about joint planning, but, as in the realms of business, government, and education, they have been partial and not especially successful. It has been well said that "the American city is a veritable jungle of religious organizations."[1] In every urban center of 100,000 or over may be found from 20 to 50 denominations. Representing each denomination or sect there are varying numbers of local churches, sometimes carefully located and centrally controlled but often established and conducted with little reference to other churches even of their own faith. In general the Catholic churches are founded in accordance with a diocesan plan, while the Protestant and Jewish congregations, like Topsy, "just growed." To be sure, there are some intra- and interdenominational affiliations which promote and facilitate joint action. Among them are ministerial alliances, Sunday school associations, women's missionary unions, men's brotherhoods, and leagues of young people. But these are not planning bodies. Also, as in the matter of education, though to a lesser degree, the various municipal boundaries seem to separate the church folk of a metropolitan area.

Now, in so far as churches exist to promote certain moral codes and general theological beliefs, they should be able to work together. In fact, it seems evident that their division, mutual indifference, and occasional conflict interfere with the achievement of these common aims. Institutional glory, denominational self-satisfaction, and sectarian fanaticism, in various forms and degrees, separate religionists and render many of their efforts rather futile. The outsider finds it very difficult to reconcile the professions of brotherhood and righteousness with the aloofness and petty squabbles which so often appear on the ecclesiastical scene.

To achieve some measure of coordination there have grown up, especially in large centers, a number of city or metropolitan church federations. In 1930 about one-third of the cities over 50,000 had such organizations. But they were limited both in membership and in activity. In the first place, they were restricted to Protestant churches; no Catholic or Jewish groups were included. Sometimes their membership was even more narrowly confined to "evangelical" churches. These include those that believe in the Trinity and hold to the importance of a special emotional experience called conversion; it excludes

[1] H. Paul Douglass, *Protestant Cooperation in American Cities*, p. 14, 1930.

Unitarians, Lutherans, and Christian Scientists. In addition Negro churches are frequently left out, as are non-English-speaking congregations. Sometimes we note the absence of fundamentalist groups, small churches, and suburban parishes. The lines are not consistent, but universally church federations omit many religious groups.

The functions of church federations are of two general kinds. The first covers joint activities in evangelism (*e.g.*, revival meetings), religious education (*e.g.*, daily vacation Bible schools), social service (*e.g.*, girls' protective leagues), and moral reforms (*e.g.*, prohibition). The second is called comity, and is really an attempt to engage in social planning as it pertains to religion.[1] Sometimes comity is involved in new situations, as when several denominations unite directly or through a federation to make a religious survey of a newly developed suburban district. Or they may consult together with reference to the organization of new congregations, the selection of church sites, the establishment of missions or Sunday schools. Sometimes comity has to do with existing churches when there are problems of relocation, mergers, splits, transfers of a congregation from one denomination to another, and federation. It may be concerned with new policies, such as the undertaking or abandoning of work for foreign language groups. All of these provide opportunities for joint planning of religious activities and facilities.

The federation movement may be said to have started with the Evangelical Alliance just after the Civil War. In the eighties and nineties it was promoted through the establishment of ministerial alliances. In 1900 a National Federation of Churches was founded; in 1908 it became the Federal Council of Churches. This body promoted the formation of local federations. Then came the Men and Religion Forward Movement, followed by special wartime commissions, further stimulating cooperation among Protestant churches. In fact, nearly one-third of the existing federations were started during and immediately following the World War. The New York City Federation has functioned continuously since 1895, but most of the others date from the decade ending 1920.

The Catholic Church, being established on a hierarchical basis, with highly centralized control, does plan the location of parishes

[1] H. Paul Douglass, *Church Comity*, 1929.

carefully, though it does not display such unified action in the founding and conduct of its charities. The Jewish congregations exercise a large degree of local autonomy. Protestants, Catholics, and Jews have in no city combined to make comprehensive plans for religious work.

Social Work Planning

Possibly the most comprehensive planning of social institutions in cities that we have had so far is that pertaining to social work. To be sure, the structure of social work, like that of business, government, education, and religion, has grown up without coordinated planning; but in recent years there have been real attempts to view the field as a whole and to plan for its orderly development. Councils of social agencies have attempted since 1909 to cover social case work, group work, institutions in the narrow popular sense, and a multitude of miscellaneous activities. The case work with which they are concerned includes relief giving, family counseling, child care, visiting teaching, vocational advice and placement, probation and parole, and medical social work. The group work includes the promotion and guidance of clubs, classes, and less formal groups of young and old, supervision of recreational activities, leadership and administration of social centers. The institutions include homes for children, old people, delinquents, mental defectives, and physically handicapped persons. In addition councils of social agencies have engaged in research, propaganda, lobbying, and in general the promotion of legislative changes, administrative efficiency, and moral reforms. Sometimes these are merely a lot of separate interests that happen to converge in one office. But sometimes their interrelations are studied and comprehensive programs are developed. Occasionally a large-scale survey is conducted to view the metropolitan situation as a whole and plan social work accordingly. Such a survey was recently carried out in Pittsburgh.[1]

Perhaps it is only fair to say that councils of social agencies are for the most part just what their name implies. They are asso-

[1] Philip Klein, *A Social Study of Pittsburgh: Community Problems and Social Services of Allegheny County*, 1938. Strictly speaking this survey was not conducted by the Council of Social Agencies but by specialists brought in from the outside by a sponsoring citizens' committee and financed by the Buhl Foundation.

ciations of organizations established to carry on social work. They usually accept the existing situation and seek to promote teamwork, raise standards, and increase public interest. But out of the coordinating function has grown some social planning, or at least the planning of social work. Several limitations of these councils were discussed in Chap. XII. They commonly devote most of their attention to private agencies; they usually deal with only a part of a metropolitan area; they are frequently dominated by people who are more interested in maintaining the *status quo* than in planning social reorganization.

Unfortunately many people have used the words "social planning" and "community organization" as synonyms of social work planning. Now the last would be a significant part of comprehensive social planning and it would overlap the promotion of local communities, but it is after all somewhat specialized. The whole matter would be clarified by a more careful use of terms.

Neighborhood Planning

Social workers have sometimes engaged in what might be called neighborhood planning. Thus the social settlements in blighted areas are often intended to be the headquarters of neighborhoods, actual or potential. It is generally assumed that the people living near a settlement house either do or should constitute a neighborhood. Sometimes this appears to be a fairly accurate characterization, but often the nigh dwellers are a heterogeneous and mobile lot, who have little to do with one another Under such circumstances the settlement becomes a social service station rather than the center of local group life. The social workers make efforts to promote mutual acquaintance and respect between various ethnic groups, to bring united pressure to bear on public officials, and otherwise to advance civic reform and develop urban nigh dwellers into neighbors. As we indicated in Chap. XII, their labors are not wholly in vain, but they cannot point to large accomplishments in the realm of neighborhood organization.

Outside the settlements the Urban League has sometimes undertaken block organization among Negroes. The principal projects of these organized groups have had to do with the appearance of houses, yards, and streets, the promotion of health programs, adult education, and various kinds of propaganda. The degree of their success is difficult to determine. But it is probably correct to say that neighborhood planning has been subordinate to other objectives.

More genuine neighborhood planning has preceded the establishment of private streets and places, like those described in Chap. XIV. Here there has been careful design of the physical layout, selection of residents, organization of a property owners' association. Often the aims of securing a congenial group of families, of protecting property values, of escaping from traffic, and of living in a stable, attractive, and accessible neighborhood are achieved. But these advantages are available almost solely to well-to-do folk.

In the plan for New York and its environs considerable attention was given to the development of neighborhoods.[1] The metropolitan area was not laid out in potential neighborhood and non-neighborhood districts, but plans were drawn up for such neighborhoods as might come into being. These plans involved a physical aspect, an economic organization, and the development of social institutions. Arterial highways were to form the boundaries but never to pass through a neighborhood. Dwellings were to be reached by winding cul-de-sacs, preferably approaching from the rear. Houses were to face on open spaces occupied by grass and flowers and by playgrounds. Pedestrian and vehicular traffic would be separated in the interest of safety. Distinctively neighborhood institutions, such as elementary schools, would be centrally located. Those serving the population of a larger area, such as retail stores, would be located on the through streets, preferably at or near intersections. The residents of a neighborhood were expected to join a property owners' association or neighborhood improvement association. This organization was to consider not merely economic problems, but recreational, educational, and any others that might affect the group as a whole. Separate plans were designed for neighborhoods in different parts of the metropolitan area: suburban, industrial, and apartment districts. These differed both in physical plan and in economic organization. In suburban neighborhoods home ownership by individual families was anticipated. In the others corporate ownership of multiple dwellings was to be the rule.

[1] Clarence A. Perry, *et al.*, *Neighborhood and Community Planning*, 1929, vol. 7 of the *Regional Survey of New York and Its Environs.*

In view of the evident decline of neighboring in cities and the gradual substitution of functional for locality groups, it may fairly be asked: Why bother about planning neighborhoods? The answer is in part that this is a means of promoting quiet, safety, health, beauty, acceptable associates, and availability without annoyance of service agencies. Neighborhood life seems to mean most to families with small children. Perhaps it is not necessary or even desirable for groups of adults and single individuals. Even for families with small children and with adequate income there are the problems of changing business and professional connections. If urban populations become much more mobile, neighborhoods can hardly survive. Even a well-integrated neighborhood will be threatened by the removal of families from its membership. Replacements may not prove congenial or they may have so many interests in other parts of the city that they never identify themselves wholly with the neighborhood. Hence we are inclined to view neighborhood planning as idealistic, but probably not practical for large numbers of city dwellers.

Community Planning

A logical development would be the grouping of neighborhoods into communities. But as a matter of fact the planning of communities seems to be older than the effort to develop neighborhoods. All through the nineteenth century there were appearing books and pamphlets urging the establishment of model communities. Fourier in 1822, Wakefield in 1849, and Howard in 1898 urged the creation of new communities on unused land. Howard's plan in particular was to establish small urban units which might combine the advantages of city and country life. There would be single dwellings with plenty of open spaces. Separate, but close by, would be places of employment, and a shopping center. Round about would be a permanent agricultural belt. Thus the community would be to a considerable degree independent and self-sufficient. It would be suburban in location, thus having access to the facilities of the great city, but with much less commuting than is usually necessary for suburban dwellers.

In England a number of industrial towns were built along these lines, Bournville and Port Sunlight being perhaps the best known. From the writings of idealists and the accomplishments of industrialists there grew up a "garden city" movement, which gave rise to two planned suburbs, Letchworth, in 1903, and Welwyn, in 1919. In the United States there have been numerous "company towns" and a few attempts by industrialists to create model suburbs but few cases of new communities planned as integral parts of metropolitan areas.

Probably the best example we have is Radburn, N. J., about 15 miles from the heart of New York City.[1] This venture is being promoted by a limited dividend company, the City Housing Corporation. Advantage was taken of land not previously used for urban purposes, and hence available at a wholesale, "undeveloped" price. A complete town has been laid out; homes have been erected; factories have been attracted. Residential sections are planned essentially as neighborhoods. There is a conveniently located shopping center. At one side is an industrial district. The whole community occupies 1,200 acres. There cannot be a permanent agricultural belt, because Radburn is too near the heart of the metropolitan area; but it is hoped that there will always be parks on all sides. The inhabitants are expected to buy their homes, instead of leasing them, as in Letchworth. They do not get the property at "cost," but ultimately, after the fixed dividends have been paid, they will receive the increased value of the land. To exercise eventual control over the whole development the Radburn Association has been established. Every householder is expected to be a member.

Under the New Deal there has been much talk of developing "greenbelt" towns around some of our great cities. In fact, several such projects are actually under way. Among these are Greendale near Milwaukee, Greenhills near Cincinnati, Greenbelt near Washington, and Greenbrook in New Jersey.[2] Like Radburn, these are to be definite communities, relatively separate and self-sufficient yet within metropolitan areas and having access to the latters' marketing, recreational, medical, and other

[1] Clarence A. Perry, *et al.*, *op. cit.*, pp. 264–269; *Encyclopaedia of the Social Sciences*, vol. 6, pp. 569–571.

[2] Albert Mayer, "The Greenbelt Towns: What and Why," *Amer. City*, 51 (1936), 59–61; "Site Plans of Greenbelt Towns," *Amer. City*, 51 (1936), 56–59.

facilities. Surrounded by permanently open belts of woods and farms, they are guaranteed fresh air and sunshine, freedom from congestion, and ease of procuring vegetables, eggs, and other farm products. Just what will be the organization of the inhabitants as social groups we do not know.

It seems now to be assumed that communities cannot be developed in the heart of great cities. But 20 years ago there was a very interesting attempt to do this very thing. In Cincinnati the Mohawk-Brighton district was selected for the "experiment" known as the Social Unit.[1] Here was a population of 15,000 occupying 31 blocks. It was a rather stable lot of folk, mostly of German descent, many of them owners of small homes. The plan was presented to them; it aroused their interest; and to its development they gave much time and effort.

The program was not one of physical construction or reconstruction. It was a genuine scheme of community organization. Its purpose was to provide a mechanism whereby the citizens could all share in devising and carrying out programs of social action. To make this possible there was devised a system of dual representation, geographical and occupational. All the adults living in a given block were to elect a block council of seven, who were to choose their representative, to be known as the block worker, to discuss local needs and to consider proposals made by the unit executive, the occupational council, or any other individual or group. Some of the block councils seem to have met rather frequently, while others came together rarely if ever. At all events every block had a "worker," however chosen. All the block workers met as members of the citizens' council. This was really the policy-making body for the community. Since the members lived very near to their constituents and put in several hours a week seeking their opinions and guiding them to specialists whose services they might need, the citizens' council was representative in a very unusual sense.

The occupational organization was intended to include everyone whose trade or profession was conducted in whole or in part in the district, rather than the gainfully employed persons who lived in the district. They were organized first by occupations. Thus there was a physicians' council, to which dentists were

[1] Courtenay Dinwiddie, *Community Responsibility: A Review of the Cincinnati Social Unit Experiment*, **1921**.

later admitted, a nursing council, a social workers' council, and a teachers' council. The clergymen, businessmen, and wage earners never united, and they took rather less part in the whole venture than was hoped. Representatives of these professional and trades groups were to form the occupational council, which was to promote better understanding and cooperation. Members of the citizens' council and the occupational council were to meet together as the general council to consider matters of general interest.

It happened that during the three years of the experiment, 1917–1920, more attention was devoted to public health than to anything else. This was stimulated by the United States Children's Bureau, but it was enthusiastically supported by the people of the district. Had it not been for the short life of the unit, the general preoccupation with the World War, and the opposition of politicians, doubtless other phases of the local life would have received similar consideration. At all events the venture came to an end when the outside subsidy ceased, and nothing quite like it has been elsewhere developed.

During the years immediately following the World War there was much loose talk about "community organization," but the underlying ideas were rather vague. Some people identified the term with public recreation. Others meant by it the enlisting of popular support for social work organizations. Still others had in mind church unity, consolidated schools, "Americanization," and doubtless many other pet projects. All these efforts contained the germ of social planning, but none of them was sufficiently comprehensive to warrant the use of that label. Today community organization has been pretty generally eclipsed by regional planning.

The Revolutionary Nature of City and Regional Planning

If we were to have really effective physical and social planning of cities, metropolitan areas, and regions, there would have to be a thoroughgoing modification, if not abandonment, of our traditional individualism and "free" competition. To project and enforce specified land uses and institutional development would inevitably restrict the almost sacred right of every American citizen to "do as he pleases." Consider how the regulation of subdivisions would hamper the conventional real estate business, how the control of social work would cramp the style of Lady Bountiful and her Rotarian husband, how comity would interfere with the effort to lure everyone into some particular religious faith. To devise and carry out comprehensive plans for urban areas would require fundamental changes in our social philosophy. They would constitute a cultural mutation of the sort that deserves the name revolution.

We say this not to frighten any timid soul or to excite those who are already restless but to emphasize the vast difference between *laissez faire,* under which our cities have developed in the past, and social planning. We do not like our cities as they are. Are we ready to pay the price of making them over? On the answer to that question rests the future of urbanism in America.

Selected Readings

Mumford, Lewis: *The Culture of Cities,* Harcourt, Brace & Company, Inc., 1938. See Chap. 7, "Social Basis of the New Urban Order."

Gist, Noel P., and L. A. Halbert: *Urban Society,* The Thomas Y. Crowell Company, 1933. See Chap. 21, "The Basis of Social Adjustment"; Chap. 22 "Social Investigation and Reconstruction of Urban Society."

Steiner J. F.: *Community Organization,* Century Company, rev. ed., 1930. See especially Chaps. 18, 21, 22. This book deals with both theory and practice, with the community as a whole and with various phases of its life.

Zorbaugh, Harvey W.: *Gold Coast and Slum,* University of Chicago Press, 1929. Chap. 12, "Reform, Realism and City Life," questions the possibility of integrating the social elements in an urban area.

North, C. C.: *Social Problems and Social Planning,* McGraw-Hill Book Company, Inc., 1932. While not specifically dealing with city planning, this book offers many suggestions.

Dinwiddie, Courtenay: *Community Responsibility,* New York School of Social Work, 1921. A narrative and interpretation of the Cincinnati Social Unit experiment.

INDEX